ac
open water diver
MANUAL

ENGLISH

PADI

Student Diver

Address

City, State/Province

Telephone

Instructor | Date

PADI Advanced Open Water Diver Manual

Published by PADI
30151 Tomas
Rancho Santa Margarita, CA 92688-2125 USA

ISBN 978-1-61381-889-3

Printed in Canada

Product No. 79199 (Rev. 05/17) Version 1.01

Table of Contents

Introduction	4
Thinking Like a Diver	18
Underwater Navigation	36
Deep Diving	60
Altitude Diving	96
Boat Diving	114
Digital Underwater Imaging	140
Drift Diving	174
Dry Suit Diving	196
Fish Identification	222
Night Diving	238
Peak Performance Buoyancy	262
Search and Recovery	278
Underwater Naturalist	300
Wreck Diving	316

INTRODUCTION

Welcome! As a certified open water diver, you've discovered that diving is an adventure – the door to an amazing world with unique sights, sounds and sensations. But, it's actually *many* adventures and experiences, and that's what the PADI® Advanced Open Water Diver course is all about: expanding your underwater world by making dives in the pursuit of new discoveries, abilities and experiences. It's about new skills that make diving more rewarding, and opening new activities and options when you go underwater. It's about exploring dive sites you've not seen before, gaining experience with dive gear, and understanding more about how you see, feel and hear in the underwater world.

And, it's about *becoming* something more. You learn how to *think* more like an experienced diver, which builds your abilities, skills and confidence. You learn more about *yourself* – where your interests lie so you can get more out of diving. Do you have a passion for creating underwater images? Recovering what someone lost? Mastering new technologies? Probing shipwrecks? Whether you're a newly certified PADI Open Water Diver or have been one for years, the PADI Advanced Open Water Diver program develops the underwater interests you have, while you discover new ones, expand and refine your skills, and become more confident.

IT'S ABOUT DIVING

In the PADI Advanced Open Water Diver program, you learn by *diving*. Predive briefings with your PADI Instructor, this manual and Knowledge Reviews cover what you need to know for most of the Adventure Dives. There are no written exams; instead, your instructor will evaluate your learning by asking questions, having discussions and watching you put what you know into practice.

With your instructor, you'll choose the Adventure Dives you want to experience and learn from. Each builds your abilities, confidence and thinking skills while focusing on a diving specialty. There's quite a list to choose from. In this manual, you'll find a section for:

- Altitude Diving
- Boat Diving
- Deep Diving
- Digital Underwater Imaging
- Drift Diving
- Dry Suit Diving
- Fish Identification
- Night Diving
- Peak Performance Buoyancy
- Search & Recovery
- Underwater Naturalist
- Underwater Navigation
- Wreck Diving

You may have other Adventure Dives to choose from if you and your PADI Instructor meet additional prerequisites and other requirements. These may include:

- Cavern Diving
- Delayed Surface Marker Buoy (DSMB) Diving
- Dive Against Debris
- Diver Propulsion Vehicle (DPV) Diving
- Enriched Air Nitrox Diving
- Full Face Mask Diving
- Ice Diving
- Rebreather Diving
- Self-Reliant Diving
- Shark Conservation
- Sidemount Diving

something you should know

Been Dry For A While?

Keeping your dive knowledge and skills fresh is part of your responsibilities as a certified diver. If you've not been diving for an extended period, it's wise to brush up. One option is the PADI ReActivate® program, which is intended specifically for helping you get back in the water. It starts with mobile device-based scenarios that prescriptively update your knowledge, followed by a dive that lets you practice your skills. The ReActivate program helps you assess where you need to brush up, then helps you do so without wasting time on what you still remember well.

Be sure to let your instructor know how long it's been since you last went diving – whether it was yesterday or a year ago. This information helps your instructor shape the program to your needs and interests.

something you should know

About PADI and Your PADI Instructor, Dive Center or Resort

PADI is the Professional Association of Diving Instructors®, the world's largest diver training organization. PADI Worldwide® establishes training programs, materials and standards, monitors quality, certifies instructors and provides support services for PADI Instructors, Dive Centers and Resorts (PADI Members).

Your PADI Instructor is an independent professional who is qualified to conduct PADI training. To reach this leadership position, your instructor has successfully completed a series of required courses, including the comprehensive Instructor Development Course, followed by independent tests in the two-day Instructor Examination. PADI Dive Centers and Resorts are professional operations dedicated to meeting your diving needs. Visit your PADI Dive Center or Resort online and in person for help choosing and servicing gear, booking dive travel and staying plugged into the diving lifestyle.

The worldwide PADI Regional Headquarters (Offices) constantly monitor for individuals misrepresenting themselves as authorized to teach PADI courses. You can verify that the individual conducting your program is an authorized PADI Instructor.

When you take your PADI Advanced Open Water Diver course through an authorized PADI Resort or Dive Center (see the Dive Shop Locator at padi.com), it's highly likely your instructor is an authorized PADI Instructor. But, if you doubt it for some reason, ask to see your instructor's certification card. Check the photo and note the instructor number. For further verification, you may call your local PADI Regional Headquarters, or you can verify the individual is authorized to conduct the PADI program you're taking with Pro Chek™ at padi.com. You can also find consumer alerts there.

If at any time you have questions about the instructor conducting your program, please contact the local PADI Regional Headquarters using the information at padi.com.

TWO CERTIFICATIONS

This program offers two certifications: PADI Advanced Open Water Diver, and Adventure Diver. To achieve the Advanced Open Water Diver certification, you'll successfully complete five Adventure Dives: Underwater Navigation, Deep, and three Adventure Dives you choose with your instructor. If you have time or other constraints, you may elect to complete the PADI Adventure Diver certification by successfully completing any three Adventure Dives.

The goals of both courses are to:

- Build on and refine your Open Water Diver skills.
- Increase your confidence while expanding your skills into new areas.
- Provide experience under professional supervision.
- Allow you to begin training in the PADI Rescue Diver course and certain other courses (e.g., Wreck Diver, Deep Diver) with an Adventure Diver and/or Underwater Navigation Adventure Dive prerequisite.

In addition, the Advanced Open Water Diver course goals are to:

- Give you experience specifically in navigation and deep diving.
- Begin your training toward certification in these areas, and start you toward Master Scuba Diver™ (the highest nonprofessional rating in recreational diving).
- Enable you to start, or complete, training in courses that have an Advanced Open Water Diver prerequisite (or require it by a certain point within the course).
- Gain additional supervised experience applying your buoyancy, navigation and deep diving skills.

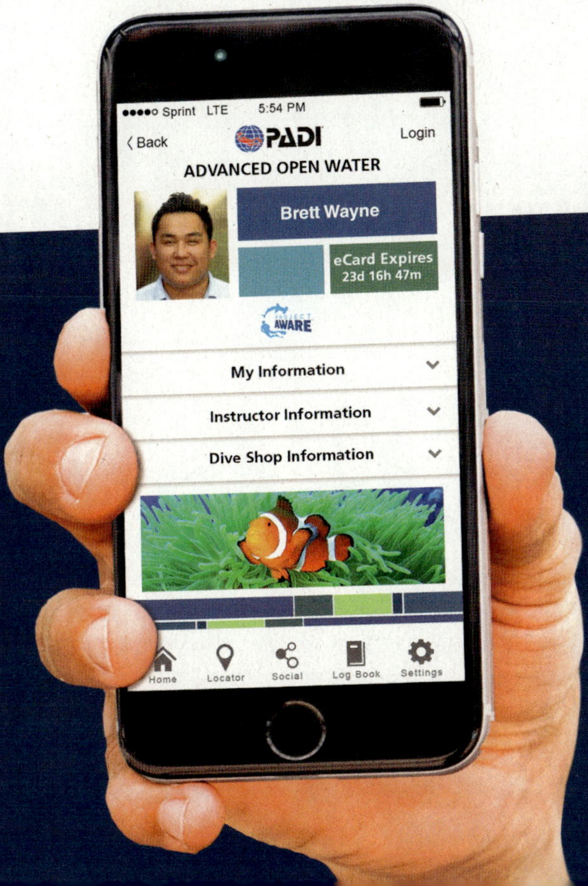

Successfully completing the Underwater Navigation, Deep, and three other Adventure Dives earns you the PADI Advanced Open Water Diver certification. You earn the Adventure Diver certification by successfully completing just three Adventure Dives.

EXPERIENCES THAT CREDIT TOWARD PADI MASTER SCUBA DIVER™

Every Adventure Dive is the first dive of the corresponding PADI Specialty Diver course, which means that your training credits toward the *entire* specialty certification. After successfully completing the Night Adventure Dive, for example, you only need two more dives to earn the PADI Night Diver certification. Similarly, if you've completed a PADI Specialty Diver course, the first dive may credit as the corresponding Adventure Dive in the Advanced Open Water Diver program.

As a PADI Advanced Open Water Diver, you will have effectively started earning five PADI Specialty Diver certifications – a huge step toward becoming a PADI Master Scuba Diver, recreational diving's highest rating. To earn this recognition, you must meet these requirements:

- PADI Advanced Open Water Diver
- PADI Rescue Diver
- Five PADI Specialty Diver certifications
- Fifty logged dives

Many PADI dive operations have programs specifically for divers who have set their sights on Master Scuba Diver. It's a great way to gain new skills and achieve recognition while gaining experience, making new friends and enjoying the diving lifestyle. Ask your PADI Dive Center or Resort about their PADI Master Scuba Diver program.

GETTING THE MOST OUT OF THE COURSE

The PADI Advanced Open Water Diver course is flexible and gives many options for locations in a sequence that consists of *water skills* and *knowledge development*. Like the PADI Open Water Diver course it applies *performance-based learning* – this means you progress by meeting specific learning objectives. It's also *student-centered*, which means the course, materials and your instructor address how *you* learn most effectively.

Meeting the objectives is what's important, not how long it takes. You must meet certification requirements, but your instructor realizes that how you prefer to learn may differ from others. So, the course pace matches what you need to become a capable and confident diver – that's student-centered learning.

If you approach learning as discussed here, you'll learn better and faster, and enjoy the process more.

Your water skills training takes place in a dive environment appropriate to the Adventure Dive you're making.

something you should know

Heart Health

Your PADI Instructor will ask you to complete the PADI Medical Statement at the beginning of your course. When completing the form, keep in mind that diving is generally relaxing, but at times it can cause elevated physical stress. Swimming hard, being in the hot sun while in an exposure suit and other factors can increase the stress on your heart and cardiovascular system. Like any other physical stress, this can cause a heart attack in predisposed individuals. Be sure to discuss this concern with your doctor if you may have a predisposition to heart disease due to age, lifestyle, body composition, family history or other factors.

WATER SKILLS

The PADI Advanced Open Water Diver program emphasizes making dives in an environment appropriate to each Adventure Dive. In a few instances, you may make a pool or confined water dive as well, but most of your diving will be in open water.

The materials introduce common techniques for many of the skills you'll learn, though your instructor may show different ones. *If you don't understand how to do something, or why you would, ask your instructor about it before the dive.* PADI courses do not have meaningless, arbitrary skills that serve no purpose, so you should understand why you're learning each skill.

Similarly, be sure your instructor knows if you have any physical challenges that affect how you may accomplish a task or skill. There are many ways to accomplish most dive skills, which allows individuals with wide ranges of physical characteristics to earn the PADI Advanced Open Water Diver and Adventure Diver certifications.

Be sure to log your dives to track your progress. Logging your dives not only records your training, but documents experience you need to participate in some courses and training levels. Go to your PADI Mobile App or visit padi.com to log your dives.

KNOWLEDGE DEVELOPMENT

Knowledge development covers principles and foundational information that you put into practice underwater with your instructor. You can complete the five Adventure Dives – three for Adventure Diver – in almost any order (there are some sequence requirements), based on logistical requirements and your interests. Some elective Adventure Dives have a required confined water dive or pool dive before going into open water. Your instructor may add confined water/pool dives for added skill assessments and/or development as well.

There is a section in this manual for each of the most popular Adventure Dives and one for Thinking Like a Diver. Start with Thinking Like a Diver and the sections for the Adventure Dives you and your instructor choose. For some Adventure Dives, your instructor will refer you to the corresponding PADI specialty diver materials.

You'll complete most of your knowledge development independently with this manual and, in some cases, one or more PADI specialty diver manuals.

something you should know

Metric and Imperial Systems

Through the course you'll see both metric and imperial measurements. Use the system you prefer, or both, but be aware that sometimes the referenced figures are not exactly equal. The reason is that divers use "round" numbers for many purposes, so the preferred figure in each system may differ slightly. For example, a general reserve air supply is 50 bar/500 psi. Fifty bar actually equals 725 psi, but 50 bar/500 psi are easy figures to reference on an SPG, so those are the figures divers commonly use in the respective systems.

Ideally, prepare *before* each Adventure Dive by following these steps:

1. **Flip through what you're going to read.** Scan the section or specialty manual quickly, generally noting headings, topics, pictures and so on. This helps you learn best by linking new information with what you already know.

2. **Read the learning objectives for each subsection, then read the subsection.** Look for the answers to each question and highlight it or write it down when you find it. This focuses you, because you're seeking the information you need. *Actually writing* speeds learning, because you immediately engage with the information and it helps you review later.

3. **Complete the exercises.** These are *not* tests, and the answers are right there. Immediately answering questions confirms learning as you go, and helps transfer what you're learning to your long-term memory. Learning as you go is important, because misunderstanding something can create learning difficulties later. If you missed a question, review the material until you understand. If you still don't get it, be sure to ask your instructor.

4. **Watch the video.** After you've read a section for the Adventure Dive, if there is one, watch the corresponding section of the PADI *Advanced Open Water Diver Video* or the corresponding PADI specialty diver video. Video and the written word have different strengths when you're learning, and repetition helps transfer what you're learning to long-term memory. If you prefer, first watch the video, then read the manual.

5. **Answer the knowledge reviews at the end of each section or specialty manual.** (There is no knowledge review for Thinking Like a Diver.) If you don't know something, review and then answer – this helps confirm and reinforce how concepts interconnect, and helps you retain what you're learning. Your instructor will go over your knowledge reviews to check that you understand the material.

6. **Get your instructor's help.** During reviews and briefings, be sure to ask about any areas in which you had difficulties or want to learn more. Your instructor will help you apply what you're learning to your needs and local diving. The better you communicate your personal interests and characteristics, the more your instructor can help.

BEYOND PADI ADVANCED OPEN WATER DIVER

After successfully completing the Advanced Open Water Diver course, the next step is PADI Rescue Diver. The PADI Rescue Diver course teaches you emergency prevention, intervention and management. But, you don't have to wait to start – you can enroll in and start your Rescue Diver training after you've successfully completed the Underwater Navigation Adventure Dive. Much of the Rescue Diver course takes place at the surface, so your instructor may integrate much of it with your Advanced Open Water Diver training.

Talk to those who've been there – almost without exception, you'll hear that the PADI Rescue Diver course is one of diving's most challenging and rewarding programs. Rescue Divers will tell you that it's a real confidence builder – an experience you don't want to miss. It's serious fun.

Once you complete the PADI Advanced Open Water Diver and Rescue Diver courses, you have two paths to continue your diving education – Master Scuba Diver or PADI Divemaster.

PADI Divemaster is the first professional level in the PADI System, and the first step in the instructor development process. During the PADI Divemaster course you will develop leadership skills and professional-level dive knowledge and abilities. Earning the PADI Divemaster certification distinguishes you as both an accomplished diver and a leader, at the doorstep of becoming an instructor if that interests you.

• PADI PROFESSIONAL

COURSE DIRECTOR
Teach the Instructor Development Course (IDC)

MASTER INSTRUCTOR
Become a dive industry leader

IDC STAFF INSTRUCTOR
Assist with instructor training

MASTER SCUBA DIVER™ TRAINER
Train Master Scuba Divers

OPEN WATER SCUBA INSTRUCTOR
Teach the world to dive

PADI ASSISTANT INSTRUCTOR
Assist instructors and gain experience teaching

PADI DIVEMASTER
The first level of a PADI Professional

MASTER SCUBA DIVER™
Become one of scuba diving's elite

RESCUE DIVER
Prepare yourself for dive emergencies

ADVANCED OPEN WATER DIVER
Build confidence and expand your skills

ADVENTURE DIVER
Complete three Adventure Dives to gain new skills and experience

OPEN WATER DIVER
Learn to scuba dive

PADI SPECIALTY COURSES

- Altitude Diver
- AWARE Coral Reef Conservation
- AWARE Shark Conservation Diver
- AWARE Dive Against Debris
- Boat Diver
- Cavern Diver
- Deep Diver
- Delayed Surface Marker Buoy Diver
- Digital Underwater Photographer
- Diver Propulsion Vehicle Diver
- Drift Diver
- Dry Suit Diver
- Enriched Air Diver
- Emergency Oxygen Provider
- Equipment Specialist
- Fish Identification Diver
- Full Face Mask Diver
- Ice Diver
- Night Diver
- Peak Performance Buoyancy Diver
- Public Safety Diver
- Search & Recovery Diver
- Rebreather Diver
- Sidemount Diver
- Underwater Naturalist
- Underwater Navigator
- Wreck Diver

Soon you'll finish the first dives and knowledge development sections of five Adventure Dives that link directly to PADI Specialty courses. Specialty Diver certification is easily within reach. As a certified PADI Advanced Open Water Diver, you have a world of opportunity, even a career in diving, in front of you. Ask your PADI Pros for more information, or visit padi.com.

• PADI DIVER

something you should know

Leading-Edge Education

Organizations in international governments and education recognize the instructional quality of PADI training. The American Council on Education's College Credit Recommendation Service (ACE Credit) independently evaluated PADI courses, and recommends many of them for college credit. Similar authoritative bodies in Australia, Canada, England, Wales, Northern Ireland, Japan and New Zealand have recognized PADI courses for academic credit, or for educational credit for competency that transfers to other fields. These acknowledgments corroborate the educational validity of PADI courses, and the PADI organization's ability to meet its educational goals. As a diver training organization, PADI is unique in having received such a broad range of academic recognition internationally.

In addition, PADI courses meet or exceed all the minimum ISO (International Standards Organization) and World Recreational Scuba Training Council (WRSTC) standards for entry-level scuba diver training.

Visit the course credits page on padi.com for current academic credit availability, links and to download applications.

something you should know

Course Evaluation Questionnaires (CEQs)

PADI Course Evaluation Questionnaires (CEQs) are student surveys that PADI uses to recognize outstanding performance by an instructor and to verify that all training elements were conducted in every course. PADI Offices distribute CEQs to some of each PADI Instructor's students via email as well as by paper. If you receive one, please help PADI maintain diving's highest training standards by taking a few moments to complete it. If you have not received a CEQ after you receive your certification card and would like to complete one, you can do so electronically at padi.com/ceq/student/ceq-paper.htm.

Standard Safe Diving Practices

This is a statement in which you are informed of the established safe diving practices for skin and scuba diving. These practices have been compiled for your review and acknowledgment and are intended to increase your comfort and safety in diving.

1. Maintain good mental and physical fitness for diving. Avoid being under the influence of alcohol or dangerous drugs when diving. Keep proficient in diving skills, striving to increase them through continuing education and reviewing them in controlled conditions after a period of diving inactivity, and refer to my course materials to stay current and refresh myself on important information.
2. Be familiar with my dive sites. If not, obtain a formal diving orientation from a knowledgeable, local source. If diving conditions are worse than those in which I am experienced, postpone diving or select an alternate site with better conditions. Engage only in diving activities consistent with my training and experience. Do not engage in cave or technical diving unless specifically trained to do so.
3. Use complete, well-maintained, reliable equipment with which I am familiar; and inspect it for correct fit and function prior to each dive. Have a buoyancy control device, low-pressure buoyancy control inflation system, submersible pressure gauge and alternate air source and dive planning/monitoring device (dive computer, RDP/dive tables – whichever you are trained to use) when scuba diving. Deny use of my equipment to uncertified divers.
4. Listen carefully to dive briefings and directions, and respect the advice of those supervising my diving activities. Recognize that additional training is recommended for participation in specialty diving activities, in other geographic areas and after periods of inactivity that exceed six months.
5. Adhere to the buddy system throughout every dive. Plan dives – including communications, procedures for reuniting in case of separation, and emergency procedures – with my buddy.
6. Be proficient in dive planning (dive computer or dive table use). Make all dives no decompression dives and allow a margin of safety. Have a means to monitor depth and time underwater. Limit maximum depth to my level of training and experience. Ascend at a rate of not more than 18 metres/60 feet per minute. Be a SAFE diver – Slowly Ascend From Every dive. Make a safety stop as an added precaution, usually at 5 metres/15 feet for three minutes or longer.
7. Maintain proper buoyancy. Adjust weighting at the surface for neutral buoyancy with no air in my buoyancy control device. Maintain neutral buoyancy while underwater. Be buoyant for surface swimming and resting. Have weights clear for easy removal, and establish buoyancy when in distress while diving. Carry at least one surface signaling device (such as signal tube, whistle, mirror).
8. Breathe properly for diving. Never breath-hold or skip-breathe when breathing compressed air, and avoid excessive hyperventilation when breath-hold diving. Avoid overexertion while in and underwater, and dive within my limitations.
9. Use a boat, float or other surface support station whenever feasible.
10. Know and obey local diving laws and regulations, including fish and game and dive flag laws.

Non-Agency Disclosure

PADI Members are licensed to use various PADI Trademarks and to conduct PADI training. Individual, dive center and resort Members are not agents, employees or franchisees of PADI. Member business activities are independent, and are neither owned nor operated by PADI. While PADI establishes the standards for PADI diver training programs, it is not responsible for, nor does it have the right to control, the operation of the Members' business activities and the day-to-day conduct of PADI programs and supervision of divers by the Members or their associated staff.

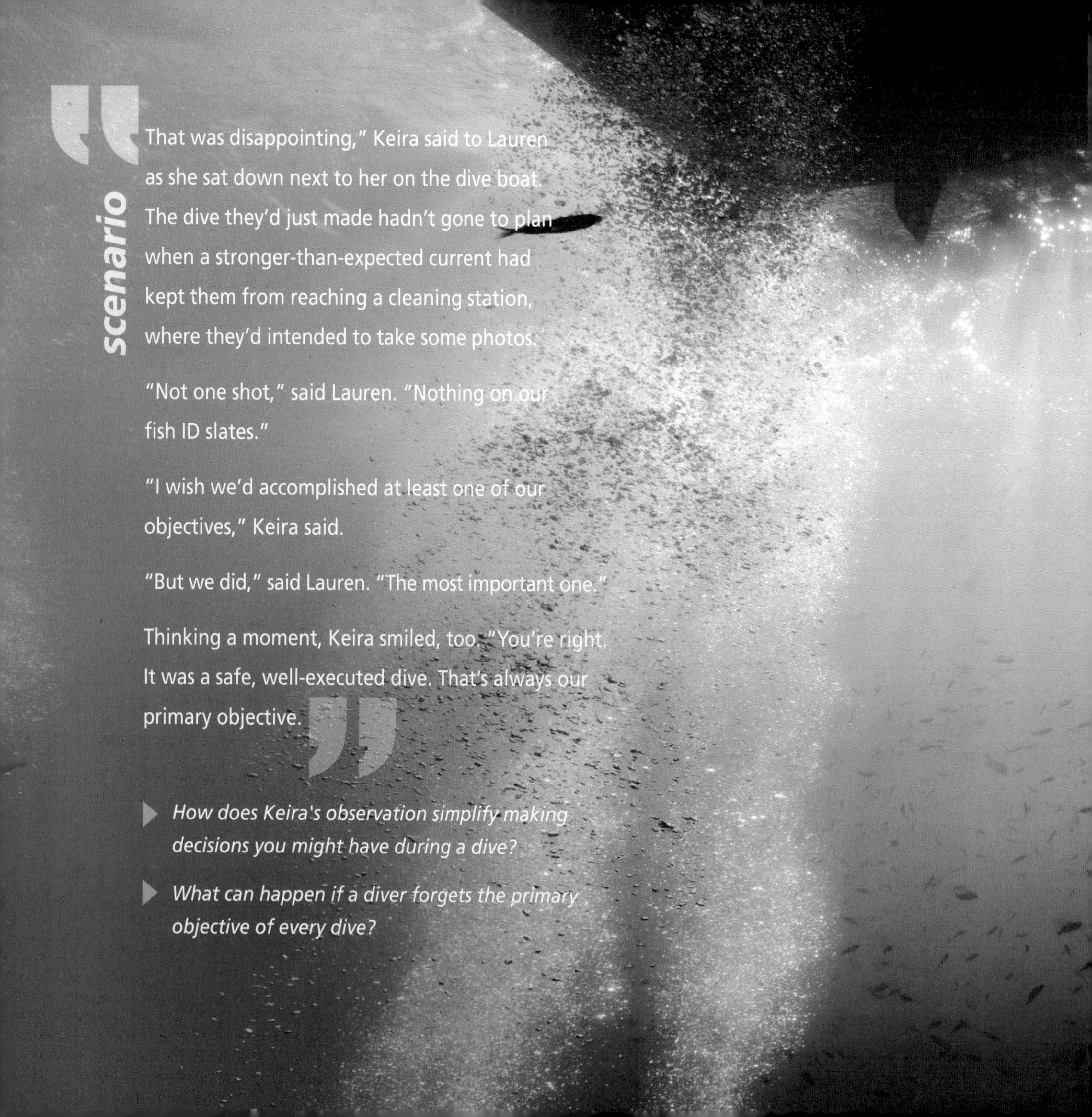

scenario

"That was disappointing," Keira said to Lauren as she sat down next to her on the dive boat. The dive they'd just made hadn't gone to plan when a stronger-than-expected current had kept them from reaching a cleaning station, where they'd intended to take some photos.

"Not one shot," said Lauren. "Nothing on our fish ID slates."

"I wish we'd accomplished at least one of our objectives," Keira said.

"But we did," said Lauren. "The most important one."

Thinking a moment, Keira smiled, too. "You're right. It was a safe, well-executed dive. That's always our primary objective."

- *How does Keira's observation simplify making decisions you might have during a dive?*
- *What can happen if a diver forgets the primary objective of every dive?*

THINKING
LIKE A DIVER
1

THINKING LIKE A DIVER

LEARNING OBJECTIVES

By the end of this section, I should be able to answer these questions:

1. What are the four central dive skills? What three characteristics do they have in common?
2. Why do I learn these dive skills?

The Four Central Dive Skills

As you gain dive experience and your skills improve, you become more aware and more confident, and your equipment use becomes second nature. Learning to think like a diver underlies this. Four central skills shape experienced, prudent divers' thinking:

1. Planning dives with secondary objectives
2. Developing and applying situational awareness
3. Managing task loading
4. Maintaining good dive habits

These (primarily) mental skills share three characteristics: First, they apply to virtually all dives to some extent. Second, they make your dives more enjoyable and more efficient, and help you reduce and manage risk. Third, they integrate with each other and all your other dive skills.

With foundational knowledge and skills mastered, you're now ready to transition from novice-thinking to experienced-thinking approaches to diving. No matter how many dives you've logged, more training in these skills helps you make the most of your experiences. It structures how you think about diving and lets you benefit from the experience of more seasoned divers.

EXERCISE-1

1. The four central dive skills include (choose all that apply):
   - ☐ a. planning dives with secondary objectives
   - ☐ b. developing situational awareness
   - ☐ c. managing task loading
   - ☐ d. maintaining good dive habits
2. I learn the central dive skills to help me transition from novice-thinking to experienced-thinking approaches to diving.
   ☐ True ☐ False

How did you do?

1. a, b, c, d. 2. True.

Every dive's primary objective is for all divers to return safely.

A secondary objective is anything you want to accomplish on the dive beyond returning safely.

LEARNING OBJECTIVES

By the end of this section, I should be able to answer these questions:

1. What is every dive's primary objective?
2. What is a secondary objective?
3. What mistake regarding secondary objectives has caused dive incidents and accidents?

Planning Dives with Secondary Objectives

Primary and Secondary Objectives

Every dive has a single, primary objective. It never changes: *Every dive's primary objective is for all divers to return safely.* A complex tec dive requires significantly more training, planning and preparation than snorkeling on a shallow reef, but both dives have this same primary objective.

This should seem obvious. But, when divers forget this primary objective, significant problems can result.

Secondary Objectives

A secondary objective is anything you want to accomplish beyond returning safely. As a new diver, your most common secondary objective was probably enjoying the sights. But, with experience, you want to do more. Examples of secondary objectives could be finding a specific organism that interests you, or learning a new skill (with professional supervision as appropriate), such as diving at night, taking photos or mapping a dive site. Some of these become part of your skill set once you master them.

Secondary objectives often (but not always) affect the dive plan, so you must plan for these effects in addition to the usual variables.

Keeping secondary objectives secondary to safety is the mark of a good diver.

The Biggest Mistake Involving Secondary Objectives

The biggest mistake involving secondary objectives is forgetting that they are secondary. This is why you see so much emphasis that the primary objective is for everyone to finish the dive safely.

Dive incidents have resulted from divers exceeding planned limits – time, depth, gas supply, etc. – because they were trying to accomplish their secondary objective. Sometimes, the divers thought it was okay to "slightly" push or exceed limits because they had "almost" reached their secondary objective.

Avoid these mistakes. **Finishing a dive safely is the primary objective** that overrides everything else. When you or your buddy(ies) reach a planned limit, turn the dive as planned, regardless of whether you've accomplished or even nearly accomplished your secondary objective.

Don't "push" your safety margin for a secondary objective; you can often plan another dive to finish it. If the secondary objective proves more difficult, time-consuming or complex than expected, it may be appropriate to cut the dive short to regroup and replan.

Always keep secondary objectives secondary to safety. Call them *secondary* to keep that mindset. If you don't accomplish secondary objectives on a dive, take satisfaction in keeping your priorities straight. It's the mark of a good diver.

EXERCISE-2

1. On a dive, I want to identify different species of angelfish on a reef, and my buddy wants to photograph soft corals. What is the dive's primary objective?
   - ☐ a. Fish identification
   - ☐ b. Soft coral photography
   - ☐ c. For both of you to finish the dive safely
2. A secondary objective is anything I want to accomplish on a dive beyond coming back safely.
   ☐ True ☐ False
3. The biggest mistake regarding secondary objectives is forgetting that they are secondary.
   ☐ True ☐ False

How did you do?

1. c. 2. True. 3. True.

LEARNING OBJECTIVES

By the end of this section, I should be able to answer these questions:

1. What is "situational awareness"?

2. How does situational awareness tend to change as I train and gain experience as a diver?

3. Why is gas management a key element of situational awareness, and what are the four basic divisions of my gas supply?

4. With respect to exertion, what is usually the appropriate response to being lower on gas than I would like during a dive? Why?

5. What eight other elements of situational awareness affect recreational divers?

6. For each element, what should I monitor as part of effective situational awareness?

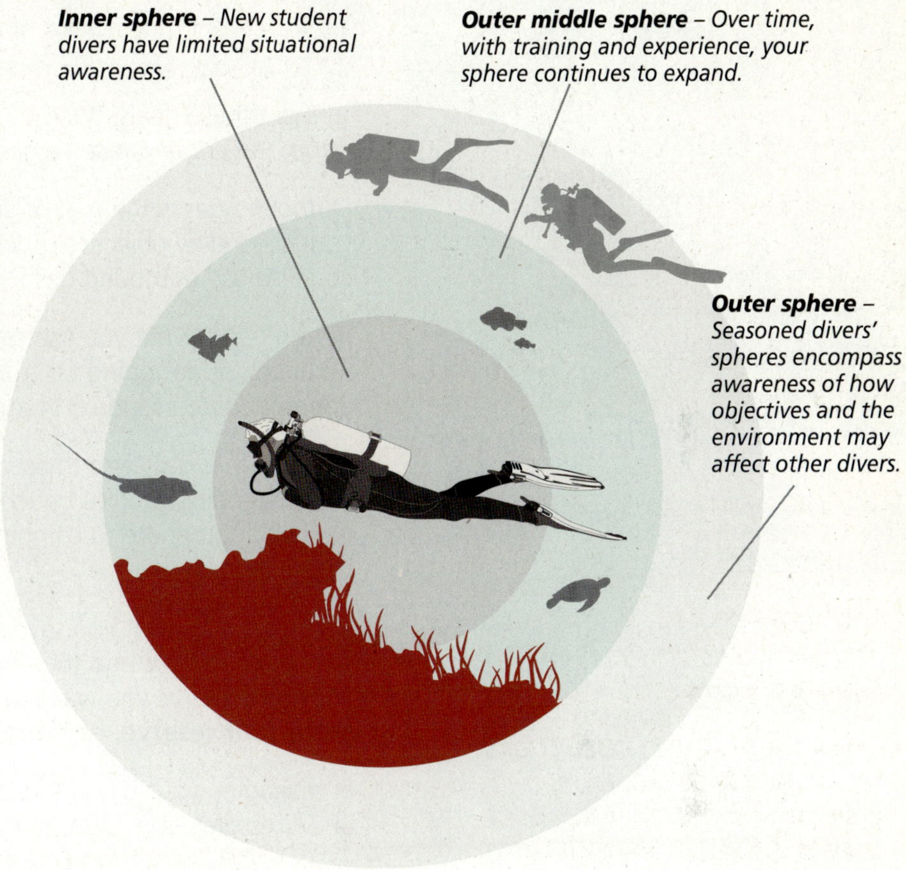

Situational Awareness

Situational awareness is your perception of what's going on around you and how it affects you. This is more complex than seeing and hearing. It is analyzing, organizing and filtering what all your senses perceive.

New student divers tend to have relatively limited situational awareness, but with training and experience, situational awareness expands. You can think of this as "spheres" that surround you.

Initially, your sphere is small, and includes primarily only you. This is because you need almost all your mental resources while learning new, unfamiliar skills. By the time you became an Open Water Diver, however, you had mastered foundational scuba skills and freed mental resources, so your sphere had expanded to include your buddy and more of your surroundings.

With training and experience, your sphere continues to expand. Seasoned divers' spheres encompass awareness of how objectives and the environment may affect other divers. Most divers reach this level by the time they complete the PADI Rescue Diver course.

You use outbound gas to descend and carry out your secondary objective. You use return gas to return to your ascent point. You use ascent gas to ascend, make a safety stop and exit the water. Reserve gas is for handling problems or emergencies.

Situational awareness applies in particular to gas management. When you were training as a PADI Open Water Diver, you learned basic gas (air) management. Gas management has these primary goals:

1. To prevent running out of gas underwater.
2. To allow a reasonable reserve for handling problems or emergencies.

To meet these goals, think of your gas as having four basic divisions: *outbound, return, ascent* and *reserve* gas. Each has a specific role in gas management.

Outbound gas is the part of your supply that you use to descend and carry out your secondary objective. If you have some distance to swim after descending, you also use outbound gas for that.

Return gas is what you use to return to your ascent point, but before you head up. If you're not going far from your entry/exit point, it may be simpler and more appropriate to include it in outbound gas.

Ascent gas is gas used to ascend, make a safety stop and exit. On long dives with ascending profiles, much of your ascent may be part of your return, so it may be appropriate to combine return and ascent gas. That's fine, as long as it's planned.

Reserve gas is what you save for problems or emergencies. The more challenging the conditions and the more complex the reasonably foreseeable problems, the more reserve you want to plan. **If the dive goes as planned, you should have your reserve, or more, left after the dive.**

In managing your gas with respect to these divisions, think in terms of three SPG pressures: *turn, ascent* and *reserve* pressures.

At *turn* pressure you turn the dive and head back toward your exit. You have used all your planned outbound gas; what remains is return, ascent and reserve gas.

When any diver in your buddy team reaches turn pressure, the dive turns. Depending upon the situation and what you're doing, you may swim directly to your ascent point, or you may continue with your secondary objective as you progress to your ascent and exit point. For example, if you're looking for specific fish; at turn pressure, you head to your ascent point, continuing to look as you go.

At *ascent* pressure you begin a direct, deliberate ascent, with safety stop, to the surface. When you reach ascent pressure, the gas remaining in your cylinder is for ascent and reserve.

Although you may often consider return gas and ascent gas together in actual practice, a separate ascent pressure can be useful. If you reach your ascent point with return gas remaining, the dive can continue in the immediate area, as appropriate, until reaching ascent pressure.

On the other hand, if you reach ascent pressure before reaching the ascent point, you know to ascend where you are and swim to your exit on the surface (as appropriate for the conditions). Remember, it's better to have a long surface swim than to run out of gas underwater. If a surface swim isn't desirable, plan extra return gas to be sure you have enough.

At *reserve* pressure you should be at the surface, or out of the water if you plan to use gas during your exit. Your remaining gas is for emergency use. You only use it if an unforeseen problem delays your ability to ascend, or if unforeseen exit conditions require you to use scuba instead of your snorkel. **If you exit the water with less than your planned reserve pressure, and you didn't have an unexpected problem, then you had a problem with gas planning or gas management.**

Note: PADI Rebreather Divers and Tec CCR Divers do not use the same gas divisions and pressures. But, they do plan corresponding divisions for all their life-support resources. (You learn to do this, as appropriate for each level, in the PADI Rebreather Diver, Advanced Rebreather Diver and Tec CCR Diver courses.)

To manage your gas supply and stay within your planned pressures, you need to account for the effects of conditions, emotions, exertion and other variables on your breathing rate and, consequently, your gas supply, but there's no precise formula.

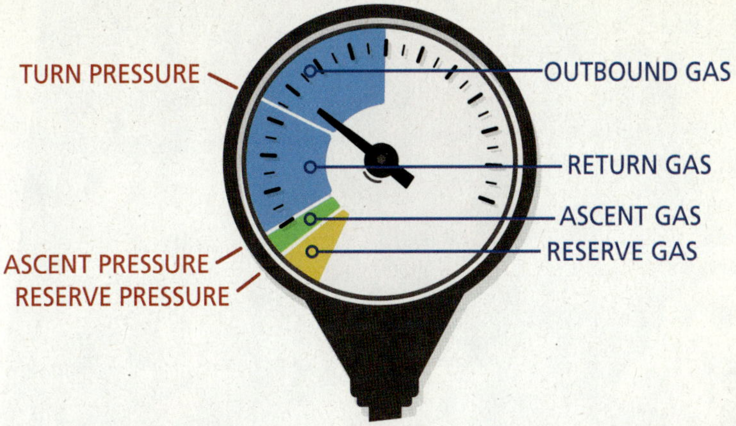

In managing your outbound, return, ascent and reserve gas, think in terms of three pressures: turn, ascent and reserve pressures.

PADI Rebreather Divers and Tec CCR Divers do not use the same gas divisions and pressures as open-circuit divers do. But, they do plan corresponding divisions for all their life-support resources.

*If your breathing's only slightly elevated, it may be acceptable to continue the dive as planned until you reach turn pressure – **but only do this if you are not in danger of overexerting.***

Handle elevated breathing and higher-than-normal gas consumption conservatively – remember the primary objective of every dive. You never want to reach the end of your gas before you get to the end of your dive. You want to end the dive safe and happy.

Fortunately, awareness and being conservative will help you manage your gas effectively. If you know you'll be breathing harder than usual (but not overexerting), you may need to plan for less outbound gas and more return gas. If you will use more gas than usual while exiting (such as through mild surf), similarly plan more return/exit gas and a larger reserve. If you find yourself breathing harder unexpectedly, on the other hand, appropriate responses depend upon the situation.

One option is to end the dive. Do this if conditions are far more difficult than expected, especially if you may overexert. **Also, end the dive if you're not sure you can reasonably manage your gas in the situation – end the dive while you have plenty of gas to do so.**

Another option is to correct the problem, resume normal breathing and continue the dive as planned. This works when you can correct or compensate for whatever's making you breathe harder, such as getting a buddy who swims too fast to slow down.

If your breathing's only slightly elevated, another response may be to continue the dive as planned until you reach turn pressure – **but only do this if you are not in danger of overexerting**, and if you will have normal, relaxed breathing after you turn the dive. The most common example of this is swimming into a mild current. After you turn the dive, the current aids your return, so your breathing rate drops. You will reach your turn pressure a bit sooner than planned, however, in such a situation.

When in doubt, *be conservative* – remember the primary objective of every dive. You never want to get to the end of your gas before you get to the end of your dive.

Note: Never allow yourself to overexert and get out of breath underwater. If you begin to feel anxious, lightheaded and/or air starved, immediately stop, signal your buddy(ies) and catch your breath. Abort the dive or continue at a slower pace.

Being lower on gas than you would like is something most divers face eventually. Reasoned responses can keep the situation from becoming an emergency. Emotional, incorrect responses can create a dynamic that makes it worse, so you want to understand and avoid the psychological dynamic that can arise when low on gas.

A diver who is lower on gas than desired at a given point (especially when already heading toward the exit) feels time pressure, especially if conditions make surfacing immediately undesirable (e.g., chop, strong current) or impossible (e.g., tec decompression or overhead environment).

What do people naturally do when they feel time pressure? They hurry. So the diver swims faster, starting a snowball effect: Faster swimming raises exertion, which increases gas consumption. This depletes the gas supply even faster, which increases time pressure, making the diver swim even faster, and so on. The diver also risks becoming overexerted.

Correct (but unintuitive) responses avoid this cycle. If you find yourself lower on gas than desired and surfacing immediately isn't the best option (in recreational diving, it should always be an option, so this is usually a judgment call):

1. Slow down. Set a pace that slows your breathing. It will take longer to reach your exit point, but you will use less gas covering the same distance.
2. If possible, ascend to a shallower level. Swimming even 3 metres/10 feet shallower may reduce gas consumption significantly. This may not be a good tactic if you're (unexpectedly) swimming against a current – current tends to be weaker near the bottom – but it is often an option.
3. Ascend. Regardless, when you or a buddy reaches ascent pressure, begin your ascent. **Do not risk running out of gas underwater.**

If you're lower on gas than you'd like and the best option is to continue to your exit underwater, slow down. By exerting less, you will use less gas to cover the same distance.

Elements of Situational Awareness

Situational awareness applies to *anything* in your surroundings that may affect you – including yourself – but, in addition to gas management, you need to consciously monitor these eight other elements as you train yourself to develop and maintain effective situational awareness.

1. **No stop time.** Remain aware of:
   - Your no stop time remaining.
   - How soon you should ascend to remain well within no stop limits.
2. **Environment.** Remain aware of:
   - Changes in wave/current/surge strength and/or the direction.
   - Increases/decreases in visibility or temperature.
   - Changes in water density – i.e., going from fresh to salt water or vice versa.
   - Your interactions – touching, disturbing or otherwise affecting aquatic life.
3. **Equipment.** Remain aware of:
   - Proper operation – note minor problems that could become major problems.
   - Adjustment/fit – especially releases that can slowly loosen.
   - Accessories, instruments, etc. – where and how they are secured.
4. **Hazards.** Remain aware of:
   - Hazards noted during dive planning.
   - Unexpected hazards.
   - Degree of hazard – is it, or has it become, higher than expected (e.g., you expected jellyfish in the area, but there are dozens, not just a couple as you expected)? Can you avoid it, or should you end the dive?
5. **Depth.** Remain aware of:
   - Your present depth.
   - Your rate and direction of depth change.
   - How far you would descend before being stopped by a physical barrier.
   - The consequences of descending that far.
6. **Navigation, orientation and location.** Remain aware of:
   - Where you are and where you came from.
   - The most direct route to your ascent point/exit.
   - Where you're going.
7. **Buddy status and location.** Remain aware of:
   - Buddy's(ies') location.
   - Communications.
   - Factors that may affect buddy(ies) – e.g., gas supplies, hazards, thermal comfort, etc.
8. **Secondary objective.** Remain aware of:
   - Secondary objectives staying secondary.
   - How soon you must quit your secondary objective due to gas use, no stop time or other dive limits.

That may seem like a lot, but you already do it to a large extent. You'll also learn to prioritize your awareness when problems arise – we cover that in the next subsection.

EXERCISE-3

1. Situational awareness is my ability to perceive what's going on around me and
   - ☐ a. to plan the next dive.
   - ☐ b. how it affects me.
   - ☐ c. remember it.
2. As I train and gain experience as a diver, my sphere of awareness tends to
   - ☐ a. solidify.
   - ☐ b. stabilize.
   - ☐ c. contract.
   - ☐ d. expand.
3. Elements of situational awareness in recreational diving include (choose all that apply):
   - ☐ a. gas.
   - ☐ b. equipment.
   - ☐ c. depth.
   - ☐ d. navigation.
4. Examples of remaining situationally aware would include knowing how close I have come to a no stop limit, and the most direct route to my exit point.
   ☐ True ☐ False

How did you do?:

1. b. 2. d. 3. a, b, c, d. 4. True.

LEARNING OBJECTIVES

By the end of this section, I should be able to answer these questions:

1. How does knowing where to put my attention first help me resolve multitasking conflicts while diving?

2. What is the order for what I pay attention to first, second and third?

Managing Task Loading – Know What to Do First

You and a buddy are at 12 metres/40 feet in a free descent without reference to 18 metres/60 feet. The visibility is 5 metres/15 feet, so you can't see the bottom or the surface.

You notice the following happening at the same time:

- Your buddy waves to get your attention.
- You realize you've lost too much buoyancy and are beginning to descend out of control.
- You've lost your sense of direction.

What do you do first? Second? Third? To answer this, you apply a thinking strategy that prioritizes what you observe through situational awareness. Remember:

> **Dive** First >> **Situation** Second >>> **Communicate** Third

Dive First, Situation Second, Communicate Third resolves what to do first by sorting the priorities so you don't have to figure them out. You respond faster, better and with reduced stress. This strategy gives you thinking priorities – the order in which you assess the situation. The order in which you act may differ, depending on what you determine from your assessment. Notice that this strategy follows the spheres of awareness, from the inside outward.

Situational awareness applies to anything in your surroundings that may affect you.

Dive First, Situation Second, Communicate Third gives you thinking priorities – the order in which you assess the situation.

Dive First

Regardless of what is going on around you, your top priority is *functioning* well as a diver. This means having your buoyancy under control, operational scuba equipment, maintaining the ability to swim, controlling stress and breathing from your diaphragm, etc. Correct, adjust or change anything that requires it.

This is top priority, because not functioning well is an underlying cause of problems. If not the cause, it can make a problem worse, impede your ability to deal with it and impede assisting a buddy. Put another way, you take care of this first so you don't make things worse.

Situation Second

Your second priority is expanding awareness from yourself to what's around you – the external influences that can affect you. Your buddy is part of this; note your buddy's location, status and related communications. Maintain the integrity of the buddy system.

Deal with anything that demands your attention based on situational awareness according to urgency and importance. Confirm where you are, your depth and so on, as necessary.

Communicate Third

Your third priority is communicating with your buddy. This doesn't mean you're disregarding your buddy up to this point; Situation Second includes your buddy. But, *communication* comes after dealing with the situation.

There is overlap. Dealing with situational demands may naturally require buddy communication, and what a buddy communicates may be what alerts you to the situation. But, communication that's not immediately related to external factors that can affect you or your buddy comes last. You act on Dive First, Situation Second priorities, and *then* signal your buddy.

Putting It Into Practice

You should now be able to think through the opening example. First, adjust your buoyancy and restore a controlled descent rate. Get your dive under control. Second, check your computer and your compass to get reoriented to your depth and direction. Third, respond to your buddy.

Because this thinking follows your situational awareness from inward outward, you don't need to worry, for example, whether "check your depth" is part of Dive First or Situation Second.

Just start with yourself, then extend your thinking outward to your surroundings and your buddy, and everything will be in the proper order.

Let's look at a scenario in which Dive First, Situation Second, Communicate Third gives you suitable priorities. The responses described are examples; other responses may be appropriate, but the *thinking* strategy doesn't change.

Scenario: Out-of-Gas Emergency Over "Bottomless" Water

You're descending next to a wall – no bottom, for practical purposes – and begin to descend faster as your wet suit compresses. Before you can adjust, your buddy signals "out-of-gas."

Dive First: First, quickly get your buoyancy under control, because trying to share air with uncontrolled buoyancy is likely to be unsuccessful. It may make the situation worse, especially if your buddy's negatively buoyant – which is highly likely if out-of-gas.

Situation Second: But, your buddy's need to share gas is a very high and urgent situational priority. Therefore, it may be reasonable to provide your alternate air source *while also* adjusting your buoyancy. This may not be overly complicated or difficult. Dive First, Situation Second, Communicate Third assures that you *think* about the buoyancy issue so that you *can* share gas effectively, though you may not necessarily have to stop to adjust your buoyancy if you can reasonably respond to both together. Buoyancy adjustment may continue after you start sharing gas because you may need to offset your buddy's negative buoyancy.

Communicate Third: You signal "okay?" and "ascend," after your buddy is breathing from your alternate, just as you've practiced in the PADI Open Water Diver course.

EXERCISE-4

1. Dive First, Situation Second, Communicate Third helps me resolve multitasking conflicts by
   - ☐ a. telling me exactly what to do.
   - ☐ b. providing a set action strategy.
   - ☐ c. providing a set thinking strategy.
   - ☐ d. putting my buddy ahead of all else.
2. While night diving, I momentarily lose track of where I am. Just above the bottom I turn to signal my buddy, who's lagging behind. As I hover while waiting for my buddy to catch up, my fins dip and begin stirring up the bottom, and then my dive light fails. Based on Dive First, Situation Second and Communicate Third, I would first
   - ☐ a. deploy my backup light and restore my buoyancy/trim.
   - ☐ b. deploy my backup light and get a compass bearing.
   - ☐ c. signal my buddy that I am okay and deploy my backup light.
   - ☐ d. wait for my buddy to catch up to me.

How did you do?

1. c. 2. a.

Better Habits for Better Diving

Part of being a diver is accepting that problems *will* occur. You make a mistake, your buddy does or you make one together. You miscalculate conditions or they change. Equipment sometimes fails. Your training helps you avoid most of these problems, but things go wrong, so your training also helps you deal with emergencies. By studying emergency incident data, scientists have found common characteristics that lead to favorable and unfavorable responses in emergency situations.

Scientists have found that under stress, thinking tends to become *slow* and *impaired*. The more urgent the response needed, the greater the impairment. Interestingly, this happens in those who respond poorly *and* those who respond well. What makes the difference?

LEARNING OBJECTIVES

By the end of this section, I should be able to answer these questions:

1. What common characteristic of reacting to stress can work against me during an emergency?

2. How can my habits work against me or for me in an emergency? How do I learn and acquire good habits?

3. Why do divers sometimes mistakenly think they don't need to develop a habit or habits that they were trained to follow? What are the two main errors of this thinking?

4. How does each of these habits help me prevent and/or manage problems?

   - Making predive safety checks
   - Keeping the mask on and breathing from the snorkel/regulator when in the water at the surface/while exiting
   - Maintaining buoyancy at the surface
   - Turning the dive with ample no stop time remaining
   - Turning the dive with ample gas supply remaining
   - Beginning my ascent with ample gas supply remaining
   - Planning an ample reserve
   - Diving conservatively as I was trained

5. What is the most important resource when I have a problem underwater?

Scientists have found that under stress, mental processing tends to slow, causing impaired thinking. Those who respond well tend to be those who have good habits.

With reduced mental processing, people under stress tend to do what they do by habit. Having no or an ineffective habit/response tends to lead to greater stress, higher mental impairment and, potentially, to panic. A wholly or partially effective response tends to lower stress and lead to clearer thinking with better problem-solving. Good habits based on training even benefit complex situations, because knowing where to start helps reduce stress and expand thinking. This is one of the benefits of Dive First, Situation Second, Communicate Third – it is *habitual* thinking that gives you a place to start.

Whether you have developed bad habits that hinder dealing with an emergency or maintained the good habits you were taught, you will tend to follow those habits in an emergency. The habits you maintain may make a significant difference.

Suppose something tangles around a diver's fins while waiting to exit at the surface. A diver who has the habit of taking off the mask and not breathing from a snorkel or regulator while on the surface won't be able to see or breathe underwater to deal with the problem. This diver will tend to struggle without replacing the equipment. If unable to stay up and solve the problem by feel, panic and the need for rescue become likely. Putting gear back on *may* help but delays the response and requires (under stress-related, impaired thinking) recognizing the need to do it.

Alternatively, by habitually wearing a mask and breathing through a snorkel or regulator at the surface, the diver will see and breathe – face in the water – and deal with the entanglement. The diver likely handles it quickly, with little or no stress. In this example, the poor-habit diver's emergency is merely an annoyance for the good-habit diver.

Good Habits

In diving, you *learn* good habits primarily through training, but you *retain* them by continuously repeating them beyond training. Training teaches you habits that help you prevent and manage problems, or that reduce the effects of making a mistake – you are human, so you *will* make mistakes.

Training also connects good habits with responses that help you in an emergency. For instance, you learned to secure your alternate air source (AAS) in the triangle formed by your chin and rib cage corners. In an out-of-gas emergency, your AAS location/securing habit allows you to share gas immediately, because you don't grope to find it, and it's not filled with mud or sand due to dragging.

Any habit, good or bad, requires repetition to acquire. To develop a good habit, repeat it until you do it automatically. The habit you learn first tends to be the strongest, so establish good habits from the start. It is more difficult to unlearn a bad habit and replace it with a good one.

Some situations, like becoming tangled in a trail line, may be stressful problems for divers with poor habits, but little more than annoyances for divers with good habits.

Divers sometimes mistakenly think they don't need the habits they learned in training. They may think these habits are unnecessary, or think they'll simply follow a procedure, or carry required equipment when they need it. This thinking reflects two errors.

The first is believing (emotionally, if not consciously) that you are not going to make a mistake. Being in and underwater has significant potential risk simply because humans cannot breathe water; the potential for a mistake to have severe consequences is high (you've learned and accepted this and other risks). And again, because you are human, you will make mistakes. It is inevitable.

Despite this, diving has an impressive safety record. This is because it usually requires a series of multiple, small and unresolved errors/problems that snowball, and/or very severe errors, for an accident to occur. Divers are trained to follow procedures and have equipment that not only reduce errors and problems, but which also help keep your inevitable mistakes from becoming the first link in a chain of unfortunate events. This works, but only if you follow the procedures and equip yourself as you were trained. If you fail to do this, the probability of a serious incident rises substantially, because the probability of serious errors, or multiple errors leading to a "snowball," rises.

Since someone can make many dives without a serious problem related to particular equipment or procedures (habits), the diver may begin to consider certain procedures/equipment as "optional." Other divers role-modeling the same poor habits may reinforce the mistake. However, unless you assume that you, your buddies and your equipment are flawless (obviously not), eventually, failing to follow procedures and equipment requirements catches up with you.

Because some procedures are so simple, the second error is thinking you can override bad habits and do the right thing when you need to. This is not true.

Remember, clear thinking declines under stress. A diver likely will not, in the moment, reliably process and make correct choices. Lots of data support this. You will likely do what you do by habit – so have the right habits.

Habits That Help You

These habits can help you prevent and manage problems. Some may seem unnecessary on many dives – except that you're trying to develop and maintain habits so they're in place when you need them.

1. *Conduct predive safety checks.* Problems often begin with gear issues, so make predive safety checks with your buddy a standard part of starting every dive. Predive safety checks help confirm that you and your buddy have all your equipment, and that it's set up and working properly. They also help familiarize you and your buddy with each other's gear, so you're better able to assist each other.

2. *Keep the mask on and breathe from your snorkel/regulator whenever you're in water too deep in which to stand.* This allows you to see and keep your face submerged to deal with or prevent problems without having to replace them first. This speeds responses to problems below the surface and reduces the risk of splashes momentarily impairing your vision, or accidentally inhaling/choking on water, especially in choppy conditions. You're also less likely to lose your mask. If a situation calls for having no mask, you can remove it much faster than you can put it on. Using your snorkel at the surface conserves your gas supply, not only for the dive, but for handling problems. Breathing from your regulator while exiting allows you to breathe if you fall back in the water. Remove the mouthpiece to talk if necessary, but replace it when you're done speaking.

Keep your mask on and breathe from your snorkel or regulator whenever you're in water too deep in which to stand.

3. *Maintain buoyancy whenever you're at the surface.* Being buoyant allows you to relax and conserve energy. If you need to assist another diver, you're already buoyant and, as you learn in the PADI Rescue Diver course, you're in a better position to deal with a panicked diver.

4. *Turn the dive with ample no stop time remaining and ample gas supply remaining. Begin your ascent with ample gas supply remaining. Plan ample reserve.* The most important resource when you have an underwater problem is time. Your gas supply and no stop time remaining give you this resource. Plan more no stop time and gas supply for returning from the dive than you think you will need. You can usually use any excess near your exit and/or at a shallower level and surface with your reserve intact. Because you are human, one day you *will* need this reserve. Unfortunately, you won't know the dive on which this will happen ahead of time – so always have it.

5. *Dive conservatively, within your limits.* Follow all the procedures and have all of the equipment you were taught to have. If other divers don't, that's their business. Don't follow their examples. If other divers – especially local divers – appear to be *more* conservative, *do* follow their examples, or at least find out if what they do applies to you. Diving conservatively as you were trained helps assure that you maintain the procedural and equipment "safety nets" that reduce the risk of a serious incident.

Turn the dive with ample no stop time and gas remaining. Surface with your reserve intact.

Follow all the procedures and have all of the equipment you were taught to have. If other divers do not, that is their business. Do not follow poor examples.

EXERCISE-5

1. People who have good habits think faster under stress.
   ☐ True ☐ False
2. Under stress, people tend to do what they
   ☐ a. were taught to do.
   ☐ b. do by habit.
3. A good habit is to choose to have surface signaling devices on the dives when I'm most likely to need them.
   ☐ True ☐ False
4. I'm on a dive boat in a new area. As I confirm that I have a visual and an audible signaling device, I notice all the local divers have two of each. I should (choose all that apply):
   ☐ a. find out why in case I should have two of each, too.
   ☐ b. get one more of each kind myself.
   ☐ c. disregard the local divers and do as I was taught.

How did you do?

1. False. People with good habits respond better under stress, but still tend to have slowed thinking. 2. b. 3. False. Accidents do not announce themselves before the dive. Make a habit of having the gear you're supposed to have on all dives. 4. a, b.

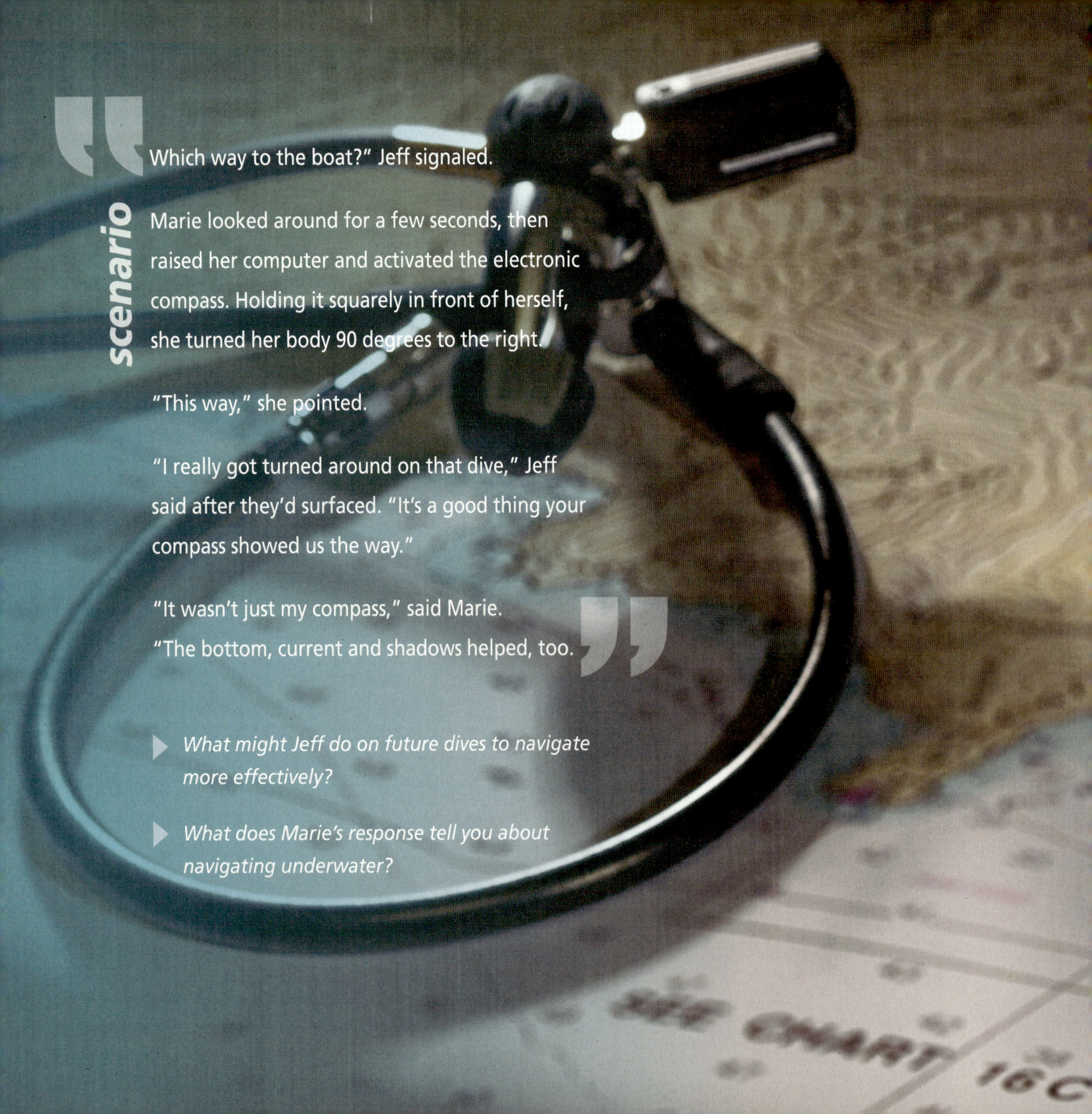

scenario

"Which way to the boat?" Jeff signaled.

Marie looked around for a few seconds, then raised her computer and activated the electronic compass. Holding it squarely in front of herself, she turned her body 90 degrees to the right.

"This way," she pointed.

"I really got turned around on that dive," Jeff said after they'd surfaced. "It's a good thing your compass showed us the way."

"It wasn't just my compass," said Marie. "The bottom, current and shadows helped, too."

- *What might Jeff do on future dives to navigate more effectively?*
- *What does Marie's response tell you about navigating underwater?*

UNDERWATER NAVIGATION 2

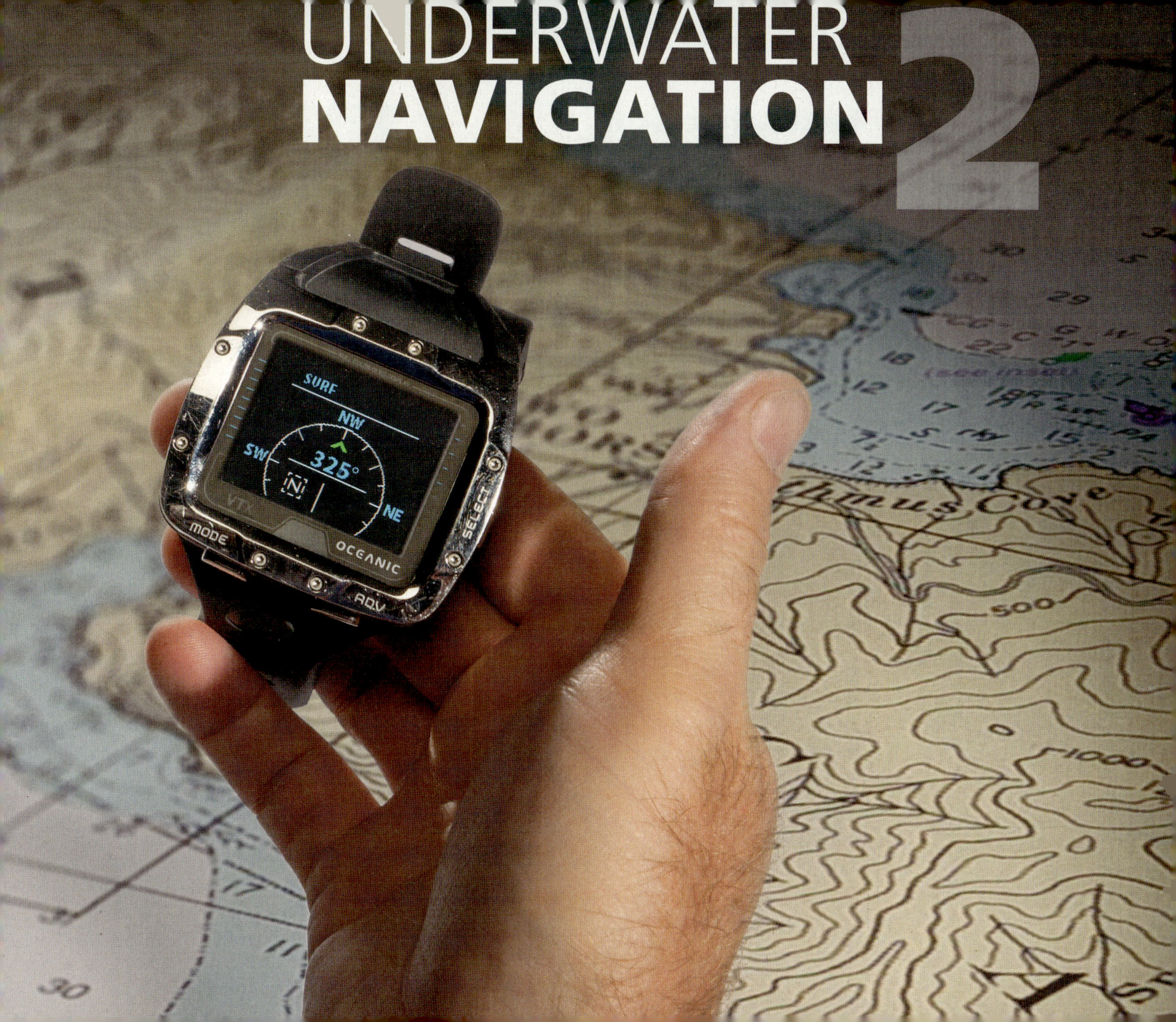

UNDERWATER **NAVIGATION**

Introduction

Remember your first open water dive? More than likely, you were thrilled with your first venture beyond a confined water or pool dive, but perhaps somewhat disoriented. Depending on the dive site, you might have been surprised to discover that even though you were unsure about direction, your instructor knew exactly where you were. Your instructor demonstrated *underwater navigation*, an important diving fundamental that, as you discovered on your subsequent dives, you learn and apply easily through a few principles and practice.

LEARNING OBJECTIVES

By the end of this section, I should be able to answer this question:

1. What are five benefits of mastering underwater navigation?

The Underwater Navigation Dive takes the rudimentary skills you're already familiar with and expands on them, so you can use those skills with greater accuracy and under wider circumstances.

Almost any diver can wander around in a general direction and eventually end up in the right place, but you'll want greater precision because effective navigation has at least five distinct benefits:

The Navigation Dive takes the rudimentary skills you're already familiar with and expands on them, so you can use those skills with greater accuracy and under wider circumstances.

1. Reduces Anxiety and Confusion

If you've ever been completely disoriented underwater, you know it can create anxiety, especially if you're low on air and would prefer to avoid surfacing (due to boat traffic or chop, for example); you don't know which way to go, which can be disquieting because you're not sure where to head if you need to cut the dive short. On the other hand, you may have a general idea of where you are but are confused about where you're trying to go – this can be irritating as your gas supply drops while you search. It's annoying to find the dive's hot spot, only to have to immediately leave due to low gas.

Navigation eliminates stress and confusion, because you'll always know where you are, which way to go, and how far you are from the boat or shore.

2. Helps Avoid Long Surface Swims

If you're not good at underwater navigation and your dive objective is far from the boat or shore, the only way to reach it without losing your way is to swim on the surface and then descend. Likewise, if you get turned around during a dive, when you run low on gas you have no alternative but to ascend where you are and swim back on the surface. Not only are surface swims more tiring and less interesting than swimming underwater, but in some areas with high boat traffic they may also be more hazardous.

3. Increases Dive Plan Effectiveness

Navigation helps make a plan more effective, by reducing guesswork about the time and gas needed to reach your objective and return. For example, if you and your buddy plan to take pictures on a familiar part of a reef, you can swim straight there rather than waste time searching for it. You use more of your time doing what you came to do and less time trying to find your way.

Mastering navigation helps reduce anxiety and confusion, and avoids long surface swims. It increases dive plan effectiveness, helps keep you with your buddy and conserves your breathing gas.

4. Helps Avoid Buddy Separation

When you and your buddy plan a dive, navigation takes you together along the same path to an agreed-upon destination, reducing the likelihood that you'll be separated from one another due to distractions or other influences. If you stray apart momentarily, you both know where to look and are more likely to find each other within a minute. This avoids spending time and gas reuniting on the surface.

5. Conserves Gas

Anything that saves you time in turn saves your gas, as does anything that helps you to be more confident and relaxed. More gas means more time doing what you like – taking pictures, observing fish, etc. – and makes for a more relaxing underwater swim back to the boat or shore, instead of a not-so-relaxing surface swim.

Besides these practical benefits, underwater navigation is a rewarding challenge. For example, navigating 100 metres/300 feet in limited visibility to a particular spot, then back to a specific exit point without surfacing or getting disoriented isn't necessarily easy. But, with training and experience, you can learn to do it repeatedly and reliably.

EXERCISE-1

1. Mastering underwater navigation benefits me by (choose all that apply):
   - ☐ a. helping reduce confusion and anxiety.
   - ☐ b. making surface swims more fun.
   - ☐ c. making my dive plan more effective.
   - ☐ d. helping me stay with my buddy.
   - ☐ e. helping conserve my breathing gas.

How did you do?

1. a, c, d, e.

LEARNING

OBJECTIVES

By the end of this section, I should be able to answer this question:

1. What are three techniques for estimating distance underwater, and how do I execute them?

Distance Estimation

To navigate, you really only need to know two things: which way you're headed, and how far you've gone. Learning to navigate means learning the techniques for both of these. Let's start with distance estimation, i.e., knowing how far you travel. There are several methods commonly used; we'll look at three.

Kick Cycles

One of the most convenient ways to gauge distance is to count kick cycles. A kick cycle is the distance you cover when both of your legs complete one fin stroke. To track kick cycles, choose either leg and count each time that leg returns to the same position. The distance you travel in one kick cycle is usually consistent.

During your navigation dive, you'll count your kick cycles as you swim a known distance. If it takes you 40 kick cycles to swim 30 metres/100 feet, for example, you know you travel about 0.75 metres/2.5 feet with each kick cycle. Then, if you were to swim 100 kick cycles, you'll know you'd have traveled approximately 75 metres/250 feet.

Gauge your kick cycles by swimming with the same relaxed pace you use when diving normally. Measure kick cycles while swimming fully submerged, because surface swimming is slower, so your kick cycles will differ from your underwater swimming measurements. You'll find that kick cycles are most accurate in calm, still water. A current will affect accuracy, though in surge they're moderately accurate if you maintain a steady pace, because the back-and-forth water motion tends to cancel itself out.

Kick cycles are particularly useful for measuring medium to long distances, and have the advantage of allowing you to stop, if necessary, and then resume your distance estimation. However, changes in your gear may affect kick cycles from one dive to the next. The size and stiffness of your fins, drag from a larger cylinder or accessories like cameras, or diving overweighted will affect the distance you cover with each cycle. If you change fins or anything that alters how streamlined you are, you'll need to re-measure your kick cycles, though they'll still be consistent within the same dive.

A kick cycle is the distance you cover when both of your legs complete one fin stroke. To track kick cycles, choose either leg and count each time that leg returns to the same position. This is one kick cycle.

Elapsed Time

You can also gauge distance underwater by measuring the time it takes to swim a known distance. If you know it takes you 30 seconds to swim about 30 metres/100 feet, for example, you can estimate your travel distance by timing your swim. So, in addition to kick cycles, you'll measure how long it takes you to swim a known distance during your underwater navigation dive.

As with kick cycles, swim at your normal, relaxed pace. The primary disadvantage of measuring distance with elapsed time is that if you stop or pause, you can throw off the measurements. As with kick cycles, current will affect elapsed time, but surge will not affect it much if you swim at a steady rate.

Cylinder Pressure

You can use gas pressure to measure distances much as you use elapsed time, because at about the same depth and activity level, your gas consumption is relatively uniform. For example, to swim a square you could swim until you've used 15 bar/200 psi, turn 90 degrees and swim until you've used another 15 bar/200 psi and so on until you return to your starting point.

A specific distance per bar/psi is only accurate at a relatively constant depth and breathing rate. This makes using gas consumption less useful for measuring metres/feet when the depth changes significantly over the distance you're measuring, or if your exertion level changes while swimming.

On the other hand, it's common to use cylinder pressure to measure distance in a relative sense over changing depths when following a course you plan to return on. This works, because the depth changes for the outbound and return trips cancel out, making the pressure you used a useful distance measure. This integrates well with gas management and your planned turn pressure – you limit how far you go based on what you need to return, plus the gas you need for the ascent and a reserve.

You learn other ways to measure distance, such as arm spans and lines, in the PADI Underwater Navigator course.

Besides kick cycles, you can use elapsed time or cylinder pressure to estimate distance while diving.

EXERCISE-2

1. While measuring distance using kick cycles, I count one cycle each time my leg
   - ☐ a. moves up or down.
   - ☐ b. returns to the same place.
   - ☐ c. moves up or down twice.
2. My buddy and I need to measure 60 metres/200 feet while following a slope from 12 metres/40 feet to approximately 18 metres/60 feet. Which of the following methods is probably our best bet?
   - ☐ a. Kick cycles
   - ☐ b. Gas pressure

How did you do?

1. b. 2. a.

Natural Navigation

Natural navigation is navigation based on what you observe in the environment – that is, navigation that isn't based on an instrument. From your previous dive experience, you've probably already begun to learn natural navigation, even if you don't know it. Finding direction from patterns in the sand, following the slope of a reef, or swimming against the current are all forms of natural navigation. Any dive site has features you can use as navigational references. It's just a matter of paying attention to the small details and environmental features that tell you where you are. You'll learn to use these references even when you're using your compass.

LEARNING OBJECTIVES

By the end of this section, I should be able to answer these questions:

1. What four predive observations can I make to assist with natural navigation?
2. How do I descend in a manner that assists me with natural navigation?
3. What six natural references do I commonly use to navigate underwater?

Predive Observations

Natural navigation begins before you dive, by looking at the environment for navigational references. From the surface, you can usually tell a great deal about what you'll encounter underwater, and you can use that information to determine where you are when you're diving.

Water motion

The direction of waves, currents and tides, while changeable, usually remains consistent over the length of a dive (though directions change once in a while – especially tidal flow). You can determine wave and current direction by watching floating debris, and in the case of tides by consulting tide apps or online tide tables. Once you know which way the water flows, you can orient yourself by swimming relative to the flow.

Sun direction and angle

Before getting in to the water, check how shadows fall and where the sun is in relation to your planned travel direction. Even in turbid water you can usually determine where the sun is, and use it to orient yourself.

Objects and formations

It's useful to note the position of reefs, piers, kelp beds, buoys and other objects so that you know where you are when you encounter them underwater. In clear water, you may see a submerged reef or wreck from the surface. Waves breaking offshore may indicate a shallow reef or sandbar, giving you reference even if the reef or sandbar does not reach the surface.

Depth finder

If you're diving from a boat with a depth finder, you'll be able to see a picture of the bottom. Depth finders can show you bottom contours, wrecks and reefs, all of which can be references that indicate where you are during the dive. Most depth finders give you a relative idea of depth changes, but not usually a wide area picture (though there are some types that do).

Natural navigation begins before you dive by looking at the environment for navigation references. From the surface, you can usually tell a great deal about what you'll encounter underwater, and you can use that information to determine where you are when you're diving.

Besides these predive observations, you may find maps of popular dive sites online at padi.com or posted by PADI Dive Centers and Resorts that lead divers to the area.

Descents

You improve navigation by maintaining your orientation as you descend. Start by orienting to your travel direction – know whether it's to your right, left, ahead, etc. If possible, either you or your buddy descends facing that way. Ideally, descend with your head level with or slightly above your feet, which helps maintain your sense of direction.

Often, you can follow a directional reference as you descend, such as a sloping mooring/anchor line or bottom. Note the strength and relative direction of the current (if there is one) as you descend.

You improve navigation by maintaining your orientation as you descend. Descend oriented to your travel direction, with either you or your buddy facing that way if possible. Ideally, descend with your head level with or slightly above your feet.

Natural References

Once underwater, you orient yourself through a variety of natural references. The six most common of these are light and shadows, water movement, bottom composition and formations, bottom contours, plants and animals, and sound.

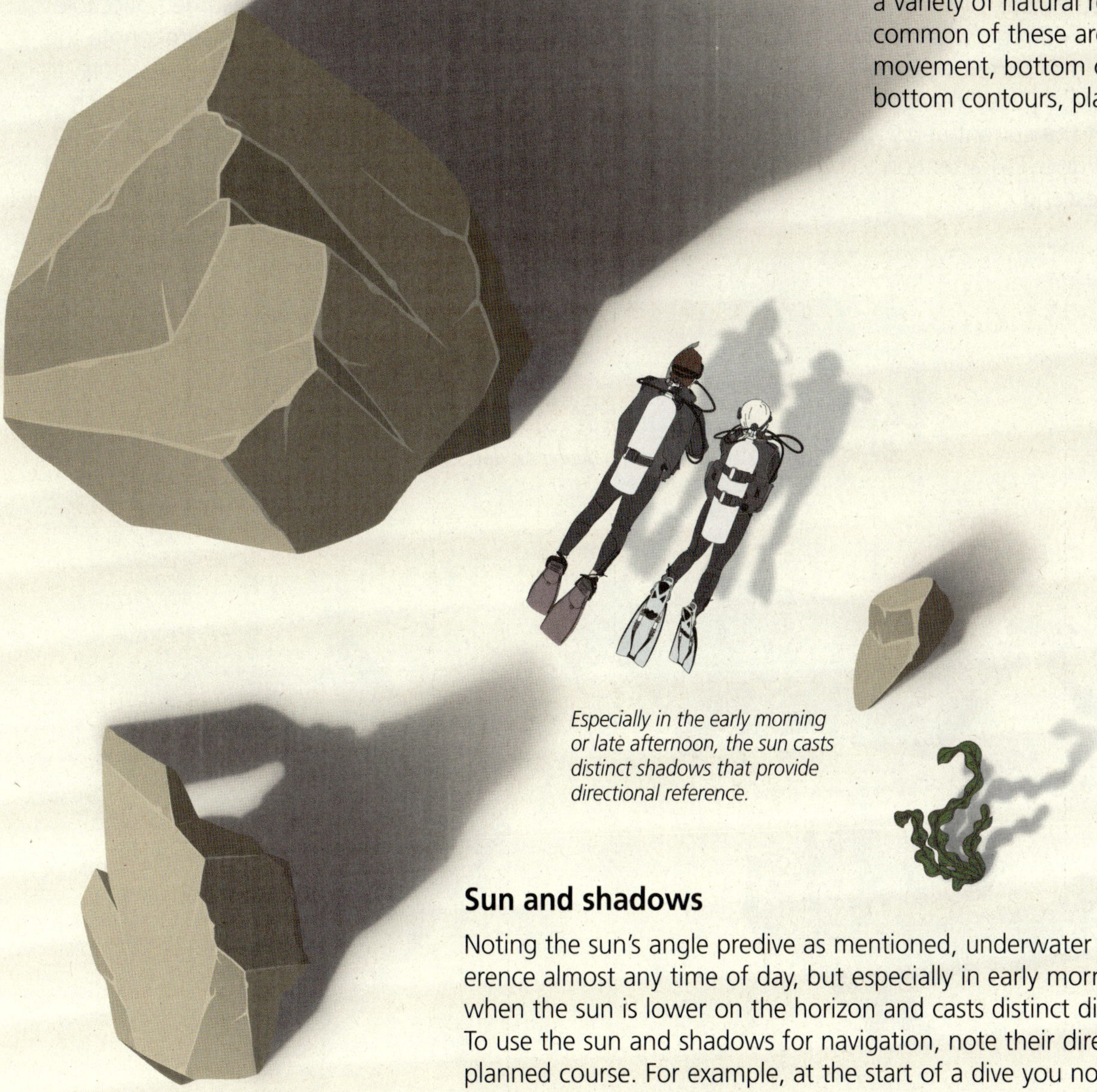

Especially in the early morning or late afternoon, the sun casts distinct shadows that provide directional reference.

Sun and shadows

Noting the sun's angle predive as mentioned, underwater you have a visual reference almost any time of day, but especially in early morning or late afternoon when the sun is lower on the horizon and casts distinct directional shadows. To use the sun and shadows for navigation, note their direction relative to your planned course. For example, at the start of a dive you note the sun is on your right and/or underwater shadows are to the left. If you get disoriented during the dive, turn so the sun's on your right and shadows are to your left. This faces you in your original direction. If you turn so the sun's on your left, you face the direction you came from. Changes in light intensity can cue you to depth changes.

Water motion

Currents provide a sure method of underwater navigation. If you're drift diving (ask your PADI Instructor about the Drift Diver course and Adventure Dive), the current naturally navigates for you, carrying you where it will. In most cases, however, you swim against the current, with the flow giving a constant bearing. Be aware that currents can shift direction during a dive, especially when tides change. Plan your dive with this in mind, so that the current helps you return to your exit at the end of the dive. Pay attention to current direction and speed as you descend.

Waves passing overhead cause surge. Surge is a reliable reference because the back-and-forth motion swings to and from shore or shallow areas. You feel it most strongly in shallow water. However, large swells can make surge noticeable in even relatively deep water. When diving in surge, note the water movement to determine the direction toward shore. If you're disoriented to the point that you don't know which "swing" is shoreward, follow the surge in one direction and watch your depth gauge. In the majority of cases, shoreward will be shallower and seaward will be deeper, but it helps to know the dive site beforehand.

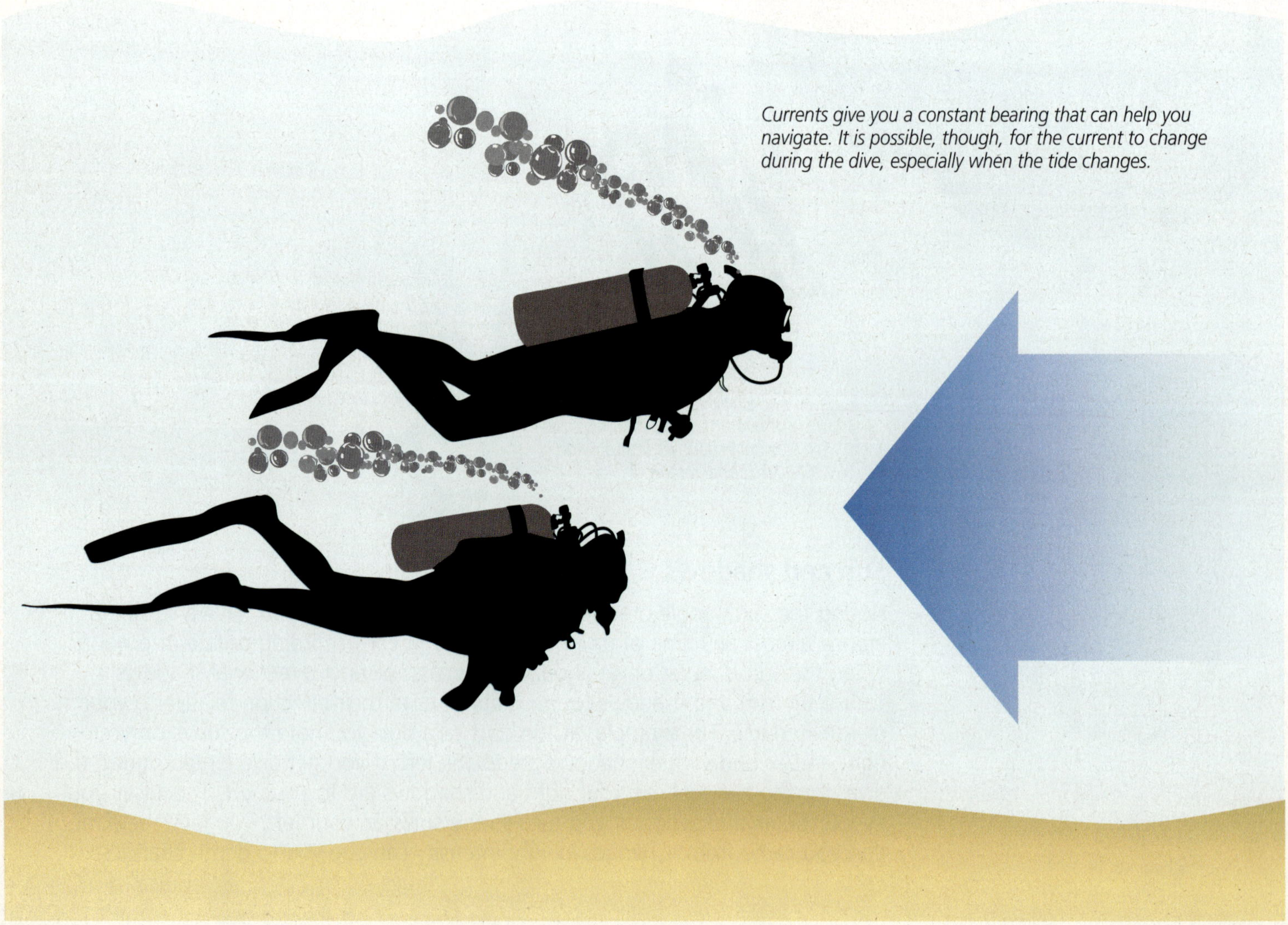

Currents give you a constant bearing that can help you navigate. It is possible, though, for the current to change during the dive, especially when the tide changes.

Bottom composition and formations

Changes in bottom composition are something else to note during a dive. You may find that various areas have distinctly different bottoms, ranging from rock to sand, mud or reef, depending upon the environment. Plant life (discussed shortly) can vary with the bottom type.

Even when the bottom composition is the same, water movement may create patterns you can use for navigation. Sand ripples are a good example; they form perpendicular to the water flow. In lakes and the ocean near a shoreline, sand ripples generally lie parallel to shore; by swimming perpendicular to the ripples, you'll head toward or away from shore usually (easily judged by whether you're getting deeper or shallower). Swimming along them, you travel parallel to shore.

Bottom contour

The bottom almost always has notable contours suitable for navigation. You can follow a natural slope toward deeper water; rock ridges, coral reefs, kelp beds and, in lakes, even sunken logs can form natural paths you can swim along. To follow a contour, simply keep the slope or other reference on your right or left. To reverse your course, turn around and keep the contour on the opposite side.

Sand ripples generally lie parallel to shore; by swimming perpendicular to them, you'll head toward or away from shore. Swimming along them, you travel parallel to shore.

Sea fans face in the same direction as their neighbors and always grow perpendicular to prevailing currents.

Sound

As you learned in your Open Water Diver course, it's difficult to determine sound direction. But, you can still use sound as a navigation aid by paying attention to its strength and your relative distance from it. Organisms on a reef sometimes click or crackle, telling you that you're approaching or leaving it. The sound of a boat compressor or generator, the clanking of a mooring/anchor chain, or rocks tumbling in the surf can all provide reliable information about your distance from the boat or shore.

Plants and animals

Aquatic plants and animals often have specific natural niches or characteristics that provide clues you can use for navigation. Some organisms live only at specific depths, cuing you to deeper or shallower water nearby. Other examples include sea fans, which always grow perpendicular to prevailing currents, and sand dollars (when alive), which typically orient themselves perpendicular to shore. Finding lots of fish over open sand may suggest a reef or habitat nearby.

Through observation and training, such as offered in the PADI Underwater Naturalist Specialty course and during the Underwater Naturalist Adventure Dive, you recognize the different organisms that provide information about your location underwater. Note how these organisms lie relative to your position and travel direction at the start of your dive, and you can use them as a reference to maintain your direction or reorient yourself.

EXERCISE-3

1. My buddy and I are preparing for a dive. Which of the following predive observations may help us navigate? (Choose all that apply.)
   - ☐ a. Sun direction
   - ☐ b. Horizon
   - ☐ c. Waves
   - ☐ d. Offshore objects
2. To help us with navigation, my buddy and I descend
   - ☐ a. head low, facing away from our planned travel direction.
   - ☐ b. head above feet, facing our planned travel direction.
3. While swimming on a reef, my buddy and I get a bit disoriented, but after swimming a bit we find ourselves over sand with ripples. That may help us, because sand ripples generally lie
   - ☐ a. parallel to shore.
   - ☐ b. perpendicular to shore.
   - ☐ c. in line with prevailing currents.

How did you do?

1. a, c, d. 2. b. 3. a.

LEARNING OBJECTIVES

By the end of this section, I should be able to answer these questions:

1. Which underwater compass features are essential? How do conventional and electronic compasses differ in how they provide these features?

2. How do I hold and use a compass to maintain an accurate heading while swimming?

3. What tips can I use to make compass navigation more effective?

Today, there are two kinds of compasses: the conventional analog compass, and the electronic compass, usually built into a dive computer.

Compass Navigation

Although you can navigate on many dives using only natural navigation, you navigate most effectively by also using a compass. This is because it gives you a directional reference even when there are no other references. A compass also gives you the most precision when you need it, such as when traveling over a featureless bottom.

Compass Features

Today, there are two kinds of compasses: the conventional analog compass and the electronic compass, which is usually built into a dive computer. Fundamentally, you use both the same way.

Besides being created for scuba diving – designed to withstand water pressure – all analog or electronic compasses have features you need for the most accuracy:

- Dampened response
- Indicates direction even when not perfectly level
- Provides degree numbers (not just north, south, east and west)
- Readable in low light
- Actual or virtual lubber lines and bezels

Dampened response means the compass readings are "cushioned" so they don't jump significantly due to the normal motions of diving, especially when you're swimming.

The needle of an analog compass locks if you tilt it too far from level, so dive compasses have a high tilt tolerance. The electronic versions usually tolerate being off level more than analog models.

For precision, you need a compass that reads degree headings in numbers. Precision analog compasses typically show degree headings in 30-degree increments, with smaller increments in between. Electronic dive compasses typically read the heading number digitally, often in one-degree increments (very precise), often displaying a virtual compass similar to an analog compass.

You'll use a compass night diving and in low visibility, so you want to be able to read it easily under those conditions. Analog compasses usually have luminous markings. Electronic compasses are commonly part of computer dive screens with internal illumination.

In the PADI Open Water Diver course, you learned basic compass navigation and may recall that the lubber line – actual or virtual – indicates your travel direction, and the bezel – again, actual or virtual – helps you hold a steady heading while swimming. Analog compasses designed for precision navigation have a lubber line and bezel, whereas those intended for general reference only may not. Electronic compasses usually accomplish both functions without an actual marked lubber line or bezel – these functions are there, but are virtual in the way you use them (more about this shortly).

Holding the Compass

You use all dive compasses similarly. The exact way you read and set them varies somewhat, but the basic steps for using analog compasses apply to most models, including electronic models. If you're not sure about the specifics for setting your compass, see your PADI Instructor and/or the manufacturer literature.

As you probably remember, hold your compass level, facing your travel direction. Align the lubber line – an imaginary line through the center of the compass, though it may be marked – squarely with your body centerline, pointed in your travel direction.

Set the bezel by rotating it until the index marks straddle the needle. This provides a visual reference that you're on course. If you turn from the desired direction, the needle leaves the index marks; turn back to re-center the needle between them. With electronic compasses, you may use a virtual bezel setting. This simply means noting the heading (e.g. 273 degrees). If you turn from the desired direction, the number changes – turning back returns to the original heading. (Electronic compasses vary in this – again, see the manufacturer literature.)

A suitable dive compass has these features:

1. *Dampened response*
2. *Lubber line*
3. *Bezel with index marks*
4. *Degrees in numbers*
5. *High tilt tolerance*
6. *Readable in low light*

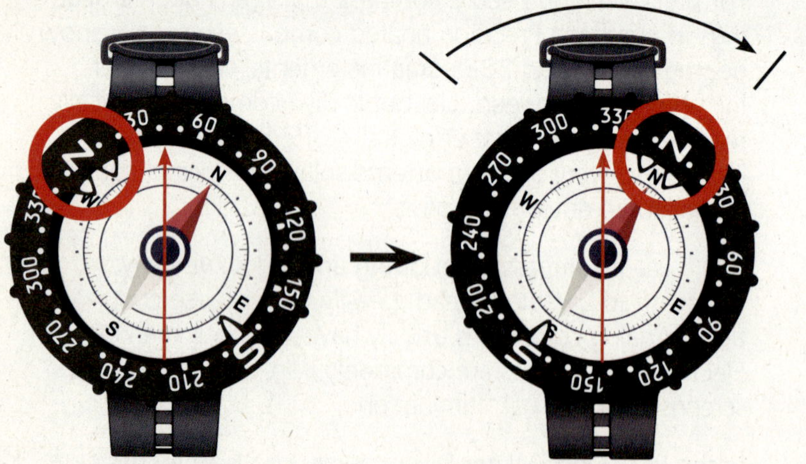

Set the compass by pointing the lubber line in your travel direction, then rotate the bezel until the index marks straddle the needle.

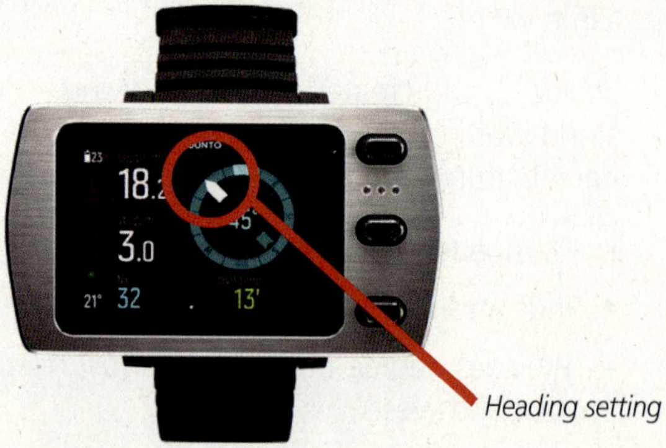

Electronic compasses allow you to set a heading, though they vary somewhat in how you do so.

To swim holding a heading, keep the compass centered with your body and travel along the lubber line (the needle *always* points north and the lubber line is *always* your travel direction) keeping the needle within the index marks (analog) or following the heading number (electronic). Look *over* the compass as you swim, so you watch where you're going. It's usually most effective if one buddy navigates and the other escorts.

If you have a physical challenge that requires you to swim with your arms, it is hard to keep the compass centered and swim at the same time. One technique is to strap the compass to your hand (so you can swim with open palms and still see it). After each breast stroke, as you glide and reach forward for the next, quickly center the compass in front of you and check your orientation.

PROJECT AWARE

When navigating and swimming with a compass, remember to control your buoyancy, staying well off the bottom and avoiding damage to sensitive aquatic life.

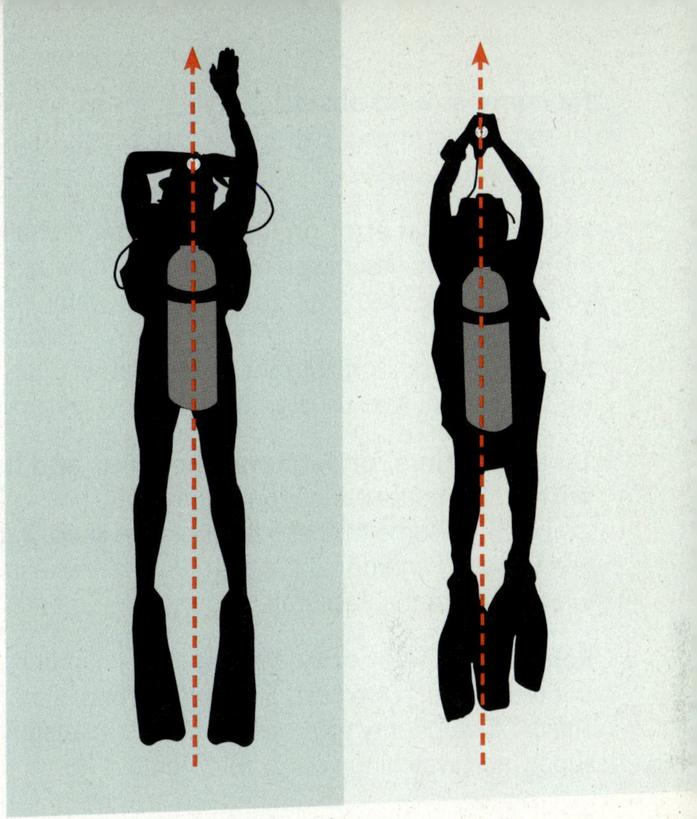

To swim holding a heading, keep the compass centered with your body and travel along the lubber line, keeping the needle within the index marks (analog) or following the heading number (electronic). Look over the compass as you swim.

Compass Use Tips

Here are a few pointers that will make using a compass easier and more accurate.

Trust your compass. If you're new to compass navigation, sometimes it feels like it's misleading you. More often than not, the compass is right and your sense of direction is off.

Use natural references. The combination of natural navigation with compass navigation is the most effective navigation. The compass closes gaps where you can't effectively navigate with landmarks, and natural navigation helps offset any mistakes you make using your compass.

Practice on land. If you're not used to how your compass works, give it a dry run on land. It works exactly the same at the surface, so you can get used to it without wasting dive time.

Allow for the effects of currents. A compass helps you swim in a straight line, but water movement such as currents or surge can carry you off course. If currents are common in your local area, your instructor may teach you how to navigate accordingly.

Share responsibilities midwater. If you're navigating in midwater, have one buddy read the compass and the other monitor depth. The depth buddy can hold the compass buddy's arm to keep the team together while watching instruments. If you're in a three-person team, you can make life even easier by further dividing responsibilities.

Use patterns. Although you can effectively navigate a random pattern without losing your way, it's easier to follow a basic course. (We'll look at patterns shortly.)

Navigate around obstacles. When following any course, don't let something in your path throw you off. Detour around it and resume your course.

Use intentional error on long distances. If you're looking for a small, specific destination a long distance away, chances are you're going to miss. Even the best underwater navigation just isn't that precise when you start swimming hundreds of metres/feet. So, aim for slightly to the right or left of your target. If you miss your mark (you usually do), you know which way to search.

Take your time, understand the limits and have fun with it. Compass navigation will not zero you in like GPS (more about some of these technologies shortly), but with practice you can find your way to within several metres/feet – which is more than accurate enough.

Remember the priority. Navigation is an important skill, but remember "Dive First, Situation Second, Communicate Third." Give priority to proper buoyancy, managing your gas supply and watching your no stop time.

EXERCISE-4

1. It's important that a dive compass indicates direction even when not perfectly level.

   ☐ True ☐ False

2. I'm using a compass to navigate for our buddy team over a featureless bottom with no current. To maintain an accurate heading, I should align the actual or virtual compass lubber line with

   ☐ a. the compass needle.
   ☐ b. either side of my body.
   ☐ c. the midline of my body.
   ☐ d. my buddy's cylinder.

3. My buddy and I want to navigate to an underwater sculpture placed about 200 yards/metres away. We have about 4 metres/12 feet of visibility and will use a compass heading to get there. My buddy thinks we should
   intentionally aim a little bit to the left. Is this a good idea?

   ☐ Yes ☐ No

How did you do?

1. True. 2. c. 3. Yes.

Get used to using your compass on land. It works exactly the same underwater, so you can master the basics without wasting dive time.

LEARNING OBJECTIVES

By the end of this section, I should be able to answer these questions:

1. What four patterns do divers use for underwater navigation?

2. How do I set a compass to navigate a reciprocal course and a square/rectangle?

3. What are six ways to use an underwater pattern effectively?

Using Navigation Patterns

It's much easier to know where you are and where you're going if you follow a predetermined pattern instead of swimming about randomly. This might sound restrictive, but you actually see more than you would by wandering aimlessly. You use your limited gas and bottom time more effectively when you use a pattern suited to the dive site. Out-and-back lines, squares/rectangles, triangles and circles are commonly used navigation patterns, each with its own characteristics. We'll discuss the out-and-back line and squares/rectangles. See the PADI *Underwater Navigator Manual* for more about triangles and the PADI *Search and Recovery Diver Manual* to learn about circular search patterns.

Out-and-Back Lines

Out-and-back lines are the simplest and perhaps most common patterns. You follow a straight line out, then reverse course and follow the same (or a close parallel) line back to your exit. You may follow a compass heading or natural formations that are long and narrow – e.g. reef grooves, the side of a wreck, etc. – or a combination of these. Using natural references, the "line" can be somewhat irregular if you have a distinct path to follow, such as the edge of a winding reef. When you reach turn pressure, you reverse and come back the way you came. You may do this several metres/feet to one side or the other if possible so you can spot some different features on the return.

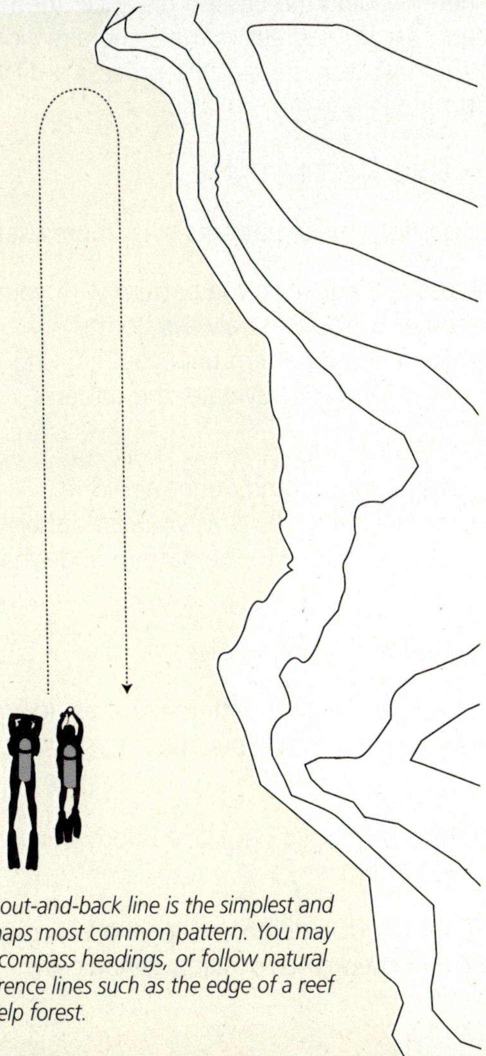

The out-and-back line is the simplest and perhaps most common pattern. You may use compass headings, or follow natural reference lines such as the edge of a reef or kelp forest.

Setting a Reciprocal Course

Using a compass, you return using a *reciprocal* course to follow an out-and-back line pattern. You learned this in the PADI Open Water Diver course, but to refresh:

- Outbound, follow your compass along a single heading as you learned in the previous discussion.
- At your turn point, rotate the bezel (analog compass) 180 degrees, then turn until the needle is again within the index marks. You're facing your return heading; swim along the lubber line.

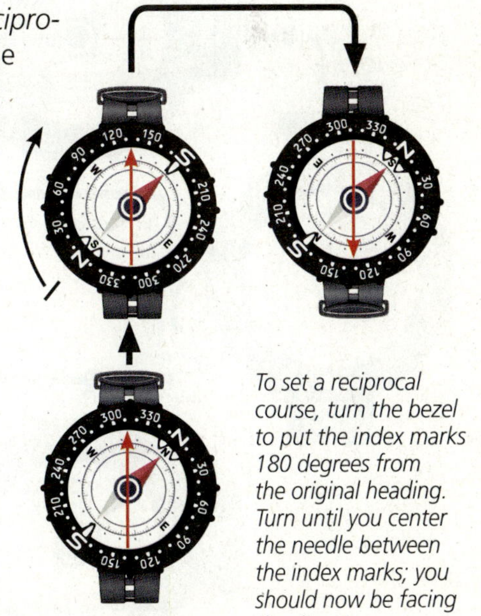

To set a reciprocal course, turn the bezel to put the index marks 180 degrees from the original heading. Turn until you center the needle between the index marks; you should now be facing the direction you came.

Some analog compasses have two sets of index marks so you don't have to reset the bezel. Simply rotate yourself to put the needle between the opposite set of marks.

Squares and Rectangles

Squares and rectangles cover more area, and suit both natural and compass navigation. Three legs of a square/rectangle are usually the easiest way to navigate around an obstacle. You may or may not have to measure distance to get a useable pattern.

An example of a natural navigation rectangle pattern would be to swim out from shore, turn 90 degrees and swim parallel to shore, then turn 90 degrees toward shore. In shallow water, you turn 90 degrees to swim parallel to shore toward your entry point. Using depth, contours and other navigation cues around you, and with a large entry/exit area, you may

When navigating a square/rectangle, use your compass to make three 90-degree turns, returning you to your starting point. In this case, your initial heading is 50°, followed by 140 °, 230 ° and 320 °.

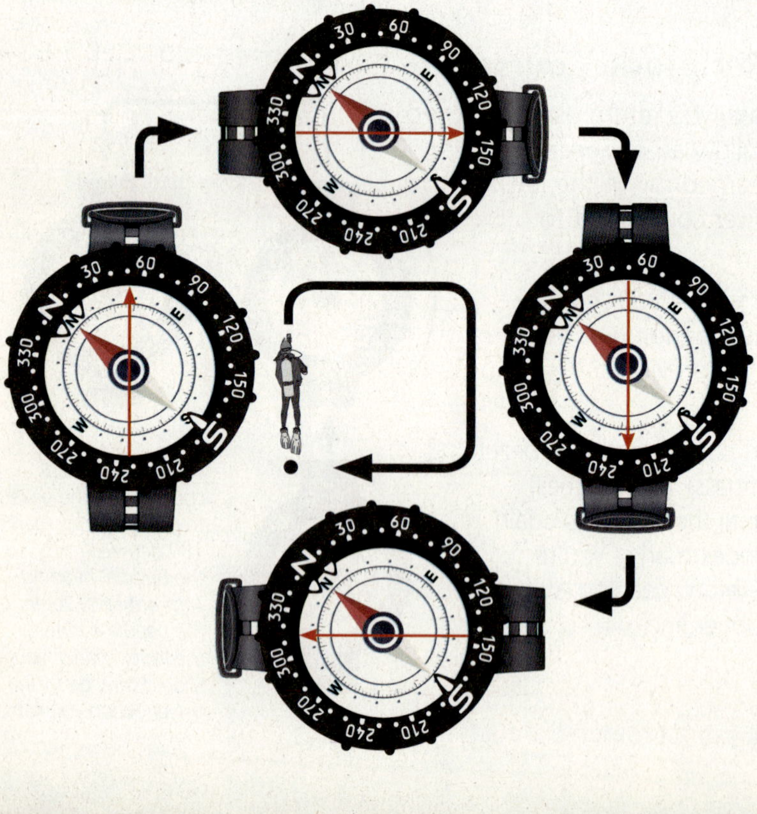

be able to navigate this pattern effectively without using your compass or measuring distance. But, if you need to follow the pattern very precisely (perhaps to return to a line for your ascent), then using your compass and measuring kick cycles may be more useful.

To compass navigate a square or a rectangle, begin by setting a heading for the first side and swimming the desired distance – use kick cycles, time or cylinder pressure to measure. Rotate the bezel 90 degrees and turn to realign the needle within the index marks. Add 90 degrees for a right turn, or subtract 90 degrees for a left; this is also how to find your headings when using an electronic compass that shows only headings. When adding, due North is 0 degrees; when subtracting it is 360 degrees.

Swim along the new heading the desired distance, then rotate the bezel another 90 degrees in the same direction (right or left) for the next turn. Repeat the process until you complete the pattern.

Tips for Effective Pattern Use

The following suggestions make patterns even more useful.

1. If possible, discuss and agree on the pattern with your buddy before the dive. You can't always do this – you may not know you need a pattern until you're diving – but doing so settles who will navigate, the pattern direction, etc.
2. Visualize the pattern prior to and during the dive. If you create a mental birds-eye view, you can get an idea of where you are relative to the pattern and what's around you.
3. Keep patterns small and move slowly.
4. When you must deviate from a pattern (such as going around an obstacle), remember your heading so you can return to it.
5. It's generally most effective to have one buddy in charge of navigating the pattern.
6. As appropriate for the dive depth and location, it may help to surface and check your position periodically.

EXERCISE-5

1. Probably the most common navigation pattern is the
   - ☐ a. out-and-back line.
   - ☐ b. square/rectangle.
   - ☐ c. triangle.
   - ☐ d. circle.
2. Within the confines of a natural harbor, my buddy is navigating a square pattern with a compass, measuring distance with kick cycles. At the turn point, we should turn _______ degrees.
   - ☐ a. 60
   - ☐ b. 90
   - ☐ c. 120
   - ☐ d. 180
3. My buddy and I plan to take turns navigating each leg of an underwater rectangle. Generally, is that recommended for best accuracy?

   ☐ Yes ☐ No

How did you do?

1. a. 2. b. 3. No.

LEARNING

OBJECTIVES

By the end of this section, I should be able to answer this question:

1. What type of technology is providing new options for precise underwater navigation?

Other Navigational Devices

You can use tools that expand your ability to navigate. Your PADI Dive Center or Resort can show you some of these, and you can learn more about them in the PADI Underwater Navigator course.

Among these, electronics are giving rise to underwater navigation options that are easier to use and more accurate than compass navigation. GPS (Global Positioning System) is a challenge for underwater use, because the signals don't penetrate water. To provide GPS-like convenience, however, a growing number of systems use a transponder hanging from a boat, buoy or dock. The transponder emits signals that diver-carried instruments (including some dive computers) use to track your relative position. While these are not entirely new, this is an emerging area of underwater technology in recreational diving that will become increasingly common.

Even with electronic underwater navigation, for the immediate future there will be many circumstances in which these devices are impractical and/or unavailable. Therefore, natural navigation and compass navigation will likely remain important, useful dive skills for the foreseeable future.

PADI UNDERWATER NAVIGATOR SPECIALTY

The Underwater Navigation Adventure Dive credits toward the PADI Underwater Navigator Specialty course. The course gives you more opportunities to apply and practice compass and natural navigation skills, including:

- More distance estimation methods
- Triangle patterns
- Relocating dive sites

Remember to log your training dives with the PADI Mobile App or at padi.com.

Knowledge Review – Underwater Navigation

Answer the following questions by selecting the best choice (or choices) from those provided. Be prepared to discuss the material at your next training session.

1. I'm planning a dive in moderately low visibility (2-3 metres/6-10 feet) and I want to maintain buddy contact. Skill in underwater navigation will help me with this.
   - True
   - False
2. When measuring distance with kick cycles, you count when
   - each leg returns to the same position.
   - the same leg returns to the same position.
3. When estimating distance with elapsed time, you measure how long it takes to cover a fixed distance while swimming
   - somewhat slower than normal.
   - at a normal, relaxed pace.
   - faster than normal.
4. My buddy and I are diving from a boat that's moored in an area popular for diving. Which of the following predive observations may assist us with natural navigation during the dive? (Choose all that apply.)
   - The divemaster tells us the boat is pointed directly into the current.
   - It's 3:30 p.m. and the sun is setting to the west.
   - There's a large buoy moored directly behind the boat.
   - The boat's depth finder shows 15 metres/50 feet directly under the boat.
5. To maintain my orientation and benefit from natural navigation, descend
   - feet above head, shoulder pointed in travel direction.
   - head above feet, shoulder pointed in travel direction.
   - feet above head, facing travel direction.
   - head above feet, facing travel direction.
6. While navigating with natural references, which of the following can help me? (Choose all that apply.)
   - Light and shadows
   - Water movement
   - Bottom composition and formations
   - Plants and animals
   - Noise/sounds
7. I'm navigating with a compass. To maintain an accurate heading, keep the ______________ aligned with my body's centerline.
   - index marks
   - compass needle
   - bezel
   - lubber line
8. With a standard analog compass, the __________ always indicates your travel direction. The ___________ always points to magnetic north.
   - a. compass needle; lubber line
   - b. lubber line; compass needle
   - c. index marks; bezel
   - d. bezel; compass needle
9. To set a reciprocal heading, turn the compass to a heading that is ____________ from the original heading.
   - a. 45°
   - b. 90°
   - c. 135°
   - d. 180°
   - e. 225°
   - f. 270°
   - g. 295°
   - h. 360°
10. During a dive, I'm following my compass but my sense of direction makes it feel like I should be going more to the right. Without any other information, the best tip would be to
    - trust the compass.
    - go more to the right.

11. Which of the following usually make compass use more effective? (Choose all that apply.)
- Practice on land.
- Allow for current effects.
- Navigate around obstacles.
- Midwater, your buddy monitors depth while you navigate.
- Swim rapidly.

Student Statement

I completed this Knowledge Review to the best of my ability. For any questions I answered incorrectly or incompletely, I reviewed the explanation provided and now understand the material. In the case of anything about which I still have questions, I will review the material again and, if necessary, discuss it with my instructor at our next session.

☒ I agree ☐ I disagree

Name Josh Leopold

Date 10/16/18

scenario

"The ship's bell is on the foredeck at 30 metres," said Sylvia. "I'd like to get some close-up shots of it, and some of Ella and Javier next to it as well. Maybe some video too."

"Sounds good," Lee said, "but we don't know exactly where the bell is, and the visibility's crummy, so we'll have to search a bit first."

"Great idea," said Javier. "After we find it and you're done taking photos and video, let's map the area so we don't have to search every time we dive it."

"Hold on," Ella interrupted, "this is a dive to 100 feet – we don't have the gas or time to do all this. Let's find the bell and note where it is so we can return to it easily. We'll come back for the photos tomorrow."

- *Everyone except Ella overlooked a basic principle of deep diving. What is that principle?*
- *What does this tell you about planning deep dives?*

DEEP DIVING 3

Introduction

Definition of a "Deep Dive"

Mention a deep dive, and most divers get excited. For some, it's an exciting challenge in itself. For others, it's a means to an end – a way to visit new dive sites to see and do things you can't do on shallower dives.

In discussing deep diving, it helps to start by defining "deep." With respect to recreational diving, a "deep dive" is a dive deeper than 18 metres/60 feet to an absolute maximum depth limit of 40 metres/130 feet. The maximum depth is based on recreational dive gear, the short no stop time and rapid gas use you have on deep dives, and the training requirements.

Other forms of diving apply different definitions and limits because they apply different training and equipment. Tec divers use multiple life support systems and helium-based gases to dive far deeper than recreational limits – at this writing, dives to 100 metres/330 feet are no longer uncommon, with some divers going to 200 metres/660 feet and deeper. Commercial divers use even more extensive technologies to achieve depths approaching 800 metres/2400 feet. These types of diving require not only the equipment, but substantial training and progressive experience.

With respect to recreational diving, a "deep dive" is a dive deeper than 18 metres/60 feet to an absolute maximum depth limit of 40 metres/130 feet.

Your Depth Limits

Although 40 metres/130 feet is the *maximum* depth for recreational diving (ideally, with certification as a PADI Deep Diver), 30 metres/100 feet is the recommended limit for Advanced Open Water Divers and, in any case, is considered the optimal recreational depth limit.

There are several reasons for this. Even with dive computers and using enriched air nitrox, the no stop time deeper than 30 metres/100 feet is very short. Most divers begin to find gas narcosis noticeable deeper than 30 metres/100 feet – staying shallower helps avoid narcosis problems. There's an increased risk of decompression sickness because it is easier than in shallower diving to reach the no stop limits, yet not have enough gas for an adequate emergency decompression stop. And, in many environments, light and temperature fall dramatically with depth. Deeper than 30 metres/100 feet, darkness and cold may complicate diving; in some environments, these are issues even shallower.

Besides this guideline, you set a *personal* depth limit within the limits of your training and experience, based on a number of factors. Your limit may vary from day to day, and dive to dive. There is no hard rule for this; use good judgment, be conservative and set your personal depth limit based on at least these factors:

- Environmental conditions (e.g., a cold, low-visibility quarry versus a warm, clear, tropical wall).
- Your physical and mental state. You should be healthy and may feel challenged, but should not have undue anxiety or lack confidence in your ability to make the dive safely.
- Previous dives. You should have ample no stop time for the planned depth so you don't push your limits. If using enriched air nitrox, you also need to pay attention to oxygen exposure limits (learn about these in the PADI Enriched Air Diver course).
- Time/distance to emergency assistance, proper first aid resources and medical treatment. The longer it would take to reach these, the shallower and more conservative you'll want to plan your dive.
- Your dive buddy's training and experience. Plan the dive within the limits of the diver with the least training/experience.

LEARNING OBJECTIVES

By the end of this section, I should be able to answer these questions:

1. What is a recreational "deep dive"? Why do tec diving and other types of diving have different limits?
2. What are the four reasons that 30 metres/100 feet is recommended as the optimal depth limit for recreational diving?
3. What are five factors to consider when determining my personal depth limit?
4. What is the difference between a proper and an improper deep dive objective?

Tec divers and commercial divers use multiple life support systems and helium-based gases to dive far deeper than recreational limits. Divers within these disciplines have progressive limits based on technology, training and experience.

You set a personal depth limit within the limits of your training and experience, based on a number of factors. It may vary from day to day, and dive to dive. There is no hard rule for this; use good judgment and be conservative.

Deep Dive Objectives

Because deep dives are short, appropriate deep diving objectives are nearly always *singular* and *simple*. Whatever you choose, remember it is your *secondary* objective. The primary objective is *always* for all divers to return safely from the dive.

Deep dives are fun challenges, but diving deep to set personal records is *not* a proper objective. Proper deep diving objectives may include exploring the deep portion of a wreck, drift diving along a wall, photographing deep-water creatures, sightseeing and training/gaining experience to gradually extend your depth limit in a given environment.

EXERCISE-1

1. A recreational deep dive is defined as a dive deeper than ____ to a maximum of _________.
   - ☐ a. 18 metres/60 feet; 30 metres/100 feet
   - ☐ b. 18 metres/60 feet; 40 metres/130 feet
   - ☐ c. 30 metres/100 feet; 40 metres/130 feet
   - ☐ d. 30 metres/100 feet; 60 metres/200 feet
2. I'm planning a deep dive that I will limit to the recommended optimal depth of 30 metres/100 feet. This is recommended because (choose all that apply):
   - ☐ a. allowable dive time deeper is very short.
   - ☐ b. most divers start to find narcosis noticeable at that depth.
   - ☐ c. most dive computers will not function deeper.
   - ☐ d. light and temperature may be issues.
3. My personal depth limit depends upon conditions, or even how I feel that day.
   - ☐ True ☐ False
4. A proper deep dive objective is usually
   - ☐ a. complex with multiple tasks.
   - ☐ b. simple with a singular task.
   - ☐ c. to set a personal depth record.

How did you do?

1. b. 2. a, b, d. 3. True. 4. b.

It's your personal responsibility to inspect and check your gear before diving, and to not dive with gear that isn't or doesn't seem to be working properly.

LEARNING OBJECTIVES

By the end of this section, I should be able to answer these questions:

1. How do I determine whether my equipment is suitable and optimal for deep diving?
2. What five pieces of equipment can be especially important when deep diving, and what do I use each for?
3. What are my options for having an extra gas supply and extra weights available when deep diving? When is an extra gas supply considered mandatory?
4. What six guidelines should I follow with respect to using dive computers?
5. What are four common misconceptions regarding dive computers?

Equipment for Deep Diving

As scuba technology has advanced, so has the performance and quality of the equipment available. Virtually all modern scuba equipment is adequate for diving to 40 metres/130 feet – the limit of recreational deep diving. Rather than adequate, you need to consider whether it's *suitable* and *optimal* for deep diving.

Whether your gear is *suitable* relates primarily to whether it is in good working order and appropriate for the local environment. Whether it is *optimal* relates to features that give it superior performance at deeper depths.

Confirm suitability by taking care of your gear, by inspecting and checking it before diving, and by not diving with anything that isn't or doesn't seem to be working properly. Have all the gear required by the local environment. As you learned in the PADI Open Water Diver course, these are your personal responsibilities.

Optimal equipment for deep diving relates primarily to your regulator, alternate air source and cylinder:

Top-of-the-line regulators perform the best at deeper depths, so they're your best choice for deep dives. Choose a manufacturer's highest-performing first stage – your PADI dive shop can identify these among the various brands they stock.

Regulators

Top-of-the-line regulators perform the best at deeper depths, so they're your best choice for deep dives. Choose a manufacturer's highest-performing first stage – your PADI dive shop can identify these among the various brands it stocks.

High-performance second stages include balanced adjustable models, Venturi-assisted models and pilot-valve second stages. Look to your PADI Professional for guidance regarding the latest models and options.

Alternate Air Sources

The most popular alternate air sources are the extra second stage and the alternate inflator regulator, both of which are acceptable for recreational deep diving. Secure it as you learned as an entry-level diver: It should be visible and buddy-accessible in the triangle formed by your mouth and lower rib cage corners.

Ideally, choose a brightly colored second stage (yellow is common) to help make it more conspicuous. H-valves are alternate air source spinoffs from tec diving. They allow you to mount two independent regulators on a single cylinder. If you were to have a freeflow, you or a buddy could shut off the affected regulator, and you would ascend using the other.

Another option (usually in *addition* to having an alternate second stage) is a pony bottle, which is a small cylinder – typically 2-4 litre/12-30 cubic foot, but sometimes larger – with its own regulator. It provides additional gas, and you can use it to rescue yourself in an out-of-gas emergency. You wear a pony bottle clipped to a chest and a hip D-ring on the left (some divers prefer right) side, so it rides against your left side under your left arm. Bungee or elastic secures the second stage hose along its length so you can quickly pull it free if needed. At one time, divers mounted pony bottles on the main cylinder (some divers still do this), but based on tec diving stage/deco cylinder configuration, clipping as described has become preferred.

Some divers have an extra-long hose (up to two metres/ seven feet long) on the alternate second stage. This makes it easier to share gas; you secure the extra length so that it doesn't dangle or protrude, yet deploys quickly if needed. Another option is two-cylinder recreational side-mount diving, which gives you two equal-sized gas sources. Ask your instructor about the PADI Sidemount Diver course to learn more about this configuration.

Finally, in a few areas, recreational divers use double cylinders with dual-outlet valves, which come from tec diving. Like H-valves, these valves allow you to mount two independent regulators.

You wear a pony bottle clipped to a chest and a hip D-ring so it rides against your side under your arm.

H-valves allow you to mount two independent regulators on a single cylinder.

One option for deep diving is two-cylinder sidemount, which gives you two equal-sized gas sources.

Cylinders

Because the deeper you dive, the faster you use your gas, for deep diving you usually want a 12-litre/71.2-cubic-foot or larger cylinder. Some high-capacity cylinders hold about 1.5 times as much gas as a standard single 12-litre/71.2-cubic-foot cylinder, making them good choices for deeper dives. Another benefit of two-cylinder sidemount is that you can use two full-size cylinders and double your available gas.

Exposure Suits

Choose your exposure suit based on the temperature at depth, which in some environments may be significantly cooler than in shallower depths. You may want a thicker wet suit, or a dry suit, for a dive that you could otherwise make with less insulation at a shallower depth.

Remember that a wet suit compresses and loses some of its ability to insulate as you go deeper. This isn't always a major issue, but one advantage of most (but not all) types of dry suits is that they have little insulation loss with depth. Before using one on a deep dive, however, learn to dive a dry suit in the PADI Dry Suit Diver course.

Especially Useful in Deep Diving

The following five pieces of equipment can be helpful in any diving situation, but may be especially useful in deep diving:

1. **Reference line.** This can be a descent/ascent line, the mooring/anchor line or other line you follow to and from depth. When shore diving, it may be a line you lower from a buoy, or unreel and reel in. A reference line is especially useful when you can't see the bottom from the surface, because you can follow the line and, in some cases, use it to assist your descents and ascents. It also aids descents, ascents and safety stops when there's a current. You can use the relatively fine line used on wreck/cave reels in many instances, but a thicker rope (1.25 cm/0.5 in) is easier to grasp if you'll be using it to help control your descent/ascent in a current.

2. **Dive light.** In some environments, such as in many inland lakes, you may need a light because there is little or no light at depth. For such dives, you would use a full-size dive light (see the PADI *Night Diver Manual* and *Night Diving* video for more about lights and diving in darkness). Even in clear water, however, you can use a light to reveal color, look in holes/cracks, etc. A small, compact light usually works well for this.

3. **First-aid kit and emergency oxygen.** As you know, having these is recommended for all diving, but their importance increases when deep diving away from immediate professional medical assistance. In addition to what you've already learned as an Open Water Diver, you can learn more about first aid, emergency oxygen administration and handling dive emergencies in the Emergency First Response Primary Care (CPR) and Secondary Care (First Aid), PADI Emergency Oxygen Provider, and PADI Rescue Diver courses.

4. **Extra gas supply.** An extra gas supply is an emergency reserve in a separate scuba system. It helps assure adequate supply for a safety stop or, if necessary, an emergency decompression stop. It may be a carried gas supply, or a staged gas supply.

As you learned earlier, a carried gas supply may be a pony bottle. The advantages of a carried supply are that you can use it at depth for self-rescue, and that you have it regardless of where you ascend.

A reference line is especially useful when you can't see the bottom from the surface, because you can follow the line and, in some cases, use it to assist your descents and ascents. It also aids descents, ascents and safety stops when there's a current.

An extra gas supply is an emergency reserve. It helps assure adequate supply for a safety stop or, if necessary, an emergency decompression stop. It may be a carried gas supply, or a staged gas supply.

A staged gas supply is left where you can access it during a safety stop (or emergency decompression stop). It is commonly a cylinder suspended from a boat or float, but it may also be a long hose suspended from a boat, supplied from the surface (often with a horizontal bar to aid safety/emergency decompression stops). The advantages are that it is available to multiple buddy teams (a carried supply can only be relied on by the team that has it), and if surface-supplied, can have a higher capacity.

An extra gas supply is considered optional for most recreational deep diving. For rebreather diving, however, a carried extra supply is considered *mandatory* for almost all models when diving deeper than 18 metres/60 feet (some models and types of rebreather diving require it shallower, or for all diving).

5. **Extra weights.** If you're properly weighted, you should not need to change your weight for a deep dive. Nonetheless, sometimes divers accidentally underweight and find themselves uncomfortably buoyant while trying to make a safety stop with a near-empty cylinder. To assist with this, in some locations you may leave extra weights with a staged extra air supply. (Don't carry more weight than you actually need.) These may be loose weights that you put in a BCD pocket, or may have bolt snaps so you can clip them to D-rings.

Dive Computers

Generally, you use your dive computer on a deep dive much as you do on shallower dives, but on a deep dive note that no stop time is more likely to limit your dive time than is your gas supply (but watch both, of course). In areas where you can gradually ascend, such as along a wall or slope, you will see a significant increase in no stop time as you and your buddy(ies) work your way up from the deepest depth. In these instances, gas supply may also be the limiting factor.

Follow these six guidelines with respect to your computer:

1. Read the manufacturer instructions and use your computer as directed.
2. Use your computer to stay within no stop (no decompression) limits. In recreational diving, required decompression should be an emergency situation only.
3. As you've learned, don't share a computer. Every diver needs at least one.
4. The buddy team ascends based on the shortest no stop limits in the team.
5. If your computer fails during a dive, you may continue the dive if you're also diving with a backup computer. If you don't have a backup, make a normal ascent and safety stop (gas supply permitting). Follow the manufacturer's recommendations regarding resuming diving, which may require waiting 12 or more hours.
6. Don't follow your computer blindly. Although computers differ somewhat, there shouldn't be huge differences between your and your buddies' computers if you've been diving similar profiles. Be cautious if you see significant differences – this could indicate a computer problem.

Don't follow your computer blindly. Although computers differ somewhat, there shouldn't be huge differences between your and your buddies' computers if you've been diving similar profiles.

Although highly reliable, mathematical models used in dive computers are not perfect and cannot account for individual differences. This is why you dive conservatively, well within the computer's limits.

It's worth noting four common misconceptions about dive computers to be sure you don't have incorrect information.

Misconception 1: Computers measure the actual nitrogen in your body. Computers use a mathematical model to estimate *theoretical* nitrogen based on depth and time information. Although highly reliable, mathematical models are not perfect and cannot account for individual differences. **This is why no dive computer or dive table can guarantee that decompression sickness will never occur, even within model limits.** It's also why you dive conservatively, well within the computer's limits.

Misconception 2: Computers are more reliable than tables (or vice versa). Both computers and tables apply the same basic mathematical models. Computers are easier to use and more versatile, but neither is inherently more reliable than the other.

Misconception 3: The more expensive computer is safer than the cheaper one. The relative cost of dive computers relates to features, not reliability.

Misconception 4: The computer says it, so I can do it. When you apply common sense and dive conservatively well within computer limits as you've been trained, your computer will give you highly reliable information. If you "push" computer limits, ignore the manufacturer guidelines, etc., the reliability declines and the risk of DCS goes up, even though you are within the computer's limits.

EXERCISE-2

1. It's my responsibility to confirm that my equipment is suitable for deep diving by checking it before diving, and not diving with it if it doesn't seem to be working properly.
   - ☐ True ☐ False
2. A(n) ____________ allows me to mount two independent regulators on a single cylinder.
   - ☐ a. pony bottle
   - ☐ b. alternate air source
   - ☐ c. sidemount configuration
   - ☐ d. H-valve
3. Planning a deep dive, which of the following equipment may be especially useful? (Choose all that apply.)
   - ☐ a. Reference line
   - ☐ b. Dive light
   - ☐ c. Submersible camera
   - ☐ d. Extra gas supply
4. A ___________ extra gas supply has the advantages of being available to multiple buddy teams and the possibility of a higher capacity.
   - ☐ a. carried
   - ☐ b. staged
5. While on a dive, my computer fails, but I'm wearing a backup computer so I can continue the dive.
   - ☐ True ☐ False
6. My dive computer directly measures the actual amount of nitrogen dissolved in my body tissues.
   - ☐ True ☐ False

How did you do?

1. True. 2. d. 3. a, b, d. 4. b. 5. True. 6. False. Dive computers estimate theoretical nitrogen based on depth and time information. They don't measure anything actually in your body.

LEARNING OBJECTIVES

By the end of this section, I should be able to answer these questions:

1. Why may losing contact with a buddy often mean the dive is over? What are two techniques for maintaining contact with my buddy during a deep dive?

2. How should I weight myself for a deep dive?

3. How should I adjust my buoyancy while descending and ascending on a deep dive?

4. How does a head-above-feet descent benefit me on a deep dive?

5. What are two ways I can slow or stop a descent or ascent along a mooring, anchor or reference line while leaving both hands free?

6. What are four techniques to apply while descending or ascending without a visual or tactile reference while deep diving?

7. How can I confirm an appropriate ascent rate without looking at my dive computer? Why may I want to do so?

Deep Diving Techniques: Buddy Contact, Weighting and Buoyancy, Descents and Ascents

Buddy Contact

As you know, if buddies separate they should immediately take steps to reunite. The rule of thumb is to search no longer than a minute, then reunite on the surface. In a buddy team of three, this is true even for the two buddies who are still together.

On a deep dive, buddy separation often ends the dive because you don't have enough gas and no stop time to find each other and then continue the dive. So, it's best to *maintain* contact. Do this by staying close and keeping visual contact during descents and ascents. On the bottom, it helps to swim side by side. If you're leading the team, swim slowly and check with your buddy frequently. In low visibility, use physical contact if necessary – hold hands, hang on to a BCD strap, etc., to keep you physically together by feel. Even in clear water, remember the rule of thumb: Stay within two seconds of your buddy(ies).

On a deep dive, buddy separation often ends the dive because you don't have enough gas and no stop time to find each other and then continue the dive. So, it's best to stay close and maintain contact.

Signal If You Can't Equalize

If you have ear discomfort or other equalization problems, be sure to signal your buddy or instructor immediately. Your buddy or instructor have no way of knowing that you have a problem unless you signal.

Weighting and Buoyancy

As mentioned previously, you should begin a dive properly weighted – that is, in all your gear and with an empty BCD, you should float at eye level holding a normal breath and sink slowly when you exhale. Add two kilograms/five pounds after adjusting if you check with a full cylinder. Depending upon your exposure suit, you may experience more buoyancy loss on a deep dive as the material compresses and loses buoyancy, but don't use less weight as a result or you'll likely be too buoyant at the end of the dive to make an effective safety stop.

Adjust your buoyancy frequently as you descend and ascend. Delaying adjustments risks rapid descents and ascents. You should arrive at the bottom and your safety stop, respectively, neutrally buoyant or nearly so. Descend *slowly* to reduce the risk of mask, ear, sinus or dry suit squeeze. Ascend slowly to reduce the risk of decompression illness. Be a S.A.F.E. Diver – Slowly Ascend From Every Dive.

You learn more about weighting and precision buoyancy control in the PADI Peak Performance Buoyancy course and Adventure Dive.

Descents and Ascents

It's usually easy to keep your orientation when descending into deep water when you can see the bottom. But, if you have to descend without the bottom in sight, it may help to descend with your head above your feet. That's because this position reduces vertigo and helps you stay oriented (and many divers find they can equalize more easily).

This doesn't mean you have to be vertical, though. A diagonal "skydive" orientation, head slightly above foot level, may be more natural and stable, though vertical is fine if that's best for the situation and doesn't risk environmental damage. Beyond this, it's good to set your compass heading to your travel direction before leaving the surface.

Although you want to use buoyancy control to primarily regulate your descent and ascent rate, there are times, such as diving in current, you may want to slow or stop your descent/ascent without losing contact with a line. Normally you grab the line, of course, but if your other hand is occupied, or you need both hands free, you can't do much. There are two methods you can use in this situation. The first is to lock your elbow on the line. You can do this relatively quickly, it's good for slowing, and easy if you don't need to stay for long; but it is tiring and awkward if you have to do something that takes more than a moment, like readjust a weight system.

The second method is to wrap your leg around the line. It takes a little longer to set this position and it is mainly for stopping. However, once in position you can usually remain this way quite easily for several minutes, if necessary.

Another method for stopping hands-free on a line is to wrap your leg around it. This takes a moment, but you can usually stay in place for several minutes easily, if necessary.

To stop hands-free while ascending or descending along a line, one method is to lock your elbow on it. You can do this quickly and it works for short stops.

Descents and Ascents without a Reference

Although it's best to follow a line or bottom contour to and from deep water, that's not always possible or necessary. If you must descend or ascend without a visual reference, follow these four steps:

1. Maintain a head-above-feet position as just described to help stay oriented.
2. Descend or ascend so you and your buddy(ies) can see each other, and descend/ascend close together. Maintain eye contact or touch contact (use your right hands to keep your left available to control your BCD) and control your buoyancy to avoid rapid depth changes.
3. Watch your dive computer so you don't exceed your maximum depth while descending.
4. Ascend no faster than the rate specified by your computer, or 18 metres/60 feet per minute, whichever is slower. Watch your computer to confirm a proper rate, but most can be set to provide audible alarms so you can monitor your ascent without looking – if you hear it, you know to slow your rate. This can be handy if you're watching overhead, and other circumstances like holding on to a line in a current, etc.

If you have to ascend following a computer failure and you have no backup, ascend at the same rate as your buddy's(ies') computer requires. Watch overhead as you ascend, and listen for boats. Make a three-minute (or longer) safety stop at 5 metres/15 feet (or depth specified by the computer manufacturer). Reach up and turn, or look around, as you near the surface for the final part of your ascent.

Keep in mind that an extra-slow ascent does not replace your safety stop. However, within the realm of no stop diving, you can't ascend too slowly – feel free to take your time coming up (assuming nothing else, like your gas supply, is an issue).

EXERCISE-3

1. I'm leading the buddy team on a deep dive. I should (choose all that apply):
   - ☐ a. check with my buddy frequently.
   - ☐ b. swim slowly.
   - ☐ c. stay within two seconds of my buddy.
   - ☐ d. use touch contact in poor visibility.
2. I should wear less weight on a deep dive than I would on a shallower dive.
   - ☐ True ☐ False
3. My buddy and I descend on a deep dive, adjusting our buoyancy as we go. Ideally, we should arrive at the bottom __________ buoyant.
   - ☐ a. negatively
   - ☐ b. neutrally
   - ☐ c. positively
4. A head-above-feet descent helps me maintain my orientation on a deep dive.
   - ☐ True ☐ False
5. While ascending along a line, my buddy needs help to adjust a loose weight system. I need both hands to provide it, and it will take a couple of minutes. Probably the best method for stopping on the line would be to
   - ☐ a. grasp the line with one hand.
   - ☐ b. lock my elbow on the line.
   - ☐ c. wrap my leg around the line.
6. Descending into deep water without a reference to follow, it helps if my buddy and I descend
   - ☐ a. back-to-back.
   - ☐ b. so we can see each other.
   - ☐ c. head first.
7. An audible ascent rate alarm on my computer can help me monitor my ascent rate without looking at it.
   - ☐ True ☐ False

How did you do?

1. a, b, c, d. 2. False. You check your buoyancy and adjust your weight the same on a deep dive as for a shallower dive. 3. b. 4. True. 5. c. 6. b. 7. True.

Deep Diving Techniques:

Breathing and Gas Use, EANx, On the Bottom and Wall Dives

Breathing on Deep Dives

As discussed in the PADI Open Water Diver course, and expanded on in Thinking Like a Diver, it is important to breathe slowly, deeply and continuously, and to avoid overexertion while diving. This particularly benefits you on a deep dive. The deeper you are, the denser the gas, which increases the energy required to breathe. The faster you breathe, the more energy you use. Trying to breathe rapidly (such as due to strenuous activity) can make you feel air starved – like the regulator can't deliver enough gas.

Effective breathing, as you learned, is deep, slow and efficient breathing from the abdomen. Breathing this way fills your lungs from the bottom up, which gives the best gas exchange with the least energy used. It is the most relaxed breathing; breathing this way helps you maintain optimal breathing techniques.

Managing Your Gas Use

As you know, the deeper you dive, the faster you use your gas. This calls for conservative gas planning on deep dives. Plan your turn pressure with adequate return, ascent, safety stop and reserve gas. It's often wiser to plan a larger than usual reserve. In many places, you start the dive deep, but finish shallow, often with most of the dive shallow. In these cases, plan your turn pressure conservatively. Then, assuming you have no unforeseen issues, you ascend to a longer, extended shallow part of the dive. This lets you plan your gas cautiously, yet still enjoy a reasonably long, satisfying dive.

As you may imagine, low-on-gas or out-of-gas emergencies become critical faster on a deep dive. Fortunately, it's easy to avoid these situations with a simple habit: **Check your remaining gas supply frequently.** The deeper you are, the more often you should check it. Although you don't usually need SAC (Surface Air Consumption) rate to plan recreational dives, some divers use SAC apps to help plan deep dives.

LEARNING OBJECTIVES

By the end of this section, I should be able to answer these questions:

1. How does slow breathing from the abdomen benefit me on a deep dive?
2. Why do I want to plan my gas use more conservatively on a deep dive? What habit during the dive reduces the risk of a low-on-gas or out-of-gas situation?
3. What are the benefits of using enriched air nitrox for recreational deep dives? What are the drawbacks?
4. What is a "wall dive"? What three guidelines should I follow when making one?

Check your SPG frequently. The deeper you are, the more often you should check it.

DETERMINING YOUR GAS CONSUMPTION

How can you determine how long your gas will last at a given depth if you've never been that deep? By using some simple mathematics. All you need is your gas consumption rate at a shallower depth, the charts listed here and a sharp pencil or calculator.

Start by obtaining a record of your gas consumption from your dive log. The more dives you work with, the more accurate your calculations will be. Also, dives made primarily at a single level will be more useful than multilevel dives. For each dive, record how many bar/psi you use, the actual dive time and the depth.

Gas Consumption Calculation METRIC

CONVERSION FACTORS

Metres	Pressure at Depth (bar)
0	1.0
3	1.3
6	1.6
9	1.9
12	2.2
15	2.5
18	2.8
21	3.1
24	3.4
27	3.7
30	4.0
33	4.3
36	4.6
39	4.9

1. Determine your gas consumption rate at the surface in litres per minute with this formula:

$$\frac{\textbf{bar used x cylinder volume (litres)}}{\textbf{actual bottom time x pressure at depth (bar)}}$$

Example: A diver using a 10-litre cylinder uses 100 bar on a dive to 12 metres for 20 minutes. What is the gas consumption rate at the surface?

$$\frac{\textbf{100 bar x 10 litres}}{\textbf{20 min x 2.2 bar}} = \textbf{22.73 litres/minute surface rate}$$

By recording your litre-per-minute surface rate over several dives and averaging them, you can determine your normal gas consumption rate.

2. To determine your gas consumption at your planned depth based on your surface rate, multiply your surface rate by the pressure (in bar) for your planned depth, and then divide the gas available by that.

Example: Suppose the diver from the previous example plans to dive to 30 metres. Approximately how long would you expect a 10-litre cylinder filled to 200 bar to last (before allowing for your reserve)?

gas available = 10 litres x 200 bar = 2000 litres

gas use at 30 metres = 22.73 l/min x 4.0 bar = 90.92 l/min
2000 litres ÷ 90.92 l/min = 22 minutes

Therefore, you would expect the cylinder to last 22 minutes before allowing for your reserve. To account for your reserve pressure, simply subtract it from your starting pressure. In this example, gas available would then be 10 litres x 160 bar = 1600 litres; 1600 litres ÷ 90.92 l/m = 17.6 minutes.

Gas Consumption Calculation IMPERIAL

CONVERSION FACTORS		
Feet	Converting from Surface Rate	Converting to Surface Rate
0	1.00	1.00
10	1.30	0.76
20	1.60	0.62
30	1.91	0.52
40	2.21	0.45
50	2.52	0.40
60	2.82	0.35
70	3.12	0.32
80	3.42	0.29
90	3.73	0.27
100	4.03	0.25
110	4.33	0.23
120	4.64	0.21
130	4.94	0.20

1. Determine your psi per minute surface rate with this formula:

$$\frac{\text{psi used}}{\text{actual bottom time}} \times \text{conversion factor (converting to surface rate for dive depth)} = \text{surface air consumption rate}$$

For example, on a 40-foot dive for 20 minutes, in which the diver uses 1500 psi, 1500 psi used divided by a 20-minute bottom time x 0.45 = 33.7 psi-per-minute surface rate.

By recording your psi-per-minute surface rate over several dives and averaging them, you can determine your normal gas consumption rate. Note: Make all your calculations with the same type cylinder. If you use different size and/or pressure-rated cylinders, you must determine your gas consumption for each independently.

2. To convert your surface rate to your planned depth rate, multiply your surface rate by the Converting from Surface Rate conversion factor (at left) for the planned depth.

Based on the previous example, if you plan to dive to 100 feet, you can expect your gas consumption to be about 136 psi per minute (33.7 x 4.03 = 135.8). If your cylinder is filled to 3000 psi, you could expect it to last about 22 minutes (before allowing for your reserve).

When calculating gas supply, keep in mind that excitement, activity and cold all increase your breathing rate, so allow room for error in your dive planning, and always watch your SPG closely. With experience, you'll become proficient at predicting how long a cylinder will last you at a given depth.

Enriched Air Nitrox (EANx)

You may recall that EANx is air with an increased proportion of oxygen and a decreased proportion of nitrogen, which can benefit deep dives because you have significantly longer no stop times – the higher the oxygen and the lower the nitrogen, the more no stop time at a given depth. Even if your dive is limited by gas, EANx decreases the residual nitrogen you accumulate, making repetitive dives longer.

The primary drawback to EANx is that you have to manage oxygen exposure – the higher the oxygen content, the shallower the maximum useable depth. For example, diving with EANx32 (32 percent oxygen), the maximum depth is 33 metres/110 feet. With EANx36 (36 percent oxygen), it's 28 metres/95 feet. Enriched air also has special considerations related to equipment, cylinder markings and analyzing your gas.

Because of these issues, you must be certified as a PADI Enriched Air Diver to obtain and dive with EANx. During the PADI Enriched Air Diver course, you learn to manage oxygen exposure and about the equipment issues. Ask your PADI Dive Center for more information.

Recall that EANx is air with an increased proportion of oxygen and a decreased proportion of nitrogen, which can benefit deep dives because you have significantly longer no stop times.

Wall Dives

Wall dives are dives along vertical or near-vertical reef, often over "bottomless" water – i.e., a bottom hundreds or thousands of metres/feet deep. Wall dives are exhilarating and fun, especially in very clear water. Three guidelines apply:

1. Watch your depth closely and control your buoyancy – it's easy to exceed depth limits and/or your planned depth. If a current begins to push you down the wall (downwelling), put air into your BCD and swim directly away from the wall until free of the current, then readjust your buoyancy. This is very rare, but it's reassuring to know what to do.

2. Stay next to the wall to provide a visual reference and reduce vertigo.

3. Don't stay too close to the wall, though. Many walls are habitats for sensitive aquatic life – avoid touching, kicking or otherwise harming it.

Wall dives are exhilarating and fun, especially in very clear water, but watch your depth closely because it's easy to exceed your planned depth.

EXERCISE-4

1. While deep diving to 27 metres/90 feet, and while diving to any depth, I make a point of breathing slowly and deeply from my diaphragm/abdomen because it (choose all that apply):
   - ☐ a. helps me relax.
   - ☐ b. is the most efficient way to breathe.
   - ☐ c. uses less energy.
   - ☐ d. fills my upper lungs first.
2. The habit that reduces the risk of running out of gas is to
   - ☐ a. check my SPG frequently.
   - ☐ b. breathe slowly and deeply.
   - ☐ c. use EANx.
3. The benefit of using enriched air nitrox (EANx) is that it gives me significantly longer no stop times.
   - ☐ True ☐ False
4. My buddy and I are making a deep dive along a wall. We should stay
   - ☐ a. far from the wall.
   - ☐ b. close to the wall.

How did you do?

1. a, b, c. 2. a. 3. True. 4. b.

LEARNING

OBJECTIVES

By the end of this section, I should be able to answer these questions:

1. How do I make a safety/emergency decompression stop at 5 metres/15 feet, with and without a reference line?

2. What should I do if I accidentally miss an emergency decompression stop?

Deep Diving Techniques:

Safety Stops, Emergency Decompression Stops

You've already learned you should make safety stops a normal part of your ascents. Safety stops reduce your risk of decompression illness by giving your body extra time to release excess dissolved nitrogen before surfacing. Stopping also helps you establish proper buoyancy control before going through the final 5 metres/15 feet, which can help you control your ascent rate better.

As you know, a safety stop is recommended on all dives. But, it's especially recommended when deep diving, when you get close to a no stop (no decompression) limit or any other limit of your computer or the Recreational Dive Planner – e.g. within three pressure groups of the RDP limit – or when your computer indicates a safety stop.

Another important benefit of safety stops is they help you reduce the risk of accidentally missing a required emergency decompression stop. During your safety stop, double check that you and your buddy(ies) are within

During your safety stop, double check that you and your buddy are within no stop limits. If you find you accidentally exceeded them, stay at the stop until you have completed the indicated emergency decompression.

no stop limits. If you find you accidentally exceeded the limits, stay at the stop until you have completed the indicated emergency decompression.

Maintaining Stop Depth with a Reference Line

It's easiest to make safety stops with a reference, such as following an ascending bottom or along a line. If you use a line, watch your computer until you find the 5-metre/15-foot depth on the line. Ideally, keep this depth at approximately midchest level; a horizontal position is theoretically optimal, but close to this depth and in any comfortable position is fine. In clear water without current, you may choose to hover near the line, which allows several divers to use the line as a depth reference together. With current, you may need to hold the line continuously, all the way to the surface.

Maintaining Stop Depth without a Reference Line

To make a safety stop midwater without a reference, ascend slowly, adjusting your buoyancy so you arrive at 5 metres/15 feet neutrally buoyant. Keep an eye on your computer to maintain your depth. Buddies can work together holding on to each other – one maintains depth while the other(s) navigates or watches overhead for the boat, etc.

If you have a Delayed Surface Marker Buoy (DSMB), you can deploy it (usually as you start your ascent) to provide a reference and to make your location visible at the surface. Maintain a comfortable position and avoid overexertion.

To make a safety stop midwater without a reference, ascend slowly, adjusting your buoyancy so you arrive at 5 metres/15 feet neutrally buoyant. Watch your computer to maintain your depth.

Emergency Decompression

If you have to make an emergency decompression stop, your computer will tell you how long to stop and the depth before surfacing. Using the RDP, follow these procedures if you accidentally exceed no stop limits:

1. If you exceed the no stop (no decompression) limit by no more than five minutes, make an eight-minute stop at 5 metres/15 feet. Do not dive again for at least six hours.

2. If you exceed the no stop (no decompression) limit by more than five minutes, make a stop at 5 metres/15 feet for at least 15 minutes (gas supply allowing) and do not dive for at least 24 hours.

Your depth is more critical with an emergency decompression stop than with a safety stop. Stay at or deeper than the stop depth shown on your computer.

With the RDP, stay as close to 5 metres/15 feet as possible. If you don't have enough gas to complete the stop, there's no emergency supply available, and your buddy doesn't have enough gas to share, make the stop as long as you can (use some of your reserve), but save enough gas to surface and exit safely. **Do not run out of gas underwater.** After surfacing, notify your buddies and breathe emergency oxygen if available as soon as possible. Monitor yourself for decompression sickness symptoms.

If you accidentally miss all or part of an emergency decompression stop, stay calm. Tell your buddies and/or the divemaster, and monitor yourself for DCS symptoms. Breathe 100 percent oxygen if available. If any signs or symptoms develop, immediately seek emergency medical assistance. Do not re-enter the water. Procedures for omitted decompression are not recommended for recreational divers; they are intended for commercial groups or expeditions with dedicated surface support teams and specialized equipment.

EXERCISE-5

1. Making a safety stop, I want the stop depth to be about __________ level.
   - ☐ a. eye
   - ☐ b. neck
   - ☐ c. midchest
   - ☐ d. waist
2. After a dive, I find I accidentally exceeded no stop limits, and my computers say I missed five minutes of emergency decompression. I should
   - ☐ a. reenter the water and complete the stop.
   - ☐ b. alert my buddy, breathe oxygen and monitor for DCS symptoms.

How did you do?

1. c. 2. b.

If you accidentally miss all of, or part of, an emergency decompression stop, stay calm. Alert your buddies and/or the divemaster, and breathe emergency oxygen while monitoring yourself for DCS symptoms.

LEARNING OBJECTIVES

By the end of this section, I should be able to answer these questions:

1. At what depth range does gas narcosis generally affect divers? What can make it occur shallower?
2. What are seven symptoms and five signs of gas narcosis?
3. What five factors can speed the onset of, or intensify the effects of, gas narcosis?
4. How do I prevent gas narcosis, and what do I do if it occurs?

Most divers feel narcosis at approximately 30 metres/100 feet to 40 metres/130 feet, but can still perform routine tasks. However, the ability to handle a stressful, new or complex situation may be impaired.

Gas Narcosis

Gas narcosis (sometimes less properly called "nitrogen narcosis") is the narcotic property that results from breathing air or enriched air nitrox under pressure. The exact cause isn't fully understood, but has been linked to the absorption of gas into the nerve cell structure, interfering with normal nervous system transmission. All gases, including nitrogen and oxygen, are thought to cause narcosis if they penetrate the cell lipid (fat) structure in sufficient concentration.

Narcosis is a variable physiological phenomenon. This means its intensity varies from one person to another, and within the same person from day to day. Most divers feel narcosis at approximately 30 metres/100 feet to 40 metres/130 feet, but can still perform routine tasks (buoyancy control, etc.). However, the ability to handle a stressful, new or complex situation may be impaired; you may not notice its effects until attempting something that requires concentration or fine coordination.

Sometimes divers experience narcosis shallower than approximately 30 metres/100 feet, and one cause can be certain drugs, which combine with narcosis and make it more noticeable. But while rare, sometimes people feel it shallower than 30 metres/100 feet without an apparent explanation.

Symptoms (What You Feel) of Narcosis Include:

- Rigid, inflexible thinking and difficulty concentrating (being unable to adapt to unexpected conditions)
- Loss of good judgment and a false sense of security
- Short-term memory loss
- Lack of concern for a specific task or personal safety
- Unjustified elation
- Drowsiness or feeling intoxicated
- Anxiety

Signs (What You See in Another Diver) Include:

- Inappropriate behaviors that are not normal for the diver
- Short attention span, slowed thinking, trouble understanding computer or hand signals
- Impaired vigilance and a disregard for safety
- Stupor and semi-consciousness
- Failure to follow the dive plan

Physiological and/or psychological conditions can speed the onset of narcosis or intensify it. Hard work, overexertion and improper breathing may elevate carbon dioxide – a very narcotic gas – in the body, contributing to narcosis. Experience with deep diving seems to build a temporary compensation for narcosis effects, so inexperience with deep diving, or lack of recent deep dives, seems to make narcosis more likely or stronger.

As mentioned, certain drugs can make narcosis occur shallower. In particular, these include drugs that cause drowsiness including tranquilizers, barbiturates, sleeping pills, some decongestants and alcohol. These chemicals also impair nerve impulse transmission and combine with narcosis. Obviously, never dive under the influence of alcohol; consult a physician about diving while taking drugs, even nonprescription drugs.

Anxiety creates perceptual narrowing and other reactions that intensify the effects of narcosis. For some divers, low visibility, cold or dark water contributes to anxiety, and therefore to narcosis. Finally, just as drugs and alcohol may affect you more when tired, gas narcosis may affect you more at these times as well.

Anxiety creates perceptual narrowing and other reactions that magnify the effects of narcosis. For some divers, low visibility, cold or dark water contributes to anxiety, and therefore narcosis.

Preventing Narcosis

In recreational diving, you prevent narcosis by diving at shallower depths – usually 30 metres/100 feet or shallower – even shallower if taking a prescription drug that might combine with narcosis. Deep diving experience helps compensate for narcosis. Build your experience gradually and continue your training in the PADI Deep Diver course.

If narcosis occurs, don't ignore it. If it becomes a factor, ascend to a shallower depth. It will normally subside on its own with no aftereffects. If it doesn't, or as otherwise necessary, end the dive.

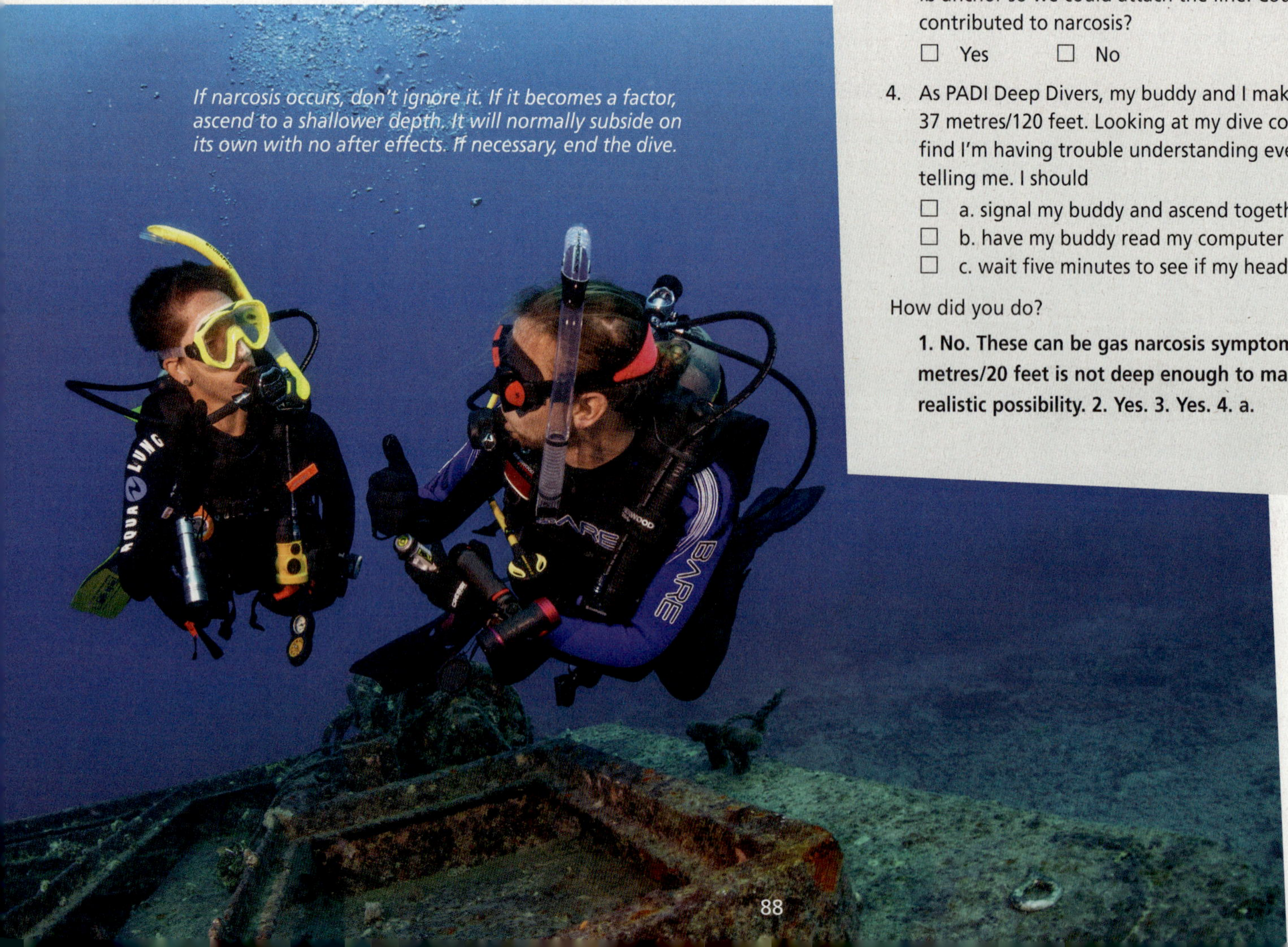

If narcosis occurs, don't ignore it. If it becomes a factor, ascend to a shallower depth. It will normally subside on its own with no after effects. If necessary, end the dive.

EXERCISE-6

1. My buddy and I descend to 6 metres/20 feet, where I notice I'm having trouble remembering what we're supposed to do, and also feel anxious. Are these likely the effects of gas narcosis?
   ☐ Yes ☐ No
2. On a deep dive to 29 metres/97 feet, I notice my buddy having difficulty tying a bowline, a knot my buddy knows well. Is this likely a sign of narcosis?
   ☐ Yes ☐ No
3. Just before tying the bowline as described in Question 2, my buddy had to work hard flipping over a 10 kg/25 lb anchor so we could attach the line. Could this have contributed to narcosis?
   ☐ Yes ☐ No
4. As PADI Deep Divers, my buddy and I make a dive to 37 metres/120 feet. Looking at my dive computer, I find I'm having trouble understanding everything it's telling me. I should
   ☐ a. signal my buddy and ascend together.
   ☐ b. have my buddy read my computer for me.
   ☐ c. wait five minutes to see if my head clears.

How did you do?

1. No. These can be gas narcosis symptoms, but 6 metres/20 feet is not deep enough to make narcosis a realistic possibility. 2. Yes. 3. Yes. 4. a.

LEARNING OBJECTIVES

By the end of this section, I should be able to answer these questions:

1. What is the primary reason recreational divers get decompression sickness?
2. What are six symptoms and seven signs of decompression sickness?
3. What 10 factors are thought to increase the probability of getting decompression sickness?
4. What can I do to reduce the risk of getting decompression sickness?
5. What is the recommended emergency care for a diver suspected of having decompression sickness?
6. What are five reasons why a diver suspected of having decompression sickness should not be recompressed underwater?

Decompression Sickness (DCS)

Recall that decompression sickness (DCS) is a serious medical condition that results when nitrogen dissolved into body tissues during a dive comes out of solution faster than the body can eliminate it safely, resulting in the formation of bubbles within tissues. Depending on where they form, these bubbles can cause pain, paralysis and, in extreme cases, death. You probably also remember that lung overexpansion injuries and DCS can be very similar in their signs and symptoms. For this reason, together they're called *decompression illness* (DCI). When dealing with an emergency involving either condition (discussed shortly), it's not important whether the underlying cause is DCS or lung overexpansion injury, but this discussion looks at DCS in particular.

Recall that decompression sickness (DCS) is a serious medical condition that results when nitrogen dissolved into body tissues during a dive comes out of solution faster than the body can eliminate it safely, resulting in the formation of bubbles within tissues. Depending upon where they form, these bubbles can cause pain, paralysis and, in extreme cases, death.

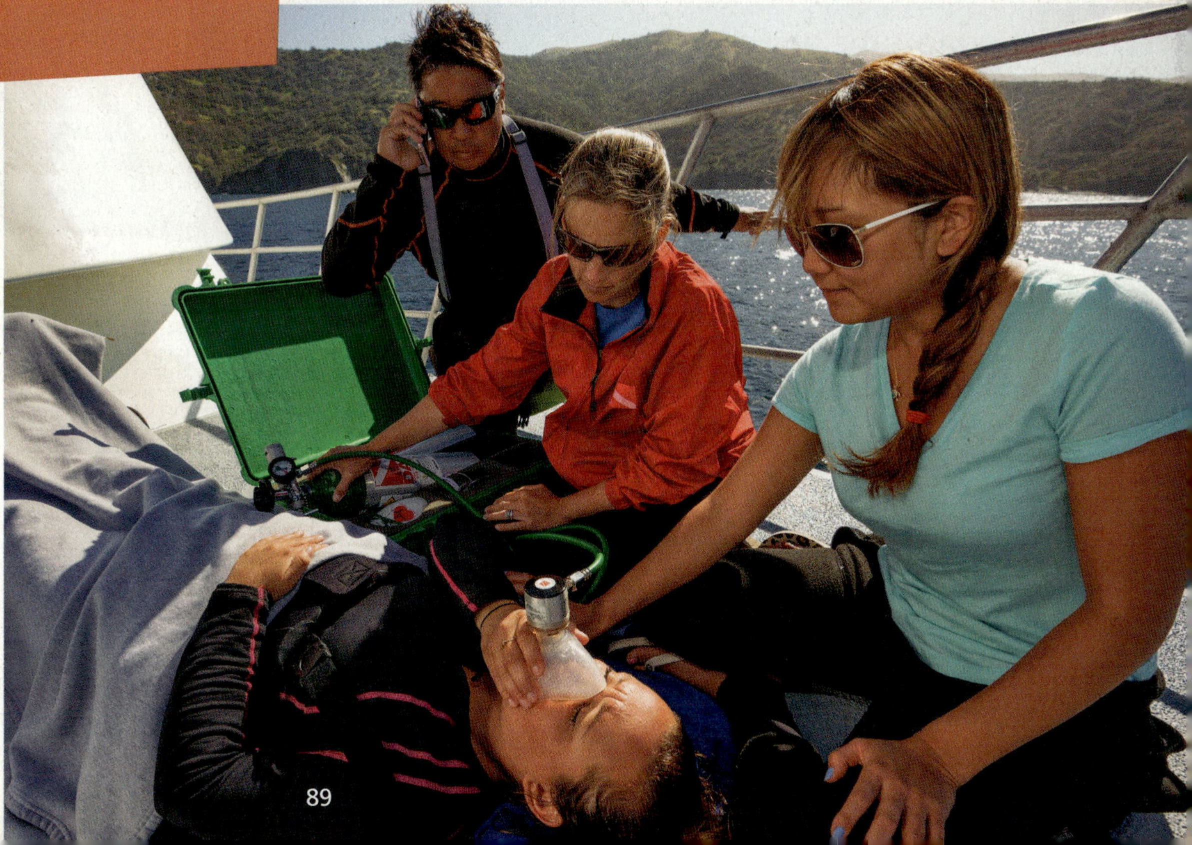

The Primary Cause of Decompression Sickness

In the discussion on dive computers, you learned that there's always some risk of decompression sickness. Nonetheless, the *primary* reason recreational divers get DCS (and lung overexpansion injuries) is *diver error*; sometimes, several errors contribute to the situation. Errors may cause a diver to absorb more nitrogen than expected during the dive, or fail to release as much as expected before surfacing.

Diver errors leading to DCS include misuse of (or not using) dive computers/tables, exceeding proper ascent rates, omitting emergency decompression stops, disregarding factors that predispose you to DCS, and failure to follow conservative diving practices (like staying well within computer/table limits). Running out of gas can also contribute by leading to rapid ascents and/or skipping emergency decompression stops. Avoiding these errors greatly reduces DCS risk, but as discussed previously, some risk always remains.

DCS Symptoms and Signs

When a diver gets decompression sickness, multiple symptoms/signs may be present together, or the diver may suffer only one symptom. Common symptoms include:

- Pain, often in the limbs and also often (but not necessarily) in the joints. The pain can change location and intensity over time.
- Numbness, tingling or paralysis
- Unusual fatigue or weakness
- Skin itch
- Shortness of breath
- Dizziness and vertigo

Signs you may observe in another diver include:

- Favoring an arm or leg, or rubbing a joint

In most cases, DCS occurs at the surface within one to two hours of the dive, though signs and symptoms can occur underwater at a shallow depth, or can be delayed as long as 48 hours.

- Paralysis
- Unconsciousness
- Staggering
- Collapse
- Coughing spasms
- Blotchy skin rash

In most cases, DCS occurs at the surface within one to two hours of the dive, though it can occur underwater at a shallow depth, or can be delayed as long as 48 hours.

Reducing the Risk of Decompression Sickness

There are several factors thought to predispose a diver to DCS. There is no way to quantify their effects, but the more of these that apply to you, the more conservatively you should dive.

1. **Dehydration.** This reduces the quantity of circulating blood, which is needed to eliminate dissolved nitrogen.

2. **Excess fat and poor fitness.** Fat tissue holds more dissolved nitrogen, and poor fitness impairs circulatory and respiratory efficiency. Both reduce tolerance to physical stressors.

3. **Age.** The circulatory system becomes less efficient with age, theoretically, so nitrogen elimination slows. Maintaining personal fitness, however, appears to slow this change.

4. **Heavy exertion immediately before, during or after a deep dive.** Before and after the dive, exertion can cause micro bubbles in the tissues. These can act as "bubble seeds" and grow as excess nitrogen dissolves into them. Exertion during the dive also speeds circulation and the body may take up more nitrogen than usual.

5. **Injuries and illness.** These can affect circulation and the ability to eliminate nitrogen.

6. **Alcohol use.** Before diving, alcohol promotes dehydration. After diving, consuming alcohol alters circulation, possibly promoting bubble growth.

7. **Cold water.** To save heat, the body restricts circulation to the extremities and skin, which may mean areas with less circulation do not eliminate nitrogen as effectively.

8. **Hot showers or baths immediately after a dive.** These cause skin capillaries to dilate, altering normal circulation as blood flows rapidly into these areas.

9. **Carbon dioxide increase.** Caused by exertion/overexertion or improper breathing, elevated carbon dioxide levels have been associated with increased DCS risk, possibly because carbon dioxide interferes with the body's ability to eliminate nitrogen.

10. **Exposure to altitude.** Altitude exposure lessens the pressure surrounding the diver after a dive, which may allow bubbles to form when they would not have at sea level. Follow current recommendations for flying after diving or driving to altitude after diving, and use altitude diving procedures when diving at altitude.

You *greatly* reduce your DCS risk by diving conservatively, well within computer or dive table limits at all times. If any predisposing factors apply, dive even more conservatively. Start your ascent with ample gas remaining, ascend slowly and make safety stops, as discussed previously.

You greatly reduce your DCS risk by diving conservatively, well within computer or dive table limits at all times. If any predisposing factors apply, dive even more conservatively.

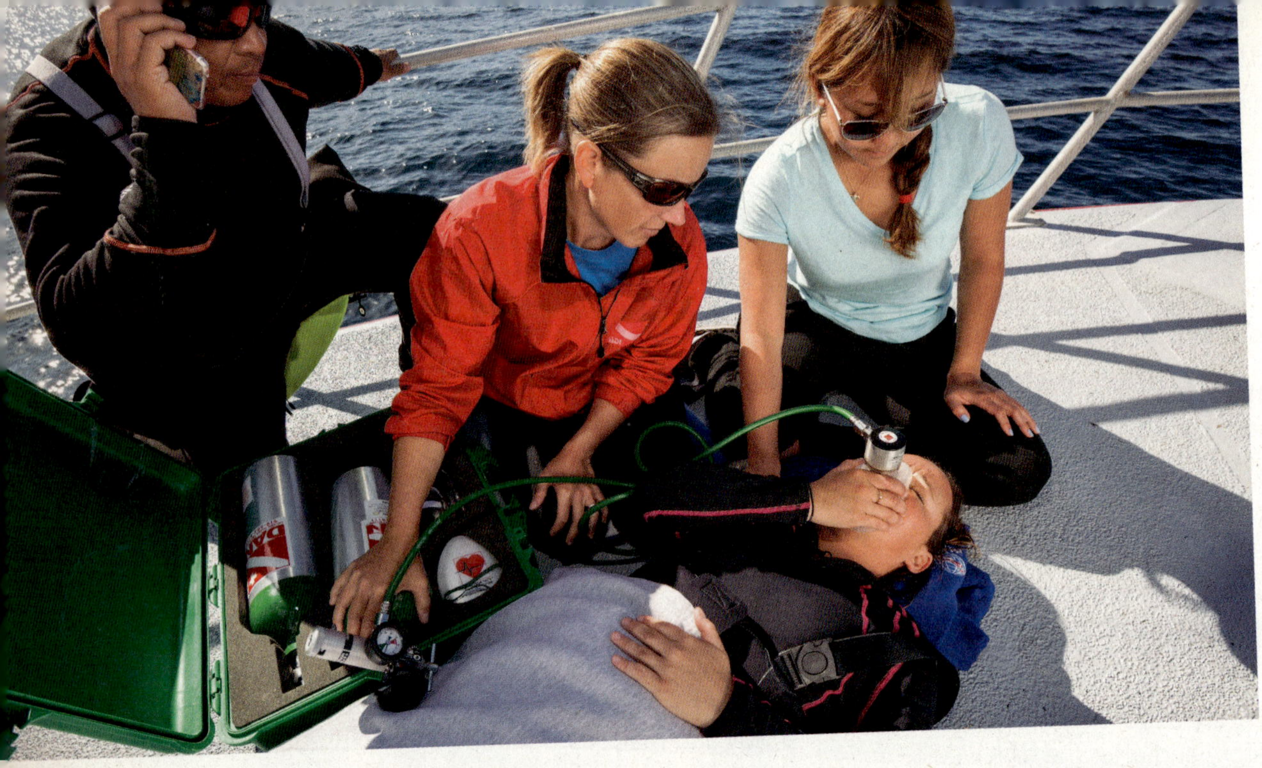

Have the diver lie down and breathe 100 percent oxygen if available. Contact the local EMS, and monitor the patient's breathing and circulation, providing CPR if it becomes necessary, until medical care arrives. Give emergency oxygen until emergency care arrives (supply allowing), and treat for shock.

DCI First Aid and Treatment

If a diver is suspected of having DCS (or lung overexpansion injuries – that is, any form of decompression illness), follow these steps:

1. Have the diver lie down and breathe 100 percent oxygen if available. The diver may lie on the side or face up, but should avoid sitting up because this can make symptoms worse.

2. In severe cases, a patient who has no breathing and no signs of circulation will need CPR. The patient must be face up on a firm surface for chest compressions.

3. Put an unresponsive breathing diver in the recovery position, left side down.

4. After beginning first aid – or before, if the diver is unresponsive and you're alone – contact the local emergency medical system (EMS) or other appropriate emergency aid. Monitor the patient's breathing and circulation, providing CPR if it becomes necessary, until medical care arrives. Give emergency oxygen until emergency care arrives (supply allowing), and treat for shock.

To better prepare yourself for managing DCS and other diver emergencies, complete the PADI Rescue Diver and Emergency Oxygen Provider courses, and the Emergency First Response Primary (CPR) and Secondary (First Aid) Care courses. Ask your PADI dive shop for course schedule information.

Medical treatment usually requires putting the diver back under pressure in a recompression chamber. Recompression reduces the bubbles and forces them into solution. Accompanied by oxygen, drug therapy and fluids, treatment brings the diver back to surface pressure at a slow (typically several hours), controlled rate. More than one treatment may be needed. To arrange for recompression at the closest available facility, contact the local diver emergency service. (Your instructor will tell you what diver emergency services cover your area.)

Although recompression is the usual treatment, *do not* put a diver with suspected DCI back into the water, for several reasons. Recompression often requires extreme pressure – the equivalent of 50 metres/165 feet (well beyond safe recreational diving depths). Oxygen and drug therapy are impossible or at best very difficult underwater. Treatments may also

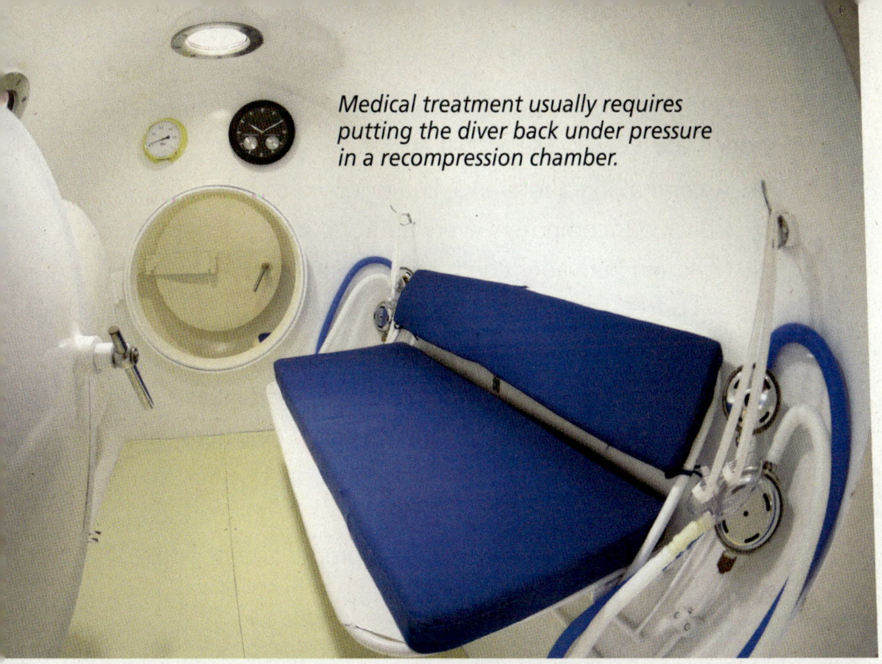

Medical treatment usually requires putting the diver back under pressure in a recompression chamber.

PADI DEEP DIVER SPECIALTY

At your instructor's discretion, the Deep Adventure Dive credits toward the PADI Deep Diver Specialty course. The course gives you more opportunities to apply and practice deep diving skills, including:

- Descents into deep water with and without references
- Observing pressure-sensitive objects
- Timing tasks to check for narcosis effects
- Simulated emergency decompression

Remember to log your training dives with the PADI Mobile App or at padi.com.

take six to 10 hours, longer than a diver can reasonably endure heat loss even in very warm water, assuming there is sufficient gas for such duration. And, underwater treatment makes observation by medical personnel difficult or impossible. A failed (incomplete) attempt at underwater recompression will make someone worse and/or delay the patient reaching proper medical care. There are some protocols for recompressing divers in water, but these require special equipment, procedures and training, and exist for exploratory divers in remote locations – not for recreational divers.

EXERCISE-7

1. The primary reason divers get decompression sickness is
   - ☐ a. diver error.
   - ☐ b. malfunctioning dive computers.
   - ☐ c. gas narcosis.
   - ☐ d. no safety stop.
2. After a dive, a diver complains of feeling unusually fatigued and weak, and says there's marked pain in the knee. Are these possible DCS symptoms?
   ☐ Yes ☐ No
3. Which of the following factors are thought to increase the risk of DCS? (Choose all that apply.)
   - ☐ a. Dehydration
   - ☐ b. Poor fitness
   - ☐ c. Injuries/illness
   - ☐ d. Altitude
   - ☐ e. Carbon dioxide increase
   - ☐ f. Gas narcosis
4. My buddy and I are planning a deep dive and will stay well within limits at all times. This should help reduce our DCS risk.
   ☐ True ☐ False
5. After a dive, a diver has suspected DCS signs and symptoms. The diver is breathing and fully responsive. We should assist the diver by providing emergency oxygen, contacting emergency medical care and having the diver sit comfortably until help arrives.
   ☐ True ☐ False
6. One reason I don't put a diver with suspected DCS back in the water for recompression is that recompression takes hours – far longer than a diver can endure, even in reasonably warm water, without special equipment.
   ☐ True ☐ False

How did you do?

1. a. 2. Yes. 3. a, b, c, d, e. 4. True. 5. False. The steps are correct, except the diver should lie down, not sit. 6. True.

Knowledge Review – Deep Diving

Answer the following questions by selecting the best choice (or choices) from those provided. Be prepared to discuss the material at your next training session.

1. Which of the following factors would I consider when determining my personal deep-diving depth limit? (Choose all that apply.)
   - ☐ Environmental conditions
   - ☐ My physical/psychological fitness
   - ☐ The effect of previous dives on my no stop (no decompression) limit
   - ☐ Distance from emergency care
   - ☐ My buddy's personal limits
2. It's summer and I've been diving in the local area for several days, reaching a maximum depth of 12 metres/40 feet. Today, my buddy and I plan to dive to 30 metres/100 feet. Which of the following statements is true?
   - ☒ My exposure suit may not be adequate.
   - ☐ Cylinder size is not a major consideration.
   - ☐ I can divide required instruments between my buddy and me.
   - ☐ There's little benefit to a balanced first stage regulator.
3. Which pieces of specialized equipment are recommended for deep diving? (Choose all that apply.)
   - ☒ Emergency breathing equipment
   - ☐ Ankle weights
   - ☒ Underwater light
   - ☐ Compass
4. When descending into deep water, the recommended general body orientation is
   - ☒ head above feet.
   - ☐ feet above head.
   - ☐ position makes little difference.
5. My buddy and I are ascending from deep water. To ascend at a proper rate, we (choose all that apply):
   - ☒ Ascend along a reference line or upward slope.
   - ☒ Check our computers every metre/few feet.
   - ☒ Maintain buoyancy control by adjusting our BCDs frequently.
   - ☐ Remove some weight at depth.
6. My buddy and I lose our way on a deep dive and must surface without a reference. Steps for doing this include (choose all that apply):
   - ☐ ascending back-to-back.
   - ☒ using our computers to gauge a proper ascent rate.
   - ☒ adjusting our buoyancy frequently.
   - ☐ not making a safety stop.
7. The primary way I avoid low-on-air or out-of-air emergencies on a deep dive is to limit dive time to 30 minutes.
   - ☐ True
   - ☒ False
8. My buddy and I are making a safety stop while ascending from a boat dive. The seas are calm but there's a current, so we're holding on to the mooring line. Ideally, we hold the line so 5 metres/15 feet is at ____________ depth, and stay for ____ minutes or longer.
   - ☐ face; three
   - ☐ face; five
   - ☒ chest; three
   - ☐ chest; five
   - ☐ waist; three
   - ☐ waist; five
9. My buddy and I are at 33 metres/110 feet. I feel intoxicated and notice I have trouble concentrating when I try to read my computer. To alleviate this, I should
   - ☒ breathe slowly and deeply.
   - ☐ switch to my buddy's alternate air source.
   - ☐ surface immediately, breathe oxygen and seek medical care.
   - ☒ ascend to a shallower depth until symptoms/signs subside.

10. Choose all that are symptoms or signs of decompression sickness.

- ☒ Pain in arm, legs or torso
- ☒ Staggering
- ☐ Inappropriate laughter
- ☒ Paralysis
- ☒ ~~Hyperactivity~~ no
- ☒ Skin itch
- ☒ Dizziness/vertigo
- ☒ Coughing spasms
- ☐ Cherry-red lips

11. The primary reason divers get decompression illness is

- ☐ computer malfunction.
- ☐ residual nitrogen.
- ☒ diver error.
- ☐ equipment failure.

12. As responsible divers who want to reduce the risk of decompression sickness, my buddy and I (choose all that apply):

- ☒ ascend no faster than permitted by our computers.
- ☒ use our computers and tables (RDP, eRDPML™) accurately.
- ☒ remain well within no stop (no decompression) limits.
- ☒ make safety stops at the end of all dives (deep or shallow).
- ☒ avoid/account for predisposing factors.

Student Statement

I completed this Knowledge Review to the best of my ability. For any questions I answered incorrectly or incompletely, I reviewed the explanation provided and now understand the material. In the case of anything about which I still have questions, I will review the material again and, if necessary, discuss it with my instructor at our next session.

☒ I agree ☐ I disagree

Name Joshua Leopold

Date 10/16/18

scenario

"My dive computer's running a surface interval," Chloe said as she unloaded gear from her car and started unpacking her dry suit.

"Mine doesn't do that," said her buddy, Sean. "I have to set it for altitude."

"I love the mountains," Chloe said, taking a deep breath as Sean set his computer. "What a gorgeous lake. We're at about 900 metres, right?"

"The sign we passed said 2900 feet, so yes," Sean nodded as he finished with his computer.

The pair strolled to the lake edge to assess the site. "Wow, look at that. The visibility looks endless," Sean said.

"This should be a great dive," said Chloe. "I can't wait to get i n the water."

- *What does this exchange tell you about altitude diving?*
- *Does this scenario change your perceptions about where you can find good diving?*

ALTITUDE DIVING 4

ALTITUDE DIVING

Introduction

The vast majority of diving takes place at sea level, but diving well above sea level is popular in many areas. This adds considerations to planning and making your dives, because the decompression models used in most dive computers and dive tables – including the Recreational Dive Planner – were developed for diving at sea level.

Altitude becomes a consideration because you surface to a lower atmospheric pressure than at sea level. This makes the accuracy and reliability of calculations of dive tables and computers intended for sea level less certain. Some altitude isn't a problem, but dives between 300 metres/1000 feet to 3000 metres/10,000 feet above sea level are considered altitude diving and have special considerations. Below 300 metres/1000 feet, dive as you would at sea level. Dives above 3000 metres/10,000 feet are generally above the range for most altitude procedures, though some dive computers will calculate to approximately 6000 metres/20,000 feet.

Reduced Atmospheric Pressure

To dive at altitude, you apply special procedures and calculations that adjust for the reduced atmospheric pressure. This is because the decompression models used by dive computers and tables reduce decompression sickness (DCS) risk by keeping the estimated dissolved nitrogen in the body's tissues within acceptable limits. If this limit is exceeded, nitrogen may come out of solution after a dive faster than the body

LEARNING OBJECTIVES

By the end of this section, I should be able to answer these questions:

1. How do I determine that a dive is an "altitude dive"?
2. Why do I need to follow special dive table and computer procedures at altitude?
3. How far can any decompression theory be relied on to acceptably reduce the risk of decompression sickness, and why?

Most diving takes place at sea level, but altitude diving is popular in many areas above 300 metres/1000 feet.

can safely eliminate it, creating an unacceptable DCS risk. At altitude, a greater difference between the dissolved nitrogen and the surrounding pressure means that after a dive, nitrogen comes out of solution more rapidly than at sea level. To stay within limits, the maximum dissolved nitrogen allowed must be lower than at sea level.

Your no stop limits need to be lower at altitude, and the higher the altitude the greater the reduction compared to sea level. Dive computers typically handle the adjustment internally – you set the computer for altitude (or it sets itself), and then use it much as you normally would.

Simply put, this means your no stop limits need to be lower at altitude, and the higher the altitude the greater the reduction compared to sea level. Various tables and computers make this adjustment differently. Dive computers typically handle the adjustment internally – you set the computer for altitude (or it sets itself), and then use it much as you normally would. With dive tables, you typically convert your actual depth to a deeper "theoretical" depth that you use on the table. Either way, these adjustments shorten your no stop times compared to sea level, so that when you dive within them, you reduce the maximum dissolved nitrogen in the body.

As you learned in the PADI Open Water Diver course, all decompression models are models – they do not measure anything actually happening in your body. Rather, they extrapolate theoretical DCS-free profiles based on human dive data. This means that no dive computer or dive table can guarantee that decompression sickness will never occur, even within its limits. This is why you dive conservatively, well within limits.

It also means we can only rely on decompression models to acceptably reduce the risk of DCS within the data upon which they are based – this becomes important in altitude diving, because there are fewer data (we'll come back to this shortly), making it important to stay well within limits, particularly at altitude.

EXERCISE-1

1. I'm diving in a lake that sits at 270 metres/900 feet of altitude. Compared to diving at sea level, I will plan and make the dive
   - ☐ a. using special procedures and reduced no stop limits.
   - ☐ b. much as I would at sea level.
2. The reason I need reduced no stop times at altitude is the reduced atmospheric pressure, which affects diving because
   - ☐ a. it causes my body to absorb more nitrogen.
   - ☐ b. after a dive, nitrogen dissolves from my tissues faster.
   - ☐ c. dive computers miscalculate the depth.
3. We can only rely on decompression models to acceptably reduce DCS risk
   - ☐ a. within the data upon which they are based.
   - ☐ b. to the limits of mathematical calculation.
   - ☐ c. at sea level.

How did you do?

1. b. 2. b. 3. a.

Flying After Diving and Driving to Altitude After Diving

Before going into altitude diving procedures, let's revisit flying after diving. It may seem they would be similar, because both involve exposure to altitude after diving, but they differ from a decompression model perspective.

During altitude diving, you ascend to altitude *before* the dive. You begin and end the dive at the *same* altitude surface pressure. When flying after diving (or driving to altitude after diving), however, you dive at sea level, surface at sea level and *then* ascend to a lesser pressure.

Yet another issue is flying after altitude diving. In this case, follow the same flying-after-diving procedures that you would follow after sea level diving. (And still another issue is repetitive diving at two different altitudes – it's recommended you avoid making a dive followed by a repetitive dive at a higher altitude. This is because there are very few human test data on this type of diving, though your computer may calculate such dives.)

LEARNING OBJECTIVES

By the end of this section, I should be able to answer these questions:

1. What are the theoretical and practical differences between altitude diving and flying after diving?
2. What are the current recommendations for flying after diving?
3. What are the current recommendations for driving to altitude after diving?

Flying After Diving Recommendations

As a review, here are the current flying-after-diving recommendations. The hyperbaric medical community revises flying-after-diving recommendations periodically. Stay up to date with current recommendations.

For dives within the no stop limits:

- Single dives – a minimum preflight surface interval of 12 hours is suggested.
- Repetitive dives and/or multiday dives – a minimum preflight surface interval of 18 hours is suggested.

For dives with required (emergency) decompression:

- A minimum preflight surface interval greater than 18 hours is suggested.

As with dive tables and computers, no flying-after-diving recommendation can guarantee that decompression sickness will never occur. These guidelines presently represent the best estimate for a conservative minimum preflight surface interval for the vast majority of divers. There always may be an occasional diver whose physiological makeup or special dive circumstances result in DCS despite following the recommendations. As with all dive practices, apply the recommendations conservatively. If your dive computer gives a different time before flying, use the most conservative option.

Driving to Altitude After Diving

Currently, there are no formal recommendations for driving to altitude after diving, whether after an altitude dive to a higher altitude, or from sea level to altitude. The most prudent practice is to be conservative: The longer you wait before ascending to altitude after diving, the lower the risk. You may check with a local dive center, resort or instructor to see if local divers follow a particular recommendation or protocol.

Although altitude diving and flying after diving both involve altitude, they differ from a decompression model perspective.

EXERCISE-2

1. Altitude diving and flying after diving differ, because altitude diving involves starting and ending a dive in reduced atmospheric pressure, whereas flying after diving involves going to reduced atmospheric pressure sometime after the end of a dive.

   ☐ True ☐ False

2. It's 9 a.m. and I've just finished a single dive. This is the only dive I've made in more than a week. According to the current recommendations, the soonest I should fly is after

   ☐ a. 9 p.m. tonight.
   ☐ b. 3 a.m. tomorrow.
   ☐ c. 9 a.m. tomorrow.

3. The recommendations for driving to altitude after diving are the same as for flying after diving.

   ☐ True ☐ False

How did you do?

1. True. 2. a. 3. False. There are no formal recommendations, so be conservative. The longer you wait, the lower your DCS risk.

LEARNING OBJECTIVES

By the end of this section, I should be able to answer these questions:

1. Aside from decompression sickness, what are two potential detrimental physiological conditions possible from altitude diving, what causes them and how do I avoid them?

2. What is the first aid for these two conditions should they occur?

Physiological Concerns at Altitude

Besides needing to use procedures to manage DCS risk, diving at altitude has two other primary physiological concerns: hypoxia and hypothermia.

Hypoxia

At altitude, air has less pressure and density, so the partial pressure of oxygen is lower. That is, each breath you inhale has fewer oxygen molecules, even though it still makes up 21 percent of air. This lower partial pressure makes it harder for your body to meet its oxygen demands. When there's insufficient oxygen to meet the body's demands, hypoxia results.

Hypoxia at altitude may result from heavy exercise like carrying and donning gear, walking, entering the water and swimming at the surface. Signs and symptoms include fatigue, shortness of breath, light-headedness, faintness and exhaustion. People who live at altitude resist hypoxia better because their bodies adapt over time to the lower pressure by increasing the red blood cells that carry oxygen.

To avoid hypoxia, limit exercise. Take your time, and don't let yourself get out of breath. Rest frequently. If you experience hypoxia symptoms, stop all activity and rest. Resume activity at a lower exertion level after you fully recover normal respiration.

Rest and fully recover at the surface before your descent to avoid overexertion and overbreathing your regulator. Going underwater restores the oxygen partial pressure.

When surfacing from a dive, you return to thin air. If you've been exerting yourself near the end of the dive, or you have a strenuous exit, you may find it difficult to catch your breath. Again, stop and allow yourself to fully recover. Some divers use and breathe EANx (enriched air nitrox) while entering and exiting the water to help avoid hypoxia (more about using EANx at altitude shortly).

When surfacing from a dive, you return to thin air. If you've been exerting yourself near the end of the dive, or you have a strenuous exit, you may find it difficult to catch your breath. Stop and allow yourself to fully recover.

Hypothermia

As you learned in the PADI Open Water Diver course, hypothermia occurs when you become significantly chilled. It results when the body's core temperature begins to drop. Without sufficient insulation, hypothermia can occur in any temperature water, and it's potentially life-threatening. However, it is particularly a concern in altitude diving, because freshwater lakes at altitude tend to be colder, with distinct thermoclines. (There are some warm-water altitude dives, but these are uncommon.)

Hypothermia signs/symptoms include shivering, numbness and blueness, which may be hard to see with dive gear on. As the body's core temperature drops, coordination declines followed by weakness, confusion, unconsciousness and, eventually, death.

Prevent hypothermia by wearing adequate exposure protection, by allowing yourself to rewarm between dives and by ending the dive immediately if you begin shivering. Shivering is a warning sign – never ignore it.

⚠ **A diver suspected of slight-to-mild hypothermia should exit the water, get into a warm, dry area and dress in warm clothes while re-warming.** More severe cases may require CPR, shock management and emergency medical treatment. If you're not already trained in CPR and first aid, see your instructor about the Emergency First Response Primary Care (CPR) and Secondary Care (First Aid) courses.

EXERCISE-3

1. _____________ can be caused by low oxygen partial pressure at altitude coupled with exertion.
   - ☐ a. Hypoxia
   - ☐ b. Hypothermia
   - ☐ c. Decompression sickness
2. After a dive, my buddy is shivering uncontrollably and has blue lips. My buddy should
   - ☐ a. stop, rest and recover.
   - ☐ b. get into a warm, dry area and dress in warm clothes.
   - ☐ c. breathe emergency oxygen.

How did you do?

1. a. 2. b.

Prevent hypothermia by wearing adequate exposure protection, by allowing yourself to re-warm between dives and by ending the dive immediately if you begin shivering.

Planning and Making Altitude Dives

As discussed earlier, dive computers used at altitude adjust for the pressure difference within their calculations. So, your primary consideration with using a dive computer at altitude is that the computer is designed for doing so.

Some computers automatically adjust, but you have to manually set others for altitude. See the manufacturer literature for the model you'll be using, and use the computer as directed by the manufacturer. A few (primarily older) computers aren't designed for altitude use. These may still be useable as timers and depth gauges, however, allowing you to altitude dive using the RDP or eRDPML™ with altitude diving procedures (discussed in the next section).

Your computer may have different safety and emergency decompression stops at altitude compared to sea level. In theory, the ideal stop depth gets shallower as the altitude gets higher, so use the stop depth indicated by your computer. If your computer doesn't give safety stop depths, a useful guideline is to make the stop between 4 metres/12 feet and 3 metres/10 feet.

Decompression stop depths are more critical: Make emergency decompression stops at the depth your computer indicates. As always, consult the manufacturer literature for the specific procedures for your computer.

LEARNING OBJECTIVES

By the end of this section, I should be able to answer these questions:

1. How do dive computers account for altitude? What considerations do I have planning dives and diving with a dive computer at altitude?

2. Why does the interval between arriving at altitude and diving matter?

3. What is the prevailing thinking regarding the use of enriched air nitrox at altitude? What benefit do I have at the surface with enriched air nitrox?

4. How does altitude affect depth gauges? What do I do about these effects?

5. In what two ways may altitude affect my buoyancy?

6. Why is it important to dive conservatively, well within limits, when altitude diving?

7. What is the recommended maximum number of dives a day at altitude?

In theory, the ideal stop depth gets shallower as the altitude gets higher, so use the stop depth indicated by your computer. If your computer doesn't give safety stop depths, a useful guideline is to make the stop between 4 metres/12 feet and 3 metres/10 feet.

Arrival at Altitude Interval

With most computers (and dive table altitude procedures), your no stop times are shorter if you arrive at your dive altitude several hours before the dive, compared to if you dive immediately. This is because you have "surfaced" from the higher pressure at sea level. You have more nitrogen in your body than can remain in solution at altitude, and this affects your no stop dive time for that altitude. Much like a surface interval between dives, over time at altitude your nitrogen levels decline to the normal levels for that altitude. At this point you are an *acclimated diver* with respect to your nitrogen levels.

How you address this depends upon your computer – see the manufacturer literature. Some computers require you to wait a minimum interval before diving. Some models adjust automatically – **but this assumes you use a computer you bring with you from sea level.** Such a computer that is *already* at altitude (such as one kept at a local dive center, etc.) will not "know" that you have just reached altitude. Because the procedure for this situation varies with the computer, again, you need to check and follow the manufacturer recommendations for the computer you use.

Because EANx has a higher oxygen percentage and therefore a higher oxygen partial pressure, using it helps avoid hypoxia when exerting yourself at the surface.

Enriched Air Nitrox and Altitude Diving

Because altitude diving shortens your no stop time, divers often ask whether they can use EANx, which extends no stop time, to offset the difference. That's a good question and, in theory, this should work. But, to this point there are few significant, scientifically organized human dive data upon which the hyperbaric medical community can base judgment with reliability.

Therefore, the recommendation is to use air no stop limits even when diving with EANx at altitude. Since altitude dives tend to be relatively short (due to temperature) anyway, in practice the shorter no stop times usually make little difference.

Despite the recommendation, some computers will adjust for longer EANx no stop times longer at altitude, and divers commonly use EANx to offset shorter no stop times at altitude. There have been no widespread problems reported; the recommendation to use air no stop limits is based on a relative lack of information – not on any known problems.

Even remaining within air limits when altitude diving, as mentioned in the hypoxia discussion, EANx has benefits – at the surface. Because EANx has a higher oxygen percentage and therefore a higher oxygen partial pressure, using it helps avoid hypoxia when exerting yourself at the surface. For example, up to 3000 metres/10,000 feet, using enriched air with at least 32 percent oxygen (EANx32), the oxygen partial pressure gives you almost the same oxygen partial pressure you have breathing air at sea level. With more than 32 percent, the partial pressure is higher than at sea level.

With this in mind, at altitude some divers use EANx and breathe from their regulators during entries, surface swims and exits when they might otherwise use their snorkels. This is fine. Follow all the EANx equipment and handling

Neoprene wet suits and dry suits are more buoyant at altitude because the closed-cell neoprene material from which they're made expands, making the suit more buoyant at the surface. This means you'll need a little more weight compared to diving in fresh water at sea level.

procedures, and stay within oxygen exposure limits you learned in the PADI Enriched Air Diver course. (You need to be certified or supervised by a PADI Enriched Air Instructor.) When planning your gas use, plan for the added gas you'll use at the surface. Even when using EANx within air no stop limits, remember to manage your oxygen exposure.

Altitude Effects on Depth Gauges

If your dive computer doesn't work at altitude and can't be used as your timer/depth gauge, you may still dive using the eRDPML or the RDP following altitude procedures, a conventional depth gauge and a watch or timer. A consideration is that altitude affects the accuracy of many depth gauges.

Electronic depth gauges may adjust automatically or may need to be set for the altitude (like a computer) – see the manufacturer literature. Bourdon tube (mechanical analog) depth gauges read *shallower* than the actual depth at altitude. Some bourdon tubes have a dial for resetting the gauge to read accurately; if not, you have to adjust for it. The rule of thumb is to add 0.3 metres/1 foot to the shown depth, plus 0.3 metres/1 foot for each 300 metres/1000 feet of altitude (write the appropriate correction on a slate or wet book for dive reference).

If in doubt, the simplest solution is to dive and compare your depth gauge against a gauge known to be accurate, or with a measured line. Note that most gauges are saltwater calibrated. You do *not* need to adjust for this with the RDP, however, because the RDP is calibrated for salt water, too.

Buoyancy Effects

Diving at altitude can affect your buoyancy in two ways. The first is that you're in fresh water, which you need to consider if you're used to diving primarily in salt water. You'll need to adjust your weights, because virtually all altitude diving is freshwater diving, so you would need comparably less weight.

More specific to altitude, however, is that neoprene wet suits and dry suits are more buoyant at altitude. This is because the closed-cell neoprene material from which they're made has gas trapped in it. At a lower pressure, this gas expands, making the suit more buoyant at the surface. This means you'd need a little more weight compared to diving in fresh water at sea level. Though water pressure offsets this extra buoyancy by compressing the material when you descend only a metre/few feet or so, you'll still want to weight properly.

Conservative Diving at Altitude

As mentioned, it's especially important to dive conservatively at altitude because, while there exists ample human experience with altitude diving procedures to be reasonably confident in their reliability, this experience base is quite small compared to sea level diving and testing.

Another reason for being conservative is that factors thought to contribute to decompression sickness are common at altitude. In particular, altitude dives are in cool conditions (the potential to get cold). And, if you're not adapted to thin air, your cardiovascular system has to work harder for the same exertion level, which may also be a factor.

Finally, as the altitude increases, theory and reality seem to separate with respect to decompression modeling. Although altitude diving procedures appear reasonably reliable to as high as 6000 metres/20,000 feet (or the limit of the computer or table that you're using), the higher the altitude, the more conservative you will want to be.

Keep these recommendations in mind:

- Turn the dive when you start to feel chilled – avoid getting cold.
- Ascend slowly – 9 metres/30 feet per minute (or slower, if required by your computer) – and make safety stops. Ideally, simply explore your way shallower along an ascending slope, spending at least three minutes in the safety stop range as you come up.
- Get the dive time you want by limiting your depth – shallow water is usually the best diving anyway at most altitude sites.
- Allow ample time between dives to rewarm and to release nitrogen from your body.
- It is recommended that you make no more than two dives a day at altitude.
- The maximum depth for recreational diving at altitude is a theoretical depth of 40 metres/130 feet (see the Theoretical Depth at Altitude Chart), with a theoretical 30 metres/100 feet the recommended maximum.
- If making two dives at two different altitudes, make the dive at the higher altitude first.
- Remember that concerns about flying after diving and driving to a higher altitude also apply to altitude dives, not just to sea level dives.

EXERCISE-4

1. My primary consideration for using a dive computer at altitude is
   - ☐ a. using sea level no stop limits.
   - ☐ b. how cold affects battery life.
   - ☒ c. using a computer designed for it.
2. I've just arrived at a dive site at 900 metres/3000 feet altitude. This means that my no stop times are shorter than they would be if I were to wait several hours before diving.
   ☒ True ☐ False
3. The recommendation to use air no stop times when diving with enriched air nitrox at altitude is based on
   - ☐ a. hyperbaric studies that found enriched air doesn't work at altitude.
   - ☐ b. the higher reliability of air no stop times.
   - ☐ c. frequent problems reported by enriched air divers at altitude.
   - ☒ d. a lack of scientific, organized test data about enriched air diving at altitude.
4. Compared to sea level, at altitude, mechanical Bourdon tube depth gauges read ________
   - ☐ a. deeper.
   - ☐ b. the same.
   - ☒ c. shallower.
5. Altitude diving can affect my buoyancy due to being in fresh water versus salt water, and because neoprene exposure suits expand at altitude.
   ☒ True ☐ False
6. The experience base for altitude diving is quite small compared to sea level diving and testing.
   ☒ True ☐ False
7. My buddy and I want to make several dives in a lake at just over 2400 metres/8000 feet altitude. Based on the recommended maximum, we would plan no more than ____ dive(s) per day.
   - ☐ a. one
   - ☒ b. two
   - ☐ c. three
   - ☐ d. four

How did you do?

1. c. 2. True. 3. d. 4. c. 5. True. 6. True. 7. b.

Using the RDP at Altitude

This section covers use of the Recreational Dive Planner (RDP) for altitude diving, which you may use for planning your dives with or without an altitude-capable dive computer. You may use either the RDP Table or eRDPML with these procedures. With the RDP, you must use these special procedures for altitudes at or above 300 metres/1000 feet. The maximum altitude is 3000 metres/10,000 feet.

Ascent Rate and Safety/Emergency Decompression Stops

At altitude, the maximum ascent rate with the RDP is 9 metres/30 feet per minute. The depth for safety and emergency decompression stops gets shallower with altitude; see the Theoretical Depth at Altitude Chart for the depth. A safety stop is mandatory on all dives at altitude.

When arriving at an altitude dive site from sea level, you have "surfaced" from a greater pressure to a lower pressure and the nitrogen pressure in your tissues is higher than the surrounding pressure. You need to account for this residual nitrogen in planning an altitude dive just as you would in planning a repetitive dive.

LEARNING OBJECTIVES

By the end of this section, I should be able to answer these questions:

1. What's the altitude range for using the RDP with altitude diving procedures?
2. What is my ascent rate and safety stop depth when using the RDP at altitude?
3. How do I determine the proper repetitive group on the RDP when arriving at altitude from sea level?
4. How do I determine the theoretical depth for a corresponding actual depth at altitude using the Theoretical Depth at Altitude chart (imperial or metric)? What is the eRDPML's advantage over the Table for planning altitude dives?
5. How do I calculate no decompression limits for single and repetitive dives at altitude, when diving less than six hours and more than six hours after arriving at the dive site?

Arriving at Altitude

As discussed earlier, when arriving at an altitude dive site from sea level, you have surfaced from a greater pressure to a lower pressure and the nitrogen pressure in your tissues is higher than the surrounding pressure. You need to account for this residual nitrogen in planning an altitude dive just as you would in planning a repetitive dive.

With the RDP, your first option is to wait six hours after arriving at altitude before making your first dive. Much like after a dive when diving at sea level, for planning purposes, this clears residual nitrogen.

To dive sooner than six hours, however, you account for the nitrogen by determining a pressure group letter for use on the RDP Table or eRDPML. You use the pressure group to plan your dive exactly as you do making a sea level repetitive dive. To get your pressure group, upon arrival at the dive site altitude count two pressure groups for each 300 metres/1000 feet of altitude. After determining your pressure group, you may allow a "surface interval," if you wish, to reduce your residual nitrogen. For dives above 2400 metres/8000 feet, wait six hours in all cases. If arriving to a higher altitude from a lower altitude, determine your pressure group as if arriving from sea level, which conservatively addresses the change. (You learn a more specific procedure in the PADI Altitude Diver course.)

Examples

1. You plan to altitude dive at 1500 metres/5000 feet. What is the pressure group upon arrival at the dive site altitude?

Answer: *J – Count 10 pressure groups (two for each 300 metres/1000 feet) to arrive at J.*

2. If you waited 90 minutes after arriving at the dive site altitude, what would the new pressure group be?

Answer: *B. Table 2 of the RDP Table or the Dive Planning Mode (PG Before SI) of the eRDPML™ shows that after 90 minutes, pressure group J moves into pressure group B.*

3. You plan to dive at an altitude of 2680 metres/8792 feet. What is the pressure group upon arrival at the dive site altitude?

Answer: *You can't determine a pressure group for altitudes greater than 2400 metres/8000 feet. The diver must wait six hours before diving.*

PADI ALTITUDE DIVER SPECIALTY

At your instructor's discretion, the Altitude Adventure Dive credits toward the PADI Altitude Diver Specialty course. The course gives you more opportunities to apply and practice altitude diving skills, including:

- Calculating ascents between altitudes with the RDP
- Additional dive planning practice
- Extended altitude diving experience with supervision

Remember to log your training dives with the PADI Mobile App or at padi.com.

Determining and Using Theoretical Depths

To accommodate altitude, you convert your actual depth to a theoretical depth that you use with the RDP. Use the Theoretical Depth at Altitude Chart (metric or imperial) to make these conversions.

- Use the exact or next greater number.
- Round altitudes up to the next 300 metres/1000 feet.
- Round depths to the next greater depth. This means a depth is rounded entering the Theoretical Depth at Altitude Chart, and then again when applying the theoretical depth to the RDP. The eRDPML, with its two metres/five foot depth increments, helps reduce the unnecessary rounding in altitude diving, and is therefore the recommended RDP for altitude use.

Examples

1. You plan to dive at an altitude of 1000 metres/3300 feet to an actual depth of 15 metres/47 feet. What is the depth used on the RDP for planning this dive?

Answer: *18 metres/60 feet. Round up 1000 metres/3300 feet to 1200 metres/4000 feet on the Theoretical Depth at Altitude Chart. Round 15 metres/47 feet to 16 metres/50 feet in the "Actual Depth" column, then move right into the 1200 metres/4000 feet column. The theoretical depth shown is 18 metres/58 feet. An 18-metre/58-foot dive rounds to 18 metres/60 feet on the RDP.*

2. At what depth would you make the required safety stop?

Answer: *4 metres/13 feet. Find 4 metres/13 feet listed under 1200 metres/4000 feet in the Safety/Emergency Decompression Stop Depth portion of the chart.*

3. If you arrived from sea level and made the dive 15 minutes after arriving at the dive site, what is the no decompression limit for the planned actual depth of 15 metres/47 feet?

Answer: *36 minutes. Upon arrival at the dive site, count eight pressure groups (two for each 300 metres/1000 feet) for group H. On Table 2 of the RDP Table, or in the Dive Planning Mode (PG Before SI) of the eRDPML, find or enter H and a surface interval of 15 minutes. This moves you into group F. Table 3 of the RDP Table, or continuing in Dive Planning Mode with the eRDPML, shows that in group F, planning a dive to a theoretical depth of 18 metres/60 feet has a no decompression limit of 36 minutes.*

Theoretical Depth at Altitude

METRIC

Altitude (in metres)

ACTUAL DEPTH	300	600	900	1200	1500	1800	2100	2400	2700	3000
10	10	11	11	12	12	12	13	13	14	14
12	12	13	13	14	14	15	15	16	17	17
14	15	15	16	16	17	17	18	19	19	20
16	17	17	18	18	19	20	21	21	22	23
18	19	19	20	21	22	22	23	24	25	26
20	21	21	22	23	24	25	26	27	28	29
22	23	24	25	25	26	27	28	29	31	32
24	25	26	27	28	29	30	31	32	33	35
26	27	28	29	30	31	32	34	35	36	38
28	29	30	31	32	34	35	36	38	39	40
30	31	32	33	35	36	37	39	40	42	
32	33	34	36	37	38	40	41			
34	35	37	38	39	41	42				
36	37	39	40	42						
38	39	41	42							
40	41									

Safety/Emergency Decompression Stop Depth

	300	600	900	1200	1500	1800	2100	2400	2700	3000
Stop Depth	4.4	4.3	4.1	4.0	3.8	3.7	3.5	3.4	3.3	3.2

Theoretical Depth at Altitude

IMPERIAL

Altitude (in feet)

ACTUAL DEPTH	1000	2000	3000	4000	5000	6000	7000	8000	9000	10,000
10	10	11	11	12	12	12	13	13	14	15
20	21	21	22	23	24	25	26	27	28	29
30	31	32	33	35	36	37	39	40	42	44
40	41	43	45	46	48	50	52	54	56	58
50	52	54	56	58	60	62	65	67	70	73
60	62	64	67	69	72	75	78	81	84	87
70	72	75	78	81	84	87	91	94	98	102
80	83	86	89	92	96	100	103	108	112	116
90	93	97	100	104	108	112	116	121	126	131
100	103	107	111	116	120	124	129	134	140	
110	114	118	122	127	132	137				
120	124	129	134	139						
130	135	140								

Safety/Emergency Decompression Stop Depth

	1000	2000	3000	4000	5000	6000	7000	8000	9000	10,000
Stop Depth	14	14	13	13	12	12	12	11	11	10

Knowledge Review – Altitude Diving

Answer the following questions by selecting the best choice (or choices) from those provided. Be prepared to discuss the material at your next training session.

1. With most dive tables and computers, an altitude dive is a dive made at an elevation higher than ____________ above sea level.

   ☐ 100 metres/330 feet
   ☒ 300 metres/1000 feet
   ☒ 1000 metres/3300 feet
   ☐ 3000 metres/10,000 feet

2. Practically and theoretically, flying after diving and diving at altitude are the same thing.

   ☐ True
   ☒ False

3. Based on current recommendations, if I make repetitive no stop (no decompression) dives and/or dive for several days in a row, the minimum interval before flying is _______ hours.

   ☐ six
   ☐ 12
   ☒ 18
   ☐ 24

4. While carrying my gear to the shore for an altitude dive, I find myself feeling a bit breathless. I am probably feeling the effects of mild ________ and should ________.

   ☒ hypoxia; pace myself and reduce strenuous exertion
   ☐ anoxia; seek medical attention
   ☐ hyperthermia; cool off
   ☐ hypothermia; rewarm myself

5. Altitude can affect my dive instrumentation. With respect to my dive computer,

   ☐ adjustments will be automatic.
   ☐ I need to set it for altitude.
   ☐ it will not be useable at altitude.
   ☒ altitude use varies, so see the manufacturer instructions.

6. When using the RDP at altitude (Table or eRDPML™), the maximum ascent rate is 9 metres/30 feet per minute, and I make my safety stop at the theoretical depth shown on the Theoretical Depth at Altitude table.

   ☒ True
   ☐ False

7. The generally recommended maximum number of altitude dives in a day is

   ☐ one.
   ☒ two.
   ☐ three.
   ☐ there is no limit.

Optional: Use the RDP Table or eRDPML for the next questions:

8. I plan to dive to an actual depth of 18 metres/60 feet one hour after arriving to an altitude of 1090 metres/3578 feet. If I were to dive to the no stop (no decompression) limit, my no stop time (NDL) for a repetitive dive to the same depth after a 45-minute surface interval would be

   ☐ 24 minutes.
   ☒ 18 minutes (metric)/20 minutes (imperial).
   ☐ 16 minutes (metric)/18 minutes (imperial).
   ☐ not applicable: A second dive is not permitted.

9. I plan to dive to an actual depth of 24 metres/80 feet after spending seven hours at the dive site altitude of 1226 metres/4023 feet. What is my no stop time for this dive?

- ☐ eRDPML metric: 31 minutes; RDP Table metric: 29 minutes; eRDPML imperial: 30 minutes; RDP Table imperial: 30 minutes
- ☒ eRDPML metric: 20 minutes; RDP Table metric: 20 minutes; eRDPML imperial: 20 minutes; RDP Table imperial: 20 minutes
- ☐ eRDPML metric: 18 minutes; RDP Table metric: 14 minutes; eRDPML imperial: 16 minutes; RDP Table imperial: 16 minutes

10. Continuing with the previous example, if my bottom time is 15 minutes, would my no decompression limit for a repetitive dive to an actual depth of 18 metres/60 feet after a one-hour, five-minute surface interval be (use RDP of your choice):

    25 minutes (eRDPML metric)?

    25 minutes (RDP Table metric)?

    24 minutes (eRDPML imperial)?

    20 minutes (RDP Table imperial)?

- ☒ Yes
- ☐ No

Student Statement

I completed this Knowledge Review to the best of my ability. For any questions I answered incorrectly or incompletely, I reviewed the explanation provided and now understand the material. In the case of anything about which I still have questions, I will review the material again and, if necessary, discuss it with my instructor at our next session.

☒ I agree ☐ I disagree

Name ______________________

Date 1/29/19

scenario

"From the moment you step onto the dive boat's main deck, you know it's going to be special – you can feel the excitement of the other divers and, as the boat pulls away from the dock, everyone cheers.

"About 30 minutes to the first site," the divemaster says.

You and your buddy finish setting up your gear, check to make sure the cylinders are secure, then go forward to join everyone for coffee.

As everyone chats excitedly, one diver passes around a tablet with photos from the last time she dived the site. "The visibility was stunning," she recalls.

"Should be just as clear today," the divemaster says.

The half-hour flies and soon the boat is tied to the site mooring. Looking over the side, you can see to the bottom about 18 metres/ 60 feet below. Excitement builds as the divemaster completes the briefing and everyone starts to gear up. You think to yourself, *Yeah, I could get used to this.*"

- *If you've never been on a boat dive, what does this tell you about boat diving?*
- *If you have been on a boat dive, how does this description line up with your experiences?*

5 BOAT DIVING

BOAT DIVING

LEARNING OBJECTIVES

By the end of this section, I should be able to answer this question:

1. What are the benefits and advantages of diving from a boat?

Introduction

Although there's lots of great shore diving, most divers end up diving from boats, at least on occasion. Although boats vary significantly in size and layout, the procedures for diving from them are consistent (with allowances for the vessel and the environment). The Boat Adventure Dive gives you an overview that helps you dive more effectively from boats, and speeds your acclimation to unfamiliar boats.

Some divers make almost *all* their dives from boats. This is because boat diving has several advantages and benefits that make it popular. For one, boats give you access to sites beyond a reasonable reach from shore. In some areas, you can't even see the shore from the dive site; in others, the site is within swimming distance, but you don't have shore access. In some places, there is no shore diving at all – you can *only* dive from boats.

Another advantage of boat diving is that if the conditions are poor at one site, you can move easily to one where you can dive. In many areas, it is far more likely you can find acceptable conditions by boat than you could with shore-based diving. Doing so is more convenient, too – you don't have to repack, you just go.

Boat diving also usually avoids long surface swims, because you moor or anchor on (or very close to) the site. While this isn't always the case, it is more often than not. At many sites, you descend/ascend along a line – descent line or mooring/anchor line – connecting the boat to the site.

Boat diving avoids difficult shore entries and/ or long or difficult walks with your gear. You don't usually have to trudge through sand or over rocks, and you avoid long hikes in your gear or multiple trips carrying gear. Conditions like high surf may make shore diving impossible, but boat diving may still be possible.

Although boats vary significantly in size and layout, the procedures for diving from them are relatively consistent, with allowances for the vessel and the environment.

Finally, boat diving is *fun*, which is perhaps the main reason you'll want to do it. It puts you together with other divers who share your love for diving and the diving lifestyle. The experience begins when you go aboard, well before you get to the dive site, because boating is a recreation itself and a great way to spend time with friends.

Boat diving has several advantages and benefits, but the main reason to do it is that it's fun. It's a great way to spend time with other divers and friends.

EXERCISE-1

1. The benefits and advantages of boat diving include (choose all that apply):
   - ☐ a. having access to dive sites unreachable from shore.
   - ☐ b. avoiding long surface swims and hikes in gear.
   - ☐ c. the ability to relocate easily if conditions are poor.
   - ☐ d. having a lot of fun doing it.

How did you do?

1. a, b, c, d.

LEARNING OBJECTIVES

By the end of this section, I should be able to answer these questions:

1. What are a boat's bow, stern, starboard side and port side?

2. Which is the windward side of a boat, and which is the leeward side?

3. What do the following terms refer to on a boat: head, galley, bridge, wheelhouse (or pilothouse), transom, rail, cylinder racks, bunks (staterooms), and diving entry/exit area?

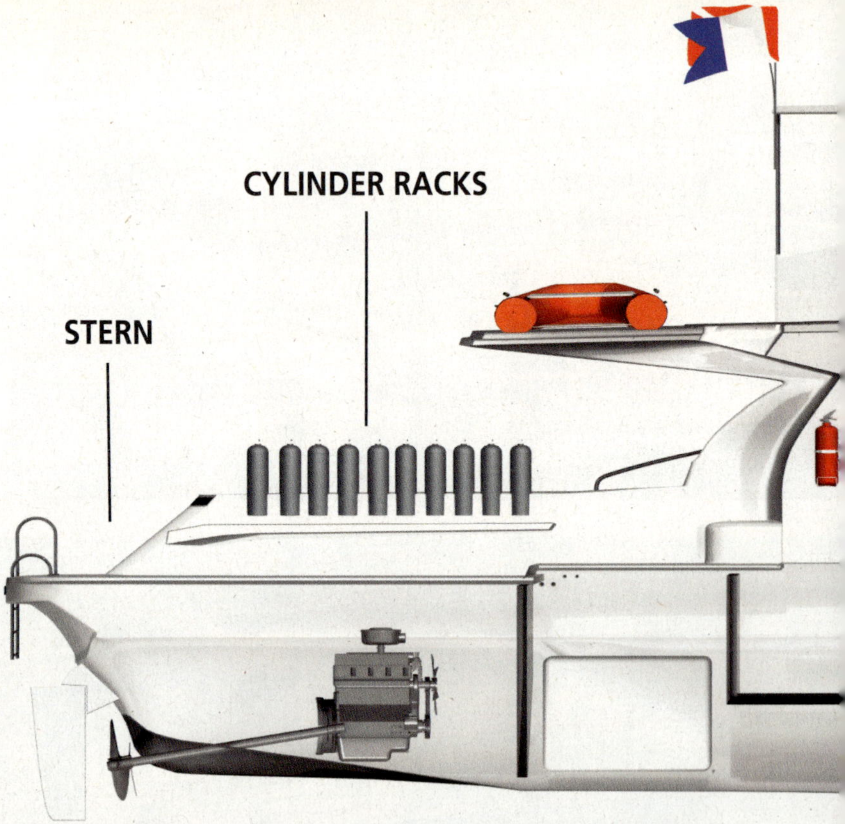

Boat Terminology

Boaters and sailors have unique terms for different locations and directions on boats. Most of these address practical considerations that you have on a boat, but others continue primarily due to tradition. Either way, being familiar with common boat terminology helps you communicate while boating, so let's start there. Here are common terms and what they mean:

Bow – The front of the boat. Going toward the bow is called "going forward."

Stern – The back of the boat. Going toward the stern is called "going aft."

Starboard – The right side of the boat, when facing the bow.

Port – The left side of the boat, when facing the bow.

Windward – The side of the boat toward the wind.

Leeward – The side of the boat away from the wind, it is sometimes pronounced "lou-ard."

Head – The restroom facilities in general, and the boat's toilet specifically.

Galley – The kitchen/cooking area.

Bridge – An elevated area from which the captain controls the boat. A "flying bridge" is an open area on top of the boat providing the captain with unobstructed views.

Wheelhouse (pilothouse) – A room with the ship's wheel (steering wheel); roughly a synonym for "the bridge."

Transom – The planking that makes up the hull's stern; normally referenced on small boats.

Rail – A rail along the outer edges of the deck. It is also called the *gunnel* or *gunwale*.

Cylinder racks – Racks that hold scuba cylinders, typically with bungee cords or other devices that keep cylinders from falling out as the boat rolls.

Bunks (staterooms) – Beds on boats that make overnight trips.

Entry/exit area – The location(s) where you enter and exit the water. On some boats you enter and exit at the same place; on others, you enter from one place and exit the water from another.

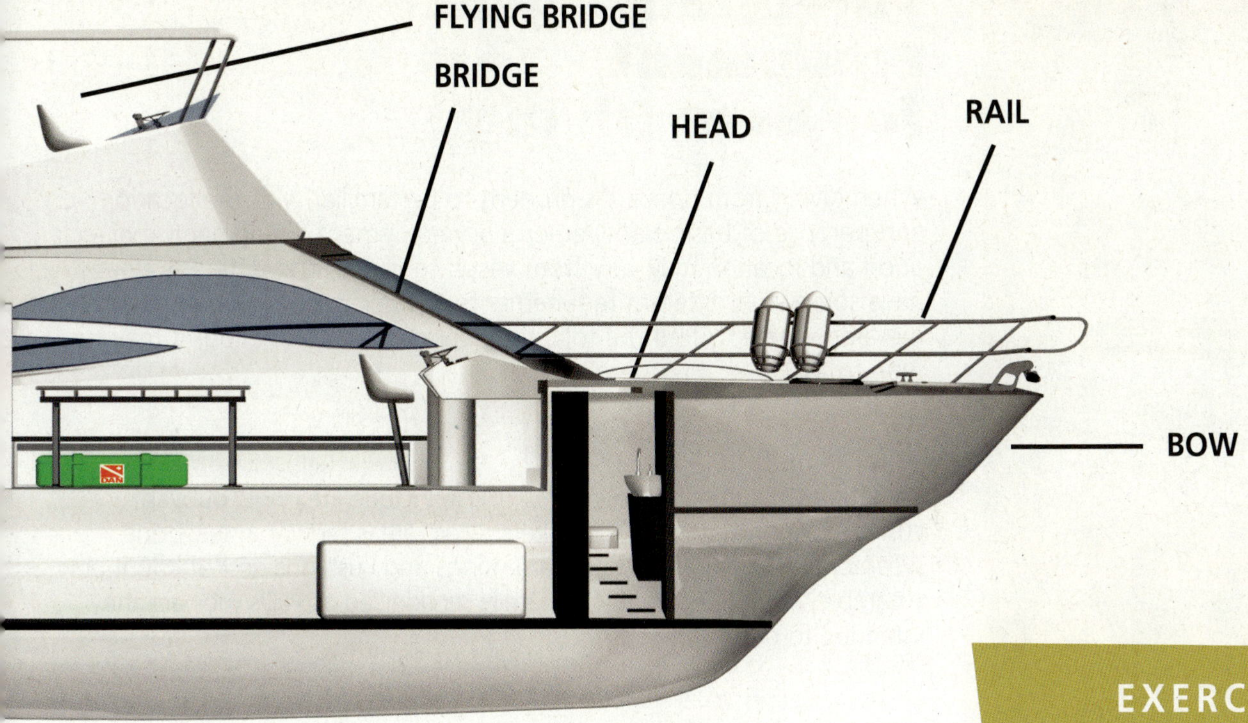

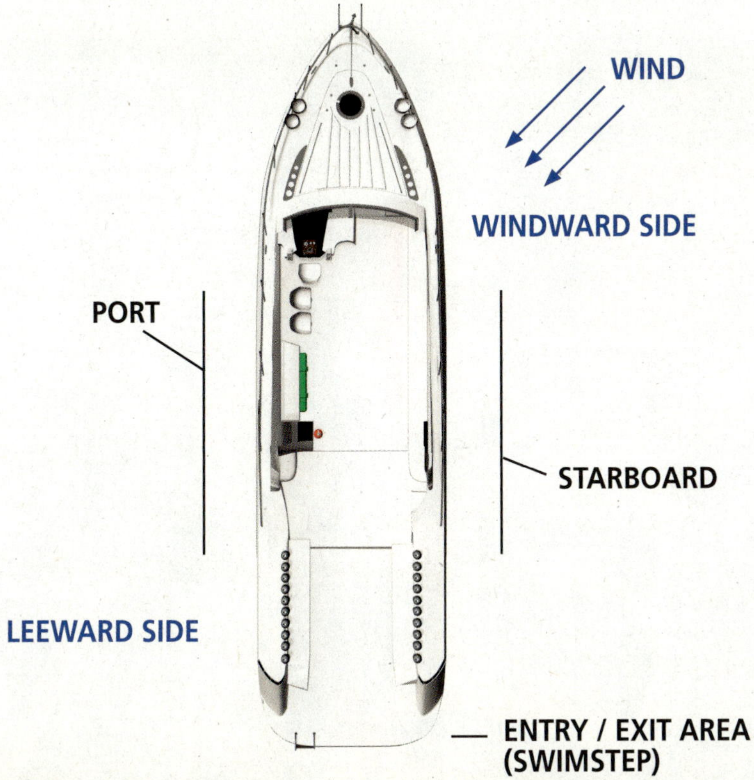

EXERCISE-2

1. I'm standing on a boat facing the bow. _______ is on my right and _______ is on my left.
   - ☐ a. Starboard; stern
   - ☐ b. Starboard; port
   - ☐ c. Port; stern
   - ☐ d. Port; starboard
2. I'm on the leeward side of the boat facing the water, so the wind blows against my
   - ☐ a. face.
   - ☐ b. back.
   - ☐ c. left side.
   - ☐ d. right side.
3. I'm on a larger boat and I'm hungry. I would normally go to the _________ for something to eat.
   - ☐ a. galley
   - ☐ b. transom
   - ☐ c. rail
   - ☐ d. wheelhouse

How did you do?

1. b. 2. b. 3. a.

LEARNING OBJECTIVES

By the end of this section, I should be able to answer these questions:

1. What eight pieces of basic emergency equipment are typically found on dive boats?

2. Where would I typically find each of those eight pieces of emergency equipment?

3. How do I operate the marine radio on board a dive boat according to local regulations and procedures?

Safety/Emergency Equipment for Boat Diving

When diving from boats, it's prudent to be familiar with the location and purpose of basic safety/emergency equipment. Equipment operation and location may vary from vessel to vessel, and different areas have somewhat different requirements. If the crew/divemaster doesn't mention where to find the following items during a briefing, it may be wise to ask.

Personal Flotation Devices (PFDs)

Sometimes called "life preservers," these include life rings, buoyant cushions, ring buoys and life jackets. Most areas require at least one *wearable* PFD per person on board. Rings and cushions do not count as wearable, and BCDs are not generally recognized as PFDs (nor are they intended to be).

When diving from boats, it's prudent to be familiar with the location and purpose of basic safety/emergency equipment.

On smaller boats, you usually find PFDs tucked somewhere visible, but out of the way. On larger vessels, they are usually kept in marked, easily accessible locations. Larger vessels usually have life rings out, as well, available to throw to someone who has fallen overboard.

Fire Extinguishers

Fire on a boat is serious, because there is no place to go (except overboard) to escape a fully engulfed vessel. Take fire precautions seriously, including smoking restrictions. The crew may include fire procedures during the safety briefing, so pay attention.

Most larger dive boats will have one or more extinguishers. Small boats with little to burn may not have one, though at least one is always recommended. Fire extinguishers are generally visible and kept near the engine, galley and other areas with the highest risk of fire. Large boats may have additional internal extinguishing systems for their engines. These are usually triggered from the bridge.

Sound Signaling Devices

Sound devices used for signaling include bells, horns and whistles. These are used to warn other vessels (required in certain circumstances), to summon divers or to signal distress. On larger vessels, the captain usually controls the ship's horn from the bridge. Smaller vessels may use a simple whistle, or a hand-held air horn.

The audible surface-signaling device you carry while diving can serve this purpose if, for some reason, the boat's device isn't available.

Take fire precautions seriously, including smoking restrictions. The crew may include fire procedures during the safety briefing, so pay attention.

Visual Distress Signals

Visual signal devices include flares, flare guns, signal lights and signal mirrors. They signal distress over longer distances than sound can carry. You usually find these near the bridge with other emergency supplies.

In an emergency with bright sun, anything that reflects will work: a piece of mirror, aluminum foil, polished flat metal, etc.

Bilge Pump or Bailer

All boats take on water as a normal part of operation, and therefore have one or more means of removing it. These become emergency devices if the amount of water onboard is excessive, and/or if a leak develops so water begins coming aboard at an unacceptable rate. Small boats – runabouts, inflatables, etc. – often use a bucket or bailing scoop of some kind. Large vessels typically have electric pumps. But, they usually also have hand pumps as backup or to assist the electric pumps if needed.

Most bilge pumps work automatically and run when water in the bilge reaches a certain level. You typically find manual switches near the captain's station on the bridge.

Most bilge pumps work automatically and run when water in the bilge – the lowest point in the boat – reaches a certain level. You typically find manual switches near the captain's station on the bridge. You usually find manual bailers with the emergency equipment. Installed manual pumps are typically below decks so they are at a low point on the hull.

First-Aid Kit

In many areas, regulations require first-aid kits on all vessels with passengers. Most kits have general dressings, bandages, etc. On dive boats, the kit may also include a pocket mask as well as vinegar, hot compresses and other supplies for marine stings.

The kit's location varies on each vessel. The crew will usually tell you where to find it during the safety briefing. On boats, first-aid kits should be kept in sealed, moisture-proof containers to protect them from splashes and wet divers accidentally dripping water onto them.

Oxygen Equipment

Emergency oxygen has become the community standard for dealing with suspected DCI (decompression illness) and certain other diving emergencies. It is not a boating requirement, but specific to diving. So, when diving from a vessel other than a commercially operated dive boat, you will usually need to supply emergency oxygen equipment yourself.

You'll typically find oxygen equipment near the first-aid kit in a sealed box that's usually orange or green. You'll learn more about oxygen systems and their use in the PADI Rescue Diver, Emergency Oxygen Provider and Emergency First Response® Primary Care (CPR) and Secondary Care (First Aid) courses.

Marine Radio

Vessels larger than a runabout will usually have a marine radio; local regulations may require it depending upon the boat size and other factors. The marine radio is normally near the captain's station on the bridge; for convenience, a vessel may have two or more located in different places. Following certain protocols, it's used for both routine communications and emergencies. With this in mind, it's important to know what qualifies as an emergency.

Emergency oxygen has become the community standard for dealing with suspected DCI (decompression illness) and certain other diving emergencies.

An emergency is a situation with immediate threat to life or the ability for the vessel to remain "viable" (this usually means afloat but, for example, passengers may have to evacuate a burning boat even if it is afloat) – loss of power, running out of fuel, etc. are not emergencies. The captain may call for aid using regular marine radio protocols, but not emergency protocols.

If a situation qualifies as an emergency, including a diver emergency, and you must use the marine radio to summon help:

- Go to the local emergency channel. In most areas, this is channel 16.
- Say, "Mayday, Mayday, Mayday. This is [vessel name (repeat three times)] with a [type] emergency." Then say "over" to indicate you're waiting for a reply.
- An appropriate authority (e.g., the US Coast Guard in US waters, the Maritime and Coast Authority in the UK, the Japan Coast Guard in Japan, Australian Marine Safety Authority in Australian waters, etc.) will reply, asking for more information about the emergency, the vessel and your location. Be ready to provide GPS coordinates. Vessels in the area may also respond and be willing to assist as able.
- If you receive no reply, repeat the Mayday call. You can also try your mobile telephone if within its service area.

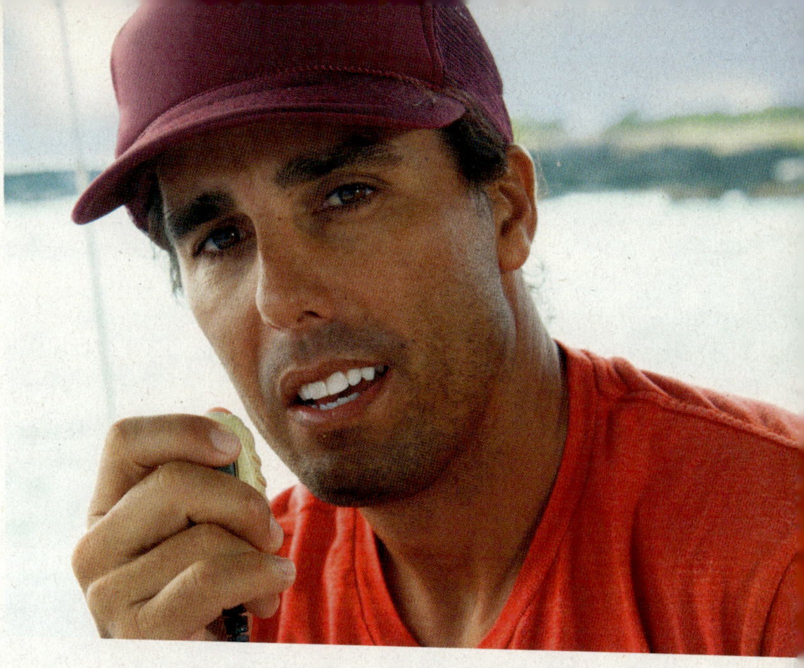

The marine radio is normally near the captain's station on the bridge; for convenience, a vessel may have two or more located in different places.

EXERCISE-3

1. My buddy and I are renting a small boat to go diving. We have all our dive gear, a fire extinguisher, air horn, flares, a bailing bucket, a first-aid kit, an emergency oxygen kit and a hand-held marine radio. Do we have all the emergency equipment typically found on a dive boat?

   ☐ Yes ☐ No

2. I'm on a friend's boat and it's taking on more water than is desirable. I'm assisting my friend, who asks me to manually switch on the bilge pumps. I would typically expect to find this switch

   ☐ a. below decks near the pump.
   ☐ b. somewhere around the transom.
   ☐ c. just inside the head.
   ☐ d. near the captain's station on the bridge.

3. To call for distress on marine radio, I should say,

   ☐ a. "Help, help, help."
   ☐ b. "SOS, SOS, SOS."
   ☐ c. "Mayday, Mayday, Mayday."
   ☐ d. "Over, over, over."

How did you do?

1. No. You need a PFD for each of you. 2. d. 3. c.

LEARNING OBJECTIVES

By the end of this section, I should be able to answer these questions:

1. How do I prepare my equipment for a boat dive?
2. Why should I confirm I have an audible and a visual signaling device when boat diving?
3. How do I prepare myself for a boat dive?

Inspect your gear before packing it in reverse order, so you can work out of your bag without emptying it. Use a checklist to reduce the chance of forgetting something.

Boat Diving Preparation

Once you're on board and the boat is underway to the dive site, you usually have to wait until the boat returns to the dock if you're unprepared for the trip in any way. For example, if your gear doesn't work, you may miss the dives. An enjoyable boat dive therefore starts with preparing your gear and yourself properly.

Preparing Your Equipment

Space is limited on a boat, so prepare your gear with this in mind. Collapsible gear bags take up the least space, just don't put your weights in them. Inspect all your gear to confirm it's in good working order, and do so far enough ahead of time that you can get something serviced if you find a problem.

Set up anything you can in advance to save time and space on the boat. For example, if you need to replace your mask strap, do it as you're preparing and packing. Be sure you have your surface signaling devices. In some conditions, it can be hard to attract the crew's attention and make yourself visible without them – especially if you're some distance from the boat.

Mark your gear so you can identify it among other divers' gear on a crowded dive boat, and use a checklist – there's one on the PADI App and in the PADI Logbook – to reduce the chance of forgetting something. Once you're on the boat and en route to a dive site, if you forgot something there's a good chance you're going to miss the dives.

Pack your gear bag in reverse order, so what you need last goes in first, and what you need first goes in last. This lets you set up and gear up without unloading the entire bag, which saves a lot space onboard. But, keep personal items such as a certification card, phone, tablet computer, log book, sunscreen, money, etc. in a separate container, like a dry bag.

Although you're trying to save space, bring your save-a-dive kit. If space is very limited, two or three divers can collaborate on a single set of spare parts and tools. Finally, if the boat doesn't provide cylinders, make sure the one (or ones) you're bringing is already filled.

Preparing Yourself

To prepare yourself, start by being adequately nourished (avoiding any foods that may cause stomach upset) and rested for a day on the boat. Get adequate sleep the night before, eat well and avoid dehydration by drinking plenty of nonalcoholic liquids. Avoid excessive alcohol the night before a day of boat diving.

Leave contact information – boat name, location and destination – with someone before departure, as well as your mobile number if you will be in a service area.

Use sunscreen, beginning early in the day. Sunburn is undoubtedly the most common preventable malady in boat diving. See your PADI Dive Center or Resort about environmentally friendly sunscreen to reduce potential harm to marine organisms.

If using a seasickness medication, take it sufficiently in advance according to the instructions or your physician's directions (more about this in the next subsection). Finally, confirm that you know where you will go to meet the boat, and the schedule, at least a day ahead.

Use environmentally friendly sunscreen often, beginning early in the day. Sunburn is probably the most preventable malady in boat diving.

EXERCISE-4

1. In preparing for a boat dive, I should (choose all that apply):
   - ☐ a. inspect my gear.
   - ☐ b. pack my bag in reverse order.
   - ☐ c. use a checklist.
   - ☐ d. pack personal items separately.
2. It's important to have surface signaling devices because, depending upon conditions, it can be hard for the crew to locate me some distance from the boat at the surface.
   - ☐ True ☐ False
3. ______________ is undoubtedly the most common preventable malady in boat diving.
   - ☐ a. Back injury
   - ☐ b. Sunburn
   - ☐ c. Seasickness
   - ☐ d. Vertigo

How did you do?

1. a, b, c, d. 2. True. 3. b.

LEARNING

OBJECTIVES

By the end of this section, I should be able to answer these questions:

1. How do I avoid seasickness?
2. What should I do if I get seasick?

Seasickness

If there's anything that keeps some people away from boats, it's the possibility of seasickness. Seasickness is a form of motion sickness that can cause severe nausea, dizziness and vomiting. The only "cure" for seasickness is solid ground, but you can prevent it. The most common and effective preventative is to use seasickness medication.

In most areas, you can buy seasickness medications without a prescription. However, it is always a good idea to consult your physician, especially if you take other medications. Be sure to follow the instructions on the medication or follow your physician's directions, and read all the medication warnings. Some seasickness medications have side effects, such as drowsiness, that you may want to avoid while diving. For most people, it's too late to use seasickness medication once they're already seasick. Therefore, take it sufficiently ahead of boarding for it to take effect (this is usually part of the instructions).

Besides taking seasickness medication, there are some other tips that many people find help reduce seasickness. Seasickness is more likely if you don't feel well to begin with, so be adequately rested and fed, and avoid alcohol before the trip. While onboard, stay in fresh air, and away from engine fumes.

Many people find that it helps to avoid tasks like reading or setting up a camera housing while the boat is underway. It may also help to look at the horizon.

If You Get Seasick

If you do get sick, realize that while it is unpleasant, you will get through it, even though you may feel miserable. Do not go to the head if you are going to vomit. The cramped indoor space and atmosphere will likely make you feel worse. Instead, if you think you're going to vomit, go the leeward rail to do so. In rough seas, have someone come with you to hold your belt or arm as a precaution against falling overboard. Avoid being on deck alone, especially at night or when underway.

Stay in the most stable part of the boat, which is as close to the center of the boat and as low in the boat (close to the waterline) as possible, while still outside in fresh air.

After being sick, sipping water may help settle your stomach and avoid dehydration. Stay in the most stable part of the boat, which is as close to the middle of the boat and as low in the boat (close to the waterline) as possible, while still outside in fresh air.

EXERCISE-5

1. If you are prone to seasickness, the most common and effective prevention for seasickness is
   - ☐ a. staying in fresh air.
   - ☐ b. avoiding intricate tasks.
   - ☐ c. looking at the horizon.
   - ☐ d. seasickness medication.
2. If I get seasick and may vomit, I should go to the ________, with someone there as a precaution against falling overboard.
   - ☐ a. head
   - ☐ b. stern
   - ☐ c. windward rail
   - ☐ d. leeward rail

How did you do?

1. d. 2. d.

LEARNING OBJECTIVES

By the end of this section, I should be able to answer this question:

1. What are the general boarding procedures for a charter dive boat?

Charter Boat Boarding Procedures

Charter dive boats vary in their procedures, but the basics discussed in these subsections apply to most boats in one form or another. Let's start with general boarding procedures.

Plan to board and check in at least half an hour before departure (or earlier, if advised by the operator to do so). Upon arrival, ask for permission to board and wait until invited to do so – the crew may still be preparing the boat and it may not be safe for passengers yet.

Once aboard, stow your gear as appropriate. If you don't know where and how – procedures for this vary greatly – ask a crew member, but assume that anything left on open deck will get wet. Usually, you store dry items forward, under cover in the cabin or below decks, as appropriate for the vessel. On small, entirely open boats, use a dry bag or leave anything that can't get wet ashore.

Most charter boats have sign-in sheets and/or a liability release (assumption of risk/acknowledgement of risks form). Read and sign these prior to departure. Be sure your name is listed on the roster showing you're aboard.

Depending upon the boat and environment, the crew may have other pre-boarding or pre-departure activities. For example, you may set up your scuba kit before departure, to save space, because you have a very short trip to the site, or because it will be easier than doing so on a rough sea.

Prior to departure, many dive boats will have a boat briefing to orient you to safety and emergency procedures and equipment location. Listen closely, even if you've been on the specific boat before, because procedures and equipment locations can change. The pre-departure briefing may include a roll call to ensure everyone listed on the roster is aboard, and to be sure everyone aboard is listed on the roster. Do not answer for another person, even if you are "sure" the person is aboard.

Once aboard, stow your gear as appropriate. If you don't know, ask where and how, ask.

EXERCISE-6

1. I'm boarding a charter dive boat. I should assume that anything left on the open deck will get
   - ☐ a. wet.
   - ☐ b. stowed below.
   - ☐ c. placed on the dock.
   - ☐ d. moved.
2. As part of charter boat boarding procedures, I should be sure my name is on the roster showing I'm aboard.
   ☐ True ☐ False

How did you do?

1. a. 2. True.

LEARNING OBJECTIVES

By the end of this section, I should be able to answer these questions:

1. Why are pre- and post-dive roll calls by divemasters or crew members important?

2. What is the procedure for suiting up and gearing up on a dive boat?

Predive Procedures

Briefings and Roll Calls

When diving from a charter dive boat, you can also expect a dive area orientation in the form of a predive briefing. Larger boats usually have more extensive briefings and, as mentioned, depending upon the situation, the briefing may be part of a pre-departure briefing, or it may be a separate briefing once the boat reaches the first dive site.

With large boats and groups, roll calls are commonly formal procedures in which everyone gathers while the divemaster calls out names and people respond. With small groups, the divemaster may simply check off names as divers enter and leave the water.

The briefing generally covers a boat orientation, recommended entry and exit procedures, safety considerations, safety equipment and other information specific to the boat. It also usually covers a dive site orientation and may provide other dive information – such as maximum dive duration, depth, etc. – conditions expected (such as the direction of the current), points of interest and possible hazards to avoid. After the briefing, you plan the dive with your buddy.

When making two or more dives, there is usually a briefing for each dive. However, briefings after the first are usually shorter, because a lot of information doesn't need to be repeated (e.g., where to enter and exit the water).

The divemaster or crew will call roll before each dive, or will get your name and note on the dive roster that you've entered as you and your buddy go in. After the dive, there's a roll call or other procedure to be sure that everyone who went diving is back aboard.

With large boats and groups, this is commonly a formal procedure in which everyone gathers while the divemaster calls out names and people respond, especially after the dive. With small groups, the divemaster may check off names as divers enter and leave the water. It's important to be present for roll calls before and after each dive.

- Never allow anyone to answer for you during a roll call.
- Never answer for someone else during a roll call.
- Be sure your name is called.

Take pre- and post-dive roll calls seriously. Roll calls (or other accounting systems for divers leaving and returning to the boat) are important safeguards for reducing the risk of accidentally leaving a diver at a dive site.

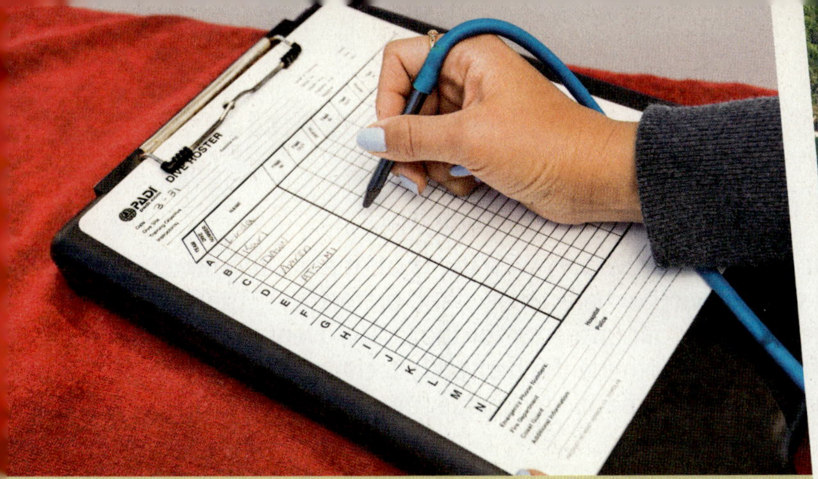

Be sure your name is listed on the roster showing you're aboard. The pre-departure briefing may include a roll call to ensure everyone listed on the roster is aboard.

With small boats that don't have a lot of space, it's common to set everything up before departure. You may put on your exposure suits (at least partially) before departure, then put on your gear once on site, and enter the water.

Suiting Up and Gearing Up

When you suit up and gear up while boat diving depends upon the environment, the boat and the time to the dive site.

With small boats that don't have a lot of space, it's common to set everything up before departure. You may put on your exposure suits (at least partially) before departure, then put on your gear once on site, and enter the water. If it's too hot to put on exposure suits early, a common practice with small vessels is to put your gear overboard on lines after you arrive. This clears the limited deck area so you have more room for getting into your suit. In this case, it's common to enter the water and then put your scuba kit on at the surface.

With larger boats, it's common to set up your gear before or soon after departure, and leave it set up for the day (except to change cylinders, etc.), most commonly secured in a cylinder rack. You don your suit as the boat nears the dive site, or soon after it is securely moored or anchored.

If the boat has cylinder racks with seats, when ready, you and your buddy(ies) get into your scuba kits while seated and conduct your predive safety check. Stay seated until ready to enter the water. If the boat lacks seats, you get into your scuba kit by having someone hold it for you. Do this only after you have everything else you need to be ready to enter the water.

When holding gear for someone else, use proper lifting techniques and be careful to not lose your balance, especially when the boat is rolling.

Go to the entry area and complete your predive safety check if you have not yet done so. Don your mask and then your fins just before entering. Avoid walking on deck with fins on.

Procedures for suiting up and gearing up may vary somewhat, depending upon the boat and the environment. The crew or your instructor will brief you on techniques for the dive you're making.

EXERCISE-7

1. Pre- and post-dive roll calls are important, because they reduce the risk of
   - ☐ a. missing the dive.
   - ☐ b. being left at the dive site.
   - ☐ c. using the wrong entry.
   - ☐ d. diving from the wrong boat.
2. On larger boats that have cylinder racks and seats, you usually want to stand up to get into your scuba kit.
   ☐ True ☐ False

How did you do?

1. b. 2. False. If you have seats for getting into your kit, you usually get into your rig sitting down.

LEARNING **OBJECTIVES**

By the end of this section, I should be able to answer these questions:

1. What are the general guidelines for making entries from various types of boats?
2. What *are mooring/anchor lines, trip lines, descent lines, gear lines, current lines,* and *tag lines* used for?
3. What are the procedures for descending while boat diving?
4. In which direction should I generally head when boat diving?
5. What are the general guidelines for ascents while boat diving?
6. What are the general guidelines for exiting the water onto a boat?

After you enter, switch to snorkel, signal you're okay and clear the area while waiting for your buddy.

Boat Diving Procedures

Entries

Boat entry techniques vary with the boat, the environment, and your individual characteristics and preferences. The divemaster (or your instructor for the Boat Adventure Dive) can help you determine the best entry technique for you. Regardless of the specific technique, the same general guidelines apply:

1. When ready to enter, be sure your buddy(ies) is ready, too.
2. On a charter dive boat, make sure the boat's specific logging or other communication process has been completed to show you are entering the water.
3. Go to the entry area with your buddy(ies) and partially inflate your BCD.
4. Breathe from your regulator as you enter (unless putting your scuba kit on in the water, of course), make sure the entry area is clear and hold your mask using an appropriate entry technique.
5. Have someone hand you accessories (e.g. a camera or DPV) after you enter.
6. After you enter, switch to snorkel, signal you're okay (assuming you are) and clear the area so other divers can enter while you wait for your buddy.

From small boats, generally, the seated back-roll is the easiest entry if you can't stand up (or at least do so easily) due to the boat's small size, poor stability and limited deck space. Depending upon the situation, you may enter wearing your scuba kit, or put it on in the water after entering. If donning it in the water, put on your weight system after donning your scuba kit and making sure you have ample buoyancy.

From larger boats on which you can stand, the most common entry is the giant stride, though another option is the seated back-roll from the swim step (if the boat has one) or some other area that's not too high above the water. If you have a physical challenge that limits your ability to wear scuba out of the water, the crew can usually assist with an alternate entry technique, such as putting on your scuba kit on a swim step after entering using the controlled seated entry.

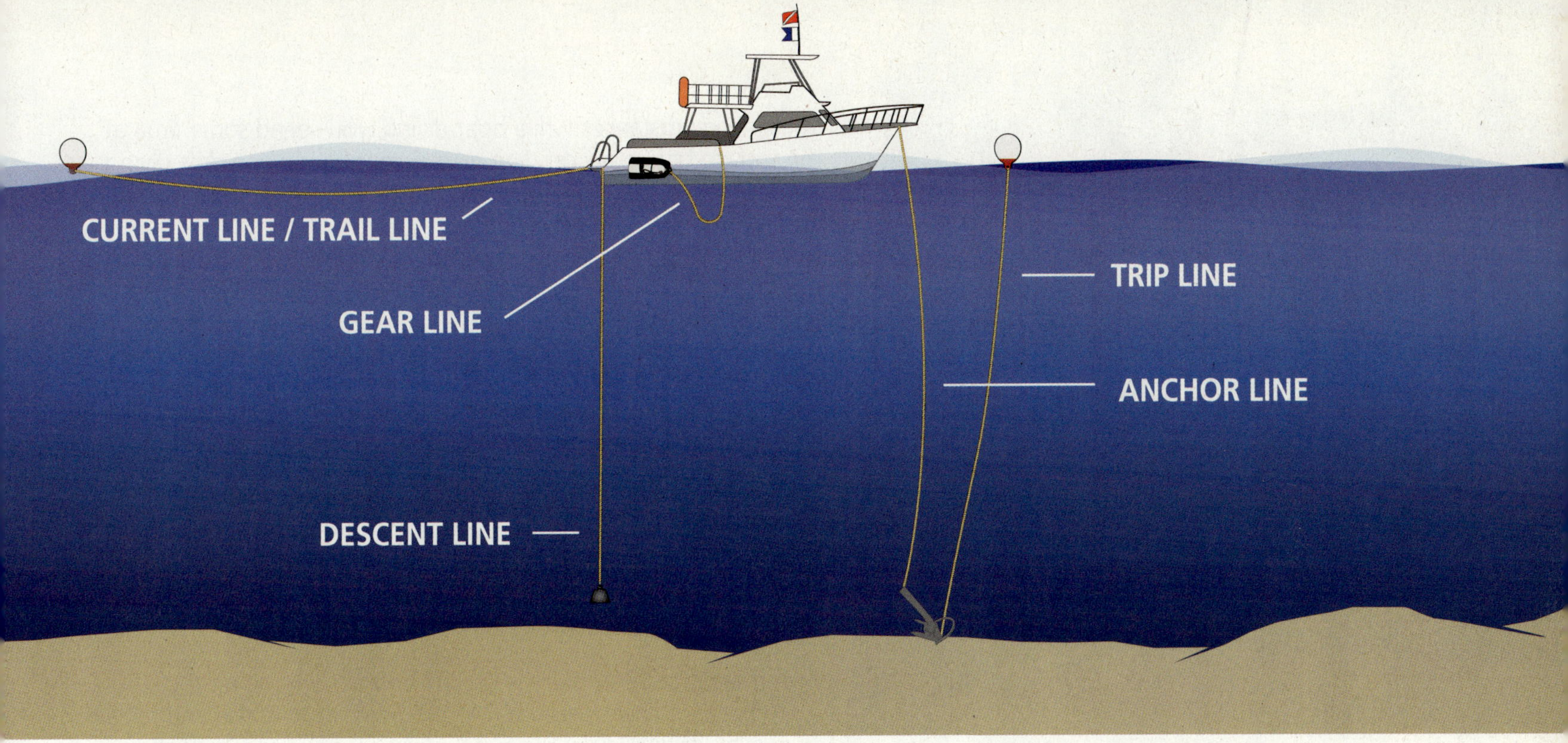

Lines Used in Boat Diving

When diving from a boat, it's common to use one or more lines to assist your dive. You probably recall many of these from the PADI Open Water Diver course. Except when drift diving, you will at least have a *mooring*, or *anchor line*, holding the boat in place. You can use it to guide your descents and ascents.

Trip lines are not commonly used, but you may see one on occasion. These are buoyed lines attached to the anchor used to "trip" it for easier retrieval. You can use a trip line for descents and ascents, but avoid pulling on it with much force because you could dislodge the anchor.

Descent lines are weighted lines hanging vertically from the boat, typically near the entry/exit area. You use these to guide descents and ascents, especially when the boat is over the dive site instead of moored/anchored into the site. They are also used for diver convenience in making safety stops.

Gear lines are any lines used to hold equipment at the surface or underwater until you retrieve it.

Current lines, which are also called trail lines or *stern lines*, are buoyed lines that trail behind the boat at the surface. Use these to keep from drifting away in a current after entering and before exiting the water. If you surface away from the boat in a current, the line gives you a larger target to reach while swimming across the current. Within practical limits, the stronger the current, the more current line the crew puts out.

Tag lines, also called ***swim lines***, are used when the current is difficult to swim against. Tag lines run from the entry area to the mooring/anchor line. After entering, you pull yourself along the tag line to the mooring/anchor line, then descend hand over hand along the mooring/anchor line. Reverse this for ascending and exiting. Depending upon conditions and logistics, the tag line may connect with the mooring/anchor line at the surface, or underwater (commonly about 5 metres/15 feet deep). The aft end of the tag line may be secured to the boat near the exit ladder, or to the current line.

The crew will usually include the recommended line-use techniques in the dive briefing.

It is common to follow the mooring/anchor line to the bottom. If there is little current, use the line primarily as a visual reference.

Descent lines tend to rise and fall abruptly with the boat, so use one as a visual reference if it is jerking up and down significantly due to surface conditions.

Descents

In most circumstances while boat diving, you spend some time at the surface before descending. (An exception is when drift diving. You can learn about drift descents in the Drift Adventure Dive and the PADI Drift Diver specialty course.) Before descending, orient yourself to the boat and/or the shore (if visible) with your compass and natural navigation cues. Complete the rest of the five-point descent with your buddy(ies), just as you would on any dive.

It is most common to use a line for a boat diving descent. Often, you use the line to reach a relatively shallow bottom, then follow the bottom topography to deeper water.

Mooring/anchor-line descent. It is common to follow the mooring/anchor line to the bottom. If there is little current, use the line primarily as a visual reference. Diving from small vessels with small anchors, you can dislodge an anchor by pulling on it (this is not an issue with a mooring).

If there is current, there is usually enough tension on the line to keep an anchor secure. Mooring/anchor lines rise and fall as waves lift and lower the boat, so be cautious to avoid letting this jerk you up and down suddenly, which can cause injury. Tension from current and from the chain at the bottom of the line help to dampen and reduce this rise and fall.

Descent-line descent. You follow a descent line vertically to the bottom; it usually stops just above the bottom.

Descent lines tend to rise and fall abruptly with the boat, so use one as a visual reference if it is jerking up and down significantly due to surface conditions. In calm water, you can hold on to it for guidance or to assist in stopping your descent momentarily.

You usually don't use reference lines when there is significant current because, unless they are significantly weighted, they tend to swing upward when divers hang on to them to maintain their places.

Free descent. In conditions without significant current, you can often simply descend without following a line. This is particularly common when you can see the bottom from the surface. Take care to avoid disorientation, use your BCD to control your descent rate and maintain buddy contact.

On the Bottom

As you near the bottom, adjust your buoyancy so you arrive neutrally buoyant. Stay off the bottom to preserve the visibility and to avoid harming sensitive aquatic life.

Recall from the PADI Open Water Diver course that you *generally* swim into the current (if present), ahead of the boat for the first part of the dive, and then return with the current. There are some exceptions, however. One of these is when drift diving, because you're intentionally drifting with the current.

Another exception is that in areas with steeply sloped bottoms near shore, the anchor may be in deep water away from shore, with the boat in shallower water closer to shore. In this case, it is typical to dive *behind* the boat. Either way, the divemaster may recommend a course or courses to follow during the dive as appropriate for the site and conditions, which you and your buddy may choose to follow. On some boats and in certain conditions, the divemaster may carefully define a dive's route, depth, maximum bottom-time limit, etc. In such situations, carefully adhere to the instructions.

If there is no significant current, you have more latitude in the direction you choose. Even so, you ideally want to return to the boat underwater to avoid a long surface swim. Charter boats will try to moor or anchor close to the best spots so you shouldn't have to go far. (The farther you go from the boat, the more effective your navigation must be to relocate it without surfacing.)

Regardless of how far you go from the boat, turn the dive with more than adequate gas remaining to comfortably relocate it. If you reach your ascent point with more gas than planned, you can explore the area around it until you must ascend. On the other hand, if your gas runs low and you reach ascent pressure before you locate the boat, ascend where you are. A long surface swim is better than running out of gas underwater.

Ascents and Exits

In many instances when boat diving, you ascend and exit following the same lines you used to enter and descend. This is particularly true when you need to use lines in a current. But, if there is no current, you may elect to ascend immediately behind or beside the boat. Recall that if you cannot relocate the boat while diving in a current that is too strong to swim against, ascend and surface, then swim *across* the current to the current line. Don't swim against the current trying to reach the boat itself if doing so may risk overexertion.

You generally swim into the current (if present), ahead of the boat for the first part of the dive, and then return with the current.

Keep your mask on and breathe from your regulator (or snorkel if low on gas, etc.) as you exit. Remove your fins only after handing up accessories and after you have firm contact with the ladder and/or boat. Either hand up your fins, or slip them over your wrists.

Remember to make a safety stop at 5 metres/15 feet for three minutes or longer. This is good practice on any dive, but particularly when boat diving, because you often tend to stay at deeper depths. When boat diving in a current, you usually make the stop on the mooring/anchor line. With no significant current, you can stop midwater or along the descent line. Many dive boats hang a bar and/or extra gas at 5 metres/15 feet to assist with safety stops. The extra gas may be a suspended cylinder with a regulator, or may be long hoses supplying air to second stages from the surface.

After the stop, surface near the boat (so you're close to the dive flag). Look up to be sure you do not come up under the boat and **stay well away from the propellers at all times.** If diving in a current, you usually do your safety stop on the mooring/anchor line.

Follow the mooring/anchor line to the tag line, and the tag line to the exit area. Wait your turn to exit on the current line.

On larger boats, you will usually exit the water via a ladder at the stern or on the side of the boat. Keep your mask on while waiting your turn, and breathe from your snorkel or regulator. Stay out from under a diver who's climbing the ladder, in case the diver slips and falls, or the diver's cylinder slips loose.

When it's your turn, time the swell or waves (if present) to help lift you onto the first step or swim platform as appropriate. If you have a physical challenge that limits your ability to climb a ladder wearing gear, an option may be to slip out of your scuba kit and pass it up before exiting. Some smaller dive charter boats will have you remove and pass up your scuba gear and weights prior to climbing the ladder as standard procedure.

Keep your mask on and breathe from your regulator (or snorkel, as is appropriate for the boat and situation) as you exit. This lets you see and breathe if you fall back in. Remove your fins only after handing up accessories and after you have firm contact with the ladder and/or boat. Either hand up your fins, or slip them over your wrists (if they're open-heel fins).

You may encounter different procedures, depending upon the boat and location, which would be explained to you in the briefing.

Once aboard the boat, sit down as soon as possible. If that's not possible, have someone help you remove your scuba kit. As much as possible, avoid walking on deck with your scuba kit on, particularly in rough conditions.

Diving from small, private boats, you typically slip out of your scuba kit in the water and secure it to a gear line (or have a buddy hold it). With some small boats, buddies may need to counterbalance the boat for each other during exits.

The usual technique for boarding is to lift and kick to rise from the water – this is why you keep your fins on – then turn and sit on the side. Another technique is to lift and kick so you end up with your stomach on the side (not appropriate on all vessels), then scoot forward while rolling face up.

The usual technique for boarding a small boat is to lift and kick to rise from the water, then turn and sit on the side.

EXERCISE-8

1. My buddy and I are making seated back-roll entries from a small boat. We have our scuba gear on, and should breathe from our
   - ☐ a. regulators.
   - ☐ b. snorkels.
2. There's a moderate current running, so after entering at the stern my buddy and I will pull ourselves along the _______ line to the _______ line for our descent.
   - ☐ a. tag; reference
   - ☐ b. tag; mooring/anchor
   - ☐ c. current; reference
   - ☐ d. current; mooring/anchor
3. There's a moderate current and the boat is sitting over the dive site. This is an instance in which one option may be to descend along a descent line.
   - ☐ True ☐ False
4. My buddy and I reach the bottom after descending on a boat dive. Generally, we will start our dive heading
   - ☐ a. into the current, ahead of the boat.
   - ☐ b. with the current, behind the boat.
   - ☐ c. across the current, to either side of the boat.
5. When boat diving in a current, in many instances I ascend and exit along the same lines I used to enter and descend.
   - ☐ True ☐ False
6. I'm exiting in all my scuba gear up a ladder onto a large boat. As I exit, my mask should be _______ and I should breathe from _________.
   - ☐ a. around my neck; nothing
   - ☐ b. around my neck; my regulator
   - ☐ c. on my face; my snorkel
   - ☐ d. on my face; my regulator

How did you do?

1. a. 2. b. 3. False. You generally don't use a descent line in a current, and would instead descend along the mooring/anchor line. 4. a. 5. True. 6. d.

LEARNING OBJECTIVES

By the end of this section, I should be able to answer these questions:

1. How should I repack and stow my gear after a dive from various sized boats?

2. Why should I listen to post-dive roll calls by divemasters or crew members?

Once you're back aboard, stow your gear and keep the deck clear. After the last dive, on larger boats you usually disassemble your kit and pack it into your gear bag; on smaller boats, you might keep everything together until reaching shore.

Post-Dive Procedures

Once you're back aboard, stow your gear and keep the deck clear. As you take off your gear, don't drop your weights, because doing so can damage the deck, or injure someone's foot. Remember to secure your cylinder so it can't slide or fall.

After the last dive, on larger boats you usually disassemble your kit and pack it into your gear bag; on smaller boats, you might keep everything together until reaching shore.

On charter boats, the divemaster or crew will call roll (or use some other appropriate procedure) after each dive. Stay on deck until your name is called and you're checked in. Again, *never* answer for another diver. The roll call is for your safety; it greatly reduces the risk of accidentally leaving a diver at the dive site. When there are only a few divers, the divemaster/crew may complete this process visually, without a formal roll call.

EXERCISE-9

1. On large dive boats, after the last dive I will usually disassemble and stow my gear into my gear bag.
   - ☐ True ☐ False
2. Diving from a large dive boat, I am below decks disassembling an underwater video system when the crew conducts the roll call on deck. I should
   - ☐ a. have a buddy let them know I'm aboard.
   - ☐ b. listen to the roll call from where I am.
   - ☐ c. stop what I'm doing and go on deck for the roll call.

How did you do?

1. True. 2. c.

BOAT DIVER SPECIALTY

At your instructor's discretion, the Boat Diver Adventure Dive credits toward the PADI Boat Diver Specialty course. The course gives you more opportunities to apply and practice boat diving skills, including:

- Entry and exit techniques
- Packing for a boat dive
- Procedures for diving from a boat
- Line use

Remember to log your training dives with the PADI Mobile App or at padi.com.

Knowledge Review – Boat Diving

Answer the following questions by selecting the best choice (or choices) from those provided. Be prepared to discuss the material at your next training session.

1. A boat's bow is the __________ while the stern is the __________ of the boat.
   - ☐ left side; right side
   - ☐ right side ; left side
   - ☐ windward side; leeward side
   - ☐ leeward side; windward side
   - ☐ front; back
   - ☐ back; front
   - ☐ control room; kitchen
   - ☐ kitchen; control room

2. Port refers to the_______ and starboard refers to the _______ of a boat.
   - ☐ left side; right side
   - ☐ right side; left side
   - ☐ windward side; leeward side
   - ☐ leeward side; windward side
   - ☐ front; back
   - ☐ back; front
   - ☐ control room; kitchen
   - ☐ kitchen; control room

3. After everyone is on board, the boat captain gives a safety briefing that typically points out which of the following safety/emergency equipment? (Choose all that apply.)
   - ☐ PFDs (personal flotation devices)
   - ☐ First-aid kit and emergency oxygen unit
   - ☐ Seasickness medication
   - ☐ Fire extinguishers
   - ☐ Marine radio
   - ☐ Swim step

4. How do I prevent seasickness? (Choose all that apply.)
   - ☐ Use seasickness medication.
   - ☐ Don't eat before a trip.
   - ☐ Take along reading material to keep you busy.
   - ☐ Stay in fresh air away from engine fumes.

5. If I become seasick, I should go to the leeward rail to vomit and have someone hold on to me so that I don't accidentally fall overboard.
   - ☐ True
   - ☐ False

6. Which of the following are typical predive procedures on a dive boat? (Choose all that apply.)
   - ☐ Work from your dive bag so you save space as you suit up.
   - ☐ Always put on my exposure suit first before preparing other equipment.
   - ☐ Watch my balance – stay seated as much as possible or use handholds.
   - ☐ Secure my scuba cylinder so it doesn't roll around.
   - ☐ Conduct a predive safety check with my buddy.

7. In general, when entering the water from a larger dive boat I should (number the following steps in their proper order):
   - __ Signal "okay" and clear the area.
   - __ Partially inflate my BCD and have my regulator in my mouth.
   - __ Check that my buddy is ready.
   - __ Hold my mask firmly and make sure the entry area is clear.

8. Draw a line from the type of line to its purpose.

Tag/swim line	Help release the anchor
Gear line	Maintain position behind boat in a current
Trip line	Secure gear or accessories when diving from a small boat
Current/trail line	Pull yourself from the entry area to the anchor/mooring line

9. My buddy and I surface with a group of divers behind a dive boat. While waiting our turn to exit, which of these procedures should we follow? (Choose all that apply.)
   - ☐ Avoid positioning ourselves under a diver on a ladder.
   - ☐ Hold on to the current line to maintain our position.
   - ☐ Remove our fins well before we reach the boat.
   - ☐ Take our masks off before boarding.
   - ☐ Hand up cameras and accessory equipment.

10. After the last dive on a large dive boat, it's best to take off and disassemble my equipment, putting each piece in my gear bag as I go.
    - ☐ True
    - ☐ False

11. During the post-dive roll call, I notice that a diver answers for his buddy, even though his buddy is not nearby and I'm not sure I've seen his buddy on board. Is this the proper procedure?
    - ☐ Yes, it's fine as long as his buddy is sure that the diver is aboard.
    - ☐ No, all divers need to be physically present for roll call.

Student Statement

I completed this Knowledge Review to the best of my ability. For any questions I answered incorrectly or incompletely, I reviewed the explanation provided and now understand the material. In the case of anything about which I still have questions, I will review the material again and, if necessary, discuss it with my instructor at our next session.

☐ I agree ☐ I disagree

Student signature ______________________________

Date ______________________________

scenario

"Check this photo out," Ivan said, holding his camera up for Sandy to see.

"I think I shot some video of those angelfish spawning, too," she said, scrolling through her camera. "See, the male's displaying."

"I also shot some video, but my stills are better," Ivan said.

"When we get home, let's edit my videos and your stills together for a short video to show at the club meeting next week," said Sandy.

"Awesome!" Ivan said. "After, we should post it on YouTube, too."

▶ *What does this conversation tell you about taking, editing and sharing underwater photos and video?*

DIGITAL
UNDERWATER
IMAGING
6

DIGITAL UNDERWATER IMAGING

LEARNING OBJECTIVES

By the end of this section, I should be able to answer these questions:

1. What two kinds of imaging can I get with most modern cameras?
2. What are the basic differences between shooting stills and video?
3. What are the components of an underwater photography system?
4. Why do I choose my camera and housing together?
5. What are some considerations in choosing an underwater photography system?

Introduction to Underwater Imaging

Stills and Video

The digital age has revolutionized our lives in many ways, and that especially includes shooting pictures and video underwater. In the early days, if you could get well-exposed, sharp images while diving, you were practically a professional. But today, digital imaging technology makes it easier than ever for people to get good quality snapshots and casual video – including underwater.

The Digital Underwater Imaging Adventure Dive is intended for anyone who wants to get good snapshots and casual video underwater, but without getting into the technical settings any more than necessary. (If you do want to learn more about the technical aspects of underwater imaging, ask your instructor about the full Digital Underwater Photographer course.)

Because most modern cameras allow you to shoot still images and video images, you'll learn the basics for casual imaging with both. Besides differences in the best way to set the camera, there are some important differences between how you shoot stills and how you shoot video. With stills, you're capturing a *moment*, and you have more composition options, like turning the camera for vertical (portrait) framing. With video, you're capturing *sequences that connect with other sequences.* You keep the camera horizontal (vertical shooting is becoming more common, but mainly for short, isolated videos), but have more story-telling potential than with stills.

Although you can create a still by "pulling a frame" from video, due to technical and technique differences this doesn't usually work well. You get better stills and video imagery by shooting whichever of the two you want. (That said, the still images you get pulling video frames may be acceptable for your purposes.)

Today, digital imaging technology makes it easier than ever for people to get good quality snapshots and casual video – including underwater.

Underwater Photography Systems

The starting place with underwater imaging is your photography system. Underwater photography systems have two required components: a camera and a housing. There are also some optional components.

Cameras range from smartphones to professional models; the Digital Underwater Imaging Adventure Dive emphasizes using smartphones and compact, point-and-shoot cameras.

Even water-resistant cameras need a housing, because while they tolerate getting wet, they're not designed to resist pressure. Note that you choose your camera and housing together, because *not all cameras have a housing available.*

Optional components include lighting. For example, for still photography you may be able to choose a separate, external strobe (flash) to use instead of (or with) the one built into the camera. For video imaging (and for stills, to some extent), you can mount external, continuous lights on some housings. But, with technical advances, today's cameras are more sensitive to color and light than in the past, so there's less need to use external lights with video.

Besides choosing your camera and housing together, there are some other options to consider as well. Some cameras have programmed underwater mode settings. These are highly desirable, because they simplify setting the camera for underwater use. If choosing between housings (some cameras only have a single housing available), a housing that is more compact is easier to transport and swim with, all else being equal. External strobes/lights are useful in low light and help bring out colors (more about this shortly), but add cost, maintenance and bulk.

Cameras range from smartphones to professional models.

EXERCISE-1

1. Most modern digital cameras allow me to shoot both still and video images.
   - ☐ True ☐ False
2. When shooting ___________, I am capturing a moment.
   - ☐ a. stills
   - ☐ b. video
3. The two required components of an underwater photography system are the camera and the housing.
   - ☐ True ☐ False
4. I choose my camera and housing together, because not all cameras have underwater housings available.
   - ☐ True ☐ False
5. Underwater mode settings are desirable, if available, because they simplify setting the camera for underwater use.
   - ☐ True ☐ False

How did you do?

1. True. 2. a. 3. True. 4. True. 5. True.

LEARNING OBJECTIVES

By the end of this section, I should be able to answer the following questions:

1. How does water affect sharpness? What do I do about it?
2. What is "backscatter" and how do I avoid it?
3. How does water affect the amount of light? What do I do about it?
4. How does water affect color? What do I do about it?

Suspended particles in the water affect picture sharpness, and can cause backscatter and reduce the amount of light you have.

How the Underwater World Affects Imaging

In the PADI Open Water Diver course, you learned that water affects light. The two ways that concern you as an underwater photographer are suspended particles and light absorption.

Suspended Particles

Suspended particles in the water affect picture sharpness, and can cause *backscatter* and reduce the amount of light you have.

Even in very clear water, light is deflected by particles in the water through which it travels. This reduces sharpness; the more water the light passes through, the more sharpness you lose. The solution is to set your camera for the widest view (wide angle) and get as close to the subject as possible. Avoid using less wide (telephoto) settings.

Another effect of particles comes from your camera's built-in flash, or external light close to the lens. Light reflects off the particles, causing a "snowstorm" effect called "backscatter." One solution is to only use a flash or external light in very clear water with few suspended particles. Another solution is to use external strobes/lights mounted away from the lens, aiming the strobe so it hits the subject, but very little light passes between the subject and the camera. You can learn more about this in the Digital Underwater Photographer course.

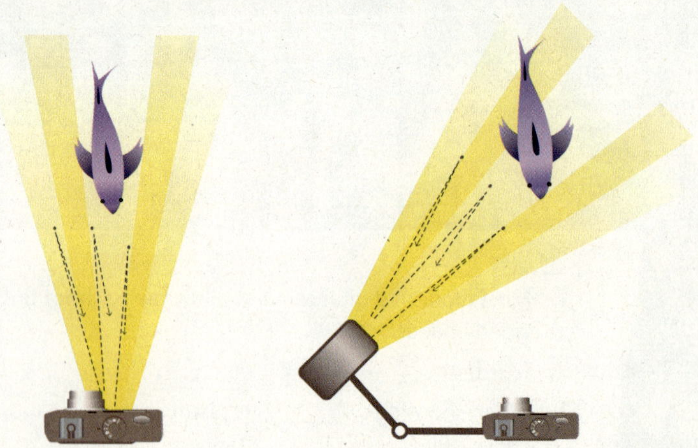

Backscatter is caused by flash (or other light) reflecting off particles. The solution is to only use flash or external light in very clear water, or to use external strobes/lights mounted away from the lens.

Light Absorption

Particles block light penetrating the water, reducing the light available, but water itself absorbs light and light also reflects off the water's surface – all of which reduces how much light you have underwater. There are several solutions, and you often apply more than one together:

1. Set the camera to be more light sensitive (i.e., a higher ISO; more about this shortly).
2. Use the camera's flash and/or external lighting.
3. Dive when maximum sunshine penetrates the water (roughly, between 10 a.m. and 3 p.m.).
4. Get close to your subject.

You probably recall that water not only absorbs light, but also absorbs some colors faster than others. First red is absorbed, followed by orange, yellow, green, blue, indigo and violet. The more water that light travels through, vertically and horizontally, the more color you lose. This can make underwater images blue, green or blue-green with not much other color visible. There are several solutions, again, sometimes used together:

1. Stay shallow and stay close to your subject to reduce the water through which light travels.
2. Set your camera to adjust for the color absorption (i.e., white balance; more about this shortly).
3. Use the camera's flash or external light.
4. Use a special filter to adjust the color.

DEPTH & COLOR

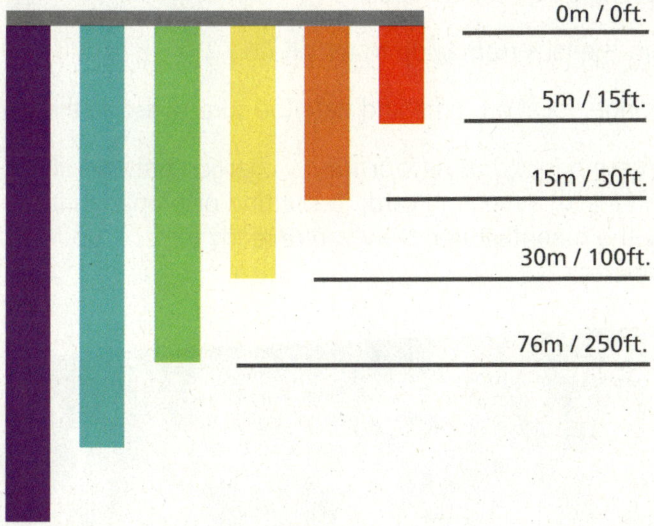

As water absorbs light, it absorbs some colors before others. The more water that light passes through, the more color you lose.

EXERCISE-2

1. To make my images as sharp as possible underwater, I should _______ my subject.
   - ☐ a. get close to
   - ☐ b. back away from
2. Backscatter is caused by flash or another external light close to the lens reflecting off particles into the camera.
   - ☐ True ☐ False
3. The only cause of light loss underwater is blockage by suspended particles.
   - ☐ True ☐ False
4. Due to color absorption, without taking steps to correct it, my underwater images will tend to be
   - ☐ a. red, orange or red-orange.
   - ☐ b. orange, yellow or orange-yellow.
   - ☐ c. yellow, green or yellow-green.
   - ☐ d. blue, green or blue-green.

How did you do?

1. a. 2. True. 3. False. Water itself absorbs light, and light reflects off of water. 4. d.

LEARNING OBJECTIVES

By the end of this section, I should be able to answer the following questions:

1. Where do I learn about how to set up my camera for basic shooting, including battery, memory and general setting concerns?

2. How do I set my camera for the proper exposure underwater?

3. How do I set my camera for the proper focus underwater?

4. How do I set my camera for good color underwater?

5. What is the best way to initially learn to use my camera for underwater photography?

6. How do I upload images from my camera to a mobile device, computer or directly to a website?

Setting Your Camera for Underwater Imaging

Getting Started – Setting Up Your Camera for General Shooting

Shooting stills or videos starts with getting to know your camera and setting it up for good results. Although modern cameras are similar in many ways, there are many models, each with its own way of accessing and using basic functions. Start by consulting the manufacturer literature for your camera for the specifics on setting it up, including:

- Where and how to set shooting modes (e.g., automatic, programmed, manual, stills, video, etc.)
- Automatic focus (autofocus)
- White balance
- Memory card requirements
- Battery types/charging requirements
- How to zoom the lens from wide to telephoto
- Setting language, location, time and date (be sure to set all these)

After learning these basics, put new or freshly charged batteries in your camera and install a memory card, formatting or preparing it as stipulated by the manufacturer. Now you're ready to set it up for shooting underwater.

After learning these basics, put new or freshly charged batteries in your camera and install a memory card, formatting or preparing it as stipulated by the manufacturer. Now you're ready to set it up for shooting underwater.

Proper Exposure

Some cameras have only one exposure setting, but most have several. If your camera has an underwater program mode, set it for that. Otherwise, set it for Program or Auto exposure. On some cameras, you set the exposure for stills and video independently. If this is the case for your camera, be sure to set it for both.

On Program modes, most cameras have automatic ISO. ISO is a number that represents the setting for the camera's light sensitivity. The higher the ISO the more sensitive the setting, but at the loss of some image quality. Set your camera for auto ISO if the Program/Auto system doesn't set it automatically.

Next, check how to turn your flash on and off (if allowed by the Program/Auto setting). You may be using your flash, but you want to choose when to do so (you'll learn more about this later). If using an external submersible strobe, consult the manufacturer instructions about settings so your camera controls it – you may have to put the camera in the underwater housing to do this.

Many cameras have a shake warning indicating the shutter speed is too slow. This means your pictures will be blurry, because you can't hold the camera steady enough. Auto ISO will prevent this, except in very low light. If you get a shake warning, or your pictures are blurry due to motion, try these fixes:

- Be sure you have Auto ISO set. If your camera doesn't have Auto ISO, set your ISO to a higher number until the shake warning disappears.
- Use your flash (stills) or external lights (video).
- Go somewhere with more light, like shallower water – the change in light levels can be dramatic.

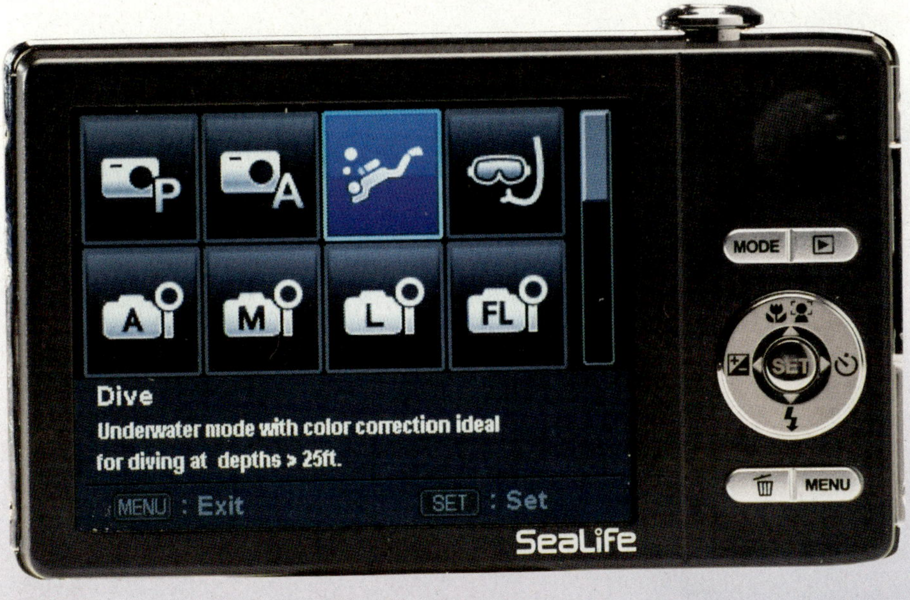

If your camera has an underwater program mode, set it for that. Otherwise, set it for Program or Auto exposure. On some cameras, you set the exposure for stills and video independently. If this is the case for your camera, be sure to set it for both.

Proper Focus

Set your focus to Autofocus (the default on most cameras). Some Program modes also set your autofocus. Zoom your lens to the widest view. Use these settings unless your housing requires specific settings; see the manufacturer instructions.

You know that objects look closer than they really are underwater. This doesn't affect your images, because your camera will autofocus on the apparent distance for a sharp image, just like your eyes do. Note that some cameras are *focus-free*, meaning they have a wide focus range and don't need to do any focusing at all. However, they sometimes require a special lens for proper focus when used underwater – these are usually supplied with the housing.

Setting for Good Color

White balance is how your camera adjusts colors to look normal. Program modes may set your white balance for you. This is particularly true with an underwater program mode. Underwater, set your white balance for automatic (if it's not set by the Program/Auto mode or underwater program mode).

This is important because the white balance settings you normally use for daylight or flash will give you photos that are too blue underwater, unless you use flash or external lights. With flash/external lights, whether you use auto white balance or daylight/flash depends upon the circumstances, your camera and the lights. See the manufacturer instructions for the lights, but you may have to try both settings while diving to see which gives you the best color.

Another way to help your color underwater is to use a filter. Some camera housings come with filters, which mount in front of the lens or inside the housing lens port – see the manufacturer instructions on how and when to use them.

Learning to Use Your Camera

The best place to initially learn to use your camera underwater is at the surface, before taking it underwater. This allows you to try different settings, check the manufacturer instructions and so on without also paying attention to depth, time, your buddies, etc.

Start by taking pictures and shooting video using the various settings, flash, etc., and check your results. Emphasize using the settings you expect to use most of the time underwater.

Next, put your camera in its housing and practice shooting. Most cameras feel a bit different in a housing and some controls may not be available – this is good to know before you dive with it. Be sure to also take test pictures/video with the external strobe or lighting if you'll be using one. We'll look at setting up your housing in the next subsection.

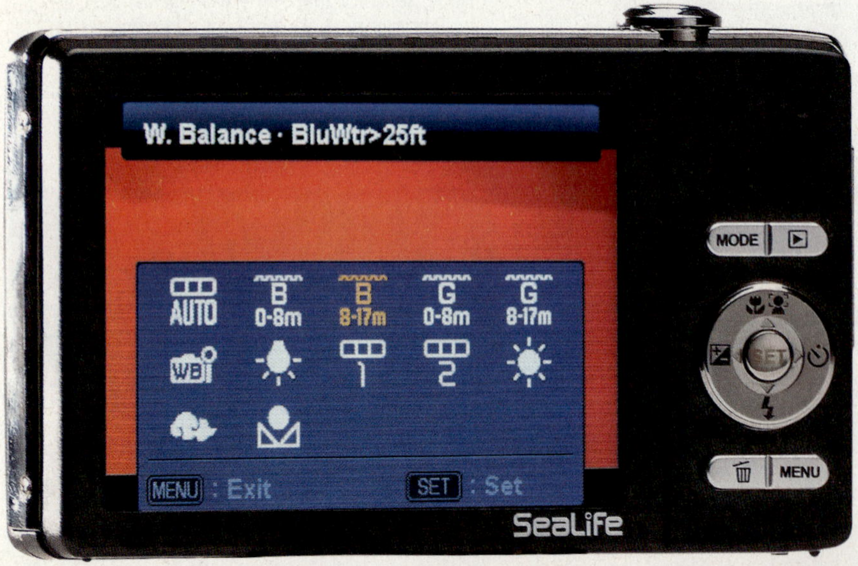

White balance is how your camera adjusts colors so they look normal. Underwater, set your white balance for automatic if it's not set by the Program/Auto mode or underwater program mode.

Uploading

Today, it's easier than ever to get your images from your camera to a personal computer, mobile device or directly online. Most personal computers and mobile devices now come with software for editing, organizing and making basic adjustments to still and video images.

In most cases, you connect the camera to the computer or device via hardwire, like a USB port, Thunderbolt, etc., or wireless like Bluetooth, WiFi, etc. A wireless connection is especially useful because you can transfer images at the surface without opening the camera housing. With smartphones and many cameras, you can also upload images directly to social media and other sites via the internet.

Regardless of how you transfer your images, get in the habit of organizing them so you can locate them later. This is one reason it's important to have your camera set for the correct date and time. Also get in the habit of backing up your images to a website or another device/drive.

See the instructions for your devices and your camera for your image transfer and organization options.

EXERCISE-3

1. To learn the basics for setting up my camera, I should start with manufacturer literature.
   ☐ True ☐ False
2. My camera does not have an underwater program mode. I would probably set it for ________ exposure mode.
   ☐ a. Program or Auto
   ☐ b. Manual
   ☐ c. Shutter Preferred
   ☐ d. Aperture Preferred
3. For underwater, I should set my camera for manual focus.
   ☐ True ☐ False
4. For underwater, I should set my white balance to ________ if it's not set by an underwater program mode or Program/Auto mode, and I'm not using a flash or external light.
   ☐ a. daylight
   ☐ b. flash
   ☐ c. cloudy
   ☐ d. automatic
5. The best place to learn to initially learn to use my camera for underwater photography is at the surface.
   ☐ True ☐ False
6. There are many options for uploading my images to a computer, mobile device or a website. I should see the instructions for my devices and camera to learn about these.
   ☐ True ☐ False

How did you do?

1. True. 2. a. 3. False. Set your camera for autofocus (usually the default setting). 4. d. 5. True. 6. True.

Regardless of how you transfer your images, get in the habit of organizing them so you can locate them later. Also get in the habit of backing up your images to a website or another device/drive.

Setting Up and Caring for Your Underwater Housing

Setting Up Your Housing

After you've set up and become familiar with your camera, you're ready to put it in its underwater housing. Do this in a clean, well-lit area, ideally with low humidity. Inspect the disassembled housing to be sure there's no dirt or debris inside, especially the lens port through which you shoot. Otherwise, dirt inside the port may be visible in your pictures and video. If necessary, clean inside the port following the guidelines in the manufacturer instructions.

Before actually setting up your housing, read the manufacturer instructions for doing so. Although the instructions are generally similar, each has its own specifics that are important to proper setup, and this is where you learn what they are. For instance, you may need to remove accessories or set the camera into specific modes.

And, how you insert the camera into place and secure it may be very specific. Improper setup can make it so you can't use your camera (best case) or cause it to flood with water (worst case), so take the time to do it right according to the manufacturer instructions.

After you've set up your housing a few times, it becomes second nature, but take your time and follow the steps while you learn. After the first time you put your housing together, *remove your cam-*

After you've set up your housing a few times, it becomes second nature, but take your time and follow the steps while you learn. Improper setup can make it so you can't use your camera (best case) or cause it to flood with water (worst case), so take the time to do it right according to the manufacturer instructions.

LEARNING OBJECTIVES

By the end of this section, I should be able to answer the following questions:

1. Where do I get the specific information I need for setting up my housing?
2. How do I remove, clean, lubricate and replace an o-ring?
3. Where should I put my camera system before and after a dive?
4. How do I enter and exit the water with a camera system?
5. What are my options for carrying a camera system underwater? What are the pros and cons of each?
6. What is the primary care my underwater system needs after a dive?

era and then test it underwater – in a shallow tub, bucket, etc. – for leaks, *before you dive*. This confirms there's no defect (unlikely) or errors in assembly (more likely) without risk to your camera.

Once you've put your housing together and installed the camera according to manufacturer guidelines, take a few test shots (with external lighting, if used) and operate all the controls to confirm proper assembly and function. Check your test images for vignetting – dark corners due to the camera lens seeing the edges of the port. If you see vignetting, zoom so the lens is slightly less wide – just enough to get rid of the vignette.

Immerse the system to check for leaks. With some housings, you can see any water inside easily, but others are more difficult. Hold the systems so that if there is leakage, it will pool somewhere it is less likely to do damage. With many systems, this is with the lens port facing down. If your system has a leak detector, hold it so the sensor is at the lowest point.

Keep the system submerged for several seconds, then remove it and look closely for any signs of water entry. If necessary, on a dive you can do this at the surface after entering the water, ready to exit/hand it up if you see any moisture inside. But, it's better to do it in a tub or rinse barrel ahead of time when you can.

If you won't be diving for some time, power down the system and put it some place out of direct sunlight, where it can't fall.

After assembling your system, immerse it to check for leaks. Keep the system submerged for several seconds, then remove it and look closely for any signs of water entry.

How to Remove, Clean, Lubricate and Replace O-rings

All housings use o-rings to keep the openings and controls watertight, so proper o-ring maintenance is critical to keeping your housing (and anything else sealed with o-rings) from leaking. Housings have user-accessible o-rings – housing cover, battery covers, etc. – and captured o-rings on most controls. Generally, you clean and lubricate the user-accessible o-rings; you care for captured o-rings by rinsing the system properly, but cleaning, lubrication, etc., is done by your dive center or the manufacturer, typically annually (see the manufacturer literature).

Here's how to service a user-accessible o-ring:

1. Remove the o-ring from its groove by sliding your fingers toward each other along the o-ring to form a bulge that you grab, and ease the o-ring out gently. Alternatively, use the corner of a credit card or certification card to lift it. Do *not* use a sharp metal object, because it can damage the o-ring, or worse, the housing's groove in which the o-ring fits. This could make it impossible for the housing to seal.

2. Use a cotton swab to gently remove dirt/excess grease from the groove. Inspect the groove carefully to be sure there is no hair, etc., remaining.

3. Gently clean the o-ring with a soft, clean cloth. Be careful not to stretch it excessively, and to not grind sand or grit against it. Remove any lint or debris on it.

Every time you open the housing, you risk compromising the o-ring seal. Therefore, after opening the system, always closely inspect the o-ring; if in doubt, remove, re-clean and re-lubricate it. Most modern cameras have enough battery power and memory that you don't need to open the system between dives, and that's the safest approach for the camera. If you want to take pictures between dives, after rinsing the system (more about this in a moment), take photos with the housing sealed. If you want to see the images on your computer or mobile device between dives, ideally choose a camera that allows wireless transfer so you don't have to open the housing.

4. Inspect the o-ring. Replace it if you find nicks, tears or other damage. Such an o-ring will not seal reliably and the only option is to replace it.

5. Lightly lubricate the o-ring. Put a few small dabs of manufacturer-approved grease – usually silicone, but some manufacturers have proprietary grease that you must use with their systems – and gently spread over the o-ring.

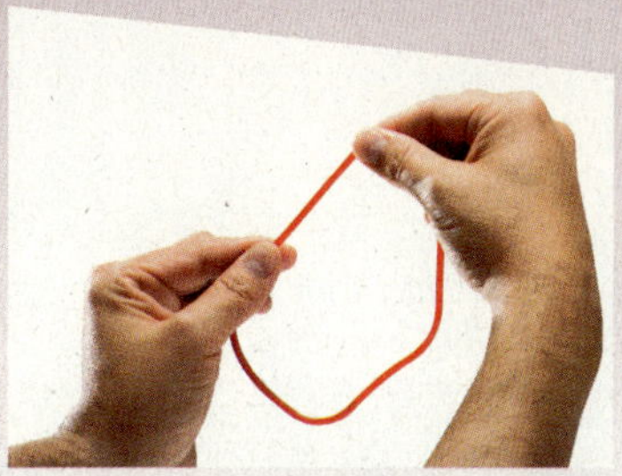

6. A properly lubricated o-ring looks shiny and wet, and has no visible grease globs. The grease does *not* make the seal; it allows the o-ring to slide into place to seal. Using excess grease makes the seal less reliable by attracting dirt.

7. Inspect the o-ring and groove again for dirt/hair/threads/lint, then replace the o-ring. Gently wipe clean the opposite seal surface and inspect it also for dirt/hair/threads before closing the housing.

Caring for Your System

At the dive site, keep the system out of the sun until you get into the water; otherwise, it can get very hot internally, causing damage. Cover the system with a towel if you have no other option. Sometimes, significant temperature changes cause fogging inside the housing. When going from indoors to outdoors, allow time for the system to gradually reach the external temperature if there's a significant difference.

On dive boats, don't let your camera go into the general rinse barrel with masks, etc., because this can be a damaging environment – not only impact damage, but mask defogs can affect some housings. Most boats have dedicated rinse tubs for camera systems.

Use the system port cover if available. Keep it on until after you enter, and replace it before exiting. This is especially important to protect the port from scratches if several cameras end up in the rinse barrel.

While diving, have some way to secure your system to free your hands and reduce loss risk. With small systems that float, a wrist lanyard works well. Larger systems that sink may require clips, though a wrist lanyard may work.

Especially when diving from boats/elevated docks, have someone hand your camera to you after entering and take it before exiting. If that's not possible, place it somewhere safe so you can reach it after entering, and put it back there for exiting.

Especially when diving from boats/elevated docks, have someone hand your camera to you after entering and take it before exiting. If that's not possible, place it somewhere safe so you can reach it after entering, and put it back there for exiting. To reduce damage and loss risk, holding your system as you enter and exit is your last option.

While diving, have some way to secure your system to free your hands and reduce loss risk. With small systems that float, a wrist lanyard works well. Larger systems that sink may require clips, though a wrist lanyard may work. Some ultra-compact cameras can be worn and shot hands-free from your chest, wrist or head with mounting devices. These are especially popular for providing diver-point-of-view video images.

After a dive, your primary care is to rinse the system thoroughly in fresh water. Ideally, immerse it fully assembled and swish it back and forth gently for at least a minute to get water to flow into small areas and remove salt. *Do not let your system dry with salt water on it.* Once the housing dries, it is much harder to remove the salt; it is better to keep your system sealed and wet in salt water until you can rinse it in fresh water.

After rinsing it, dry the housing thoroughly before opening it. Make sure your hair is dry (or wear a hat) so you won't drip into it. Make sure any small openings face down before opening them so any remaining water falls away from, rather than into, the housing.

After a dive, your primary care is to rinse the system thoroughly in fresh water. Ideally, immerse it fully assembled and swish it back and forth gently for at least a minute. Do not let your system dry with salt water on it.

EXERCISE-4

1. I get specific information I need for setting up my housing from the manufacturer instructions for housing setup.
   - ☐ True ☐ False
2. A properly lubricated o-ring looks
   - ☐ a. dry.
   - ☐ b. shiny and wet.
   - ☐ c. coated, with visible grease globs.
3. The best place for my camera system on a dive boat is in the barrel used for masks and other accessories.
   - ☐ True ☐ False
4. My buddy and I are entering the water from a platform 1.5 metres/4 feet above the water. I have a camera system, so the best option is to __________ I enter.
   - ☐ a. hold it in my right hand as
   - ☐ b. have someone hand it to me after
   - ☐ c. drop it in right before
5. My buddy has a small camera system that straps to his head, but this is not an acceptable way to carry it underwater.
   - ☐ True ☐ False
6. A big wave rocked the dive boat and spilled the camera rinse barrel, though fortunately there were no systems in it at the time. There's no other fresh water and my camera system has been in salt water. It will be an hour ride back to the dock. My best option for caring for the system is to
   - ☐ a. allow it to dry.
   - ☐ b. use a towel to dry it.
   - ☐ c. keep it wet in salt water until I can rinse with fresh water.

How did you do?

1. True. 2. b. 3. False. The rinse used for masks can be a damaging environment; look for a rinse tub or barrel dedicated to camera systems. 4. b. 5. False. Strapping to your wrist, head or chest is an option with some small camera systems that have specific mounts for doing so. 6. c.

LEARNING OBJECTIVES

By the end of this section, I should be able to answer the following questions:

1. Why is it important to hold my camera system steady?
2. When would I use and not use flash?
3. Why should I get close and shoot upward?
4. What is the purpose of good composition?
5. What are five basics for better composition?
6. What is the "rule of thirds"?

Shooting Stills

Now that your camera system's set up and you know the basics for taking care of it, let's get into shooting, starting with still images. (Some of what you learn in this subsection applies to video, too.)

Sharp Images

To get a sharp image, you need to have the subject in focus and hold the camera steady. If either of these is missing, your pictures will be blurry.

The autofocus system should take care of focus. If your camera has you select where it focuses – there may be a mark or indicator in the viewfinder – ideally focus on the subject's eye if taking a picture of a diver or animal. Most cameras indicate when they're in focus, and some won't let you take the shot until they're in focus.

Assuming you use the autofocus properly, the most common cause of blur is camera motion. If you move the camera excessively, it can't freeze the motion, so it's important to hold your camera steady for a sharp

If you move the camera excessively, it can't freeze the motion, so it's important to hold your camera steady for a sharp picture. Also, if your camera has a "shake" warning that comes on, use a higher ISO, external lights or flash.

picture. Also, if your camera has a "shake" warning that comes on, it's indicating there's not enough light to freeze camera motion for a sharp picture. In that case, use a higher ISO, external lights or flash.

Using Flash

Whether or not you use your (internal or external) flash depends on the situation.

You usually use it when:

- there's not enough light without it.
- you want the best color, especially the deeper you are. The flash replaces colors absorbed by the water.
- you are fairly close to your subject – within 3 metres/10 feet, ideally less.

You avoid using flash when:

- there are a lot of particles in the water and you can't get the flash away from the camera lens (i.e., avoid the built-in flash), because it causes backscatter. If you see backscatter in your images, turn your flash off.
- you need to save batteries.
- you are farther than 3 metres/10 feet from your subject, because it won't do much anyway (some strobes have an even shorter range).
- photographing very timid creatures that it would frighten.

Angles and Composition

Once you have exposure, focus and flash taken care of, you're mainly interested in taking pleasing photos. Your best general angle for most imaging (stills or video) is to get close to your subject and somewhat low, shooting at a slight upward angle. Although there are exceptions, this is the best general angle because getting close reduces the water between the camera and the subject for the best color and sharpness, and the upward angle helps separate the subject from the background, giving the image more apparent depth.

Besides this angle, you want good composition. Composition is the arrangement of elements in an image, and good composition is arranging everything for a pleasing and/or interesting picture. This is subjective, but there are five general principles that can help with both still and video imaging:

1. **Framing and cropping –** Your subject should be framed in a way that isn't distracting. If you don't show your whole subject, crop at a natural point. For example, if you photo your buddy, cropping at the ankles looks odd – come in closer and frame your buddy so the crop line is through the mid thighs or abdomen.

2. **Use negative space and eliminate distractions –** Negative space is the image portion that isn't your subject; it should balance your subject and not have anything in it that competes for attention with your subject. The blue or green water background of underwater images often creates excellent negative space without distractions.

3. **Natural direction and spacing –** Subjects that move need to have some place to go in both still and video imaging. Have a fish swimming into the picture, not out of it. Note there are exceptions, though; for example, sometimes facing outward creates a desired tension.

4. **Weighting –** This is the "balance" between the subject and the negative space. The center is rarely the best place for your subject; usually, images look better weighted to one side (where the subject is), with negative space opposite.

Negative space is the image portion that isn't your subject; it should balance your subject and not have anything in it that competes for attention with your subject.

The center is rarely the best place for your subject; usually, images look better weighted to one side, with negative space opposite.

5. **Colors –** Choosing colors that go well together gives images power. Complementary colors are opposite colors on the standard color wheel that contrast strongly in a pleasing way. Reds and oranges complement greens and blues, making these common complementary pairings underwater. Analogous colors are similar hues on the color wheel that don't contrast strongly, such as putting yellow, green-yellow and green subjects together.

6. **"Rule of Thirds" –** The "rule of thirds" is a guideline that can help you with the above principles. Imagine your viewfinder is divided horizontally and vertically with lines into thirds. Put your subject where the lines intersect, or on one of the lines (depending upon subject type). With some cameras, you can activate lines in the viewfinder to help you with this.

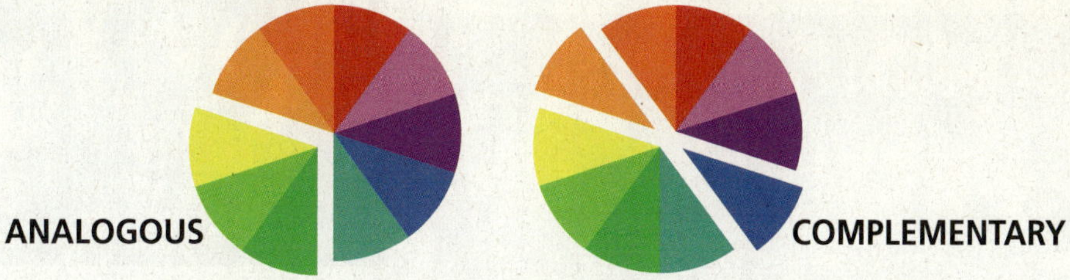

Complementary colors are opposite colors on the standard color wheel that contrast strongly in a pleasing way. Analogous colors are similar hues on the color wheel that don't contrast strongly, such as putting yellow, green-yellow and green subjects together.

To apply the "rule of thirds" guideline, imagine your viewfinder is divided horizontally and vertically with lines into thirds. Put your subject where the lines intersect, or on one of the lines (depending upon subject type).

EXERCISE-5

1. I need to hold my camera steady
   - ☐ a. to avoid disturbing aquatic life.
   - ☐ b. to reduce flooding risk.
   - ☐ c. for sharp pictures.
2. I'm taking still photos, and my buddy and I are about 18 metres/60 feet deep in clear water. I want the best color possible, so I should
   - ☐ a. use flash.
   - ☐ b. back away from my subjects.
   - ☐ c. turn off "underwater" mode.
3. In framing some stills and video, I get low and close to my subjects. This helps my images, because doing so helps (choose all that apply):
   - ☐ a. improve my colors.
   - ☐ b. make them sharper.
   - ☐ c. reduce backscatter.
   - ☐ d. create separation.
4. The purpose of good composition is to make stills and video pleasing and/or interesting.
   ☐ True ☐ False
5. Usually, I want my subject in the center of my image.
   ☐ True ☐ False
6. To use the "rule of thirds," I mentally divide the frame into thirds vertically and horizontally, and place my subject where the lines intersect, or on the lines.
   ☐ True ☐ False

How did you do?

1. c. 2. a. 3. a, b, d. 4. True. 5. False. The center is rarely the best place for your subject. 6. True.

LEARNING OBJECTIVES

By the end of this section, I should be able to answer the following questions:

1. How do I tell a story with video imaging?
2. When do I use wide, medium-wide, medium and close-up shots? How do I generally sequence them?
3. What are truck, pan, dolly, tilt, rise, and fall shots?
4. What is "the line" and why don't I cross it with my shots?
5. How do I shoot for editing?
6. How do I edit video?

Shooting Video

Telling a Story

For anything more than a short incident or event, making a watchable video relies on telling a story. To create something people enjoy watching, you shoot a series of "takes," or video sequences, based on a story you plan.

Planning your story is important; watchable videos rarely happen just by accident. The story doesn't have to be complex, and you don't have to plan everything that happens – just enough to be sure you can put a visual story together. For example, your story could be "Our Dive Outing," perhaps with sequences (scenes) that show:

1. Divers arrive on the dive boat with their gear
2. Gearing up on site
3. Predive safety check
4. Entering the water
5. On the bottom
6. Heading up
7. Everyone about to exit the water after a great dive.

Note that you don't need to include everything that happens to make a watchable sequence; just enough so viewers can follow the story (note the previous example omits anchoring, the descent, exiting or returning to port). Your viewers will mentally fill in obvious gaps, allowing you to focus on the main story – in this example, the dive itself.

Types of Shots

Telling a story visually not only requires sequencing your takes, but different types of takes (shots) that establish what's happening where, and to direct attention.

Wide shots show the viewer the overall picture, such as the dive boat at the dock with several divers boarding. *Medium-wide* shots get in closer and direct attention, such as showing the two divers you plan to feature coming aboard the boat.

Medium shots get in close to show specific action, such as showing one of the two divers lifting a cylinder into the rack, and *close-ups* show details you don't want the viewer to miss, like the diver's hand pulling the bungee over the cylinder valve to secure it.

Generally, you start each scene (new shooting location) wide, followed by medium-wide, medium and close-up as needed to tell your story. You often come back to a wider shot before going to a closer shot of something new so the viewer can follow where you're going. But, these are generalities – the important thing is that you lead the viewer's attention to avoid confusion and make it clear what you're trying to show.

Close-ups show details you don't want the viewer to miss.

Wide shots show the viewer the overall picture.

Medium-wide shots get in closer and direct attention.

Medium shots get in close to show specific action.

Underwater, you usually keep your camera at its widest zoom setting and move the camera away from or toward the subject to change from a wider to a narrow (closer) shot. At the surface, you may zoom the lens instead of move the camera.

Motion shots are important, especially underwater. They reveal different views in a single shot and allow you to stay with and reveal action.

A *truck* shot is when the camera travels left to right (or vice versa) while pointed straight ahead. Use it to follow action. A pan also follows action – the camera stays in place, but rotates left to right (or vice versa). You also use a pan to reveal a wider view.

A *dolly* moves the camera toward or away from the subject. Use it to change from wide to medium wide, etc., while videoing. This is very useful underwater, but don't overdo it.

A *tilt* is like a pan, only the camera changes angle to look upward or downward. For a *rise*, the camera goes up while shooting; for a *fall,* the camera goes down. Without specialized equipment, rise and fall shots are very limited at the surface, but underwater you can use them easily.

Motion shots can combine, such as a rise, trucking right, while also panning right to keep up with a passing sea lion. Again, you can do a lot more underwater like this than you can at the surface without special equipment.

Sequencing

Each scene usually has multiple takes (excepting aquatic life, which may not have repeatable behaviors). You change the angle and move around the scene, as long as it's clear to the viewer. Avoid crossing "the line" between takes because it confuses the viewer.

"The line" is the natural line of action in the scene; you can show the action from many angles on the same side of the line, but it becomes confusing if you cross it. As an example, you shoot this sequence of a couple diving together:

1. Medium-wide shot with male closer to camera, the shot trucks right to follow the couple.
2. Medium shot, slightly ahead looking back, male signals "okay," female replies "okay."
3. Close-up from slightly behind, male diver's hand sneaks into the BCD pocket.
4. Medium-wide shot, slightly ahead looking back, the male surprises the female with an engagement ring and underwater proposal.

You shoot all of these with the male diver closest to you, both divers swimming to camera right. If you were to shoot a take from their other side swimming to camera left, you would have crossed "the line." When edited into the sequence, it would look like they're suddenly going the other way, confusing the viewer.

Shooting for Editing

Shooting for editing means planning your takes so you can put the story together. Think about your story and be sure you have the shots you need to connect the dots. Depending upon what happens, you may need to shoot some takes that recreate steps so that everything fits together.

Follow the rules of composition; try to keep the image in the viewfinder continuously well composed. Hold the camera steady and, if moving (panning, tilting, trucking, etc.), do so slower than feels normal. Unsteady, rapidly shifting video images are unsettling and hard to watch.

Hold each take long enough to show the action, but not too long. A common mistake is shooting too short; better too long because you can adjust in editing. Don't go too long, though. A good rule of thumb is 10 to 20 seconds for most takes. A four-minute take is likely to be way too long, and you'll have difficulty (not to mention get bored!) finding the right short clip and editing it.

There are exceptions, of course, such as unique animal behaviors that require long takes. Some shots will be very short in your final video, but that's usually handled in editing.

Editing

Editing is the process of putting your takes into the story sequence. Although you generally shoot them in order, sometimes you shoot them out of order, such as when you recreate something for a complete story.

And, sometimes the "real" order doesn't tell the story well, so you change the sequence to tell it properly.

Upload your footage (all the takes) into your computer's editing software. There are many editing programs available, ranging from simple and basic to complex, professional software.

Start by dragging the takes into the proper order for the story – not necessarily the order in which you shot them. How you do this will vary with the editing program you use; go through a tutorial for the program to get started if you're not familiar with it. (You can usually find these tutorials online.)

Next, refine. Play your roughly assembled video; some takes will obviously be too long. Trim those so they don't stay on the screen as long, and so they flow smoothly from one to the next. As a very loose rule of thumb, limit shots to 10 seconds (there will be some obvious exceptions), with most shorter. Vary the lengths to keep your story moving and to hold the viewer's attention.

You can drop still images, or a series of them, into your sequence, if available, and if they make sense; some pro-

"The line" is the natural line of action in the scene; you can show the action from many angles on the same side of the line, but it becomes confusing if you cross it.

grams allow you to animate your stills (called "Ken Burns Effects"). For a more polished look, most software lets you add transitions, music and other effects, but don't overdo these. Keep them subtle so they enhance rather than distract from your story.

Editing doesn't have to be overly sophisticated or complicated, but it is important in creating enjoyable video imaging.

Editing doesn't have to be overly sophisticated or complicated, but it is important in creating enjoyable video imaging.

EXERCISE-6

1. My buddy and I are making a video of our day of diving. To make this enjoyable and watchable, we should be sure it tells a story.
   ☐ True ☐ False
2. Generally, I want to start each scene with a __________ shot, followed by _________, _________ and ___________ shots in this sequence.
   ☐ a. wide; medium-wide; medium; close-up
   ☐ b. close-up; medium; medium-wide; wide
   ☐ c. medium; medium-wide; close-up; wide
   ☐ d. medium-wide; close-up; wide; medium
3. I'm videoing the story of a professional shark feeding, and a large tiger shark swims past me. I stay where I am but rotate to follow the shark with the camera. This called a ________ shot.
   ☐ a. truck
   ☐ b. dolly
   ☐ c. rise
   ☐ d. pan
4. I'm shooting a video of two divers communicating with hand signals. To show this dialog, I shoot medium-wide shots that show both of them, medium shots that show each from the waist up, and close-ups on their hand signals. As I do this, I should shoot them so each diver is always on the same side of the camera frame.
   ☐ True ☐ False
5. To shoot for editing, I just shoot whatever comes along knowing that the story will be created during editing.
   ☐ True ☐ False
6. As a loose rule of thumb (and there will be exceptions), in my edited video each shot should be no more than ____ seconds long.
   ☐ a. 10
   ☐ b. 20
   ☐ c. 40
   ☐ d. 80

How did you do?

1. True. 2. a. 3. d. 4. True. 5. False. Shooting for editing means being sure you have all the takes you need to create a meaningful story when you edit later. 6. a.

LEARNING OBJECTIVES

By the end of this section, I should be able to answer the following questions:

1. What fundamental diving considerations do I have when diving with a camera?
2. What do I do with my camera in a dive emergency?
3. How do I protect the aquatic environment when diving as an underwater photographer?
4. What is the difference between a housing leak and a housing flood?
5. What is the priority with a housing leak or flood?
6. What causes most leaks and floods?
7. What do I do if my housing leaks?
8. What do I do if my housing floods?

Diving with a Camera

Besides the processes of shooting stills and video, diving with a camera system has some considerations that affect dive planning and how you dive.

Bulk and drag. Larger camera systems have enough drag to affect effort and gas use. Don't try to swim as fast or go as far with large systems. Plan a higher gas consumption rate. Bulk and drag aren't significant issues with most compact systems, however.

Buddy/depth/time/direction/gas awareness. Paying attention to your camera can take your mind off your diving. Diligence helps you avoid this problem. Check your buddy, depth, no stop time, orientation and gas supply after each photo sequence or take. If your buddy's using a camera system, alternate turns shooting.

In a dive emergency, ditch your camera if you must to handle the situation. Although it can represent a considerable investment, you have to think of your camera system as disposable. Fortunately, you can often recover a discarded system later; if not, no piece of equipment is worth risking injury or worse.

In a dive emergency, ditch your camera if you must to handle the situation.

Protecting the Environment

When concentrating on imaging, divers sometimes inadvertently bump, kick or otherwise damage aquatic life. Fortunately, this is easy to avoid with forethought.

Start by staying neutrally buoyant (ask your instructor about the Peak Performance Buoyancy Diver course for more about refining your weighting and buoyancy techniques). Be aware that your camera system may change your buoyancy depending upon whether it is neutral, negative or positively buoyant. Usually, you want your systems to be close to neutral, though slightly positive or negative is fine. Some systems allow you to add or remove small weights so you can adjust the buoyancy. Pay attention to your surroundings before you start shooting, especially at your fin tips.

There's a tendency to swim backwards at times, especially with video imaging. This is fine, but be sure you won't run into anything before you start your swim, and/or have your buddy help you watch where you go.

Give priority to protecting the environment. There's no image worth killing or damaging living creatures to get. It makes no sense to be destroying the beauty you're imaging.

Water in the Housing

It's useful to know what to do if your camera system leaks or floods, because if you shoot underwater long enough, it will eventually happen.

How you respond depends partly on whether your system has a leak or a flood. A leak is a small amount of water inside the housing that may get on the camera and damage it. A *flood* is substantial water with the camera partially immersed.

In both cases, safety is your priority. *Do not make a rapid ascent or otherwise risk your safety.* There is no equipment worth getting hurt for.

Most leaks and floods are caused by human error, such as allowing hair or dirt to compromise an o-ring, failing to maintain the housing properly, or improperly assembling the system.

Give priority to protecting the environment. There's no image worth killing or damaging living creatures to get.

In Case of a Leak

You know you have a leak if you see water drops inside, and/or the system's leak detector (if so equipped) alerts you. Note that leak detectors are very sensitive and rarely wrong – *assume a leak if it activates, even if you don't see water in the housing.*

Turn the system so the lowest place, where water may accumulate, is the least damaging to the camera. Often, this is with the lens port facing down. Turn the power off.

Signal your buddy and make a normal, safe ascent together. Exit the water keeping the system in the same position. Don't allow it to get rotated, which may spill water over the camera inside.

Open the housing in a dry environment, remove the camera and dry it off. Most modern cameras reasonably tolerate stray drops and splashes, so it should be fine if you see no signs of water inside the camera itself, though the prudent action is to have it examined by a professional camera technician as soon as reasonably possible.

If the camera's internal workings may have gotten wet, see the manufacturer instructions or website for guidance specific to your camera. Remove batteries and do not power the camera up until it has been dried/serviced.

Unless the leak source is obvious and easily corrected, do not use the housing again until it has been professionally serviced. Test dive it without a camera to be sure it's back in working order.

In case of a leak, turn the system so that the lowest place, where water may accumulate, is the least damaging to the camera. Turn the power off and make a normal ascent with your buddy.

In Case of a Flood

A flood will be obvious, with lots of water sloshing inside the housing. Unless it involves an immersible, water-resistant camera, the camera will likely be ruined. Either way, there's no reason to hurry. Turn the camera off and make a normal ascent.

Once you're out of the water, open the housing carefully. Wear glasses or your dive mask and, ideally, disposable gloves as you proceed, because batteries in contact with water may release gases, causing the housing to pop open when you release the catches. Don't touch the water inside, because it may have corrosive/irritating chemicals that can injure skin and eyes. Remove affected batteries and drain the water for proper disposal (see local environmental guidelines).

Remove and dry the memory card(s). These usually tolerate flooding, allowing you to keep what you shot prior to the flood.

Dry the camera and see the manufacturer recommendations (online or in the literature) for what to do before returning it for service. The housing will also require servicing before further use. If it is not an immersible camera, chances are it will not survive flooding, especially in sea water.

PADI DIGITAL UNDERWATER PHOTOGRAPHER SPECIALTY

At your instructor's discretion, the Digital Underwater Imaging Adventure Dive credits toward the PADI Digital Underwater Photographer Specialty course. The course gives you more opportunities to apply and learn underwater photography skills, including:

- basic image exposure principles and using histograms.
- setting white balance and getting good color.
- using off-camera flash.
- post processing.

Remember to log your training dives with the PADI Mobile App or at padi.com.

EXERCISE-7

1. My buddy and I are both shooting as we dive together. Ideally we should
   - ☐ a. alternate turns shooting.
   - ☐ b. shoot at the same time.
2. I'm diving with a camera system and have to share gas with my buddy in an emergency. The system is interfering with handling the situation, so I should
   - ☐ a. clip it to my BCD.
   - ☐ b. have my buddy hold it.
   - ☐ c. ditch it.
3. There's no image worth killing or damaging living creatures to get.
   - ☐ True ☐ False
4. While diving, I discover that my housing has filled more than halfway with water. This is a housing
   - ☐ a. leak.
   - ☐ b. flood.
5. I've just discovered that my housing may have a leak. The priority is
   - ☐ a. my buddy's and my safety.
   - ☐ b. protecting what I've shot.
   - ☐ c. getting to the surface.
6. Most leaks and floods are caused by
   - ☐ a. housing failure.
   - ☐ b. user error.
   - ☐ c. manufacturing defects.
   - ☐ d. contact with aquatic life.
7. If my housing leaks, I should make a/an __________ascent.
   - ☐ a. normal
   - ☐ b. accelerated
   - ☐ c. rapid
   - ☐ d. emergency
8. If my housing floods, I should make a/an __________ascent.
   - ☐ a. normal
   - ☐ b. accelerated
   - ☐ c. rapid
   - ☐ d. emergency

How did you do?

1. a. 2. c. 3. True. 4. b. 5. a. 6. b. 7. a. 8. a.

Knowledge Review – Digital Underwater Imaging

Answer the following questions by selecting the best choice (or choices) from those provided. Be prepared to discuss the material at your next training session.

1. Water affects the light reaching my camera by (choose all that apply):
   - ☐ a. reducing the amount of light available.
   - ☐ b. absorbing color.
   - ☐ c. reducing sharpness.
2. The best overall angle for underwater photography is
   - ☐ a. close to my subject, looking slightly upward.
   - ☐ b. close to my subject, looking slightly downward.
   - ☐ c. far from my subject, looking slightly upward.
   - ☐ d. far from my subject, looking slightly downward.
3. Options for good color underwater may include to (choose all that apply):
   - ☐ a. use external lighting/internal flash.
   - ☐ b. set my camera's white balance to underwater/automatic mode.
   - ☐ c. use a filter.
   - ☐ d. set my lens for telephoto.
4. I'm setting up my camera housing and notice a scratch in the main o-ring. To get a proper seal, I should
   - ☐ a. use o-ring cement to repair it.
   - ☐ b. apply extra silicone grease to the area.
   - ☐ c. apply no silicone grease to the area.
   - ☐ d. replace the o-ring.
5. Generally, it's a good idea to leave the port cover on my camera system until I get in the water, and to replace it before exiting.
   - ☐ True
   - ☐ False
6. After an ocean boat dive, I learn the freshwater rinse got knocked over and there's no fresh water. It will be about two hours to reach shore. My best bet is to
   - ☐ a. dry the system with a towel.
   - ☐ b. allow the system to air dry.
   - ☐ c. keep the system wet in seawater until I can rinse in fresh water.
7. The "rule of thirds" means
   - ☐ a. putting your subject where imaginary lines divide the frame into thirds.
   - ☐ b. shooting only a third of your subject.
   - ☐ c. taking three photos or takes of every subject.
8. For the most viewable videos, I want to shoot so that I can tell a story by editing the clips together.
   - ☐ True
   - ☐ False
9. My buddy has an out-of-gas emergency and the camera system is in the way of sharing gas. I should
   - ☐ a. give it to my buddy.
   - ☐ b. ditch it to handle the situation.
10. During a dive, I notice there's water in my housing. I should
    - ☐ a. make a rapid ascent.
    - ☐ b. make a normal ascent.

Student Statement

I completed this Knowledge Review to the best of my ability. For any questions I answered incorrectly or incompletely, I reviewed the explanation provided and now understand the material. In the case of anything about which I still have questions, I will review the material again and, if necessary, discuss it with my instructor at our next session.

☐ I agree ☐ I disagree

Name ______________________________

Date ______________________________

scenario

"Great dive!" Renee exclaimed as she sat down next to Pierce on the boat. "What a fun drift – we saw so much and hardly finned at all. Down 70 minutes and I still have about a thousand psi left."

"I've got about the same," said Pierce. "Did you see those blacktip reef sharks?"

"Where?" Renee asked.

"Hanging out over the deep water, away from the wall."

"Ready to go again?" she asked, "Maybe we can find them this dive."

"Sure, I'm not tired at all. Let me change my cylinder, get something to drink and I'm ready to roll."

▶ *What does this conversation tell you about drift diving?*

7 DRIFT DIVING

DRIFT DIVING

Introduction to Drift Diving

Drift diving is diving with the current instead of against it. It is any form of diving in mild to heavy current in which your exit point is significantly down-current from your entry. Rather than have to swim or pull yourself into the current, you let it give you a ride.

Drift diving is popular in areas with strong prevailing currents because it has four main advantages: First, you expend relatively little energy – you don't swim much or at all during most of the dive. Second, drift diving enables you to dive where it would otherwise be difficult, impossible or hazardous due to current.

LEARNING OBJECTIVES

By the end of this section, I should be able to answer these questions:

1. What is drift diving?
2. What are four advantages of drift diving?
3. What are four concerns when drift diving?

Drift diving is diving with the current instead of against it. Rather than have to swim or pull yourself into the current, you let it give you a ride.

Even where you could make a non-drift dive, a third advantage is you generally cover a wide area and see a lot of the reef. Finally, with many types of drift diving, you don't have to find a particular exit point, which simplifies navigation.

There are some concerns you have to consider, though. For one, timing is important, because drift diving requires divers to coordinate entries, exits, descents and ascents. If your buddy stops, and you're not aware of it, the current can separate you very quickly. A third concern is that you commonly need some form of surface supervision (usually from a boat). And, drift diving's not suitable everywhere, even when there's current. There are exceptions, but it is generally best suited to long, extensive bottom topography, such as a reef, river or a series of closely spaced sites.

EXERCISE-1

1. When drift diving, my exit point is significantly down-current from my entry point.

   ☐ True ☐ False

2. My buddy and I are making a 40-minute drift dive from a boat. Assuming no unexpected issues, we can expect to be ______ tired compared to a non-drift dive of the same duration.

   ☐ a. more
   ☐ b. equally
   ☐ c. less

3. My buddy and I want to make a dive on a small, local reef surrounded by sand, but there's a strong current. A drift dive is likely to be a good option for making this dive.

   ☐ True ☐ False

How did you do?

1. True. 2. c. 3. False. Drift diving is generally best suited to long, extensive bottom topography; you would probably drift past the small reef and then see little else.

LEARNING OBJECTIVES

By the end of this section, I should be able to answer this question:

1. How can current vary in intensity from the surface to the bottom?

Current Characteristics

Many forces cause currents including tides, wind, gravity and the earth's rotation. Despite this variety, a characteristic almost all currents share is they don't flow uniformly. As you recall from the PADI Open Water Diver course, it's exhausting to swim against anything but a very mild current – usually less than 1/2 knot for most divers – and current speed is *usually* slower near the bottom than at the surface because of resistance with the bottom.

Currents usually flow slower near the bottom. When drift diving, you also need to keep in mind that divers closer to the bottom will usually drift more slowly than those well above it.

You probably remember that if you must move against the current (which can be a concern whether drift diving or not), it is usually easiest to remain on or near the bottom and pull yourself along (without touching sensitive aquatic life) rather than swim. When drift diving, you also need to keep in mind that divers closer to the bottom will often drift more slowly than those well above it, because current usually slows near the bottom because of drag. Sometimes, deeper current along walls flows faster than in the shallower water in the area. Either way, this can affect keeping a group together.

The more irregular the reef, the more drag and the more the current slows. Besides this effect, when drift diving in rivers, the flow is typically faster on the inside of a bend than outside, but not always. Obstructions and depth variations – the inside of a bend is usually shallower – also affect current flow in a river.

Your instructor will give you more detail on what to expect with respect to current speed where you'll be making your Drift Adventure Dive.

EXERCISE-2

1. A current is typically slower
   - ☐ a. near the surface.
   - ☐ b. between the surface and the bottom.
   - ☐ c. near the bottom.

How did you do?

1. c.

LEARNING OBJECTIVES

By the end of this section, I should be able to answer these questions:

1. What are the three general types of drift dives?

2. Why is surface support usually recommended for drift diving? By what methods can it be provided?

Types of Drift Diving

There are several variations of drift diving, but for simplicity, we can divide them into three types:

1. Drift diving with a surface float.
2. Drift diving without a surface float.
3. Drift diving with DSMBs (Delayed Surface Marker Buoys).

Of these, diving with DSMBs (Delayed Surface Marker Buoys) has become the most common and popular. We will look at all three types because all methods are still in use, and because this will help you understand why DSMB drift diving has become the most popular.

Drift diving with a towed surface float. With this technique, divers drift along under a tethered surface float as part of either buddy teams or as a single group. In the latter case, everyone keeps the leader towing the float in sight. The dive boat either follows the float or just floats along. The group ascends together when someone reaches a dive limit. Or, buddy teams may ascend individually when they reach a limit.

This method makes surface supervision easy, and is useful in limited visibility with generally flat, unobstructed bottom. It is also good when surface conditions make it difficult to follow diver bubbles and there's no other means to be sure the boat is staying reasonably close to the divers.

Drift diving without a towed surface float. Divers travel as a group, keeping the leader in sight, with the boat staying in the general area above at the surface. Like drift diving with a float, the group may ascend together or in individual buddy teams.

This technique is useful when the surface current is much stronger than on the bottom, or when obstructions pose entanglement hazards. Both of these make towing a surface float problematic.

Drift diving without a towed surface float requires adequate visibility for the group to stay together, if diving in a group. Another consideration is that the boat must also stay close enough to keep boat traffic away from the divers, and to keep the divers within adequate range of the dive flag.

Drift diving with DSMBs. Drift diving with DSMBs combines the advantages of diving with and without a towed surface float, while avoiding most of the drawbacks of both techniques. Divers start without a towed float overhead, as a group or in buddy teams.

Drift diving with a surface float is useful in limited visibility with generally flat, unobstructed bottom. It is also good when surface conditions make it difficult for the dive boat to follow diver bubbles.

Floatless drift diving requires adequate visibility for the group to stay together.

Drift diving with DSMBs combines the advantages of diving with and without a surface float. Divers start without a towed float overhead and, upon reaching a limit, the leader (or buddy team) deploys and sends up a DSMB.

Upon reaching a limit, the leader (or buddy team) deploys and sends up a DSMB, inflating it with an accessory inflator or alternate second stage. It ascends on a reel-deployed line – your instructor may have you practice this before the dive if you'll be using DSMBs on your Drift Adventure Dive – and alerts the boat that divers are coming up. The line also provides a reference for the ascent and safety stop as the divers drift.

Surface Support

Regardless of drift diving type, you usually want surface support. Typically, it is provided by boat, though when shore drift diving it may be by motor vehicle.

Surface supervision simplifies the dive logistics by picking you up at your exit, which is generally a long distance from where you enter. This is essential when boat diving, of course, but even when shore diving you may be well beyond a reasonable walk (especially in dive gear) back to where you started. Beyond this, surface supervision can assist in an emergency, and help warn boat traffic away while you're underwater.

Boat operation for drift diving requires maneuvering and close coordination between the crew and divers, so those supporting and operating the vessel should be familiar with drift procedures.

EXERCISE-3

1. In most areas, drift diving ______________ has become the most popular technique.
   - ☐ a. with a surface float
   - ☐ b. without a surface float
   - ☐ c. with a DSMB
2. Surface support is generally recommended for drift diving because, among other reasons, I generally exit the water a long distance from where I enter.
   ☐ True ☐ False

How did you do?

1. c. 2. True.

LEARNING OBJECTIVES

By the end of this section, I should be able to answer these questions:

1. What are three types of floats used in drift diving?

2. What type of line should I use when drift diving, and how should I control it?

3. What are the two basic types of surface signaling devices, and why should I have at least one of each?

Drift Diving Equipment

The equipment you use when drift diving depends on where you're diving and the type of drift dive, though some equipment (like surface signaling devices) apply to *all* diving. (There are some additional equipment options covered in the PADI Drift Diver course.)

DSMBs

As mentioned earlier, drift diving with DSMBs is becoming the most popular drift technique. They are available in different sizes and colors, but be sure your buoy is designed to deploy underwater. Those designed for surface use only are good standard equipment for emergency signaling, but DSMBs have a non-spill design – they won't deflate if they invert while ascending – and feature over-pressure valves to release expanding gas. With a line and reel, this makes them deployable at depth.

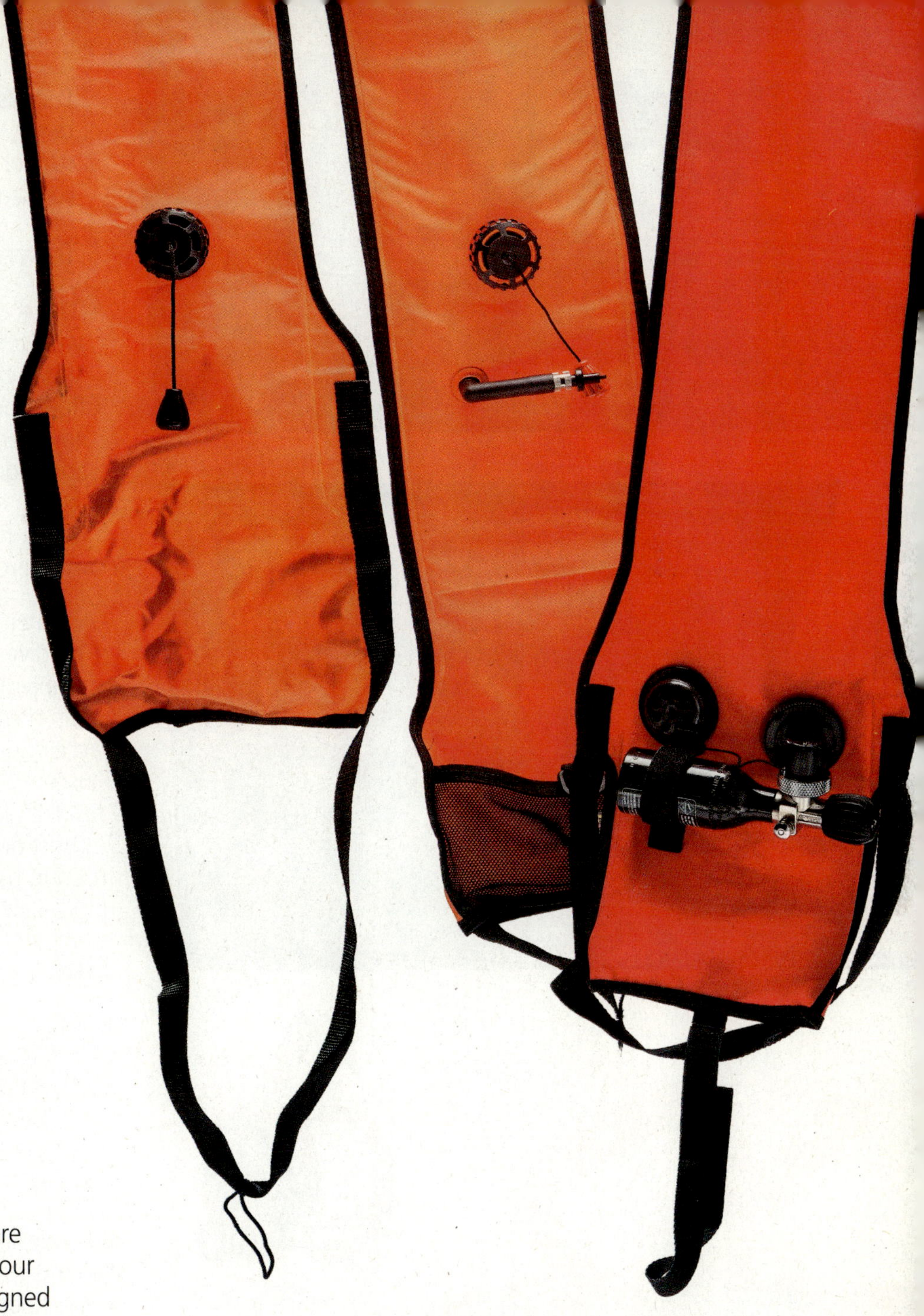

Unlike standard inflatable signal tubes, DSMBs have a non-spill design – meaning it won't deflate if it inverts while ascending – and feature over-pressure valves to release expanding gas.

Boat fenders make great towed floats because they're readily available, very buoyant and highly visible.

In drift diving, the conventional dive flag/float is commonly used when in rivers, and by smaller groups or buddy teams towing a float.

DSMBs have enough buoyancy to guide ascents by divers who control their buoyancy, but not enough to support divers at the surface. They also double as surface signaling devices (discussed shortly).

Towed Surface Floats

There are a few types of floats used in drift diving with a towed float. The first of these is the international-orange boat fender. These make great towed floats because they're readily available (most dive boats have fenders for docking), and they're very buoyant and highly visible. There are many sizes available, and they're commonly used when a group is drift diving with a float. Their main downside is they can be bulky and hard to tow, especially across a current.

Another float choice is the conventional dive flag/float. The dive flag warns off boaters and may be required to comply with local regulations. It may be easier to tow than a conventional boat fender, and you can stow extra accessories in some types. The smaller ones may be susceptible to being pulled underwater, however, and like fenders, large ones can be harder to tow across currents. In drift diving, the conventional dive flag/float is commonly used in rivers, and by smaller groups or buddy teams towing a float.

Lines and Reels

DSMBs are usually deployed using tec-diving-type reels with #36 braided nylon line. For drift diving with a towed surface float, use 0.4-1.25 centimetre/1/8-1/2-inch nylon or polypropylene line, which is a manageable, visible size that divers can use to guide descents/ascents. Control the line with a line caddy or reel.

As a rule of thumb, have approximately twice the length as the expected depth. This gives you extra in case you end up deeper than planned, and allows for the curve the current often puts in the line.

For drift diving with DSMBs, #36 braided nylon line works well. For diving with a towed surface float, use 0.4-1.25-cm/1/8-1/2-in nylon or polypropylene line. In all cases, control the line with a line caddy or reel.

Surface Signaling Devices

You should have *at least* one *visual* and one *audible* surface signaling device. Most are compact, so it's reasonable to have more than one of each. As you recall, this is standard scuba equipment for all diving, not just drift diving.

You need visual devices to make you easier to spot at long distances and in rough surface conditions. Inflatable signal tubes and surface marker buoys (most DSMBs included) work well for this. Signal mirrors help attract attention over long distances, making them useful for signaling aircraft. For night drift dives, flares and emergency lights make you visible (you learn more about these in the PADI Night Diver course).

You need audible devices to gain attention. Whistles have unlimited use and deploy quickly (attached near your BCD oral inflator works well). Low-pressure inflator-powered air horns get attention over long distances because they're loud, but you must have air in your cylinder, so also carry a whistle.

Finally, there are electronic signaling devices that use GPS to send the boat and/or rescuers your location by radio. Carried in watertight, pressure-proof containers, these are not unusual for drift diving in remote areas.

You should have at least one visual and one audible surface signaling device. As you recall, this is standard scuba equipment for all diving, not just drift diving.

EXERCISE-4

1. I'm planning a drift dive with a towed float. The floats I might choose from include (choose all that apply):
   - ☐ a. boat fenders.
   - ☐ b. dive float/flag.
   - ☐ c. lobster pot markers.
2. My buddy and I plan to use a boat fender towed with 1.25-cm/1/2-in line. We only need 18 metres/60 feet of line for our planned 9 metre/30 foot maximum depth, so it's acceptable to carry the line as a loose coil.
   - ☐ True ☐ False
3. My buddy and I need _________ surface signaling devices so we're easier to spot at long distances and in rough surface conditions, though we should carry both types.
   - ☐ a. visual
   - ☐ b. audible

How did you do?

1. a, b. 2. False. Always use a line caddy or reel to control the line. 3. a.

LEARNING OBJECTIVES

By the end of this section, I should be able to answer these questions:

1. What seven considerations go into planning a drift dive?
2. How do I navigate when drift diving?
3. What is the most important factor in preparing for a drift diving entry?
4. What are the differences between buoyant and negative drift diving entries, and when would I use each?
5. What are two procedures I can use when beginning a drift dive that will use a towed surface float?
6. When using a towed surface float and line, what techniques can I use so the group stays together while descending?
7. What are the procedures for beginning a drift dive that will not use a towed surface float?
8. When not using a towed surface float and a line, what techniques can I use to keep the group together while descending?
9. What techniques can I use to stay with the group on a group drift dive?
10. What body position do I generally maintain during a drift dive?
11. What techniques do I use and what factors do I consider when ascending as a group from a drift dive?
12. What techniques do I use and what factors do I consider when ascending as an individual buddy team from a drift dive?
13. What are the procedures for exiting the water after surfacing from a drift dive?

Drift Diving Techniques and Procedures

Drift Diving Planning Considerations

Beyond general considerations you have for any dive, there are at least seven considerations when planning drift dives.

1. Surface conditions and current intensity affect the drift technique you'll use and the distance you can expect to drift. If conditions are very choppy, you may opt to tow a float or deploy a DSMB so the boat can find you more easily when you come up.
2. Depth and visibility affect the drift technique you'll use and whether you'll travel as one large team or several smaller ones. Generally, lower visibility and a faster current make it more advantageous to dive in several smaller teams rather than one large group.
3. The secondary objective may influence the drift technique and dive team choice, but drift dives usually avoid objectives that require stopping for any significant interval.
4. The number of divers and buddy teams affects the techniques you will use. Even in conditions that work for diving as a single group, if there are too many divers it may be better to break into two or more groups.
5. Drift diving and general experience levels affect how you plan the dive. With more drift experience, you usually have more technique and site options. Lack of experience with drift diving or deep diving may influence your site options and the best techniques to use.
6. As mentioned earlier, bottom topography and the environment may influence the techniques you use. Obstacles that can entangle a line may make a floatless or DSMB drift desirable.
7. Surface support often influences drift diving. For example, an experienced crew may have no difficulty following divers without a towed float, whereas a less-experienced crew may need a towed surface float to follow. In some situations, lack of surface support makes drift diving unfeasible.

Navigation

Because you're carried along by the current, with the boat following you, most drift diving requires little navigation. One exception is shore-based drift diving because you may need to navigate so you don't miss your exit point. You would surface with ample time to reach shore and exit. If you overshoot, you usually have to exit the water and walk back.

Another exception is if there are areas where a boat can't follow you, such as in shallow water on the top of walls. In these cases, you may need to swim across the current to stay in, or get to, where the boat can go.

Drift Diving Entries: Predive

Drift diving entries take more coordination than non-drift entries. The most important factor is for divers to be ready together so they can enter together. Otherwise, the current can separate everyone – buddies, or a group – quickly.

So, before the dive conduct your predive safety check and other preparations out of the water until the entire group, or buddy team, is ready. Even when drift diving in buddy teams, you usually need all teams to be ready together.

Even when everyone's ready, wait for the divemaster or captain to clear you to enter. **Never enter the water until cleared to do so by the captain/crew. This is very important to be sure the propellers are disengaged and all divers are ready.**

Drift diving and general experience levels affect how you plan the dive. With more drift experience, you usually have more technique and site options. Lack of experience with drift diving or deep diving may influence your site options and the best techniques to use.

Drift Diving Entries and Descents

Buddy teams or groups diving together begin a drift dive either floating together before descending together, or immediately descending together. Let's look at both of these, as well as how you may handle a float with each.

Buoyant entries. Divers enter with their BCDs partially inflated. They stay together and descend together, when ready, at the leader's signal. It's common to hang on to a line deployed from the boat until everyone's ready. Buoyant entries allow final adjustments (e.g., weight check) at the surface with everyone together.

It's a good choice when the drift area's large and there's no issue delaying the descent a bit. Buoyant entries work well with less-experienced divers who need more time descending and equalizing.

Negative entries. Divers enter with their BCDs deflated and descend without time on the surface. This means everyone must enter and descend together. It's a good technique when the dive must begin at a very specific point, or when surface conditions are rough.

Negative entries are exciting and fun, but all divers must have sufficient experience to descend and equalize relatively rapidly.

Entries with a towed surface float. For buoyant entries with a towed surface float, the dive may begin with the float trailing behind the boat, like a current line. After cleared to do so, divers enter and assemble on the line with the line handler (leader) closest to the boat. When everyone's ready, the leader disconnects the line and starts down, with divers following, using the line as visual reference. There are variations on entries with a surface float.

For negative entries with a towed surface float, after cleared to enter the leader goes in with the float and line. All divers follow immediately. The leader descends, letting out line, with the group following the line, keeping the leader in sight.

One option for buoyant entries, the dive begins with the float trailing behind the boat, like a current line. When everyone's ready, the leader disconnects the line and starts down, with divers following, using the line as a visual reference.

Negative entries are exciting and fun, but all divers must have sufficient experience to descend and equalize relatively rapidly.

Descents using a towed surface float. Use these techniques while descending:

1. Use the line as a visual reference. Pulling on it can pull the reel/caddy out of the leader's grasp, or drag the leader if you're in shallower water and faster current.
2. Stay with your buddy and the line. The leader may have to swim across current to avoid obstacles; follow the line and leader.
3. If you have equalizing difficulties, ascend along the line with your buddy as necessary and try again. If you can't equalize, surface and signal the boat. Stay near the float until the boat is ready to pick you up.
4. Go around other buddy teams having descent problems, but don't descend faster than the leader.
5. The leader will wait for everyone at the bottom, either stationary out of the current (topography allowing) or drifting at a planned depth.

Entries and descents without a towed surface float. Floatless entries are often (but not necessarily) negative entries. On group dives, to keep together, all divers need to descend at once and keep the leader in sight. This is less of an issue when drifting as individual buddy teams.

Usually, you descend until you can see sloping bottom, a wall or other reference, and follow it to the planned depth. Equalization issues can be a problem, because you don't have the line to keep everyone together. How you'll handle this depends upon the group and experience, but it should be planned in advance.

Group Drift Tours Procedures

On group dives, after reaching the planned depth the leader makes sure everyone's accounted for (on group dives), confirms current strength and direction, and indicates the travel direction. Stay with your buddy and keep contact with the leader. When drifting as buddy teams, you stay with your team.

Stay neutrally buoyant and streamlined as you drift (see the Peak Performance Buoyancy section for more about refining your buoyancy, trim and streamlining). Generally, maintain a normal horizontal swimming position facing your travel direction; you do this diving in individual buddy teams, too. Stay behind the group leader.

If necessary to stop or slow (e.g., to let some of the group catch up with the leader), swim gently into the current, duck behind something out of the current, or hang on to a nonliving part of the reef. If you and your buddy are catching up with a group, swim gently with the current.

Generally, maintain a normal horizontal swimming position facing your travel direction. Stay up current, behind the group leader.

Direction changes usually involve swimming across the current to avoid or intercept something. To avoid having to fight the current, start your swim before you reach your target.

Ascending as a Group

If the plan is for the entire group to ascend together, the ascent begins when any diver reaches an agreed cylinder pressure, no stop time remaining or other limit. Using a DSMB, the leader deploys it and sends it up.

All divers signal "up" and ascend normally. Control your buoyancy with your BCD; with a towed float or DSMB, don't use the line to pull up or down. Use it as a visual reference, or with a loose "okay" around it. When ascending without a line, use the topography and your dive computer to monitor your ascent rate.

The group completes the safety stop and ascends together, then looks to the boat for directions and pickup. With a DSMB or towed surface float, the diver with the reel comes up last, taking in line while ascending.

Ascending as Individual Buddy Teams

When drifting as buddy teams, and often with group drifts, individual buddy teams ascend upon reaching a limit. This is more typical with experienced drift divers. Depending upon the situation and plan, buddy teams may send up a DSMB, follow a towed float line, or simply ascend without a line, make a safety stop, surface and look to the boat for pickup directions.

Boat Exits

At the surface when boat drift diving, stay with your buddy and/or the group. Using a towed surface float, the leader will bring in the line, but may leave a length for everyone to hold on to. (This isn't usually done with the fine line used with DSMBs, however.) Be cautious of slack line – pass over it rather than under it, if possible, to reduce entanglement issues.

Ascending along a float/DSMB line, use the line primarily as a visual reference, or make a loose "okay" around it. Don't use the line to pull up or down. The leader comes up last, reeling in the line.

Do not approach the boat until signaled to do so by the captain/crew. Stay in the group with your buddy, visible at the surface. Propeller injuries are serious and debilitating, and often fatal, so take this seriously.

Do not approach the boat until signaled to do so by the captain/crew. Stay in the group with your buddy, visible at the surface. Propeller injuries are serious and debilitating, and often fatal, so take this seriously.

The boat usually maneuvers as close as possible, then disengages the engines for boarding. The crew may throw out a line for everyone to hang on to, or there may be deployed lines for this, but in calm conditions this may not be necessary. When it's your turn, exit as you normally would. The leader is usually the last aboard.

If you become separated at the surface, stay buoyant, deploy your signaling devices and wait for the boat. In most cases you won't be that far from the boat, because you and it are drifting together; the primary force that separates you would be wind blowing the boat. You learn more about boat diving procedures in the PADI Boat Diver course.

Shore Exits

When drift diving from shore, if you have a specific exit point, surface well before reaching it so you don't miss it. Swim across the current to your exit. Ideally, be as close to shore as possible for the last hundred metres/yards or so. Exit as appropriate for the environment. You may exit as a group or spread out as individual buddy teams.

EXERCISE-5

1. I'm in a group of 10 experienced drift divers planning a dive in a very strong current and relatively low visibility. Generally, this leads us to planning the dive as
   - ☐ a. individual buddy teams.
   - ☐ b. a single group.
2. When drift diving from a boat, you usually don't need to navigate much.
   ☐ True ☐ False
3. The most important factor in preparing for a drift dive is
   - ☐ a. for all divers to be ready to enter together.
   - ☐ b. to defog our masks before entering.
   - ☐ c. adding an extra 2 kg/5 lbs of weight.
4. I'm drift diving with a group of less-experienced divers over a large dive site. We would probably use a ________________drift diving entry.
   - ☐ a. buoyant
   - ☐ b. negative
5. One common technique for buoyant drift diving entries using a towed surface float is to assemble on a line secured to the back of the boat like a current line.
   ☐ True ☐ False
6. I'm having trouble descending on a group drift dive, so I should pull myself downward on the towed surface float line.
   ☐ True ☐ False
7. When descending on a group drift dive without a towed surface float, we stay together by keeping the ________ in sight.
   - ☐ a. boat
   - ☐ b. float
   - ☐ c. bottom
   - ☐ d. leader
8. During the tour portion of a group drift dive, my buddy(ies) and I should stay _______ the leader.
   - ☐ a. ahead of/down current of
   - ☐ b. behind/up current of
   - ☐ c. below/deeper than
9. During a drift dive, I generally want to maintain a vertical or sitting position.
   ☐ True ☐ False
10. If the plan is for the entire group to ascend together, everyone ascends when any diver reaches an agreed limit.
    ☐ True ☐ False
11. It is never appropriate for individual buddy teams to surface as they reach their limits on a group drift dive.
    ☐ True ☐ False
12. To avoid serious, often fatal propeller injuries after surfacing from a drift dive, I should not approach the boat until signaled to do so by the captain/crew.
    ☐ True ☐ False

How did you do?

1. a. 2. True. 3. a. 4. a. 5. True. 6. False. Pulling up on the line can pull the reel/caddy from the leader's hand or drag the leader. 7. d. 8. b. 9. False. Generally, maintain a horizontal, normal swimming position. 10. True. 11. False. Especially with experienced drift divers, it is not unusual for individual buddy teams to ascend from a group drift dive as they reach a limit. 12. True.

LEARNING OBJECTIVES

By the end of this section, I should be able to answer these questions:

1. What constitutes getting "lost" when drift diving? What do I do to rejoin the group?

2. How can diving in currents contribute to exhaustion, stress and buddy separation? How do I avoid these problems?

3. How does the line handler avoid entanglement in a towed surface float line? What is the procedure if a diver becomes entangled?

Drift Diving Hazards and Problems

Getting "Lost"

When boat drift diving, there's usually no specific exit. With shore drift diving there may be, so staying with the group may be more important if only the leader knows where to exit. Either way, on a group drift dive, being "lost" in drift diving means you're out of contact with the group and leader. This is true even if you're still with your buddy and have a good idea of where you are.

Unless the group agrees to a different procedure during dive planning, if lost (separated), search for no more than a minute before ascending to the surface. If you think you're up current from the group, try swimming to catch up. If you think you're down current, stop or swim slowly into the current so the group catches up. Either way, if the group changed course, you might not reunite within a minute.

In that case, ascend slowly, make a safety stop and carefully surface. The boat operator may not spot your bubbles, so be cautious.

You can send up a DSMB if you have one. At the surface, establish buoyancy, signal the boat (use your signaling devices if necessary) and wait for pickup. Depending upon circumstances, the boat may help you rejoin the group. The procedure may be for the group to surface if someone gets separated, though this isn't always the case when boat drift diving.

If you don't know the exit point when shore drift diving and get lost, look for bubbles and the towed float (if used) at the surface. If you don't see the group, you may have to stay at the surface. This may make you drift faster, however, so it's common for everyone to surface if someone gets lost when shore drift diving. But, this depends upon the dive plan. The leader may also tell everyone what exit landmarks to watch for, in case of separation.

Overexertion

Overexertion (exhaustion) is the primary hazard when diving in currents. Its signs and symptoms include fatigue, labored breathing, a feeling of suffocation, headache, muscle cramping and a tendency to panic.

Avoid overexertion underwater. Don't try to fight the current, and stay well within your physical limits. If being carried in an undesirable direction in a current too strong to swim against, don't fight it. Underwater, duck out of the current or hang on to something on the bottom (avoiding sensitive organisms). If you can't do this, ascend at a safe rate, inflate your BCD, rest and signal the boat to pick you up. Swim across the current if you can reach a current line. If shore drift diving, swim across the current to shallow water.

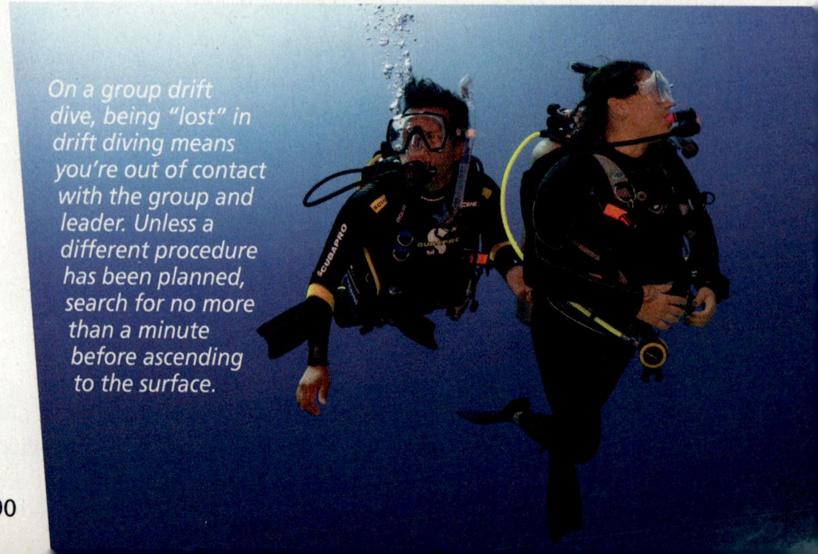

On a group drift dive, being "lost" in drift diving means you're out of contact with the group and leader. Unless a different procedure has been planned, search for no more than a minute before ascending to the surface.

Don't try to fight the current, and stay well within your physical limits. If being carried in an undesirable direction in a current too strong to swim against, duck out of the current or pull yourself along on the bottom (avoiding sensitive organisms). If you start to experience overexertion, get your buddy's attention, stop all activity and rest.

If you start to experience overexertion signs and symptoms, do as you learned in the PADI Open Water Diver course: Signal your buddy, stop all activity and rest. After catching your breath, either continue the dive with less exertion or, if necessary, abort the dive.

Psychological Stress

Currents can also cause psychological stress, primarily due to inexperience with them. Completing this dive and the rest of the PADI Drift Diver course, and the PADI Boat Diver course, provides structured training, which reduces psychological stress because you learn current-diving techniques and how to manage the potential problems. Beyond that, in drift diving, like all diving, stay within your psychological and physical limits, and gain experience slowly. Tell your instructor how you feel, especially if you feel stressed.

Buddy Separation

Currents can cause buddy separation if one diver stops or slows, carrying the other away. Avoiding this is primarily a matter of vigilance. Stay close, communicate and make a point of staying together. It also helps to stay at the same depth because a shallower diver usually tends to drift faster. The main point is that if one buddy stops or slows, the other must also.

Unless planned otherwise, if separated, follow the standard procedure of searching for no more than a minute, then reuniting on the surface.

Entanglement

Entanglement in the float line isn't common, but is possible. With both DSMBs and towed surface floats, the primary cause is slack line; to avoid the problem, the leader keeps tension on it, taking in slack as necessary.

Fortunately, entanglement in the float line while drift diving is rarely serious, but especially in a rapid current needs to be dealt with efficiently. The tangled diver should stop swimming and signal a buddy to assist. Trying to turn tends to make the problem worse. Although unlikely, if the diver is severely entangled, the group surfaces, taking up the diver and line together, and deals with it there. If the line snags on the bottom, it may be necessary to cut it free.

PADI DRIFT DIVER SPECIALTY

At your instructor's discretion, the Drift Adventure Dive credits toward the PADI Drift Diver Specialty course. The course gives you additional information and opportunities to apply and practice drift diving skills, including:

- Types and causes of currents
- Specialty activities while drift diving
- Different drift diving environments
- Applying drift diving techniques

Remember to log your training dives with the PADI Mobile App or at padi.com.

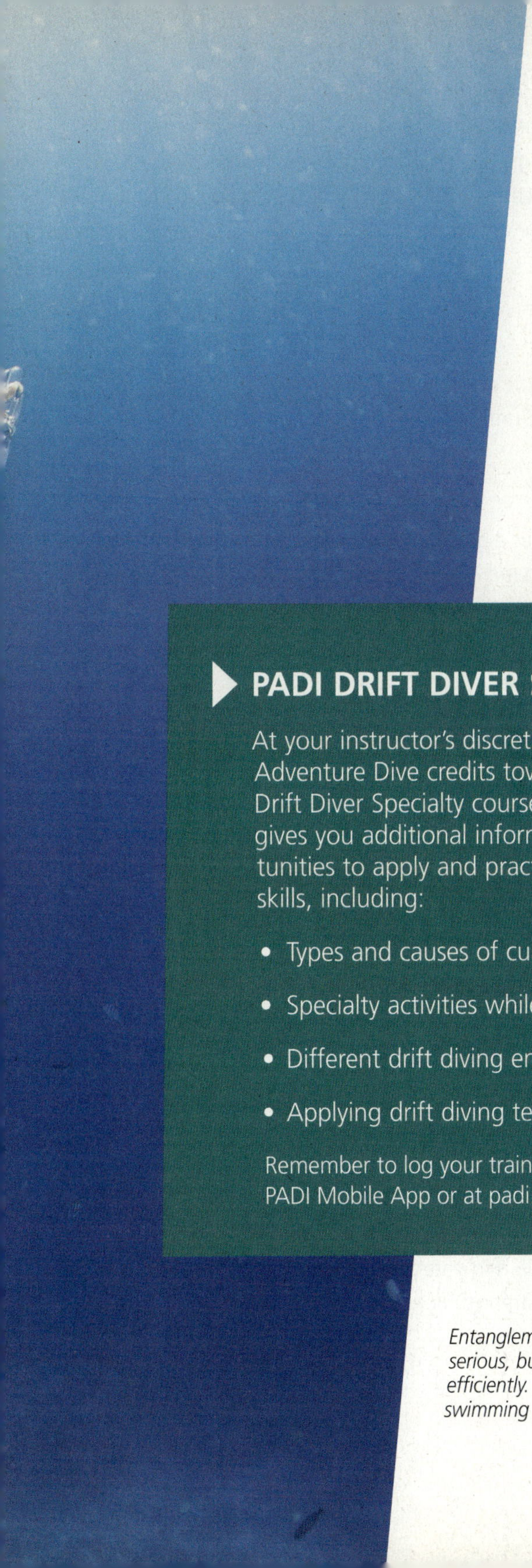

Entanglement while drift diving is rarely serious, but needs to be dealt with efficiently. The tangled diver should stop swimming and signal a buddy to assist.

EXERCISE-6

1. On a group drift dive, my buddy and I find ourselves separated from the leader and other divers, unable to rejoin them after looking for a minute. We should
   - ☐ a. continue the dive as planned.
   - ☐ b. swim across the current.
   - ☐ c. ascend to the surface.
2. During a drift dive, my buddy stops by ducking out of the flow and the current starts to carry me away. I should
   - ☐ a. fight the current by swimming into it.
   - ☐ b. also duck out of the current.
3. The primary cause of entanglement in the float line during a drift dive is
   - ☐ a. strong current.
   - ☐ b. wrong line choice.
   - ☐ c. reel failure.
   - ☐ d. slack in the line.

How did you do?

1. c. 2. b. 3. d.

Knowledge Review – Drift Diving

Answer the following questions by selecting the best choice (or choices) from those provided. Be prepared to discuss the material at your next training session.

1. What are the advantages of drift diving? (Choose all that apply.)
   - ☐ Drifting along requires little effort.
   - ☐ I can stay longer and go deeper on a drift dive.
   - ☐ I can dive even in a moderate to strong current.
   - ☐ Navigation is easier because I don't return to a specific exit point.
2. My buddy and I plan to drift dive down a local river. What should we consider as part of our dive plan specific to drift diving? (Choose all that apply.)
   - ☐ Whether the river has obstructions and sufficient depth for our planned route.
   - ☐ Where will we exit downstream.
   - ☐ The need for surface support to exit.
   - ☐ How will we maintain buddy contact.
3. When drift diving from a boat, it's important to have someone on the boat who keeps track of where the divers are.
   - ☐ True
   - ☐ False
4. I'm on a dive boat approaching a dive site where I plan to drift along a wall. The boat pauses at the entry point to allow the divemaster and divers to evaluate conditions. At this point, the divemaster decides against the drift dive and the boat heads to a different site. What could be reasons for this decision? (Choose all that apply.)
   - ☐ Most divers onboard are new to drift diving and the current appears much stronger than usual.
   - ☐ It's windy, causing surface chop and whitecaps.
   - ☐ Many divers have been to this dive site before.
   - ☐ It's cloudy and most divers don't have dive lights.
5. During the dive briefing on the boat, the divemaster describes the entry technique in which all divers enter the water together and descend as a group immediately, with no time on the surface. This is necessary, because the dive starts on a small pinnacle before we drift over to the main wall. This entry is called a ________________ entry.
   - ☐ a. buoyant
   - ☐ b. negative
6. Especially when drift diving, it's important to never enter the water from a boat until signaled by the crew to do so.
   - ☐ True
   - ☐ False
7. I'm drift diving with a group of five other divers. Which of the following can help me and the group stay together? (Choose all that apply.)
   - ☐ As I descend, maintain buddy contact, but also stay with the group leader.
   - ☐ While drifting, stay up current from (behind) the group leader.
   - ☐ Continuously hold on to the float line.
   - ☐ If the group leader stops, stop until the leader continues onward.
8. What general procedures should I follow when waiting to exit the water onto a boat after a drift? (Choose all that apply.)
   - ☐ Swim toward the boat immediately after I surface.
   - ☐ Maintain buddy contact and stay close to the group.
   - ☐ Keep my mask on and my snorkel/regulator in my mouth.
   - ☐ Don't get under a diver who is climbing up the ladder.
9. During a drift dive, my buddy pauses to look at something by ducking out of the current behind the reef. I have to swim against the current a short distance to reunite, so my best option is to swim in midwater, well above the bottom, and swim with all my strength fighting the current.
   - ☐ True
   - ☐ False

10. My buddy and I momentarily stop to take a photo while making a group drift dive. When I look up, the group seems to have drifted around a corner, so we swim a little faster to catch up. However, after rounding the corner, we can't find the group even though visibility is good. Unless planned otherwise, we should

- ☐ swim faster until we catch up.
- ☐ look for the group for no more than one minute, then surface to reunite with the group.
- ☐ stop, hold on to a nonliving object if necessary and wait for the group leader to come back for us.

Student Statement

I completed this Knowledge Review to the best of my ability. For any questions I answered incorrectly or incompletely, I reviewed the explanation provided and now understand the material. In the case of anything about which I still have questions, I will review the material again and, if necessary, discuss it with my instructor at our next session.

☐ I agree ☐ I disagree

Name ______________________________

Date ______________________________

scenario

"Can't believe we saw all those fish," Don said, standing on the lakeshore, his dry suit still wet from the dive.

"They were everywhere," Jenny said to Sophia. "They're still in the area so we're going back for another dive. Do you and Erika want to come?"

"We want to," said Sophia, "but we're not diving dry like you two. I'm too chilled for another dive in my wet suit and Erika's already back at the car, toweled off and warm."

"Bummer," Jenny said, as Don helped her into her gear. "I'll try to shoot some video for you."

- *What do Don and Jenny not have to deal with that's clearly an issue for Erika and Sophia?*
- *What does this tell you about the advantages of diving dry?*
- *Although relatively large investments, what does this anecdote tell you about how dry suits "pay for themselves"?*

DRY SUIT DIVING 8

DRY SUIT DIVING

Introduction:
Heat, Water and the Diver

Sometimes people think that cold water takes the fun out of diving, but that's not true. It's *being cold* that takes the fun out, and this is a potential issue in all but the warmest water. Without exposure protection, diving would be limited to a relatively narrow area above and below the equator, and short, shallow dives during the summer months farther north and south.

Exposure suits open diving to the majority of the world's dive sites. The coolest water calls for diving *dry* for maximum insulation so you have more dive time or, in the coldest water, so you can dive at all. Thanks to modern dry suits, though, even in very cold water you can dive in reasonable comfort.

LEARNING OBJECTIVES

By the end of this section, I should be able to answer these questions:

1. Why do I get cold underwater?
2. What is hypothermia? What are its signs and symptoms?
3. Why can mild hypothermia be a serious problem for scuba divers?
4. How do I avoid hypothermia?

Exposure suits open diving to the majority of the world's dive sites. The coolest water calls for diving dry for maximum insulation so you have more dive time or, in the coldest water, so you can dive at all.

Why You Get Cold

Recall from the PADI Open Water Diver course that water absorbs significantly more heat than air does. Because of this, without exposure protection, water at a temperature that's comfortable in air can make you dangerously cold in as little as an hour.

Exposure suits offset this by substantially slowing heat loss. With sufficient insulation and moderately warm water, they can even slow heat loss enough that your body can keep up with the loss. In these conditions, you can stay underwater indefinitely (with respect to comfort and temperature).

However, in many circumstances, while exposure suits greatly slow heat loss, you still lose heat faster than your body generates it. After enough time, you would get cold. But, assuming you wear the proper exposure suit, you can finish the dive before you lose enough heat to get cold.

Shivering is a warning sign of hypothermia. If you experience uncontrollable shivering, end the dive, exit the water and seek warmth.

Hypothermia

In the PADI Open Water Diver course, you learned that without adequate protection, or by overstaying in cold water, you're not only uncomfortable, you can suffer *hypothermia*. Hypothermia results when the body core temperature drops below normal.

Most divers leave the water before this point because it is uncomfortable. But, hypothermia can occur if the diver ignores the warning signs and symptoms, or if something delays exiting.

Shivering is a warning sign of hypothermia. **If you experience uncontrollable shivering, end the dive, exit the water and seek warmth.** Keep in mind that even mild hypothermia is a safety concern because it interferes with thinking, weakens the diver and reduces endurance. Severe hypothermia leads to unconsciousness and death.

Hypothermia signs and symptoms include:

- Uncontrollable shivering
- Numbness, especially in the hands and feet
- Blueness of the skin (which may be hard to see underwater)
- Sleepiness, drowsiness and general fatigue
- Carelessness/poor decision making

Severe hypothermia signs and symptoms also include:

- Confusion
- Shivering stops
- Unconsciousness
- Death

To avoid hypothermia, wear adequate exposure protection for the dive. If you underestimate and begin feeling cold, end the dive and get a more appropriate exposure suit before you experience hypothermia. Even with an appropriate suit, end your dive and seek warmth when you start to feel a bit too cool, *well within* your temperature comfort level. Leave enough "heat reserve" in case something delays exiting the water. Don't ignore hypothermia signs and symptoms, especially shivering.

Note that drinking alcohol or urinating in a wet suit may make you feel warm, but both practices actually *speed* cooling. This is because the body conserves heat by reducing blood flow to the skin. Alcohol dilates your skin capillaries, which is why you feel warmer. Warm fluid (urine) in your suit feels warm, so your skin capillaries dilate. In both cases, increased blood flow to the skin accelerates heat loss, even though you feel warmer for a while. (Besides the heat-loss issue, consuming alcohol before diving is an obviously unsafe practice due to impaired judgment, loss of motor skill coordination and slowed response times.)

EXERCISE-1

1. Without exposure protection, I get cold underwater, because water absorbs significantly more heat than air does.
   - ☐ True ☐ False
2. Signs and symptoms of hypothermia include (choose all that apply):
   - ☐ a. uncontrollable shivering.
   - ☐ b. numbness in the extremities.
   - ☐ c. unconsciousness.
   - ☐ d. poor decision-making.
3. Even mild hypothermia can be a safety concern, because it impairs thinking.
   - ☐ True ☐ False
4. During a dive, I begin to feel chilled. To avoid hypothermia, I should
   - ☐ a. urinate in my wet suit and plan on sitting alone on the trip back to port.
   - ☐ b. end the dive and seek warmth.
   - ☐ c. swim faster.

How did you do?

1. True. 2. a, b, c, d. 3. True. 4. b.

LEARNING OBJECTIVES

By the end of this section, I should be able to answer these questions:

1. How do wet suits and dry suits differ in how they insulate me?

2. What are at least three advantages and three disadvantages of using a dry suit compared to using a wet suit?

Wet Suits and Dry Suits

To understand how dry suit diving differs from wet suit diving, it helps to start by learning more detail about the two technologies. In the PADI Open Water Diver course, you learned that wet suits keep you warm (i.e., slow heat loss substantially) by surrounding you with neoprene foam, which is a good insulator. Water seeps in and gets trapped, after which it doesn't contribute to heat loss.

Dry suits come in a variety of materials and keep you warm by keeping you dry. The air (or other gas in the suit, like argon) trapped in an insulating undergarment and/or the suit itself (more about this shortly) slows heat loss.

Advantages and Disadvantages

Dry suits have several advantages over wet suits, and disadvantages as well.

Advantages

- Insulation – This is the biggest reason for diving dry; you dive in cooler water with more comfort, use less gas, reduce hypothermia risk and make more/longer dives. You can also vary your insulation with the same suit by changing undergarments.

- No insulation loss with depth – Wet suit neoprene compresses and insulates less as you go deeper. With most dry suits, depth has little effect on insulating ability (it does affect some types – more about this in the next subsection).
- Forgiving fit – Unlike wet suits, which must fit snuggly, dry suits allow more physical variation for a given size and cut.
- Warmer before and after the dive – This is a big advantage in cooler conditions, because you get out of the suit dry. You also don't get into a cold wet suit when making a repetitive dive.
- Easier transition to the water – Using a dry suit avoids the cold "rush" you feel entering cooler water in a wet suit. The colder the water, the more you appreciate this benefit.

Disadvantages

- Higher initial cost – This is noticeable, but in the long run dry suits are often cheaper because they tend to last longer. Usually, your cost-per-underwater-hour declines, because you make more dives and/or longer dives on each outing.
- More maintenance – Dry suits have valves and special zippers that require more post dive care than do wet suits; but, it's not significantly more.
- More drag – Most divers find that dry suits have a bit more drag and are a bit more tiring when making long swims.
- More weight – Dry suits typically need more weight than full wet suits, but not that much more for most types.

Dry suits provide superior insulation to wet suits by surrounding you with a layer of air or other gas.

One advantage of dry suits is that they have a forgiving fit compared to wet suits, which must fit snuggly. For a given size and cut, dry suits allow more physical variation.

Dry suits have a higher initial cost than wet suits, though they are often cheaper in the long run. This is because they usually last longer, and your cost-per-underwater-hour declines, because you make more dives and/or longer dives on each outing.

- More likely to overheat – Dry suits insulate so well that if the air temperature is warm (especially just before the dive), you have to be careful to avoid overheating.

Looking at the advantages and disadvantages, don't be surprised if you determine that you will still dive in wet suits more often. Many active divers have both wet suits and dry suits so they can choose the one that's best for a particular dive or dive series.

EXERCISE-2

1. ________ suits are made of neoprene and let in a little water. _______ suits are made of different materials and surround you with air or gas.
   - ☐ a. Wet; Dry
   - ☐ b. Dry; Wet
2. _______suits require a close fit. Most ________ suits do not lose insulation with increasing depth.
   - ☐ a. Wet; dry
   - ☐ b. Dry; wet

How did you do?

1. a. 2. a.

LEARNING OBJECTIVES

By the end of this section, I should be able to answer these questions:

1. What six factors should I consider when choosing a dry suit?
2. What are the two basic dry suit types and how do they differ?
3. What are the three most common types of dry suit seals?
4. How do I adjust a neck seal for proper fit?
5. What is the carotid sinus reflex, and how do I prevent it?
6. Why do dry suits have special zippers, and where are they located?
7. What two valves does a dry suit have? Why?
8. What are six considerations when choosing dry suit undergarments?
9. What options exist for my head, hands and feet when dry suit diving?

Dry Suit Types and Features

Choosing a Dry Suit

Before getting into specific dry suit types and features, there are six factors to think about when choosing a dry suit and an undergarment for it.

- Water temperature – This is the primary consideration, with influences from the five to follow.

Water temperature, your thermal characteristics, your activity level, the dive depth and duration, and the weather all influence how much insulation you need. If you notice you're feeling a bit cold on a dive, for the specific temperature, depth and duration, assume that you need more insulation.

Neoprene dry suits are very comfortable, and like wet suits lose insulation and buoyancy as you go deeper, due to compression.

- Your thermal characteristics – If you chill easily, you'll want more insulation. Go by your own personal characteristics – divers often differ a lot in this.
- Activity level – If you'll be relatively active, you'll stay warmer and need less insulation than if you rest in one place or swim very slowly.
- Depth – Water temperature generally decreases with depth, though the colder the surface water, usually the less significant the change at depth. Most dry suits don't lose insulation with depth, whereas wet suits do. But, you may need to choose your undergarment based on the depth.
- Duration – With EANx, computers, sidemount and recreational rebreathers, the door to longer no stop dives is open. Insulation that's adequate for a short dive may not be enough for longer and/or repetitive dives.
- Weather – Moderate temperature water may give you a choice between a full wet suit or dry suit. If it is bright and sunny, you may prefer the wet suit, but you may want to choose the dry suit if it's overcast or windy.

Shell dry suits keep you dry, but provide little or no insulation. You wear an undergarment for insulation.

Latex and silicone seals have a tapered cone that you will trim to fit you. Trim them in small increments, trying the seal on after each cut.

All these factors interrelate, and there's a psychological aspect to staying comfortably warm. But, if you notice you're feeling a bit cold on a dive, for the specific temperature, depth and duration, assume that you need more insulation.

Basic Dry Suit Types

In the PADI Dry Suit Diver course, you will learn that manufacturers use several different materials for dry suits. These have inherent advantages and disadvantages. Even with all these materials, we can divide dry suits into two types: neoprene dry suits and shell dry suits.

Neoprene dry suits use the same material as wet suits – neoprene rubber, usually backed with fabric on both sides – but you stay dry. The neoprene insulates you, so you often don't need an undergarment. Worn with an undergarment, they are among the warmest suits. The material stretches, making these suits very comfortable. Compared to other dry suits, they are more buoyant, and like wet suits, the material loses insulation and buoyancy as you go deeper, due to compression.

All other dry suits are **shell dry suits.** With these, the suit keeps you dry but provides little or no insulation. You wear an undergarment for insulation. Most (but not all) shell suit material has little or no stretch, so manufacturers use design features to provide mobility. Most have little buoyancy; some are negatively buoyant. The insulating characteristics and the buoyancy of the suit don't change as you go deeper, because the undergarment provides the insulation.

You can learn more about different suit materials from your PADI Dive Center or Resort, and in the PADI Dry Suit Diver course.

Seals

You need to stay dry, but have your face and hands outside your suit. To do this, dry suit seals keep water out of the suit at your wrists and neck (and sometimes face). The three common types are latex, neoprene and silicone seals.

Latex seals offer great flexibility, seal well and are easy to put on and take off, but are more delicate and need replacement more often than other seals. Neoprene seals are tough and last longer, though some divers don't find they seal as well, and they can be more difficult to don. Silicone seals are similar to latex, except made of tough silicone rubber. They don easily, seal well and last a long time – they're tougher than latex but not as tough as neoprene.

It's especially important to properly size your neck seal. Never dive with a neck seal that is excessively tight. Doing so can constrict the blood vessels passing through your neck, which can make you faint. Losing consciousness underwater is potentially life threatening, so be sure to size your neck seal properly.

Seals must fit properly or they're not comfortable and/or leak. If you choose neoprene seals, you'll buy your suit with them sized approximately, whereas latex and silicone seals have a tapered cone that you will trim to fit you. Trim latex/silicone seals in small increments, and then try the seal on. Leave some room for permanent stretch over time, though high-quality seals don't permanently stretch much. Better to leave them slightly too tight than too loose – if you trim too much, you have to replace the seal. Your instructor or dive shop can help you with this.

You don't trim neoprene seals. Instead, you adjust them by stretching them. Usually, they're initially slightly smaller than desired, so after trying them on, if they're too tight, you can stretch them for several hours by inserting an appropriately sized round object – a small scuba cylinder for neck seals, beverage can for wrists, etc. Again, leave them slightly too tight so there's room for permanent stretch with use.

Some suits have systems that allow you to quickly change out latex/silicone seals. This is useful in case of seal damage, or if you accidentally over-trim a seal. They also offer other options you'll learn about in the PADI Dry Suit Diver course.

It's especially important to properly size your neck seal. **Never dive with a neck seal that is excessively tight.** Doing so can constrict the blood vessels passing through your neck, which can make you feel ill and light-headed, and you can faint.

Some physiologists think this is the *carotid sinus reflex* – the body mistakes the pressure on your neck arteries for elevated blood pressure and slows the heart. Other physiologists think the constriction blocks blood flow leaving the head, reducing overall blood flow to the brain and causing the same symptoms. It doesn't really matter which it is – either way, losing consciousness underwater is potentially life threatening, so be sure to size your neck seal properly. Your PADI Dive Center or Resort can help with seal-sizing if you need assistance.

Dry Suit Zippers

It's the dry suit zipper that's made the modern dry suit possible – it has to be a special zipper that differs from wet suit zippers, because it must be watertight. It's also one of the most expensive parts of your suit, so care for it properly.

Zipper locations vary, each giving different ways to get into your suit. The most common locations are across the shoulders, and from behind the shoulder across the chest to the opposite hip. The shoulder entry makes the suit easy to put

The shoulder entry zipper location makes the suit easy to put on, but requires help to zip and unzip.

Across the chest is a popular zipper location that allows you to zip and unzip the suit yourself.

on, but requires help to zip and unzip. Across the chest is a popular self-don location that you can zip and unzip yourself. Other self-don zipper locations include across the waist and from the center waist in back through the crotch to mid chest, though these are not as common.

Most dry suit exhaust valves are mounted on the left shoulder or upper chest. When you ascend with your upper body above your feet and the valve at the highest point, gas vents automatically. You can also release gas manually by pressing the valve.

Inflator and Exhaust Valves

Because dry suits are air spaces, you must equalize them by adding gas as you descend to avoid a suit squeeze – a squeeze caused by the gas in your suit becoming so compressed that the suit can cause welts and bruises, and even restrict breathing. As you ascend, you need to release expanding gas to avoid uncontrolled buoyancy and a runaway ascent, just like you do with a BCD. To accomplish these, your dry suit has an inflator valve and an exhaust valve.

The inflator valve is most commonly on the chest, but may be located elsewhere. It receives gas from your regulator (or an independent inflation system) via a hose similar to the one supplying your BCD, but usually longer so it can reach the valve. When diving dry, you connect the inflator valve hose after donning your scuba kit, and release it before taking it off. This is also a consideration when assisting or rescuing a dry suit diver.

Most dry suit exhaust valves are mounted on the left shoulder or upper torso, but may also be on the forearm. You set most dry suit exhaust valves to vent automatically, controlling how much gas your suit holds (depending upon your buoyancy needs) by rotating the outside of the valve. When you ascend with your upper body above your feet and the valve at the highest point, gas vents automatically. You can also release gas manually by pressing the valve.

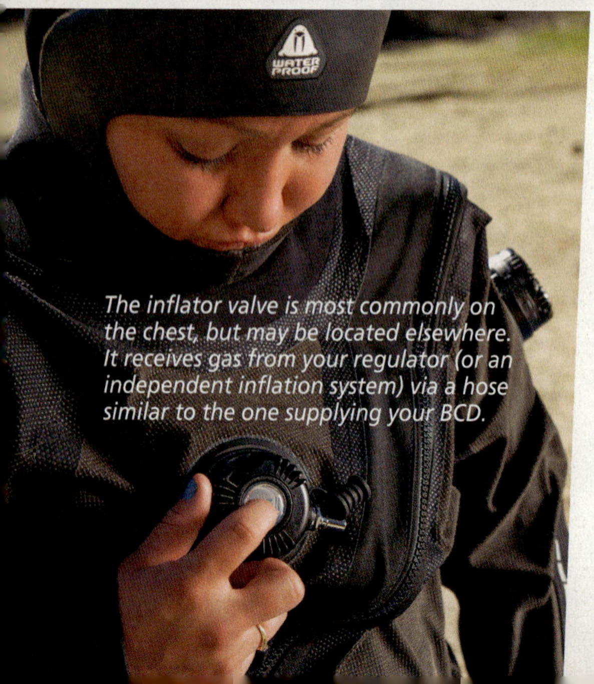

The inflator valve is most commonly on the chest, but may be located elsewhere. It receives gas from your regulator (or an independent inflation system) via a hose similar to the one supplying your BCD.

Undergarments

Modern undergarments do an excellent job of insulating you for a comfortable dive. Today, you have a wide range of styles and types from which to choose based on your personal needs. Here are six considerations to discuss with your PADI Dive Center or Resort when investing in an undergarment.

- Cost – The more you can invest, the more you get in features, insulating ability and durability. But, more expensive garments are usually less expensive in the long run because they last longer and give you more dive time.
- Insulating ability – In moderate temperatures, you can be over-insulated and uncomfortably warm, especially if you'll be active, so choose insulation based on the temperature and what you'll be doing. You may have two or more undergarments, or layers you can add and subtract, for different temperatures. Some materials and designs insulate better than others, but may require a higher investment. In extreme temperatures or on long dives (especially tec dives), battery-driven heating systems for undergarments are becoming more common.

- Insulation characteristics when wet – The best materials provide good insulation even when wet, which is a benefit if you have any seepage, but is especially important in the event of a leak.
- Care – Some undergarments have stringent care requirements; others you treat like normal clothes.
- Bulk – The best undergarments insulate well with little bulk. Lower-cost undergarments have to be bulkier for the same insulating qualities, so you may need more weight and have to deal with more drag. Some top-quality garments reduce bulk by being thicker only where gear and pressure will compress the material excessively.
- Fit – The garment should fit comfortably and give you full motion range. Beyond these, you also have choices that include one-piece or two-piece designs, pockets and special padding for added comfort.

Head, Hands and Feet

With most (but not all) dry suits, you wear a separate wet suit hood, often intended specifically for the dry suit. But, in the coolest water, divers commonly wear dry hoods that are built into the suit.

In water 10°C/50°F and warmer, divers typically wear wet suit gloves. For colder water, some divers wear dry gloves that are connected to the suit sleeves; these allow the hands to remain dry and warmer. Dry suits with quick-change seal systems usually allow you to go from wet suit gloves to dry gloves and back, depending upon the water temperature.

Your PADI Dive Center or Resort can help you choose undergarments best suited to your diving needs.

With most dry suits, you wear a separate wet suit hood. But, in the coolest water, divers commonly wear dry hoods that are built into the suit.

In water 10°C/50°F and warmer, divers typically wear wet suit gloves.

Although dry suits are more forgiving than wet suits with respect to fit, with your undergarments on, your suit should neither be overly tight nor overly loose.

Most dry suits have built-in boots. A few use separate protective boots over a built-in sock that encloses your foot, but in both cases your feet stay dry. After choosing your boots, try on your fins. It is common to need a larger size fin for your dry suit than for your wet suit boots.

Most dry suits have built-in boots. A few use separate protective boots over a built-in sock that encloses your foot, but in both cases your feet stay dry.

Overall Fit

Although dry suits are more forgiving than wet suits with respect to fit, you still need a suit that fits properly. This means that, with your undergarments on, your suit should neither be overly tight nor overly loose.

Excess slack from too loose a fit can create buoyancy problems. This is particularly true of the legs. If the legs are too long for your size, it's easier to accumulate too much gas there, which can cause an uncontrolled, feet-first ascent (more about this later).

EXERCISE-3

1. Which of the following should I consider when choosing a dry suit and an undergarment? (Choose all that apply.)
   - ☐ a. Water temperature
   - ☐ b. My thermal characteristics
   - ☐ c. Dive duration
   - ☐ d. Weather
2. ______________ dry suits often don't require an undergarment, but __________ dry suits always require one for insulation.
   - ☐ a. Shell; neoprene
   - ☐ b. Neoprene; shell
   - ☐ c. Hoodless; hooded
   - ☐ d. Rubber; canvas
3. I'm choosing a new dry suit and my PADI Pro recommends silicone seals. The advantages of silicone seals include that they
   - ☐ a. cost the least.
   - ☐ b. are the toughest seals.
   - ☐ c. adjust by stretching them.
   - ☐ d. don easily and are durable.
4. My PADI Dive Center just replaced my latex neck seal. To adjust it, I should
   - ☐ a. trim the tapered cone in small amounts until I get the correct fit.
   - ☐ b. stretch it over a small scuba cylinder.
   - ☐ c. let it stretch to fit with use.
5. I should never dive with an excessively tight, improperly adjusted neck seal, because doing so can cause me to lose consciousness, which is potentially life threatening.
   - ☐ True ☐ False
6. Dry suit zippers differ from wet suit zippers, because they must be watertight.
   - ☐ True ☐ False
7. Failure to add gas to my dry suit as I descend can cause
   - ☐ a. suit squeeze.
   - ☐ b. a runaway ascent.
8. One consideration in choosing an undergarment is how well it insulates when wet.
   - ☐ True ☐ False
9. I'm selecting a new dry suit at my local PADI shop. One thing I should check is whether my __________ still fit(s) with my dry suit, or whether I need a larger size.
   - ☐ a. fins
   - ☐ b. mask
   - ☐ c. regulator

How did you do?

1. a, b, c, d. 2. b. 3. d. 4. a. 5. True. 6. True. 7. a. 8. True. 9. a.

LEARNING OBJECTIVES

By the end of this section, I should be able to answer these questions:

1. How do I put on and take off my dry suit?
2. How do I eliminate excess air from my dry suit after I put it on?

Exactly how you put on and take off a dry suit depends upon the zipper location. It may be a little cumbersome at first, but you'll find you get into your suit fairly quickly after doing it a couple times.

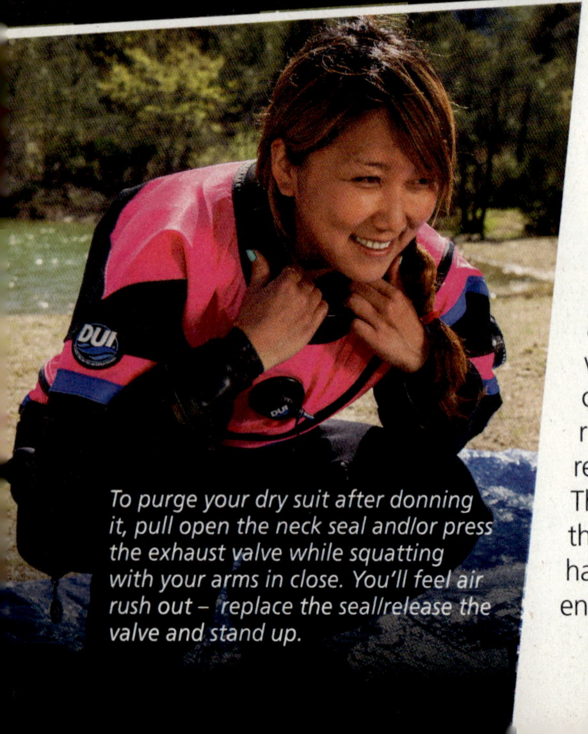

To purge your dry suit after donning it, pull open the neck seal and/or press the exhaust valve while squatting with your arms in close. You'll feel air rush out – replace the seal/release the valve and stand up.

Putting on Your Dry Suit

One of the first things most divers notice about dry suits is that they're easier to put on than wet suits, because they don't fit as tightly. Only the wrist and neck seals require a snug fit that you must deal with while putting the suit on.

Exactly how you put on and take off a dry suit depends upon the zipper location. Your instructor and the manufacturer instructions can give you the recommended method specific to your suit. It may be a little cumbersome at first, but you'll find you get into your suit fairly quickly after doing it a couple times. Regardless, there are four guidelines that apply to getting into virtually any dry suit.

The first is *timing*. Dry suits insulate very well, so don them at the last possible moment if you might overheat. You can put most types on partially, helping you keep cool until you're ready to gear up completely. If it's cold out, though, you may want to get into your suit immediately so you stay warm.

The second guideline *is be careful with seals*. Especially when putting your hands and head through seals, be careful to not damage them. Remove watches and jewelry. You may lubricate the seals with talcum powder or a manufacturer recommended lubricant (avoid petroleum-based lubricants like Vaseline®). Be sure the seals lie flat without trapping hair, which will wick water into the suit.

Third, *zip all the way*. Pull the zipper gently and steadily, making sure nothing gets trapped in it as you close it. Debris may not only cause a leak, but may damage it. Give the zipper an extra gentle tug to be sure it is closed at the end, because if it's open even a little, you'll get wet. Lubricate the zipper as recommended by the manufacturer to keep it zipping easily.

The fourth guideline is to *purge excess air*. You do this so the air doesn't balloon around your neck when you enter the water. To purge your suit, pull open the neck seal and/or press the exhaust valve while squatting with your arms crossed tightly. You'll feel air rush out. Then, replace the seal/release the valve and stand up. The suit will feel snugger with the excess air gone, but you'll still have to release some when you enter the water.

EXERCISE-4

1. How I put on my dry suit depends primarily on
   - ☐ a. my undergarment.
   - ☐ b. my BCD type.
   - ☐ c. the zipper location.
2. After putting on my dry suit, I need to purge excess air from it. To do this, I
   - ☐ a. enter the water.
   - ☐ b. add air using the inflator valve.
   - ☐ c. open a seal/the exhaust valve, then squat.

How did you do?

1. c. 2. c.

Diving with a Dry Suit

The primary difference between diving in a wet suit and diving in a dry suit is how you control your buoyancy. As discussed shortly, there are two methods for controlling buoyancy underwater with a dry suit – using just the suit, or using your BCD. Either way, the recommended technique for positive buoyancy at the surface is to use your BCD, not your suit. To float you at the surface, your suit would be uncomfortably overinflated (if it would actually hold that much gas – some won't). Beyond this, with either method of controlling buoyancy, you use your BCD to handle some dry suit emergencies (you learn about these in the next subsection).

Weighting

Because a dry suit holds gas and you're often insulating for colder water, you may need a bit more weight with a dry suit than you do with a wet suit, depending upon the suit type and undergarment. You can make it easier to handle this weight and keep yourself in proper trim by distributing weight evenly on your body in three ways:

1. Use accessory weights, like ankle weights, to redistribute weight for proper trim.

2. On a belt, use smaller weights that you can spread out instead of fewer large weights.

3. Divide your total weight between two systems, such as the BCD weight system and a weight belt or weight harness.

In an emergency, you don't have to be able to quick-release *all* weights, just enough to assure positive buoyancy.

Determining proper weight in a dry suit follows the procedures you learned in the PADI Open Water Diver course, and is the same as when wearing any other exposure suit:

- Enter the water fully suited in all your gear, including the dry suit and undergarment you will wear.

- Vent excess air from your BCD *and* dry suit. Your dry suit exhaust valve should be fully open.

LEARNING OBJECTIVES

By the end of this section, I should be able to answer these questions:

1. When do I use my BCD when diving with a dry suit?

2. What's the recommended technique for maintaining positive buoyancy at the surface when dry suit diving?

3. Why may I need more weight for a dry suit than a wet suit?

4. What three ways can I distribute weight evenly on my body?

5. How do I adjust the weight worn with a dry suit so I'm properly weighted?

6. What are the two methods for controlling buoyancy underwater while diving with a dry suit?

7. How do I add air to a dry suit underwater?

8. How do I vent air from a dry suit underwater?

- Add and subtract weight until you float at eye level holding a normal breath. When you exhale, you should start to sink slowly.
- If checking with a full cylinder, add 2.5 kilograms/5 pounds to correct for the buoyancy increase as you use up your gas.

If you are a PADI Rebreather Diver using a rebreather, follow the same procedure, but you should adjust until you just barely float, with the top of your head at the surface rather than at eye level. With an eSCR type of rebreather, you typically add 1 kilogram/2 pounds if checking with a full supply cylinder.

You always want to avoid overweighting, but it is especially important when diving dry. If you're over-weighted, you have to put too much gas in the suit, which is uncomfortable and can cause buoyancy control problems we'll look at in the next subsection.

Controlling Your Buoyancy

How you make buoyancy adjustments underwater while diving dry has evolved over the years. At present, there are two basic methods that depend upon personal preference, weighting and manufacturer recommendations (always follow manufacturer recommendations). Your instructor will show you either or both methods, as appropriate for the suit you're using, local practices and the situation.

Method One: Controlling buoyancy with only the suit. Don't use your BCD (except to deal with an emergency like a flooded suit, if necessary) until you return to the surface. This avoids suit squeeze, which is when the suit compresses painfully tight on you. If you're weighted properly, the suit adjusts your buoyancy at the same time. There will only be a slight change in the air you need in your suit as you consume the air in your cylinder over the course of the dive. You only have to control a single system (your suit) when you change

One method of controlling your buoyancy underwater is to add gas only to the suit. You don't use your BCD (except to deal with an emergency, like a flooded suit, if necessary) until you return to the surface.

The second method for controlling buoyancy is to add enough gas to prevent suit squeeze as you descend, but offset the loss of suit buoyancy by using your BCD, just as you would with a wet suit.

When it's time to ascend, start by gently swimming upward. Raise your left shoulder/arm to raise the exhaust valve, and allow expanding gas to escape as you rise. If you're using your BCD to control buoyancy, vent your BCD, too.

Correction: If your exhaust valve jams closed, to prevent a runaway ascent you'll have to vent gas through a wrist or neck seal (you may get wet). If necessary, flare your body horizontally to increase drag and slow you while you continue to exhaust gas, and use a line (if available) to slow you.

3. Accidental weight release (and can't recover weights)

Cause: You don't have to be diving dry for accidental weight release to cause a buoyancy emergency. The usual causes are improper quick-release attachment, mishandling weights, or accidentally activating a release mechanism by snagging it.

Prevention: Be sure you're familiar with your weight system and proper operation. Avoid accidental release by being cautious when you're close to the bottom, or near something that could snag and trip a release. Using multiple weight systems helps avoid extreme buoyancy if you accidentally release one. Of course, inspect your weight system for proper setup before the dive.

Correction: Flare your body horizontally to increase drag and dump as much gas as possible. Use a line (if available) to slow your ascent.

4. Over-weighted

Cause: The usual cause is failure to conduct a buoyancy (weight) check and diving over-weighted, particularly while controlling buoyancy with the dry suit. This makes it necessary to use a large gas volume in the suit to maintain neutral buoyancy. On ascent, this gas expands faster than the diver vents it, leading to a rapid ascent.

Prevention: Dive properly weighted. Conduct a weight check before starting the dive if you're not sure how much you need.

Correction: Stop an ascent that's starting to run away and allow your exhaust valve to catch up, and then continue your ascent more slowly. If necessary, you can vent gas through a wrist or neck seal, though this may let some water into the suit. If you can't control and stop a runaway ascent, slow your ascent by flaring out and/or using a line (if available). After the dive, correct your weighting.

Regardless of the cause, if you find yourself in an uncontrolled ascent, remember to breathe normally and not hold your breath.

Excess Gas in the Legs

Although not a common event because it's easily prevented, excess gas in the legs can cause a hazardous, upside-down uncontrolled ascent. The problem is that you can't vent gas from the suit with your legs above you. The suit legs become buoyant, and it becomes difficult to turn so your exhaust valve is elevated. Ascending this way can leave you floating upside down at the surface, and with some suits even make your fins come off.

Cause: Excess buoyancy and allowing the legs to get above shoulder level at the same time can cause an ascent with the legs elevated. Or, starting to ascend with legs above shoulder level can cause the problem.

Prevention: Start by avoiding excess buoyancy as just described. Do not ascend with your feet above shoulder (exhaust valve) level. Don't raise your legs when your buoyancy's in question. Some dry suits have ankle exhaust valves to help prevent excess buoyancy in the legs. Dry suits with boots that go over neoprene socks resist swelling at the feet, reducing the risk of fin loss – but you can still have an uncontrolled, legs-up ascent.

Correction: If possible, grab something to hold you in place and give you leverage to bring your legs down. Failing that, one technique is to kick hard to rotate forward and continue until you reach a head-up, feet-down position (forward roll out), or arch your back and swim upward and backward until the same position (backward roll out).

One technique for correcting excess gas in the legs is to tuck your legs up and roll sideways to your right while attempting to vent gas.

Another technique is the ball tuck. Bring your knees to your chest and tuck into a ball to squeeze air from the legs into the upper suit. At the same time, roll sideways to your right onto your back as you attempt to vent through the exhaust valve.

If you can't recover and end up floating upside down – legs up, sticking out of the water – you may not be able to swim into an upright position. Inflate your BCD to bring your chest and head to the surface, and then deflate your suit.

Flooded Dry Suit

A little bit of seepage into a dry suit from time to time isn't unusual, but if it's frequent, determine and correct the cause. A properly fitted and functioning dry suit should keep you dry the vast majority of the time. On the other hand, flooding your dry suit – taking in a substantial amount of water – is unusual and can compromise your insulation and warmth, as well as your buoyancy. Most floods are partial, dousing one body area and (typically) spreading below the leak as water collects in the feet. Catastrophic floods – water filling almost the entire suit – are rare, but possible.

Causes: There are many possible causes of suit flooding, some of which you'll notice immediately, and others that can occur well into the dive. They include a zipper that's not closed or is damaged, material caught in the zipper, seal leakage (damaged or placed improperly), and exhaust valve leakage (due to dirt, its being improperly secured to the suit or poor maintenance). Tears and holes can occur due to seam failure, chafing, tears, ripping, punctures or delamination (failure of the material).

Prevention: You prevent most leaks by donning your suit properly and carefully, and by properly maintaining it. Check the zipper for full closure before entering the water, and be careful around anything that could puncture or tear it.

Correction: Regardless of the cause, end the dive immediately. Use your BCD to restore your buoyancy if necessary and, in extreme instances, you might need to drop your weights. If you're properly weighted, though, you would not usually need to drop your weights to ascend. If you know where the leak is, keep it as low as possible to reduce gas loss.

EXERCISE-6

1. Inflating my dry suit in a long, continuous burst can cause excess buoyancy and a runaway ascent.
   ☐ True ☐ False
2. My weight system accidentally released and, unable to recover it, I am venting as much gas from my dry suit as possible as I ascend. I should also
   ☐ a. hang on to my buddy.
   ☐ b. remove my regulator and make an "ahhhhhhh" sound.
   ☐ c. flare out my body.
   ☐ d. partially inflate my BCD.
3. Excess gas in my dry suit legs can cause an uncontrolled ascent.
   ☐ True ☐ False
4. During a dry suit dive, I begin to float upward with my legs above shoulder level. One technique is to tuck into a ball and ___________ while attempting to vent gas.
   ☐ a. roll to my right
   ☐ b. swim backward
   ☐ c. swim forward
   ☐ d. lower my weights to my ankles
5. Following an uncontrolled ascent due to excess gas in the dry suit legs, a diver is floating upside down, legs up, sticking out of the water. To get into an upright position, the diver should
   ☐ a. use a knife/tool to puncture the dry suit feet.
   ☐ b. swim upright.
   ☐ c. inflate the BCD.
6. Shortly into a dry suit dive, my left arm is wet, with water running down my left side and accumulating around my left foot. However, my undergarment insulates well when wet and the water's not that cold. I should
   ☐ a. end the dive immediately.
   ☐ b. continue the dive as long as I'm comfortable.
   ☐ c. purge the water out of my suit.

How did you do?

1. True. 2. c. 3. True. 4. a. 5. c. 6. a.

LEARNING OBJECTIVES

By the end of this section, I should be able to answer these questions:

1. What are the general guidelines for dry suit care?

2. Where should I look to find out how to fix a leak on a specific dry suit?

Dry Suit Care

Every dry suit manufacturer has recommendations for the care and regular servicing of its products. These vary from suit to suit, so consult the recommendations for your suit. That said, the following general guidelines apply to most:

1. Wash the suit in fresh water after diving. If water entered the suit, wash the inside too (or as the manufacturer recommends).
2. Hang the suit open over a thick bar or other rounded surface, bent at the knees or at the waist. Allow it to dry thoroughly, out of direct sunlight, before storage. Store it rolled or folded loosely (as specified by the manufacturer) away from heat, chemicals, oil and direct sunlight.
3. Most dry suits require seal and zipper maintenance. Consult the manufacturer instructions; be aware that most manufacturers tell you to not put silicone on the zipper.
4. Launder undergarments as specified by the manufacturer.
5. Your other gear can puncture your dry suit or damage a valve, so when going diving, carry the suit separately, in its own bag.

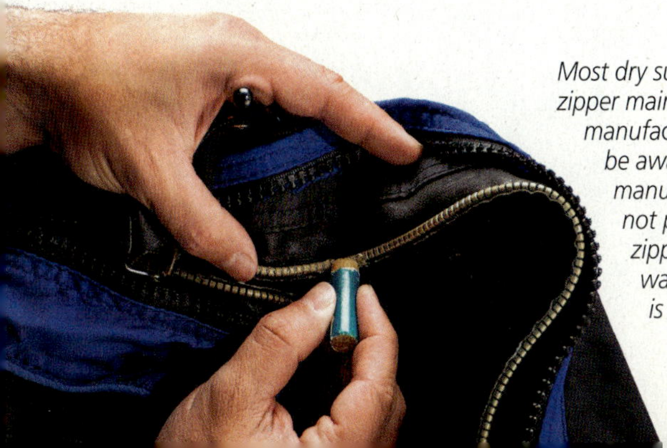

Most dry suits require seal and zipper maintenance. Consult the manufacturer instructions; be aware that most manufacturers tell you to not put silicone on the zipper. Applying special wax to lubricate the teeth is a common practice.

Most dry suits include or have a patch kit available for repairing small holes and leaks. Because different suit materials require different patches and cements, use only those recommended by the manufacturer for your suit.

You can get leak repair information from the suit's instruction booklet, manufacturer and from your PADI Dive Center or Resort. Some manufacturers have basic leak location and/or repair information online. Talk to your PADI Dry Suit Diver Instructor as well.

As mentioned earlier, some dry suits have wrist and neck seals designed to quickly release for replacement in case you damage a seal. You need to have a spare seal to take advantage of this, but it allows you to make a repair in minutes that would normally take hours.

Some dry suits have wrist and neck seals designed to quickly release for replacement in case you damage a seal. This allows you to make a repair in minutes that would normally take hours.

EXERCISE-7

1. Although dry suits vary in their recommended care, virtually all recommend you wash the suit in fresh water after use, and dry it thoroughly before storing it.
   ☐ True ☐ False
2. I should look for leak repair information for my dry suit (choose all that apply):
   ☐ a. on the manufacturer website.
   ☐ b. at my PADI Dive Center or Resort.
   ☐ c. in the instruction book for the suit.
   ☐ d. from my PADI Dry Suit Diver Instructor.

How did you do?

1. True. 2. a, b, c, d.

Dry Suit Diving Guidelines

The following guidelines have been adopted and endorsed by several dry suit manufacturers.

1. Complete a dry suit diving course from an instructor and stay current by practicing your skills often.
2. Use a BCD for surface flotation and backup.
3. Know your equipment and emergency procedures.
4. Practice your dry suit diving skills under controlled conditions until they become second nature.
5. Dive with a buddy who understands your dry suit system.
6. Use the correct amount of insulation for the water temperature in which you are diving and exercise rate.
7. Do not weight yourself heavier than neutral buoyancy with an empty cylinder. You should be able to make a safety stop with 50 bar/500 psi or less in your cylinder.
8. Inspect your valves, zipper and seals before each dive.
9. Maintain your dry suit and have it serviced by a qualified individual as recommended by the manufacturer.
10. Know your limitations and do not exceed them.
11. Water or air temperatures below 21°C/70°F constitute cold water diving. Water or air temperatures below 5°C/40°F are potentially very hazardous and require special equipment, training, preparation and procedures.

DRY SUIT DIVER SPECIALTY

At your instructor's discretion, the Dry Suit Adventure Dive credits toward the PADI Dry Suit Diver Specialty course. The course gives you more opportunities to apply and practice dry suit skills, including:

- Exposure suit overview
- Dry suit types and materials – advantages/disadvantages
- More on handling problems
- More on leak repair

Remember to log your training dives with the PADI Mobile App or at padi.com.

TUSA
NGER
ina

Knowledge Review – Dry Suit Diving

Answer the following questions by selecting the best choice (or choices) from those provided. Be prepared to discuss the material at your next training session.

1. Hypothermia occurs when a diver's core body temperature becomes __________ normal. To avoid hypothermia, always wear adequate ________ protection before, during and after a dive.
   - ☐ a. above; sun
   - ☐ b. above; exposure
   - ☐ c. below; sun
   - ☐ d. below; exposure
2. Even mild hypothermia can be a problem for divers, because it causes (choose all that apply):
   - ☐ unclear thinking.
   - ☐ poor decision making.
   - ☐ severe joint and limb pain.
   - ☐ reduced strength and endurance.
3. I'm trying on dry suits at my local PADI Dive Center and the dive pro asks me about the comfort of the neck seal. Why is the neck seal fit important?
   - ☐ It should be loose enough to allow my hood to fit underneath it.
   - ☐ It should be extremely tight.
   - ☐ If it is too tight, it can restrict blood flow and cause light-headedness and unconsciousness.
4. On a hot summer day, my buddy and I are preparing to dive in a cool mountain lake. I should put my dry suit on ____________ as I prepare my equipment to avoid ____________.
   - ☐ a. last; overheating
   - ☐ b. last; hypothermia
   - ☐ c. first; overheating
   - ☐ d. first; hypothermia
5. Regarding buoyancy control, match the following:

Positive buoyancy at surface	Add gas to dry suit
Neutral buoyancy underwater	Vent gas from suit/BCD
To prevent squeeze on descent	Add gas to BCD
Controlling buoyancy on ascent	Add gas to suit/BCD

6. After putting my suit on I must ____________ excess air so my suit doesn't ____________ when I enter the water.
   - ☐ a. add; squeeze
   - ☐ b. add; balloon
   - ☐ c. purge; squeeze
   - ☐ d. purge; balloon
7. If I set my dry suit exhaust valve correctly, I will never need to manually vent gas, even during an ascent.
   - ☐ True ☐ False
8. Which of the following is something I can do if I have too much air in my dry suit legs/feet and begin to rise feet first?
   - ☐ Rapidly tuck into a ball while rolling onto my back, then dump gas as needed.
   - ☐ Kick as hard as possible to swim to the bottom and grab hold of a nonliving object.
   - ☐ Inflate my BCD to bring my head up so that I can vent gas through my neck seal.
   - ☐ Release my weight pocket/belt and hold it against my ankles.
9. If I accidentally drop my weight system during a dive, I should (choose all that apply):
   - ☐ control my ascent by dumping as much gas as possible from my suit/BCD.
   - ☐ flare out to create drag and try to grasp the descent/ascent line, if possible.
   - ☐ vent gas continuously through my dry suit's exhaust valve or a seal as I ascend.
   - ☐ exhale/breathe normally throughout the ascent, being sure to never hold my breath.

10. During a dive, my buddy gets my attention and points to a neck seal tear, with a strong bubble stream coming from it. My buddy signals "cold." What should I do?

- ☐ Provide my buddy with my alternate air source.
- ☐ Immediately end the dive and help my buddy make a controlled ascent.
- ☐ Drop my buddy's weights and signal my buddy to swim hard to reach the surface.
- ☐ Hold the neck seal tear tightly and swim slowly toward the exit point.

Student Statement

I completed this Knowledge Review to the best of my ability. For any questions I answered incorrectly or incompletely, I reviewed the explanation provided and now understand the material. In the case of anything about which I still have questions, I will review the material again and, if necessary, discuss it with my instructor at our next session.

☐ I agree ☐ I disagree

Name ______________________________

Date ______________________________

scenario

Rob and Laura were swimming along a beautiful reef, enjoying the corals and marine life. Every few minutes Rob would stop, point to a particular fish, and give a "What's that?" shrug to his buddy. After seeing the fish Rob was pointing to, Laura would think for a second before writing down the name on her slate, then showing it to Rob.

"How did you know the names of all those fish?" Rob asked after the dive, amazed at Laura's ability to recognize everything they had seen.

"It's pretty easy," Laura said. "I learned to identify certain characteristics that let me categorize each fish. It makes each dive so much better now knowing what I'm seeing."

- *What can Rob do to become better at identifying and recognizing fish life?*
- *How can Laura's fish identification knowledge help protect fish and marine life?*

FISH IDENTIFICATION 9

FISH IDENTIFICATION

Fish Identification Strategy

Imagine you're on a one-week land safari in Africa. On the first day, you drive aimlessly around looking for animals, but don't see any. It continues like this for the second day, the third day. Then on the fourth day, you finally see a cat-like animal hunched down in the grass. Your daughter asks, "What is that animal? Why is it crouched like that?" However, you don't know and can't tell her, and you wish you knew yourself. The experience wasn't what it would have been if you knew what you were looking at.

LEARNING OBJECTIVES

By the end of this section, I should be able to answer these questions:

1. Approximately how many different fish species exist worldwide?
2. What simple strategy can I use to identify fish during a dive?

Imagine now that you're underwater, looking for a particular type of fish. If you don't know what it eats, or its habitat, you won't know where to look. Without that information, you just wander around. On an African savannah, this might be okay for a day or two, but when you dive, you're limited by gas supply and no stop time. Knowing more about fish makes the best use of your limited underwater time.

Knowing what a fish is, what it eats and where it lives makes a dive more interesting and enjoyable – it's more than simply swimming around sightseeing.

PADI Fish Identification is a good place to start expanding your knowledge about what you see underwater. Knowing what a fish is, what it eats and where it lives makes a dive more interesting and enjoyable – it's more than simply swimming around sightseeing. At an unfamiliar dive site, you're more likely to notice fish if you're aware of fish that can be found there.

Scientists estimate there are more than 21,000 fish species globally, more than 4000 of which are found on coral reefs. It would be difficult to memorize a substantial percentage of these species, so fish identification relies on a different strategy.

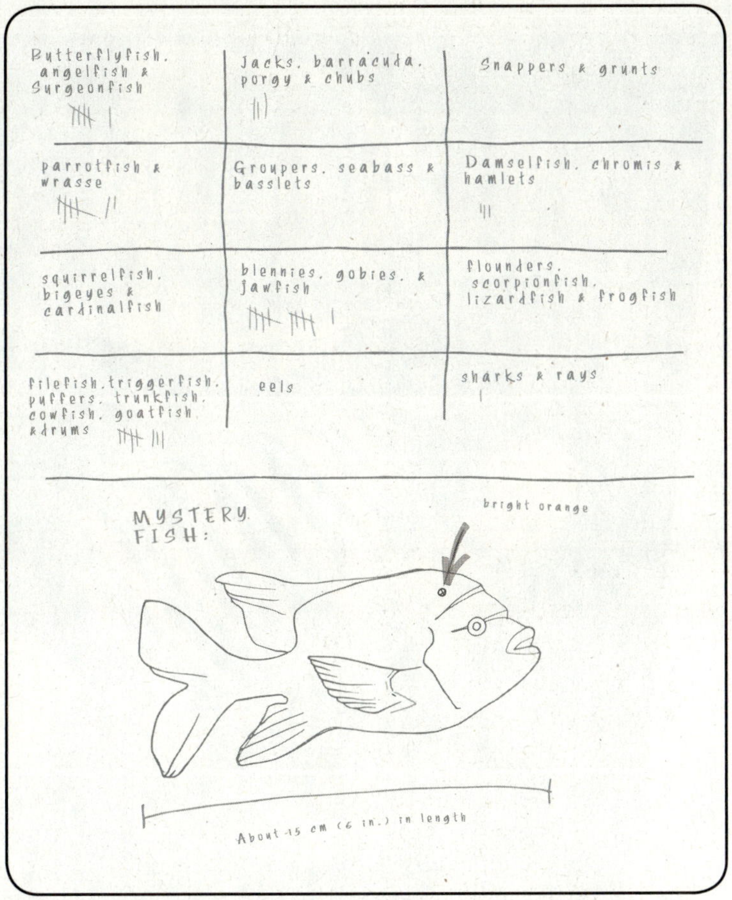

During a dive, you categorize fish as you spot them. One technique is to divide a slate or wet book pages into boxes, one for each family you expect to see, and then note in each when you spot a fish with the same or similar family characteristics.

To identify fish, you look for common characteristics that let you categorize them into 12 groups that represent 30 to 50 families. With practice, you learn to focus on the most common and representative species of different families. Understanding key characteristics, plus basic information about local ecology, provides the foundation for classifying most fish at the family level.

During a dive, you categorize fish as you spot them. One technique is to divide a slate or wet book pages into boxes, one for each family you expect to see, and then note in each when you spot a fish with the same or similar family characteristics. Fish ID slates can help you identify and categorize fish. Have a place to sketch and note physical characteristics of fish you don't recognize, so you can categorize them later.

You see more fish by being still, floating relaxed and neutrally buoyant. Chasing fish, sculling your hands and kicking up the bottom chases them away. For more about passive interactions, check out the Underwater Naturalist dive. You can also improve your buoyancy and fish-watching skills in the PADI Peak Performance Buoyancy specialty course.

EXERCISE-1

1. Scientists have identified approximately ______ species of fish in the world.
   - ☐ a. 580
   - ☐ b. 4000
   - ☐ c. 10,000
   - ☐ d. 21,000
2. To identify fish on a dive, I will look for certain characteristics that help me categorize them in particular families.
   - ☐ True ☐ False

How did you do?

1. d. 2. True.

Fish Groups and Characteristics

In tropical or temperate waters, you can usually group fish into one of these 12 family groups:

- Butterflyfish, angelfish and surgeonfish
- Jacks, barracuda, porgy and chubs
- Snappers and grunts
- Damselfish, chromis and hamlets
- Groupers, seabass and basslets
- Parrotfish and wrasse
- Squirrelfish, bigeyes and cardinalfish
- Blennies, gobies and jawfish
- Flounders, scorpionfish, lizardfish and frogfish
- Filefish, triggerfish, puffers, trunkfish, cowfish, goatfish, trumpetfish and drums
- Eels
- Sharks and rays

LEARNING OBJECTIVES

By the end of this section, I should be able to answer these questions:

1. What are the 12 groupings commonly used to identify fish in tropical or temperate waters?

2. What are the key characteristics of at least 30 of the most common fish families found in tropical and temperate waters worldwide?

Butterflyfish

Angelfish

Surgeonfish

Butterflyfish, Angelfish and Surgeonfish

Characterized by thin, oval or disk-shaped bodies, typically with bright colors and patterns.

Butterflyfish are usually round, small and have concave foreheads. They often have long snouts for feeding from crevices. Common types are the banded, foureye, raccoon, and lemon butterflyfish.

Angelfish tend to be darker in color, have long dorsal fins and rounded foreheads. They're some of the few fish that eat sponges. Common types are the queen, blue, French, gray, rock beauty, flame, emperor, and royal angelfish.

Surgeonfish, also called tangs, usually have solid color, and are typically identifiable by the spines sticking out from each side of their tail base. They eat algae, and common types include blue tang, ocean surgeonfish, doctorfish, Achilles tang, convict tang, and longnose unicornfish.

Jack

Barracuda

Chub

Porgy

Jacks, Barracuda, Porgy and Chub

These fish are usually silver and have forked tails. They are often among the largest fish on or near the reef.

Jacks, also called trevally, are large silver or bluish fish seen in open water at the reef's edge. Some species are solitary, while others school. They're strong swimming predators. Common types include bar, crevalle, bigeye, amberjack, and bluefin.

Barracuda are long, cylindrical and silver with faint markings. They have large mouths with visible sharp teeth. Large barracuda tend to travel alone, but smaller species may gather in schools. Common types include great, chevron, and Pacific barracuda.

Porgies, sometimes called sea bream, are oval shaped and have steep-sloping foreheads. They may have blue or yellow markings over a silvery base, and you may see them in sandy areas adjacent to the reef. Common types include sheepshead, saucer-eye, and double-bar sea bream.

Chub, or rudderfish, have elongated oval bodies, usually solid silver or gray/charcoal. You tend to see them in the water over the reef rather than close to the reef. Common types include yellow, Bermuda, and brassy rudderfish.

Snapper

Grunt

Snappers and Grunts

The distinguishing features of this group are long, tapered bodies, and heads that slope toward the mouth. Snappers and grunts are commercially important in many areas.

Snappers have upturned snouts and mouths, with visible canine teeth that they snap open and shut when caught (hence their name). They may be small, and travel well over the reef in loose schools. Common types include gray, cubera, dog, schoolmaster, yellowtail, twinspot, and bluestripe snappers.

Grunts got their name because they make a grunting noise when caught. You see them in small groups and large schools on the reef, or at night singly in sand flats and grass beds. They may be colorful with stripes; in some areas grunts are called sweetlips. Common types include French, bluestripe, blackspot, and oriental sweetlips.

Damselfish

Chromis

Hamlet

Damselfish, Chromis and Hamlets

These small, oval-shaped fish dart in and out of reef crevices. They're colorful, with many different patterns and shades.

Damselfish tenaciously defend their territories, including chasing larger fish and divers. They often feed on algae, and have distinct nests or living areas. The Indo-Pacific anemonefish is a damselfish. Others include sergeant major, dusky, yellowtail, sulfur, humbug and Garibaldi damselfish.

Chromis are similar to damselfish but slightly different in appearance. They feed on plankton and are less territorial. They're usually elongated, with deeply forked tails. Common types include blue, brown, purple, blue-green, and bicolor chromis.

Hamlets are actually members of the seabass family, but look more like damselfish, though they have flatter, sloping head profiles. These predators are often colorful and may have stripes or markings. Common types include barred, indigo, black, and blue hamlets.

Grouper

Basslet

Groupers, Seabass and Basslets

This group consists of (proportionately) big-bodied fish with large mouths and lips. They tend to be solitary and hang out in the shadows. They're predators and many – mainly groupers and bass – are highly sought after as food fish in some areas, making them prone to overfishing.

Groupers are often dark brown, black or reddish with splotchy markings. They can change color, markings and shade, sometimes making it hard to determine exact species. They have short, spiny dorsal fins that taper down to the tail. Common types include Goliath grouper, Nassau, yellowfin, black, peacock, coral, and potato groupers.

Seabass tend to be smaller and more elongated than groupers. They're often dark, with lighter spots and varied markings. They tend to stay near the bottom, and common types include Graysby, rock hind, Coney, harlequin, soapfish, and kelp bass.

Basslets are tiny, usually colorful fish related to the seabass family. You find them on deeper reefs and walls.

Parrotfish and Wrasse

These are colorful fish, particularly in tropical environments.

Parrotfish get their names from their beak-like teethplates and rainbow colors, much like parrots. They swim using pectoral fins, and you see them scraping algae off hard surfaces. Common types include rainbow, blue, queen, stop-light, redband, longnose, and bicolor parrotfish.

Wrasse are generally smaller than parrotfish, and more elongated. You see them foraging through sand and the reef for small invertebrates. Wrasse change colors and patterns as they grow from juvenile to adult. Some wrasse, such as the hogfish and razorfish, depart markedly from the "typical" wrasse shape. Common types include creole, yellowhead, bluehead, clown, rainbow, senorita, bird, and cleaner wrasse.

Squirrelfish, Bigeyes and Cardinalfish

This group is largely nocturnal – out on the reef by night and hiding in cracks and crevices by day. Their reddish color and big eyes make them easy to spot and identify as night-adapted fish.

Squirrelfish have a pronounced rear dorsal fin that sticks up like a squirrel's tail, hence the name. You see them under ledges and in crevices during the day. Common types include longspine, reef, giant, blackbar, and soldierfish.

Bigeyes differ from squirrelfish in that they have bigger eyes, a continuous dorsal fin and appear less scaly. Common types include glasseye, bigeye and goggleye.

Cardinalfish are small and reddish, with short snouts and two separate dorsal fins. Common types include barred, flamefish, and five-line cardinalfish.

Blennies, Gobies and Jawfish

This group has long bodies and spends time perched in small holes or on the bottom. Often, all you see is the fish's head sticking out from its hiding place.

Blennies generally perch themselves on their pectoral fins. They have fleshy appendages, called cirri, which look like bushy eyebrows. Common types include saddled, redlip, seaweed, chestnut, and leopard blennies.

Goby

Jawfish

Gobies rest on their pectorals, lying flat and motionless. Some types are cleaners, which pick parasites off other fish. Common types include neon, bridled, blue, Steinitz, maiden, and citron gobies.

Jawfish are long-bodied fish that live in burrows they construct by moving sand and stone with their mouths. You'll see them in sand near the reef. The yellowhead jawfish is a common type.

Flounders, Scorpionfish, Lizardfish and Frogfish

Flounder

Although from different families, this group consists of bottom-dwelling fish with excellent camouflage and unusual shapes.

Flounders are flat fish with both eyes on the tops of their bodies; they swim on their side. Some species can change color, and most hide by burying themselves in sand except for their eyes. Common types include peacock, eyed, gulf, and panther flounders.

Scorpionfish

Scorpionfish blend in well with their surroundings, usually resembling the local flora. They have stocky bodies, and spiny dorsal fins that carry venom. Some species are quite venomous. They're hard to spot because they remain still; injuries result when someone accidentally steps on or puts a hand on a scorpionfish. The lionfish is in this family, though it is active, visible and doesn't lie on the bottom. Other common types include the spotted and reef scorpionfish, and the stonefish.

Lizardfish have elongated bodies and large, upturned mouths. They often rest on the bottom, camouflaged, waiting for unsuspecting prey. They may be pale, with mottled colors that match the sandy bottom. Common types include the sand diver, the snakefish and the common lizardfish.

Lizardfish

Frogfish

Frogfish, sometimes called anglerfish, have bulky bodies and large upturned mouths. They blend well with the bottom, and move by walking on their pectoral fins. Frogfish have an appendage that dangles in front of their mouths, which baits prey within reach. Common types include sargassumfish, longlure frogfish and freckled frogfish.

Filefish, Triggerfish, Pufferfish, Trunkfish, Cowfish, Goatfish, Trumpetfish and Drums

All fish in this group are free swimming, meaning they don't tend to perch or lie on a substrate and are able to swim freely, and many have unusual shapes that allow them to take advantage of fauna for camouflage.

Filefish and *triggerfish* make up a family called leatherjackets, so named for their rough, textured skin. These fish have oval- or diamond-shaped bodies. Filefish have an elongated dorsal fin similar to the triggerfish, only they're more spike-like. Common filefish include scrawled, orangespot, whitespot, broom, and longnose filefish.

Triggerfish get their name from their elongated dorsal fin, which has a shape similar to a gun's trigger. Part of the leatherjacket family, these fish have oval- or diamond-shaped bodies. Common triggerfish include queen, black durgon, ocean, triton, clown, and Picasso triggerfish.

Pufferfish get their name from the fact that they can swell their bodies up like balloons. Some have spines that stand out when they do this. All species have powerful jaws; most have dark spots or blotches. Some common types include the dogface puffer, the blackspotted puffer, and porcupine puffer.

Trunkfish and *cowfish* make up the boxfish family, so named for their triangular, boxy shape. These fish move slowly with sculling fin motions. Cowfish have two "horns" that distinguish them from trunkfish. Common trunkfish include smooth, spotted, and cube trunkfish. Common cowfish include scrawled and honeycomb cowfish.

Goatfish have long, cylindrical bodies and barbels that hang from their chins, much like the beard of a goat. They feed on the bottom and may gather in schools. Goatfish have many color variations, and common species include spotted, yellow, red patch, longbarbel, and yellowsaddle goatfish.

Trumpetfish get their name from their long, tube-like bodies and long mouths. They stalk their prey by hanging head down, often near other vertical corals or growth that camouflages them from their prey. They may be blue-gray, bright yellow, brown or an intermediate shade.

Drums have long fore dorsal fins and striking, black-and-white coloring. You see them under ledges, and common types include spotted, jackknife fish, and high-hat drums. Some different drum species look very similar.

Filefish

Pufferfish

Triggerfish

Trunkfish

Trumpetfish

Goatfish

Drum

Eels

Eels are fish, though to the uninformed they may appear to be snakes.

Most eel species live in holes and crevices, but may come out to feed at night. Some have singular color, while others have distinct patterns. Perhaps the most common marine eel is the moray; moray types include green, spotted, reticulated, viper and giant morays. Other types of saltwater eel include conger, ribbon eel, dragon, and wolf eels; freshwater species include the American eel and shortfin eel.

Sharks and Rays

Sharks and rays share a group because their bodies consist of flexible cartilage and lack much true bone.

You may see many types of sharks and rays, ranging from larger species to smaller ones. Sharks swim using their tails, like other fish, whereas rays have modified pectoral fins that they use like wings, "flying" through the water. Common sharks include the nurse, white tip, black tip, and leopard sharks; common rays include the skate, southern stingray, eagle ray and manta ray.

EXERCISE-2

1. My buddy and I are diving at 10 metres/30 feet on a tropical reef, when we see a reddish fish with big eyes swimming back and forth under a ledge. With the notes we've taken on our wet books, we look in a fish ID book back on shore and would likely find this fish in the family of __________.
   - ☐ a. blennies, gobies and jawfish
   - ☐ b. squirrelfish, bigeyes and cardinalfish
   - ☐ c. parrotfish and wrasse
   - ☐ d. damselfish, chromis and hamlets
2. On that same dive, the divemaster points out a fish that's not moving, camouflaged on a coral-covered rock. The divemaster signals to remind us that the fish has poisonous spines. This is probably a
   - ☐ a. moray eel.
   - ☒ b. blenny.
   - ☐ c. scorpionfish.
   - ☐ d. filefish.

How did you do?

1. b. 2. c.

LEARNING OBJECTIVES

By the end of this section, I should be able to answer these questions:

1. What is the roving diver survey technique? Why is it a good method for recreational divers to use when surveying fish?
2. How do I record a "mystery" fish?
3. How do I record my observations?

One effective way to survey fish is the roving diver survey technique. You simply swim, spotting and recording fish you identify from the start to the end of your dive.

Fish Surveys

Some organizations, like REEF (Reef Environmental Education Foundation), have developed reef surveys that allow divers to identify and record fish they see on a dive. One effective way to survey fish is the *roving diver survey technique.* Developed by REEF, you simply swim, spotting and recording fish you identify from the start to the end of your dive. There's no need to count – simply note on your slate or wet book an "S" for single, "F" for few (2-10), "M" for many (11-100) or "A" for abundant (100-plus). If you see a "mystery" fish you don't recognize, sketch its distinguishing marks and features for later identification, or photograph it.

In fish surveys, you record only fish you can positively identify. Many divers keep fish surveys for personal interest, but you can also use them for scientific data collection by local or international institutions. Depending upon the situation, your Fish Identification Adventure Dive may simply focus on identifying fish without surveying them.

During and after the dive, you can use fish identification slates to help determine fish species. After the dive, you can use apps (there are many available, including regional ones, from which you can choose) and guidebooks to help determine fish species. Your instructor and local divers usually know many of the local species as well.

EXERCISE-3

1. One advantage of the roving diver survey technique is that I don't have to count individual fish.
   - ☐ True ☐ False
2. During a dive, I'm surveying fish and see one I don't recognize. For survey purposes, I should
   - ☐ a. ignore the fish.
   - ☐ b. sketch/note characteristics for possible identification later.
   - ☐ c. capture the fish for positive post-dive identification.
3. During fish surveys, I record fish that I
   - ☐ a. positively identify.
   - ☐ b. positively identify or reasonably guess.
   - ☐ c. see, regardless of ability to identify.

How did you do?

1. True. 2. b. 3. a.

LEARNING OBJECTIVES

By the end of this section, I should be able to answer these questions:

1. Why are scuba divers and snorkelers "natural" ambassadors for the aquatic environment?
2. What is Project AWARE®?
3. What is Project AWARE's mission and purpose?

Caring for Our Oceans

Scuba divers and snorkelers like you notice changes in the underwater world. This makes you a natural ambassador for the aquatic environment – you witness what's happening and, hopefully, have a passion for sharing and acting based on what you see.

Scuba divers and snorkelers are some of the strongest supporters of conservation programs and initiatives, including:

- Volunteer monitoring efforts
- Underwater and beach cleanups
- Supporting marine parks and protected areas
- Supporting legislative actions for sustainable fisheries and protecting endangered habitats and species

Since 1992, PADI's partnership with Project AWARE® – a global nonprofit organization – has empowered divers across the globe to become stewards for the underwater world and fight for critical environmental victories.

Project AWARE's mission is to mobilize the world's divers into a global force to protect our ocean planet. The organization is focused on the issues of sharks in peril and marine debris – two global ocean issues where scuba divers are uniquely positioned to affect long-term change. PADI encourages divers worldwide to join the movement to protect our ocean planet – one dive at a time. To get involved in current campaigns and respond to the latest calls to action visit projectaware.org.

FISH IDENTIFICATION SPECIALTY

At your instructor's discretion, the Fish Identification Adventure Dive credits toward the PADI Fish Identification Specialty course. The course gives you more opportunities to apply and practice fish identification skills, including:

- Fish identification strategies
- More on fish groups and characteristics
- Identifying locally found fish families

Remember to log your training dives with the PADI Mobile App or at padi.com.

EXERCISE-4

1. My ability to witness what's happening to the underwater world positions me as a natural ambassador for the aquatic environment.
   ☐ True ☐ False
2. Project AWARE is an international not-for-profit organization dedicated to educating divers and the public about ocean issues, and encouraging participation in marine conservation efforts.
   ☐ True ☐ False

How did you do?

1. True. 2. True.

Project AWARE involves divers and others in projects and activities to conserve aquatic environments.

Knowledge Review – Fish Identification

Answer the following questions by selecting the best choice (or choices) from those provided. Be prepared to discuss the material at your next training session.

1. Approximately how many different fish species are thought to exist worldwide?
   - ☐ Nearly 100,000
   - ☐ 50,000
   - ☐ More than 21,000
   - ☐ Less than 4000
2. What is a simple strategy for identifying fish?
   - ☐ Focus on common characteristics that help me identify a fish as belonging to a family.
   - ☐ Always take several photographs of each fish for identification later.
   - ☐ Never dive without a complete set of waterproof fish identification cards.
   - ☐ Note the depth and location of each of the fish I want to identify.
3. My buddy and I are planning a dive to a reef at 20 metres/66 feet. Our goal is to see the greatest variety of fish possible. What would be the best way to do this?
   - ☐ Swim around as fast as we can.
   - ☐ Hover over a patch of reef and let the fish come to us.
   - ☐ Calmly swim around the reef.
4. Which of the following are groupings of fish families commonly found in tropical or temperate waters? (Choose all that apply.)
   - ☐ Butterflyfish, angelfish and surgeonfish
   - ☐ Parrotfish and wrasse
   - ☐ Groupers, seabass and basslets
   - ☐ Flounders, scorpionfish, lizardfish and frogfish
   - ☐ Filefish, triggerfish, puffers, trunkfish, cowfish, goatfish, trumpetfish and drums
   - ☐ Snakes and serpents
   - ☐ Sharks and rays
5. Which characteristics may assist you in distinguishing between fish families? (Choose all that apply.)
   - ☐ Size
   - ☐ Color
   - ☐ Body shape
   - ☐ Fin configuration
   - ☐ Habitat and behavior

6. I spot a fish that has a boxy shape and two appendages that look like small horns coming out of the top of its head. This is likely to be a
   - ☐ triggerfish.
   - ☐ cowfish.
   - ☐ goatfish.
   - ☐ pufferfish.
7. I see two eyes sticking up from the sand on a fish that appears to be flat. This is likely a/an
   - ☐ eagle ray.
   - ☐ jawfish.
   - ☐ grouper.
   - ☐ flounder.
8. The "roving diver" survey technique means that I follow a strict search pattern and only identify fish that appear directly in front of me on my planned path.
   - ☐ True
   - ☐ False
9. I see a fish I can't identify and complete a sketch of it on my slate. To identify it after the dive, I can (choose all that apply):
   - ☐ consult with a more experienced fish watcher.
   - ☐ check a fish reference book.
   - ☐ compare my sketch to the local fish identification slate.
   - ☐ assume that it is an unknown species.
10. Scuba divers and snorkelers are the world's "natural" ambassadors for the aquatic environment because they see changes to favorite dive sites over time and generally (choose all that apply):
    - ☐ support the establishment of underwater parks and protected areas.
    - ☐ support legislation and regulation to protect threatened species and habitats.
    - ☐ pick up marine debris and participate in both underwater and beach cleanups.
    - ☐ care about what they love: the underwater world.
11. Project AWARE's mission is to educate divers and the public about environmental issues affecting aquatic environments, and unite them in efforts to protect and sustain them.
    - ☐ True
    - ☐ False

Student Statement

I completed this Knowledge Review to the best of my ability. For any questions I answered incorrectly or incompletely, I reviewed the explanation provided and now understand the material. In the case of anything about which I still have questions, I will review the material again and, if necessary, discuss it with my instructor at our next session.

☐ I agree ☐ I disagree

Name ______________________________

Date ______________________________

scenario

"That queen parrotfish sleeping in its mucus cocoon was pretty cool," Mei said, as she sat down on the dive shop steps after a night dive.

"They do that for protection from predators," said her buddy, Lin. "Some scientists think the cocoon helps them heal and get rid of parasites."

"Let's swap out cylinders and see if we can find it again," said Mei.

"We're only going to about 12 metres," said Lin, checking her computer, "so that works. We'll have plenty of no stop time."

- *What does this anecdote tell you about possible organism behaviors after dark?*
- *What did you learn about what makes night diving interesting?*

NIGHT DIVING 10

NIGHT DIVING

Introduction

Why Dive After Dark

Before you first learned to dive, night diving might have sounded scary – who would want to go underwater at night? But, after gaining diving experience during the day, most divers find they're interested in diving after dark. Ask why, and you commonly get at least one of five answers (though there are others):

LEARNING OBJECTIVES

By the end of this section, I should be able to answer these questions:

1. What are five reasons to go night diving?

2. What three diving specialty activities benefit from night diving?

1. **Curiosity.** Many divers just want to see what diving's like at night, which is what you would expect from adventurous people like divers.

2. **Nocturnal life.** You see organisms at night that you don't see during the day, and you witness different behaviors from some creatures compared to what you see during the day.

3. **A new look at familiar sites.** Visiting a favorite spot at night is a great way to take a fresh look at it – as if diving there for the first time.

4. **"True" colors.** Colors seem more vivid at night because they're lit by your dive light instead of natural light that's been filtered by the water. Plus, everything's draped in the black of night, creating contrast.

5. **More chances to dive.** For a lot of people, diving at night makes it possible to dive after work during the week, or to make more dives on holiday.

Divers frequently cite three activities as benefiting in particular from night diving, though you can enjoy many activities at night. The first of these is *observing nature*. This makes sense considering you see organisms and behaviors you don't see during the day: Lobsters hide during the day, but emerge into the open at night. Many fish "sleep" and you can get very close to them. In many marine environments, microorganisms emit light – bioluminescence – creating an underwater light show and "sparks" in the water.

Curiosity, nocturnal life, a new look at familiar sites, vivid colors and more dive opportunities make night diving appealing to many divers.

A second activity that benefits from night diving is *image making*. Darkness makes a dramatic backdrop for still photos and videos. Close-up imaging is especially popular at night. Ask your instructor about the PADI Digital Underwater Photographer course if you're interested in shooting pictures and videos underwater.

For many divers, *wreck diving* has extra appeal at night. Part of this is a new look at a familiar site, but night diving on many wrecks has a thrill like visiting a "haunted" house at night. Also, wrecks often make great places to observe wildlife and make images, so they make exciting sites for night dives.

Darkness makes a dramatic backdrop for still photos and videos. Close-up imaging is especially popular at night.

EXERCISE-1

1. I may find night diving appealing (choose all that apply):
   - ☐ a. because I'm curious.
   - ☐ b. to see familiar sites in a new way.
   - ☐ c. because colors are vivid and dramatic.
   - ☐ d. so I can dive more often.
2. Divers commonly say that night diving benefits include (choose all that apply):
   - ☐ a. observing nature.
   - ☐ b. photography and video.
   - ☐ c. wreck diving.

How did you do?

1. a, b, c, d. 2. a, b, c.

Things That Go Bump in the Night – Nocturnal Aquatic Life

LEARNING OBJECTIVES

By the end of this section, I should be able to answer this question:

1. How should I interact responsibly with nocturnal aquatic life?

The different organisms and/or behaviors you see on a night dive compared to a day dive affect how you interact with underwater life. As you learned in the PADI Open Water Diver course, it's important to interact responsibly with sensitive organisms to avoid harming them, to avoid injury to yourself and to avoid disrupting their normal behaviors.

Accidental contact is more likely at night, so wear adequate exposure protection to reduce the risk of scrapes and stings. For example, you may choose to wear a suit that covers you entirely, even when a shorty wet suit would be adequate with respect to insulation. Stay neutrally buoyant and move more slowly and cautiously in the dark. Use your light to check before making bottom contact to be sure the area isn't sensitive and that it's free of potentially harmful organisms.

Keep in mind that avoiding contact with organisms is as much about protecting them as protecting you. In the same spirit, be careful with your light – it can damage aquatic life if you push or prod with it. Its beam may disturb normal behavior – the disruption is usually inconsequential, but be cautious to not repeatedly disturb the same organisms or areas. Observe and then move on.

Accidental contact is more likely at night so wear adequate exposure protection, stay neutrally buoyant, and move more slowly and cautiously in the dark.

EXERCISE-2

1. Accidental contact with sensitive or potentially hazardous organisms is more likely at night, so I should wear exposure protection, move slowly and cautiously, and check the bottom with my light before making any contact.

   ☐ True ☐ False

How did you do?

1. True.

Night Diving Equipment

Most of the gear you use for day diving at a given site will be suited to night diving as well. A primary difference is that you may want more exposure protection. This is partly to reduce injury risk through accidental contact, as you just learned, so consider gloves (unless prohibited) and wet suit boots. Some divers also like elbow and knee pads. But, you may wear more protection, because in many climates surface temperatures are significantly cooler at night. In these areas, many divers like dry suits for night diving for post-dive comfort, even when a wet suit would be adequate for the dive itself.

Always have surface signaling devices; these can be more important at night, because you're harder to see. Computers and other instruments that illuminate or glow are optimum, though you can read almost any instrument with your dive lights.

For night diving, generally use equipment with which you're already familiar. If you have something new that can affect your routine dive skills – e.g., a BCD with a different inflator mechanism – it's recommended you become familiar with it diving during the day before using it on a night dive.

LEARNING OBJECTIVES

By the end of this section, I should be able to answer these questions:

1. What personal dive equipment considerations does a night dive require?
2. What is the recommendation regarding the use of new or unfamiliar equipment at night?
3. Why is it important to carry at least two lights on a night dive? Why might I carry three?
4. Why should some dive lights be switched on only underwater?
5. How do I maintain a dive light?
6. How do I care for a flooded light?
7. What are three uses for marker lights?
8. Where do I attach marker lights used to mark individual divers?
9. What do I use surface support lights for?

For night diving, use equipment with which you're already familiar. If you have something new that can affect your routine dive skills, it's recommended you become familiar with it diving during the day before using it on a night dive.

Dive Lights

The obvious piece of equipment for a night dive is a dive light. Actually, you carry at least two dive lights – your *primary* light, with which you make the dive, and a *backup* light, so you don't have to end the dive without a light if your primary has a problem. Your primary light is a powerful, full-sized light. Your backup may be smaller and more compact.

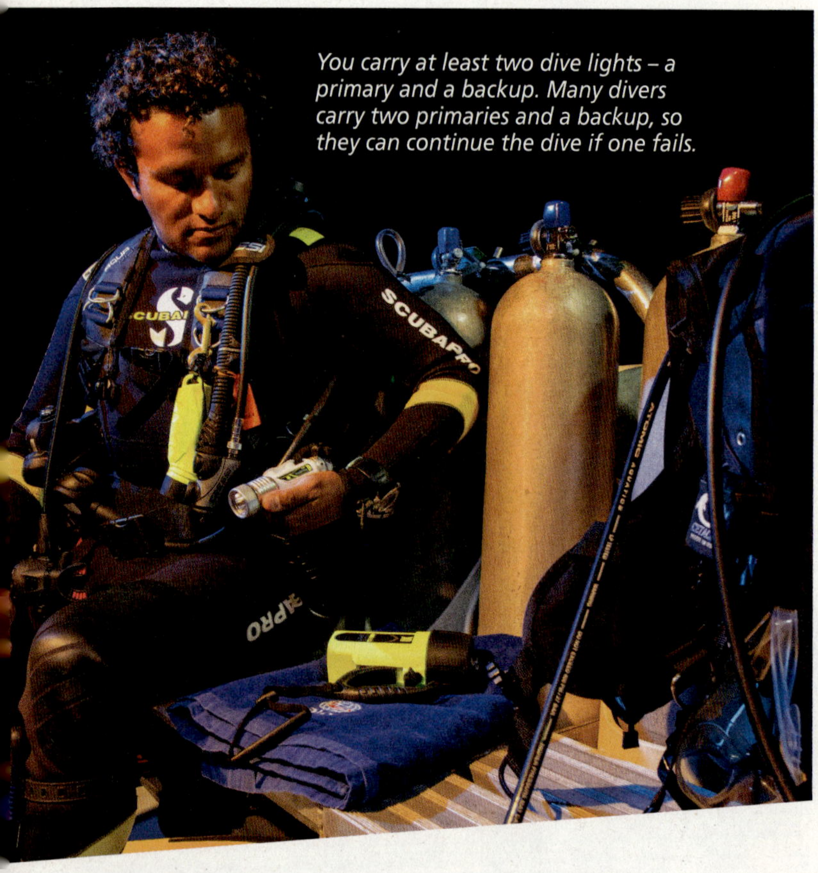

You carry at least two dive lights – a primary and a backup. Many divers carry two primaries and a backup, so they can continue the dive if one fails.

Today, many divers carry three dive lights. At one time, primary lights had to be significantly larger than the compact lights used as backups, but LED and battery technologies have made primary lights much more compact – almost as compact as backup lights once were. So, you may choose to carry three lights – two primary lights and a backup. This way, if you or a buddy has a primary light failure, you can continue the dive. You only need to end the dive using a backup if two primary lights fail – which is highly unlikely.

Features and Accessories

Dive lights have many options and features – brightness, power, rechargeable or nonrechargeable batteries, etc., as well as a range of sizes and costs. But, it must be a *dive* light – "waterproof" lights not intended for diving will not withstand pressure and fail at depth.

Be aware that some dive lights take advantage of water's cooling properties and should only be switched on in the water. Otherwise, such lights can overheat and suffer damage.

When choosing dive lights, be sure to also equip each with a clip so you can secure it. It's also a good idea to have a wrist lanyard, tether or other system to avoid loss if you release the light while using it (not necessarily intentionally).

See your PADI Retailer or Resort for assistance in choosing the latest in modern dive lights. You can also learn more in the PADI Night Diving Manual.

Maintenance

Dive light care isn't complicated. Avoid impact damage and dropping lights, and rinse them thoroughly in fresh water after each dive. Charge up rechargeable batteries according to the manufacturer guidelines.

Store dive lights out of heat or direct sunlight, and follow any other manufacturer requirements.

When choosing dive lights, be sure to also equip each with a clip so you can secure it.

How to Remove, Clean, Lubricate and Replace an O-Ring

All dive lights have at least one user-accessible o-ring seal where you access the battery, and may also have captured o-rings (e.g., on a switch) that are not user accessible. Generally, you clean and lubricate the user-accessible o-rings. You care for captured o-rings by rinsing the light properly, with periodic cleaning, lubrication, etc., by your dive center or the manufacturer (see the manufacturer literature).

To service a user-accessible o-ring:

1. Remove the o-ring from its groove by sliding your fingers along it, toward each other, to form a bulge that you grab, then ease the o-ring out gently. Alternatively, use something like the corner of a credit card or certification card to lift it. Do not use a sharp metal object, because it can damage the housing groove in which the o-ring fits. This could make it impossible for the light to seal.

2. Use a cotton swab to gently remove dirt/excess grease from the groove. Inspect the groove carefully to be sure there is no hair, other debris, etc., remaining.

3. Gently clean the o-ring with a soft, clean cloth. Be careful not to stretch it excessively, and to not grind sand or grit against it. Remove any lint or debris on it.

4. Inspect the o-ring. Replace it with a new one if you find nicks, tears or other damage. A damaged o-ring will not seal reliably and the only option is to replace it.

5. Lightly lubricate the o-ring. Put a few small dabs of manufacturer-approved grease – usually silicone; a few lights specify no lubrication – and gently spread them over the o-ring.

6. A properly lubricated o-ring looks shiny and wet, with no visible grease globs. The grease does not make the seal; it allows the o-ring to slide into place to seal. Using excess grease makes the seal less reliable by attracting dirt.

7. Inspect the o-ring and groove again for dirt, hair, threads, or lint, then replace the o-ring. Gently wipe clean the opposite seal surface and inspect it also for dirt, hair, or threads before reassembling the light.

Flooded Dive Light. Dive lights have become increasingly reliable, but a damaged or improperly maintained o-ring, or other cause, can allow one to flood. If your light floods, follow these steps:

1. Turn the light off as soon as you notice it is flooded. Go to your backup light if you're diving.

2. Once out of the water, wearing eye protection (your dive mask will work) and gloves, open the light and drain it. Rinse it internally with fresh water and drain the rinse water. Batteries can release caustic chemicals, so the eye protection/gloves are good precautions. Also, gases can build up in a flooded light due to reactions within batteries. The light can pop apart suddenly, so use caution.

3. Discard the water and disposable batteries in an environmentally appropriate manner. Especially in fresh water, rechargeable batteries may survive flooding, but isolate them – e.g., in a heavy-duty plastic bag or box – so they won't cause a hazard or damage if they do leak.

4. Leave the light apart and allow it to dry. Do not use it again until a PADI Dive Center or Resort, or the manufacturer, has serviced it.

Wear eye and hand protection when draining a flooded dive light because batteries can release caustic chemicals. Dispose of the flood and rinse water in an environmentally appropriate manner, and don't use the light again until it has been professionally serviced.

Batteries and the Environment

One of the primary concerns with batteries is they can leak heavy metals into the environment (especially a concern regarding groundwater). Rechargeable batteries are generally worse in this regard than disposables. However, over its life one rechargeable battery may replace hundreds of disposable batteries, so overall they're less of a problem for the environment. And, if you're going to be night diving a lot, rechargeables may also be a lot better for your wallet.

Regardless of type, when your batteries reach the end of their useful life, dispose of them properly. It's a simple step that goes a long way toward protecting the environment.

Marker Lights

In addition to your dive lights, it is common to use marker lights (designed for diving) to assist you on a dive. Marker lights vary in size, but are typically compact and use disposable batteries. You can get them in different colors so you can tell them apart.

You secure marker lights using rubber bands, tape, string, cable ties or a supplied attachment device, and typically use them for three purposes when night diving:

1. **Marking each diver.** Attached to your cylinder valve or snorkel, the marker light makes you more visible to a buddy(ies) regardless of which way you're pointing your light, or even if it's off.
2. **Secured to the boat or a surface float.** This makes it easier to find the boat/float at the surface, and may help alert boaters to your presence.
3. **Marking the reference line or mooring/anchor line.** Attaching a marker light makes it easier to relocate the line. It is common to put one at 5 metres/15 feet (safety stop depth), as well as several along its length.

Attached to your cylinder valve or snorkel, marker lights help make you visible regardless of which way you're pointing your light, or if it's off.

In Place of Disposables

Some primary lights, many backup lights and most marker lights you may choose for night diving use AA cells. The majority allow you to use alkaline *or* nickel-metal hydride (NiMH) rechargeables. Although NiMH cells cost about twice as much as alkalines, you can reuse them 500 or more times. In the long run, you save a lot of money, reduce electronic waste and can use them for electronics other than your dive lights when needed.

Check manufacturer literature for the light or device to be sure you can use NiMHs in place of alkalines (you usually can).

Surface Support Lights

"Surface support light" is just a way of referring to any light you use before and after the dive other than your dive lights. You may use these for kitting up, to help you enter and exit the water, and for putting everything away after the dive. Gas lanterns, vehicle lights, streetlights, street-warning flashers, etc., may all serve some or all of these purposes. Having light other than your dive lights saves your batteries for underwater use, and may be necessary when diving with lights that you can only burn underwater. Having these lights makes pre- and post-dive activities much easier.

If leaving unattended lights burning to assist with shore exits, it may be wise to put a label or sign on them to prevent removal by passers-by.

Underwater Organisms Attracted by Light

In some areas, depending on the season, your dive lights may attract small aquatic organisms. These can range from interesting organisms to those that can sting. Be careful about placing bright lights near surface entry and exit points when there's a possibility of attracting these organisms. If in doubt, check with local divers for more information before using bright surface or underwater lights.

"Surface support light" is just a way of referring to any light you use before and after the dive other than your dive lights. You may use these for kitting up, to help you enter and exit the water, and for putting everything away after the dive.

EXERCISE-3

1. My buddy and I are night diving at a site we've visited during the day. We may want more exposure protection than we wear in the daytime.
   ☐ True ☐ False
2. I'm excited to try out my new dry suit, which is a model, make and material different from any I've used before. My buddy suggests we "break it in" with a night dive. Following the recommendation for using new or unfamiliar equipment at night, I would reply that
   ☐ a. I'm ready to go for it.
   ☐ b. we should have three in the buddy team.
   ☐ c. it would be best to dive with it during the day first.
3. Going night diving, my buddy and I have two dive lights each. We have two so that if one fails we can __________the dive using the other.
   ☐ a. abort
   ☐ b. continue
4. Turning on some dive lights out of water can cause them to overheat and get damaged.
   ☐ True ☐ False
5. My buddy and I have just finished a night dive in sea water. The primary care for our dive lights is to rinse them in fresh water followed by rinsing with rubbing alcohol.
   ☐ True ☐ False
6. I was in a hurry and didn't properly maintain my dive light's o-ring, so the light flooded. In dealing with it, I should (choose all that apply):
   ☐ a. turn the light off immediately.
   ☐ b. wear eye/hand protection when opening it.
   ☐ c. be aware that the light may pop apart.
   ☐ d. not use the light until it has been serviced.
7. Common uses for marker lights include marking (choose all that apply):
   ☐ a. individual divers.
   ☐ b. the mooring/anchor line.
   ☐ c. boats/surface floats.
   ☐ d. cameras.
8. Besides my regular dive lights, for night diving it is common to attach a marker light to my lower leg or fin.
   ☐ True ☐ False
9. Uses for surface support lights include (choose all that apply):
   ☐ a. gearing up for the dive.
   ☐ b. helping me enter/exit the water.
   ☐ c. putting my kit away after the dive.

How did you do?

1. True. 2. c. 3. a. 4. True. 5. False. Rinse your lights in fresh water, followed by any other manufacturer requirements; none call for rinsing lights with alcohol. 6. a, b, c, d. 7. a, b, c. 8. False. It is common to attach a marker light to your cylinder valve or snorkel. 9. a, b, c.

Planning Night Dives

Choosing and Evaluating Sites for Night Diving

Generally, for night diving choose a site you're familiar with. Ideally, dive or snorkel the site during the same day, before nightfall. If possible, arrive before dark to make it easier to evaluate conditions. As you've learned, as appropriate for the site, among other things consider:

- visibility
- surge/current
- surf and waves
- water temperature
- tides

Reference compass headings and note entry/exit points (shore diving) as appropriate. If useful, note these on a slate or in a wet book. For additional information about the site or sites, consult your log book, check online sources such as ScubaEarth and talk to your local PADI Dive Center or Resort. Your instructor will be familiar with the Night Adventure Dive location and will provide additional information as appropriate.

Evaluating a site for night diving differs little from any other dive. The primary difference is to be more conservative; you usually want conditions to be a bit better than the least favorable you would find acceptable for a day dive. The ideal surface conditions are clear skies with a full moon because you see a lot after your eyes adjust. But, in many environments you may be able to evaluate the site more than adequately without moonlight.

LEARNING OBJECTIVES

By the end of this section, I should be able to answer these questions:

1. What should I consider when evaluating and choosing a night dive site?
2. What six environmental conditions should I try to avoid when planning a night dive?
3. What are the four general night dive planning recommendations?
4. How can I reduce and cope with stress during a night dive?
5. What should I do if my light fails during a night dive?

Evaluating a site for night diving differs little from any other dive. The primary difference is to be more conservative; you usually want conditions to be a bit better than the least favorable you would find acceptable for a day dive.

Generally, avoid the following conditions when night diving:

- **Moderate to high surf.** It can be difficult to judge changes to wave patterns, and to see oncoming waves in the dark.
- **Moderate to strong current.** It may be hard to find your way if thrown off course; if you don't return to the mooring/anchor line while boat diving, you may be hard to spot for pick up. An exception may be drift diving, but have experience drift diving during the day before doing a night drift. (See the Drift Diving section to learn more.)
- **Poor visibility.** If the visibility is so poor that it complicates navigation or reduces the chance you'll see anything interesting, it's probably not worth diving.
- **Thick kelp, nets, line or any other potential entanglement.** In the dark it's easier to get tangled and harder to free yourself, so be cautious night diving where entanglement hazards are known or likely.
- **Heavy surge.** Light or mild surge isn't usually an issue, but heavy surge can swing you into large rocks and cause disorientation.
- **Overhead environments.** Even if you're a PADI Wreck Diver or PADI Cavern Diver, stay out of overhead environments at night. At night, overhead environments are considered tec diving, because you don't have the sun as a light source to help you find your way out.

Planning Night Dives

Plan night dives following the procedures you learned in the PADI Open Water Diver course. In addition, there are four recommendations to include in your night dive planning.

The first is to *prepare your equipment in adequate light*. Complete your set up before dark or where you have ample light, because it's easier to do, and you can inspect all your gear better. Be sure you have fresh or freshly charged batteries, and secure your marker lights (but don't activate them until ready to dive).

Second, *eat a few hours before the dive*. There's a tendency to skip or delay dinner to make a night dive, but a proper meal gives you energy for the dive. To avoid stomach upset, it helps to allow two or three hours between eating and the dive.

Third, if possible, *dive with familiar buddies.* Diving with people you know makes it easier to communicate and anticipate, which can be helpful in the dark. A common exception is diving with a professional whom you may not know as well.

Prepare your equipment in adequate light. Complete your set up before dark or where you have ample light, because it's easier to do, and you can inspect all your gear better.

Fourth, *bring someone who's not diving.* It's often helpful to have someone at the surface to assist with accessories, provide additional light, help you relocate the exit and, if needed, provide emergency assistance. Charter dive boats provide this, which is one reason many divers prefer night diving from charter boats.

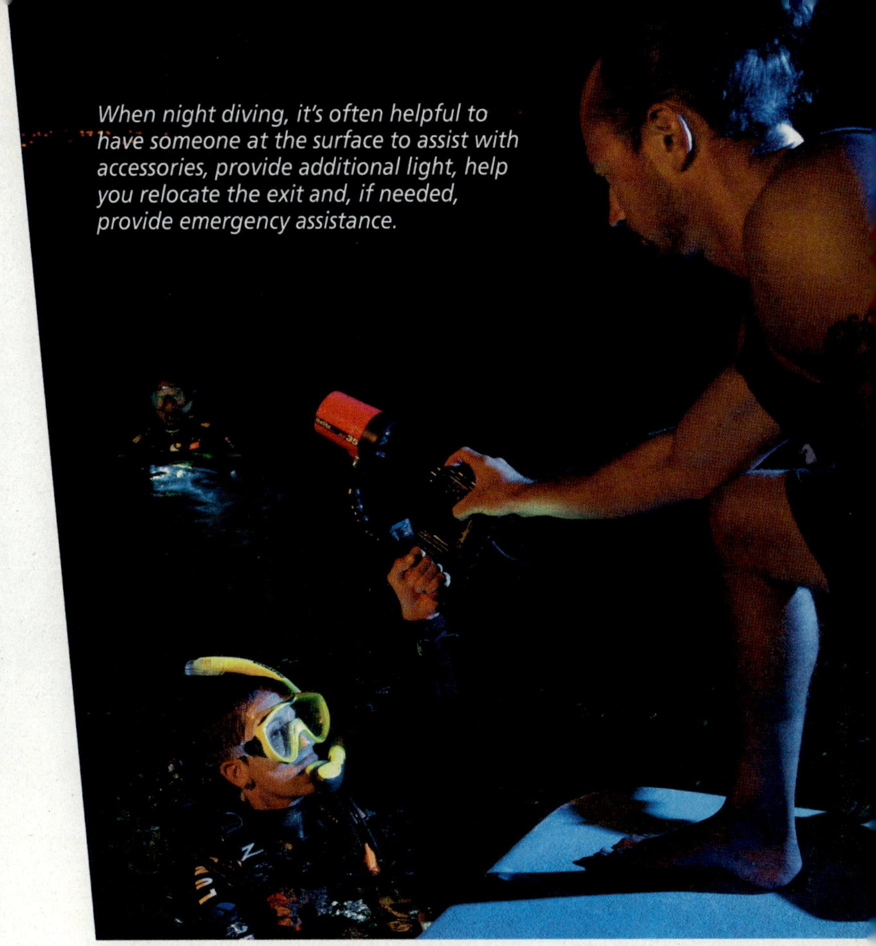

When night diving, it's often helpful to have someone at the surface to assist with accessories, provide additional light, help you relocate the exit and, if needed, provide emergency assistance.

Dealing with Night Diving Stress

When you don't have much experience night diving, it's not unusual to find it produces some stress. In fact, some stress makes night diving exciting – but too much takes the fun out of it. People may feel stress night diving because of environmental conditions that become more difficult to deal with in the dark, using unfamiliar gear, task loading by trying to do too much, or fear of the dark. (Actually, people aren't afraid of the dark, but rather fear threats or hazards they imagine are hidden in the dark.)

You reduce night diving stress through training and experience. Through both, you learn problems you may have night diving and how to handle them. You remove sources of stress by being conservative with respect to evaluating conditions, and gaining experience with significantly unfamiliar equipment by diving with it during the day first.

Remembering that your first priority is *always* safety helps to reduce task loading. This is because you more easily remember to abandon secondary objectives if you can't accomplish them. Having too many objectives can lead you to accomplish nothing, so don't try to do as much as you might on a day dive. Keeping things simple reduces stress. Completing the Night Adventure Dive and the PADI Night Diver course reduces stress by developing your abilities under professional supervision and guidance. Finally, maintaining good diving habits and situational awareness reduces stress (on all dives, not just night dives).

It's not unusual to find night diving produces some stress. In fact, some stress makes night diving exciting – but too much takes the fun out of it.

If your light fails, stop and switch to your backup light, obviously. If it's clipped or secured, turn the backup light on before releasing it so you can find it if you drop it while exchanging lights.

One common stress source is *fear of light failure* while diving at night. For those who feel this way, let's deal with it and eliminate any worry. It's little more than an inconvenience.

If your light fails, stop and switch to your backup light, obviously. If it's clipped or secured, turn the backup light on *before* releasing it so you can find it if you drop it while exchanging lights. End the dive. (Note: If you or a buddy has a second primary light, you can continue the dive if everyone still has a backup light.)

If your backup fails (*highly* unlikely, but just in case), borrow a buddy's backup. If it fails (very, very unlikely you would have a triple light failure), your buddy's remaining light is usually more than adequate for ending the dive together. But, if you must ascend in the dark for some reason, follow a reference – mooring/anchor line or ascent line, or bottom – if possible. Watch your computer; if it doesn't have an illuminated face, listen for its ascent rate alarm to help guide your ascent.

Beyond this, in environments with reasonably clear water and moonlight, you can see well without your dive light once your eyes adjust. You may find you turn your lights out just to enjoy this experience.

EXERCISE-4

1. My buddy and I are evaluating a possible site for a night dive. Other than being more conservative, doing this differs little from doing so for a day dive, and we should consider visibility, surge/current, surf and waves, water temperature and tides.
   ☐ True ☐ False
2. My buddy and I are planning a shore night dive. When we arrive before dark, the surf is moderately high, but within our capabilities when diving during the day. The recommended action is to
   ☐ a. begin the dive before nightfall.
   ☐ b. dive as planned.
   ☐ c. carry four lights each.
   ☐ d. find a site with less surf or cancel the dive.
3. Heading out for a shore night dive in a few hours, it would be a good idea to arrive at the site before sunset so we can set up our gear while it's still light out.
   ☐ True ☐ False
4. Remembering that ending the dive safely is *always* my first priority reduces night diving task loading and stress.
   ☐ True ☐ False
5. If my light fails during a night dive, I should (choose all the options that may apply, depending upon the situation) ________ and end the dive.
   ☐ a. switch to my backup light
   ☐ b. borrow my buddy's backup light
   ☐ c. share my buddy's light
   ☐ d. ascend carefully, following a reference if possible

How did you do?

1. True. 2. d. 3. True. 4. True. 5. a, b, c, d.

LEARNING

OBJECTIVES

By the end of this section, I should be able to answer these questions:

1. How do I stay with my buddy(ies) on a night dive? What should I do if I become separated?

2. What are the procedures for entering and exiting the water from a boat and from shore while night diving?

3. What techniques can I use during night ascents and descents to avoid disorientation and stress?

4. How do I signal to my buddy(ies) on a night dive? To the boat or shore?

5. What navigation techniques can I use at night?

6. What should I do if I become disoriented or lost during a night dive?

7. What are the procedures for locating an offshore dive site at night?

Night Diving Techniques

Night diving techniques are generally the same as those you use during the day, with adaptations for darkness and using a light.

Buddy System Procedures

It is easier to separate from your buddy(ies) in the dark because you may not see each other as well. But, it's also easier to stay together because, within reasonable distances, your lights pinpoint your locations.

To avoid separation, stay within touching distance. You can hold hands or wrists if helpful. This is especially helpful in lower visibility that limits how far you can see your buddy's(ies') lights.

Be aware of the glow from your buddy's(ies') light around you. This glow makes it easier to stay together – with experience, you'll quickly notice when it's missing, alerting you that your buddy(ies) may have stopped to look at something or deal with a problem.

If you do separate, stop and look for your buddy's(ies') light. Cover your light if that helps, but only for short periods, because your buddy is probably looking for you, too. If you don't see your buddy(ies), shine your light straight out and rotate to help your buddy(ies) find you.

If you don't reunite after a one-minute search, ascend cautiously and reunite on the surface (or follow another procedure, if appropriate, as agreed and planned before the dive). After reuniting, you can continue the dive, gas and no stop time permitting. When diving in a buddy team of three, remember that buddy separation procedures apply when one buddy is separated from the other two.

To avoid separation, stay within touching distance. Be aware of the glow from your buddy's(ies') light around you. With experience, you'll quickly notice when it's missing.

When entering the water at night, the first step is to turn on your primary light and secure its lanyard to reduce the risk of losing it, and to make it easier to locate if you do. Use your light to check the entry area.

Diving from a boat, enter as you would during the day. Signal "okay" after entering, clear the entry area and wait for your buddy. Keep your light pointed downward, and avoid shining it at your buddy(ies) or up at people on the boat, which can temporarily blind them.

Entering from shore, watch for rocks and obstructions. If you're entering through light surf, time your entry for a lull in the waves. Watch for waves frequently with your light as you enter. You have to watch more closely, but otherwise enter as you normally would, staying close to your buddies and being careful not to shine your light in their eyes.

Exit the water similarly as you would during the day, but using your light. Keep your light on so you can see, and in case you drop it, but be careful not to shine it up into the boat or shore support's eyes. When exiting through surf, time your exit for a lull and keep an eye out for waves as you go. If it's dark enough that you need your light to see approaching waves, realize they may be relatively close when you see them.

When entering the water at night, the first step is to turn on your primary light and secure its lanyard to reduce the risk of losing it, and to make it easier to locate if you do. Use your light to check the entry area, but keep it down and avoid shining it in anyone's eyes.

Night Diving Descents and Ascents

When night diving, a reference for descents and ascents helps avoid disorientation. If you're diving from shore, you can often follow the bottom to and from deeper water as your reference. If you're diving from a boat, or with a float, a reference/anchor line provides a good reference. But, when the water's clear enough to see the bottom from the surface, there's less need for a reference.

Descents

In good conditions, if you have to wait before descending at the surface, you may turn your light off to save batteries, or an accidental bump may turn it off. So, confirm it's on before starting down. Check the time, take a compass reading on the shore or boat lights, signal your buddy and vent your BCD.

When descending along a line, you can follow the line with your free hand and use the other to control your light, BCD, etc. – again, a lanyard or other system that lets you release your light helps. Descend slowly in a head-above-feet position (horizontal trim) to help retain your sense of direction. Adjust for neutral buoyancy often and stay close to your buddy(ies). Use your light to check what's below frequently, and watch for the bottom. An issue at night is that it's harder to judge your progress until you can see the bottom, so note the depth on your computer frequently. Check your SPG and compass frequently as well.

Ascents

If you descended along a reference line, you usually return to it for your ascent. When it's time to go up, signal your buddy(ies) and make a normal, slow ascent, using the reference to help guide and control it. Stay close and use your lights to watch overhead frequently. It may help to hold the line with the same hand holding the light, which tends to aim the beam upward. Vent your BCD to maintain proper buoyancy, and watch your computer as usual.

You may have fewer visual references on a night dive, so it may help to go more slowly than usual. After your safety stop, shine your light upward, look up and reach up for the final part of your ascent. Be cautious not to surface under the boat, swim step or other overhead obstruction. At the surface, establish buoyancy, maintain buddy contact and signal to anyone waiting on the boat or shore that you're okay, as discussed in the next subsection.

Descend slowly in a head-above-feet position to help retain your sense of direction. Use your light to check what's below frequently, and watch for the bottom. Note the depth on your computer frequently.

Night Communication

At night, you use the signals you normally use, but make sure your buddy(ies) can see them and that you don't accidentally blind them with your light. Get your buddy's(ies') attention by touch, rapping on your cylinder, etc., or waving your light back and forth. If you need to aim your light in your buddy's(ies') direction, point it low, at foot level. You can also wave your beam across your buddy's(ies') sight line on the bottom, since that's where everyone's attention usually is. Either method avoids shining a blinding light into your buddy's face. (Similarly, when passing other buddy teams, point your light away from them.)

Shine your light at the hand making the signal; waist level usually works well. To signal with your light over a longer distance, waving back and forth continuously means "help" or "emergency." Large circles with the light mean "okay." Slowly waving the light up and down means "attention."

To signal the boat, shore or other divers some distance away at the surface, hold your light overhead and shine it down on your head for "okay." Wave it to ask for help.

Navigation at Night

Even in clear water, being in darkness makes underwater navigation particularly useful at night. You apply what you learn in the Underwater Navigation Adventure Dive and/or the PADI Underwater Navigator course, with adaptations specific to night diving. You use both natural and compass navigation to find your way.

One popular night navigation technique is to follow the natural line formed by a rock reef, coral reef or other formation out and then back. As discussed in underwater navigation, sand and mud ripples run roughly parallel to shore and are excellent natural navigational aids. You may find these especially useful at night when you're away from a reef that forms a line you can follow.

Shine your light at the hand making the signal; waist level usually works well.

To signal with your light over a longer distance, waving back and forth continuously means "help" or "emergency." Large circles with it mean "okay." Waving it up and down slowly means "attention."

Pay attention to depth relative to the bottom contour; you do this navigating during the day, but it can be more useful at night when there are no other landmarks visible and you don't have the sun to indicate direction. But, while you don't have the sun, in moderately clear water or better, lights are great references at night. Note the locations of different lights from boats, on shore, etc., as well as those you place as underwater references. These significantly benefit finding your way at night, provided you're mindful to keep them in sight.

You will probably find you use your compass more on a night dive. (It's a good idea to have a compass at all times, but especially when night diving.) You learned basic compass use in the PADI Open Water Diver course, which you refined (or will refine) in the Underwater Navigation Adventure Dive.

Before descending, find the compass heading to your exit or the boat, so you can use it when it's time to turn the dive and head back. If the area is somewhat new to you, choose a single compass heading to follow out and back (out-and-back line). This lets you see a lot without complicating your navigation.

Head back to the exit early so you have plenty of time to locate it. If you find it with a lot of gas left, you can continue the dive in the immediate area until you have to ascend to your safety stop.

To signal the boat, shore or other divers some distance away at the surface, hold your light overhead and shine it down on your head for "okay." Wave it to ask for help.

In lower visibility, instead of following one course, follow several short ones to and from the exit area. Starting, for instance, at the bottom of a reference line, follow a compass heading out and back a short distance. After returning to the line, choose another heading and repeat the process. You'll see a good deal, while remaining oriented and close to your ascent point.

One popular night navigation technique is to follow the natural line formed by a rock reef, coral reef or other formation out and then back.

Head back to the exit early so you have plenty of time to locate it. If you find it with a lot of gas left, you can continue the dive in the immediate area until you have to ascend to your safety stop.

You may have to swim to your exit on the surface. So, before descending, look toward it so you know what it looks like at night.

Just as you do during the day, you usually try to plan your dives to return to your exit underwater. However, be prepared to do so swimming on the surface. To help you do this, before descending look toward your exit (the boat or shore) so you know what it looks like at night.

When swimming on the surface at night, it helps to point your lights away from you, let your eyes adjust to the dark and then use boat/shore lights to guide you. If there are boats in the area, keep your lights on and visible. Swim slowly, watch for obstructions and use your light to check the area as you exit.

Disorientation and Getting Lost

If you lose your sense of up and down midwater, without a reference, and you can't see the surface or bottom, grasp your buddy or hug yourself until the feeling passes. If necessary, discontinue the dive, using your computer to guide an ascent at a safe rate.

More common is simply losing your way at night. If this happens and you cannot determine where you are, surface with your buddy to get your bearings. Gas and time allowing, agree on a new travel direction, descend and continue the dive.

Locating an Offshore Dive Site

When night diving from shore, you may want to visit a specific spot away from shore. In fact, the main point of your dive may be to see or do something at night that you had during the day, such as observe an organism, photograph a wreck, etc. A few techniques make finding the spot easier.

The first is to follow a previously determined compass course to the dive site. You can get the heading and distance from another diver, or even better determine them yourself during a day dive as you've learned in your navigation training. Even when it's a spot to which you can easily navigate without a compass during the day, at night you may find it much more reliable to use your compass.

You can locate an offshore dive site by following a previously determined compass course. Even when it's a spot to which you can easily navigate without a compass during the day, at night you may find it much more reliable to use your compass.

In clear water at a familiar site, you can find your way to a spot based on the features around you, just as you do during the day. A map sketched on a slate or in a wet book may help.

The easiest way to relocate an offshore site is to mark it with a buoy during daylight if you can. Similarly, if you are in an area where charter dive boats operate and conduct night dives, they will usually moor or anchor on or near the best spots, effectively "relocating" sites for you.

NIGHT DIVER SPECIALTY

At your instructor's discretion, the Night Adventure Dive credits toward the PADI Night Diver Specialty course. The course gives you more opportunities to develop and practice your night diving skills, including:

- Orientation to nocturnal wildlife
- More dive light options
- Rechargeable battery systems
- Maintaining position in the dark

Remember to log your training dives with the PADI Mobile App or at padi.com.

EXERCISE-5

1. While night diving, I become separated from my buddy. I should (choose all that apply):
   - ☐ a. cover my dive light and look for my buddy's light.
   - ☐ b. surface to reunite if unable to do so after a one-minute search.
   - ☐ c. shine my light straight out and rotate.
   - ☐ d. stay where I am until my buddy finds me.
2. When entering and exiting the water on a night dive, I should keep my light pointed up at all times.
   - ☐ True ☐ False
3. Making a night dive from a charter dive boat, my buddy and I descended the mooring/anchor line. We would normally return to it for our ascent.
   - ☐ True ☐ False
4. On a night dive, I'm signaling "Direction?" to my buddy. I should shine my light
   - ☐ a. on my hand signal.
   - ☐ b. at my buddy's chest.
   - ☐ c. at my buddy's feet.
   - ☐ d. straight up.
5. To help with navigation at night, I can (choose all that apply):
   - ☐ a. note the heading to my exit before descending.
   - ☐ b. use any visible lights as references.
   - ☐ c. head to my exit with plenty of time to locate it.
   - ☐ d. look toward my exit at the surface before descending.
6. During a night dive, my buddy and I have lost our way. After searching the immediate area, we can't find anything familiar or establish the compass heading back to the boat. We should
   - ☐ a. pick a direction and swim until we find something familiar.
   - ☐ b. swim in a widening circle.
   - ☐ c. rap on our cylinders until other divers locate us.
   - ☐ d. ascend carefully and reorient on the surface.
7. Probably the *easiest* way to relocate an offshore site at night is to
   - ☐ a. anchor/moor on the site, or mark it with a buoy during the day.
   - ☐ b. follow a compass heading to it.
   - ☐ c. use a map and natural references to locate it.

How did you do?

1. a, b, c. 2. False. Keep it pointed downward to see where you're going, and to avoid blinding others with it. 3. True. 4. a. 5. a, b, c, d. 6. d. 7. a.

Knowledge Review – Night Diving

Answer the following questions by selecting the best choice (or choices) from those provided. Be prepared to discuss the material at your next training session.

1. Your buddy has just bought a new regulator and BCD and wants to go night diving with you. What would the general recommendation be?
   - ☐ Never use new or unfamiliar equipment on a night dive.
   - ☐ When possible, become familiar with equipment before using it on a night dive.
   - ☐ There is no recommendation that applies.
2. Setting up for a night dive, you and your buddy attach small marker lights to your cylinder valves. Where else might you use such lights? (Choose all that apply.)
   - ☐ On your dive float
   - ☐ Attached to the descent/ascent line
   - ☐ At a boat's swim step
   - ☐ Strapped to your right ankles
3. When choosing a potential site for a night dive, a spot you've never visited before is generally more exciting and rewarding.
   ☐ True ☐ False
4. Environmental conditions to avoid while night diving include (choose all that apply):
   - ☐ moderate to high surf.
   - ☐ cool water.
   - ☐ moderate or stronger current.
   - ☐ poor visibility.
   - ☐ heavy surge.
   - ☐ overhead environments.
   - ☐ wrecks.
5. Which of the following are general night diving planning considerations? (Choose all that apply.)
   - ☐ Prepare your equipment ahead of time in daylight if you'll be in an unlit area.
   - ☐ Eat a proper meal a few hours before the dive.
   - ☐ Dive with familiar buddies.
   - ☐ Bring someone who won't be diving.
6. You and your buddy are on a night dive. A large fish swims by and startles your buddy, causing stress. Your buddy should
   - ☐ breathe rapidly.
   - ☐ get behind you.
   - ☐ stop, think and then take appropriate action.
7. During a night dive, your light fails. Normally, you would respond by holding on to your buddy so you can share one light and end the dive.
   ☐ True ☐ False
8. About 20 minutes into a night dive, you turn and find your buddy's nowhere to be seen. You cover your light and look for the glow of your buddy's light and search for about five minutes. After failing to reunite, you ascend to reunite on the surface. Did you follow the correct procedure?
   ☐ Yes ☐ No
9. You're forced to ascend without a reference on a night dive. Which of the following steps can help you avoid or deal with disorientation midwater? (Choose all that apply.)
   - ☐ Avoid direct buddy contact.
   - ☐ Don't look down.
   - ☐ Watch your computer.
10. When entering the water on a night dive, always use a light to check the entry area before going in.
    ☐ True ☐ False
11. What are the recommendations for night diving descents that reduce disorientation and stress? (Choose all that apply.)
    - ☐ Follow a reference line or bottom contour.
    - ☐ Keep your feet above your head.
    - ☐ Descend as quickly as possible.

12. What are the recommendations for night diving ascents that reduce disorientation and stress? (Choose all that apply.)

- ☐ Follow a reference line or bottom contour.
- ☐ Look down the entire time.
- ☐ Ascend slowly.

13. You want to signal your buddy to turn a night dive and head back. You should signal at

- ☐ eye level and point your light at your hand.
- ☐ waist level and point your light at your hand.
- ☐ eye level and point your light at your buddy.
- ☐ waist level and point your light at your buddy.

14. On a night dive, your buddy's gotten a bit farther from you than you'd like, but you can still see each other's lights. As you swim toward each other, your buddy makes a big circle with a light. This means

- ☐ Zero air – need help immediately
- ☐ Oriented – follow me
- ☐ Okay – situation normal

15. To navigate effectively at night and avoid getting disoriented, (choose all that apply):

- ☐ dive the site during the day.
- ☐ get a compass heading to the exit before descending.
- ☐ do not go as far from my exit as I might during the day.

Student Statement

I completed this Knowledge Review to the best of my ability. For any questions I answered incorrectly or incompletely, I reviewed the explanation provided and now understand the material. In the case of anything about which I still have questions, I will review the material again and, if necessary, discuss it with my instructor at our next session.

☐ I agree ☐ I disagree

Student signature ______________________________

Date ______________________________

scenario

"Ten minutes into their first dive of the day, Dan signaled to Tod that he was at turn pressure. Tod signaled "okay," and "turn the dive."

Back ashore, as they were taking off their gear, a slightly out-of-breath Dan noticed that Tod's cylinder was still half full.

"You're great on gas, and you don't look tired at all. What are you doing that I'm not?" Dan asked.

"Well, I used to use more gas and diving took a lot more effort," said Tod. "Then I learned more about streamlining and buoyancy. I found I had stuff sticking out unnecessarily, and I was wearing too much weight. Tucking everything in and perfecting my weight made me more streamlined. Now I don't tire out as easily from finning hard, and I use a lot less gas. Maybe you should check your streamlining and weight, too."

- *Why does Tod's streamlining and proper weighting affect his effort level underwater?*
- *What can Dan do before his second dive to be more properly weighted?*

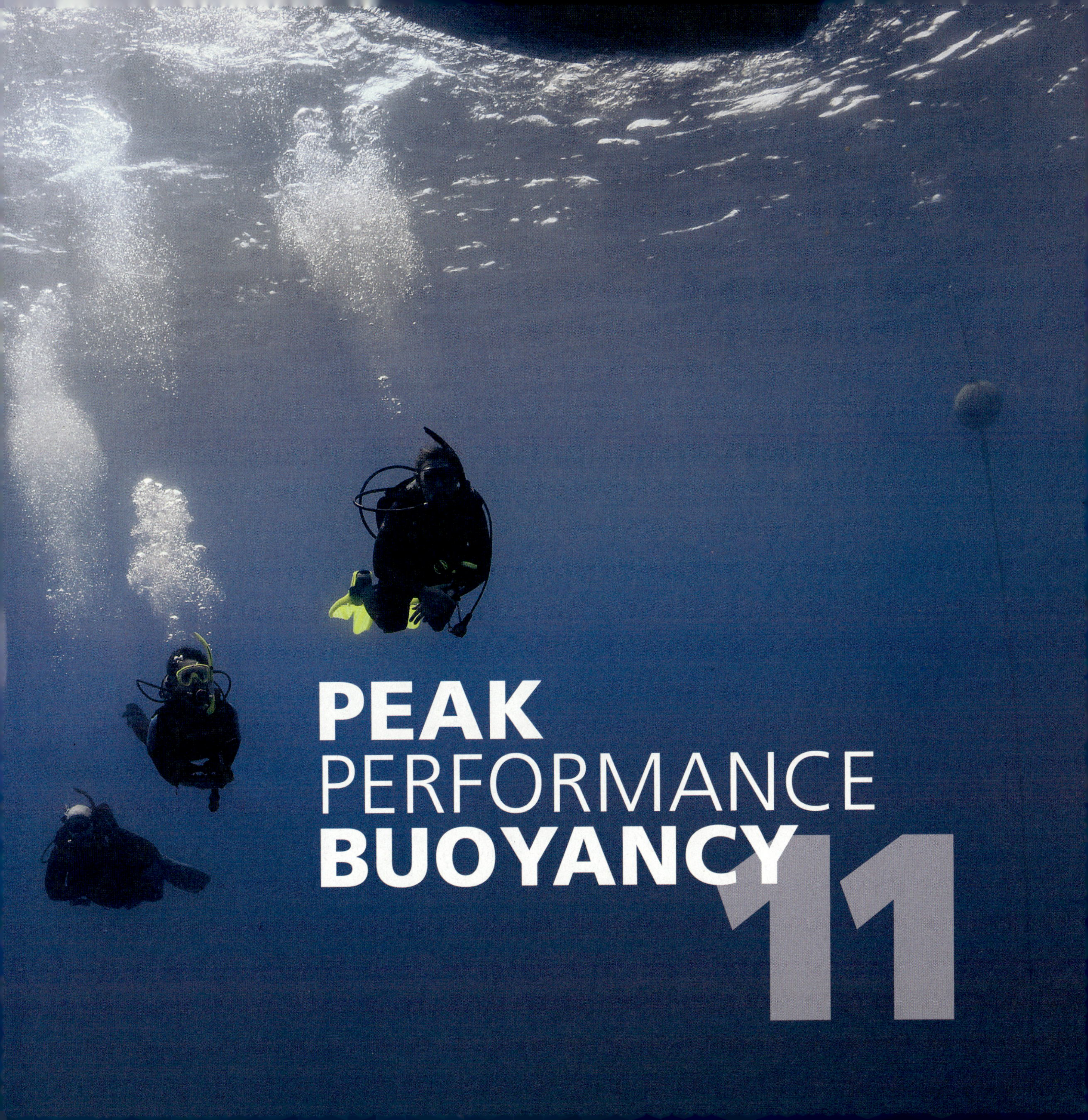

11 PEAK PERFORMANCE BUOYANCY

PEAK PERFORMANCE BUOYANCY

Buoyancy Basics – Proper Weighting

Peak performance buoyancy is the mark of an accomplished diver. It consists of proper weighting, trim, buoyancy adjustment and streamlining.

- *Proper weighting* means diving with the correct amount of weight.
- *Trim* means distributing your weight and equipment for a natural, comfortable balance in the water.
- *Buoyancy adjustment* means using your BCD or dry suit, and breathing during the dive, to accommodate buoyancy changes caused by depth changes and gas consumption.
- *Streamlining* means your scuba kit is compact with nothing dangling, dragging or protruding inappropriately.

Peak performance buoyancy is the mark of an accomplished diver. It consists of proper weighting, trim, buoyancy adjustment and streamlining.

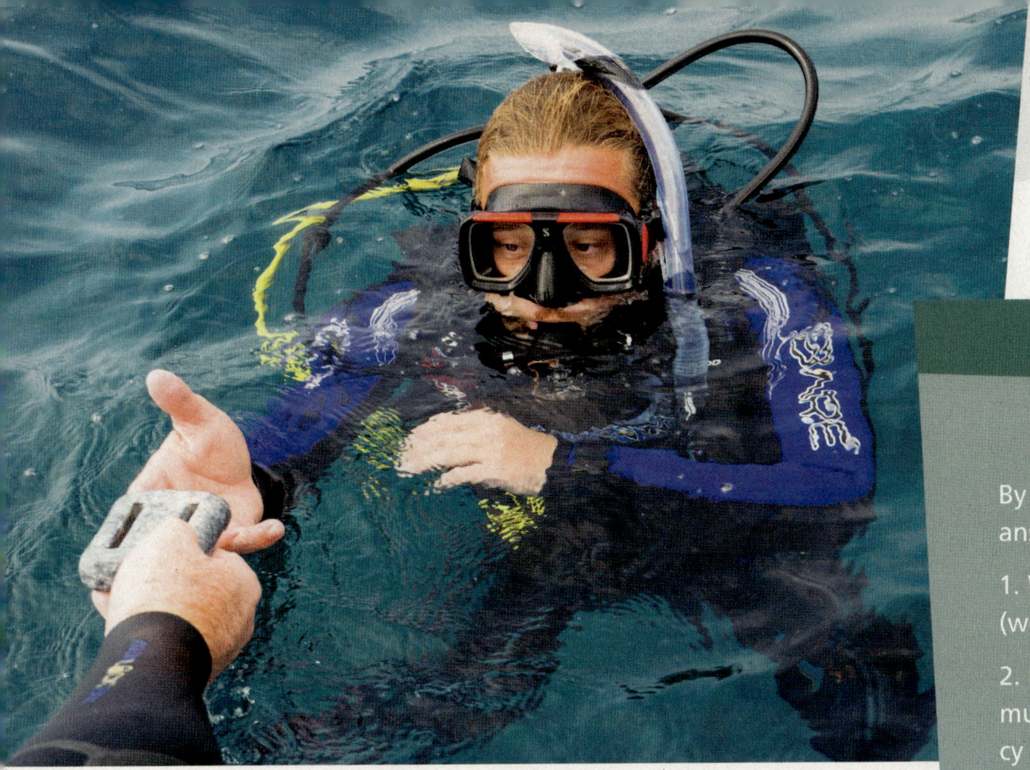

The only way to determine your weight precisely is to conduct a buoyancy (weight) check. Basic guidelines and experience will get your weight close, but for precision you still need to check.

LEARNING OBJECTIVES

By the end of this section, I should be able to answer these questions:

1. When should I conduct a buoyancy (weight) check before diving?
2. Based on basic weighting guidelines, how much weight do I need before my buoyancy (weight) check in the Peak Performance Buoyancy Adventure Dive?
3. How do I conduct a buoyancy (weight) check at the surface?
4. How does my buoyancy change as I breathe the gas in my cylinder? How do I account for this?

Peak performance buoyancy control begins with proper weighting. Your BCD can offset having too much weight, but overweighting raises your torso, lowers your feet, increases drag and magnifies your buoyancy adjustments. Too little weight means you struggle to stay down, which increases your air consumption. It gets progressively worse during the dive, and may make it difficult to control your ascent rate or make an effective safety stop.

The only way to determine your weight precisely is to conduct a buoyancy (weight) check, which is covered shortly. Basic guidelines and experience will get your weight close, but you still need to check your buoyancy for precision. Check your buoyancy when:

- using unfamiliar dive gear and/or a new configuration.
- you're in a new dive environment (especially salt water to fresh water, or vice versa).
- you have been away from diving for a while.

Use the Basic Weighting Guidelines table to estimate how much weight you need. This does not replace a buoyancy (weight) check. Instead, it gets your weight close so you can make minor adjustments instead of major ones when you do your buoyancy check. With experience, you may be able to estimate the weight you need without the guidelines.

In your log, make a habit of recording the weight you use (after your buoyancy check) and the gear you wore. Remember: The Basic Weighting Guidelines only apply to open-circuit diving; if you're using a rebreather, check your buoyancy as you learned in the PADI Rebreather Diver course.

BASIC WEIGHTING

GUIDELINES

EXPOSURE SUIT TYPE	START WITH
Swimsuit/Dive skin	0.5-2 kg/1-4 lbs
3 mm or 1/16 in. one-piece wet suit, shorties, jump suits	5% of your body weight
5 mm or 3/16 in. two-piece wet suit	10% of your body weight
7 mm or 1/4 in. wet suit w/hood, gloves	10% of your body weight, + 1.5-3 kg/3-5 lbs
Neoprene dry suit	10% of your body weight, + 3-5 kg/7-10 lbs
Shell dry suit, light undergarment	10% of your body weight, +1.5-3 kg/3-5 lbs
Shell dry suit, heavy undergarment	10% of your body weight, + 3-7 kg/7-14 lbs

SALT / FRESH WATER CHANGE

BODY WEIGHT	SUBTRACT (GOING TO FRESH)
45-56 kg/100-125 lbs	2 kg/4 lbs
57-70 kg/126-155 lbs	2.3 kg/5 lbs
71-85 kg/156-186 lbs	3 kg/6 lbs
86-99 kg/187-217 lbs	3.2 kg/7 lbs

When applying these guidelines, you should take some factors into consideration, including:

Gender – Women tend to be more buoyant than men.

Physique – Lean, muscular physiques are less buoyant, while those with a higher percentage of body fat are more buoyant.

Wet suit age – Wet suits lose buoyancy with age and use.

Cylinders – Steel cylinders are less buoyant than aluminum cylinders.

Accessories – Wet suit hoods, gloves and extra dry suit undergarment layers all add buoyancy.

The Buoyancy (Weight) Check

During the PADI Open Water Diver course, you learned to check for proper weighting. As a refresher, here are the steps:

1. Enter water too deep in which to stand, wearing all your gear and the estimated weight from the basic guidelines.
2. Breathing from your regulator, completely deflate your BCD. If you're diving in a dry suit, open the auto exhaust valve all the way.
3. Relax in a vertical position holding a normal breath at the surface. If you're weighted properly, you should float at eye level.
4. Add or subtract weight until you float at eye level. It helps to simply hold weights while you figure it out.
5. As a final check, you should sink slowly when you exhale.

Using a rebreather, follow the same steps outlined here, but you should float with the top of your head just at the surface, and then slowly descend by exhaling through your nose and venting the loop.

During the dive, your overall weight changes as you use the gas in your cylinder. For example, from full to reserve, gas in the popular 11-litre/80-cubic-foot cylinder is about two kilograms/five pounds – your buoyancy will increase this much during the dive. To account for this increase, perform your buoyancy check using a cylinder at reserve pressure, get your weight set, then fill the cylinder or switch to an identically sized cylinder that is full. This isn't always feasible, though. In that instance, adjust your weight wearing your full cylinder, and then add two kilograms/five pounds.

Either way, you should be slightly negatively buoyant at the surface at the start of the dive, and neutrally buoyant at the surface at the end with your cylinder at reserve pressure. Note that gas weighs the same regardless of the cylinder holding it. Using a steel cylinder instead of an aluminum cylinder, for example, may reduce how much weight you need in your buoyancy check. But, the weight change from full to reserve pressure will be the same for comparable capacity cylinders.

Be sure to log your weight requirements in each configuration. Even though you may need to recheck your weight, you'll start with an amount close to what you need. Use the PADI Mobile App or visit padi.com to access your online log book.

Gas weighs the same regardless of the cylinder holding it. Using a steel cylinder (right) instead of an aluminum cylinder (left), for example, may reduce how much weight you need in your buoyancy check. But, the weight change from full to reserve pressure will be the same for comparable capacity cylinders.

EXERCISE-1

1. Before diving, I should always check my buoyancy (weight) when (choose all that apply):
   - ☐ a. I'm diving in fresh water versus salt water, or vice versa.
   - ☐ b. I'm using new gear or a different gear configuration.
   - ☐ c. I've taken a long flight to the dive destination.
   - ☐ d. I haven't been diving in a while.
2. A friend has invited me for a dive in a freshwater lake where the water temperature is 12°C/54°F. I weigh 68 kilograms/150 pounds, and will be wearing a 7 mm suit with a hood, booties and gloves. Using the Basic Weighting Guidelines, how much weight should I start with before my buoyancy (weight) check?
   - ☐ a. 8.3-9.8 kilograms/18-20 pounds
   - ☐ b. 6-7.5 kilograms /13-15 pounds
   - ☐ c. 6.8 kilograms /15 pounds
3. When conducting a buoyancy (weight) check at the surface, I should (choose all that apply):
   - ☐ a. fully inflate my BCD while breathing from my regulator.
   - ☐ b. relax, holding a normal breath in.
   - ☐ c. add or subtract weight until I float at eye level.
   - ☐ d. sink slowly when I exhale.
4. As a dive progresses, I become less buoyant.
   - ☐ True ☐ False

How did you do?

1. a, b, d. 2. b. 3. b, c, d. 4. False. As you dive, your overall weight decreases as you consume gas from your scuba cylinder and you become more buoyant.

Buoyancy Basics – Controlling Buoyancy During the Dive

You learned how to constantly control your buoyancy during a dive during the PADI Open Water Diver course, but let's look at this from a peak performance buoyancy perspective. There are three variables that make buoyancy adjustment necessary:

1. **Suit compression** Wet suits and dry suits change volume as the gas in the material (wet suits/neoprene dry suits) or in the suit itself (dry suits) compresses under pressure. You add gas to your BCD or dry suit to offset this; as you ascend, the gas expands, so you release it to maintain buoyancy control.

2. **Gas consumption** You start the dive slightly negative; as you consume gas, your cylinder becomes lighter, increasing your buoyancy. Over the course of the dive, you gradually release gas from your BCD/dry suit to maintain buoyancy control.

3. **Depth change** This variable relates to suit compression, but also to gas you add to your BCD/dry suit. As you change depth, you not only adjust for the change in the gas volume in your exposure suit, but also for changes in the gas volume in your BCD/dry suit.

Rebreather divers have a fourth variable – the counterlung. Part of your training in the PADI Rebreather Diver course includes learning to keep the counterlung at the proper volume as you change depth.

LEARNING OBJECTIVES

By the end of this section, I should be able to answer these questions:

1. What three variables require me to adjust my buoyancy as needed?

2. When and how should I adjust my buoyancy?

3. As a recreational diver, how do I control my buoyancy when using a dry suit?

4. With open-circuit scuba, how does my lung volume affect buoyancy, and how do I use it to fine-tune buoyancy? Why doesn't this apply when using a rebreather?

You have to adjust your buoyancy due to suit compression, gas consumption and depth changes.

Learn to use all the exhaust valves – for example, the shoulder valve and rear dump valve – on your BCD so you can release gas without having to be in a vertical position. This saves time and energy.

Fine-Tuning Buoyancy

There are several ways to help you achieve peak performance buoyancy control. First, control your buoyancy by *anticipating* changes, especially changes in depth. Make small, frequent adjustments to your buoyancy as you dive, and maintain neutral buoyancy by adjusting when you notice small buoyancy changes.

Use your fins and breathing to change depth. If you're maintaining neutral buoyancy, a kick should start you upward, or exhaling should start you downward. And finally, learn to use all the exhaust valves – for example, the shoulder valve and rear dump valve – on your BCD so you can release gas without having to be in a vertical position. This saves time and energy.

If you're a PADI Dry Suit Diver, you know that you control buoyancy slightly differently when diving dry, because you add and release gas from your suit as well as from your BCD. You learn more about this in the Dry Suit Adventure Dive.

Breath Control and Buoyancy Control

You're almost certainly aware already that your breathing affects your buoyancy. When you inhale, your lungs expand and you displace more water, raising your buoyancy. When you exhale, your lungs contract and you displace less water, lowering your buoyancy. Depending upon your size, this can vary your buoyancy as much as three kilograms/seven pounds.

Once neutrally buoyant through proper weighting and adjusting your BCD/dry suit, you use your breathing to fine-tune. Breathe with somewhat fuller or emptier lungs for short intervals to temporarily raise or lower your buoyancy, respectively. If you need to do this for more than a moment, then you probably need to adjust your BCD/dry suit. *Never hold your breath* – fine-tune your buoyancy using breathing adjustments while *continuing* to breathe. With practice, this becomes an automatic process that you don't have to think about.

Breath control does not change your buoyancy with a rebreather. This is because, as you inhale and exhale, the counterlung contracts and expands correspondingly. Your displacement and buoyancy don't change. Instead, when diving with a rebreather you control buoyancy entirely with proper weighting and your BCD/dry suit.

Breath control allows you to fine-tune your buoyancy by breathing with somewhat fuller or emptier lungs, but never holding your breath.

EXERCISE-2

1. The three variables that affect my buoyancy are:
   - ☐ a. water currents, water temperature and depth change.
   - ☐ b. the weight of my BCD, fin type and style of regulator.
   - ☐ c. gas consumption, water temperature and water salinity.
   - ☐ d. suit compression, gas consumption and depth change.
2. To maintain neutral buoyancy while diving, I should (choose all that apply):
   - ☐ a. take long, deep breaths and hold for three seconds.
   - ☐ b. use my fins and breathing to change depths.
   - ☐ c. use all the various exhaust valves on my BCD.
   - ☐ d. anticipate change and make small, frequent adjustments.
3. When diving with a dry suit, I adjust my buoyancy exactly as I do with a wet suit.
   - ☐ True ☐ False
4. On an open-circuit scuba dive, my chest ______ when I inhale and my buoyancy ______; when I exhale, my chest ______ and my buoyancy ______. This doesn't happen when using a rebreather because of the ______.
   - ☐ a. expands, decreases; contracts, increases; scrubber
   - ☐ b. contracts, increases; expands, decreases; counterlung(s)
   - ☐ c. expands, increases; contracts, decreases; counterlung(s)

How did you do?

1. d. 2. b, c, d. 3. False. When diving with a dry suit, you have to add and release gas from the suit, which makes controlling buoyancy a little bit different. 4. c.

Trim

Trim refers to your attitude and position underwater. You may have the correct *amount* of weight, but it is your trim that determines *where* you wear it. Your equipment affects your trim – changing to a different cylinder, for example, may affect your trim. You can also adjust your trim based on what you plan to do, though the most generally useful trim is for a horizontal swimming position.

LEARNING OBJECTIVES

By the end of this section, I should be able to answer this question:

1. How do I distribute weight for better attitude and position (trim) control underwater?

Finding Your Trim

Properly weighted, adjust for neutral buoyancy and hover underwater. Relax and allow your body to roll into whatever position it wants. Once you know your current trim, you can adjust.

There are a couple of places to start when adjusting for a normal, horizontal swimming position trim:

1. If your feet are low, shift weight toward your head. It may help to move your cylinder toward your head, but not so close that your head can hit the valve.
2. If your feet are high, shift weight toward them. Heavier fins and ankle weights are options.

If you tend to roll face up, shift weight toward your front. It may also help to switch a steel cylinder for an aluminum cylinder. If you tend to roll right or left side down, you have more weight on that side; it may help to shift some weights to the lighter side.

Use BCD trim weight pockets and accessory weights to help position weight where you want it. You can distribute weight to several places – two integrated weight pockets, trim pockets and onto a weight belt. You don't have to be able to quick-release and drop *all* your weight in an emergency, just enough to assure you're positively buoyant.

To adjust your trim for low feet, shift weight toward your head. If your feet tend to be high, shift weight toward them.

EXERCISE-3

1. On the first dive of the day, I notice my trim is moderately head-down, feet-up. To correct this, I could (choose all that apply):
   - ☐ a. move my cylinder lower.
   - ☐ b. shift weights higher on my body.
   - ☐ c. use heavier fins.
   - ☐ d. move my cylinder higher.

How did you do?

1. a, c.

LEARNING OBJECTIVES

By the end of this section, I should be able to answer these questions:

1. What are four reasons for being streamlined?

2. How do I look when I'm streamlined underwater?

Streamlining

Streamlining is reducing drag by eliminating protruding and dangling equipment. Besides making you look more proficient, it has four practical benefits:

- **Streamlining makes your kicks more efficient.** Clutter on your kit can interfere with a clean kick, and you may have to compensate for disproportionate drag on one side.
- **Streamlining is more comfortable.** Everything is where it belongs, so you don't have to search for your gear, whether making a routine computer check or giving a buddy an alternate air source in an emergency.
- **Streamlining saves energy by reducing drag.** Water is dense, so it doesn't take much gear sticking out to substantially increase drag and energy expenditure.
- **Streamlining reduces damage to your gear and to the environment.** Dragging equipment over sensitive reef harms your gear as well as organisms. SPGs, alternate air sources, cameras, dive lights and slates are common items that divers dangle, but shouldn't.

Streamlining is reducing drag by eliminating protruding and dangling equipment. It makes your kicks more efficient, increases comfort, saves energy and helps protect the environment.

When you're streamlined, everything stays put when you change position.

There's a certain "look" when you're streamlined:

- Everything has the correct fit, and is adjusted correctly. Your scuba kit rides high and tight on your back.
- Your BCD or dry suit is not overinflated because you're not overweighted.
- In the water, you have adjusted for a horizontal trim.
- Your hoses are clipped and secured. Your SPG is high on your chest to take up hose slack, and your alternate second stage is secured, but visible, and quick-releases with a firm tug.
- All small accessories are stowed neatly or in a pocket. The only ones out are generally those that won't fit, or that are in use.
- Each accessory has its own clip attached so the accessory protrudes or dangles as little as possible.
- Everything stays put when you change position. When you have everything properly secured and streamlined, it doesn't move much when you roll face up, or put your feet straight up so you can look under a ledge.

EXERCISE-4

1. Streamlining is valuable because it (choose all that apply):
   - ☐ a. is more efficient.
   - ☐ b. is more comfortable.
   - ☐ c. saves energy.
   - ☐ d. makes you less visible to fish.
   - ☐ e. reduces damage to gear and the environment.
2. When I'm properly streamlined, which of the following is true? (Choose all that apply.)
   - ☐ a. My hoses are clipped and secured.
   - ☐ b. My BCD or dry suit is slightly overinflated.
   - ☐ c. The cylinder rides low on my body.
   - ☐ d. Most accessories are stowed neatly or in a pocket.
   - ☐ e. I have adjusted for a horizontal trim.

How did you do?

1. a, b, c, e. 2. a, d, e.

LEARNING OBJECTIVES

By the end of this section, I should be able to answer this question:

1. How does physical fitness relate to Peak Performance Buoyancy?

Physical Fitness

You can have proper weight, trim and streamlining yet still struggle to achieve peak performance if you're out of shape. Being out of shape affects your buoyancy in several ways:

- An out-of-shape diver has less strength and stamina; this potentially causes elevated breathing that uses gas faster and creates buoyancy by keeping the lungs full more of the time.
- Lean mass (muscle) sinks and fat tissue floats. An out-of-shape diver is more buoyant and therefore needs more weight. The same diver tends to be larger and needs a larger exposure suit, which requires even more weight.
- The out-of-shape diver has more bulk, and is less streamlined.

Overall, the out-of-shape diver has less strength and stamina. However, due to buoyancy characteristics, drag and wearing more weight, the out-of-shape diver must use more energy to swim at a given speed compared to a fit diver. Staying in shape helps you dive better: You save energy, move more efficiently and stay well within your physical limits. If dealing with a problem or emergency, you have more physical capacity to do so.

Improving your physical fitness benefits diving and many aspects of life, but always see your doctor for guidance before starting an appropriate program of exercise and healthy diet.

PEAK PERFORMANCE BUOYANCY SPECIALTY

At your instructor's discretion, the Peak Performance Buoyancy Dive credits toward the PADI Peak Performance Buoyancy Specialty course. The course gives you more opportunities to apply and practice the buoyancy skills you learned as a new diver, and includes:

- Perfecting your trim
- Techniques to improve streamlining
- How to effortlessly hover vertically or horizontally

Remember to log your training dives with the PADI Mobile App or at padi.com.

Improving your physical fitness benefits diving and many aspects of life.

EXERCISE-5

1. As long as I have proper weight, trim and streamlining, overall physical fitness doesn't affect peak performance buoyancy.

   ☐ True ☐ False

How did you do?

1. False. Your physical fitness affects how much weight you need and how much you can streamline yourself.

Knowledge Review – Peak Performance Buoyancy

Answer the following questions by selecting the best choice (or choices) from those provided. Be prepared to discuss the material at your next training session.

1. I'm about to dive in a freshwater lake. I'm using exactly the same equipment I always use in seawater, and I'm familiar with the buoyancy change to expect. Nonetheless, it would be best to conduct a buoyancy check.
   - ☒ True
   - ☐ False

2. Number the five steps for conducting a buoyancy (weight) check in the correct order:
   - __2__ Enter water too deep to stand, and deflate my BCD (and dry suit) completely.
   - __4__ Hang vertical and motionless while holding a normal breath.
   - __1__ Put on all equipment.
   - __3__ Add or subtract weight until I float at eye level while holding a normal breath.
   - __5__ As a test, exhale. I should sink slowly.

3. My buddy and I adjust for neutral buoyancy at the beginning of the dive, and continue at the same depth throughout the dive. I notice that I must occasionally let a little air out of my BCD to remain neutral during the dive. Why?
   - ☒ To compensate for the gas used from my cylinder.
   - ☐ To compensate for buoyancy changes due to exposure suit compression.
   - ☐ Because as I tire, I breathe deeper and keep my lungs more inflated.
   - ☐ Because as I tire, I kick less efficiently.

4. If diving with a steel cylinder, I do not need to account for the air I consume during the dive.
   - ☐ True
   - ☒ False

5. When I'm neutrally buoyant, I__________ slightly as I inhale and ________ slightly as I exhale.
   - ☐ a. sink; rise
   - ☐ b. sink; move
   - ☐ c. glide; rise
   - ☒ d. rise; sink

6. Besides wearing the correct amount of weight, generally I want to distribute weights so that my natural orientation in the water is as ______________ as possible.
   - ☐ vertical
   - ☒ horizontal
   - ☐ negative
   - ☐ positive

7. I want to be streamlined when diving because it helps me (choose all that apply):
   - ☐ maintain an efficient kicking style.
   - ☒ use less gas.
   - ☐ stay warmer.
   - ☒ avoid damage to gear and aquatic life.

8. If I'm wearing a lot of weight, such as with a full wet suit or dry suit, using multiple weight systems gives me more options for positioning and managing my weights.
   - ☒ True
   - ☐ False

9. In any environment, when wearing a wet suit or dry suit, I need to adjust my buoyancy as I change depths during the dive. Why does this occur?
   - ☐ Water density changes with depth.
   - ☐ My lung volume changes with depth.
   - ☐ Depth changes a suit's water volume.
   - ☒ Pressure change affects the gas bubbles in my wet suit and/or the gas volume in my dry suit.

Student Statement

I completed this Knowledge Review to the best of my ability. For any questions I answered incorrectly or incompletely, I reviewed the explanation provided and now understand the material. In the case of anything about which I still have questions, I will review the material again and, if necessary, discuss it with my instructor at our next session.

☒ I agree ☐ I disagree

Name [illegible]

Date 10/21/18

scenario

"Oh no!"

Splash.

"I can't believe I just did that." Ian said, standing up from leaning over the dive boat rail.

"What happened?" David asked.

"I was checking the visibility and forgot about the sunglasses in my shirt pocket."
"So bummed they're gone, I just bought them."

"Hmm," said David, looking over the side.
"Clear water, no current, open bottom and we know where to start. Bet we can find them in about 10 minutes, then see if we can locate those black sea bass."

Ian and David exhibit very different reactions to the situation, and it appears that David has search and recovery training, but Ian does not. What does this tell you about knowing how to search when you lose something overboard?

12 SEARCH AND RECOVERY DIVING

SEARCH AND **RECOVERY** DIVING

Introduction

Whether it's dropped while diving, knocked off a dock or tipped overboard, anyone who spends time around water eventually loses something. This highlights the first of four benefits of learning recreational-level search and recovery skills: It saves you money because, if you lose a small anchor, eyeglasses, a wallet, mask, favorite dive knife, etc., you have a good chance of finding it.

A second benefit is that learning search and recovery makes you a better-rounded diver, because you apply the skills beyond looking for lost objects. For example, you apply search techniques in the PADI Rescue Diver course, and use them for mapping in the PADI Divemaster course.

LEARNING

OBJECTIVES

By the end of this section, I should be able to answer these questions:

1. What are four benefits of learning recreational-level search and recovery skills?

2. What are the differences between professional and recreational divers engaged in searches and recovering submerged objects?

3. What considerations apply to objects of historical interest?

By learning search and recovery, not only can you find small objects you've lost, but you often enjoy the search as a rewarding challenge.

The third benefit is that search and recovery can be rewarding and challenging. It's enjoyable and satisfying to plan and execute a search, and what you're looking for doesn't even have to be particularly important or valuable.

Finally, a fourth benefit is that learning recreational search and recovery gives you a glimpse into, and a foundation for, professional underwater salvage. It broadens your understanding of what professionals have to do.

Professional and Recreational

The Search and Recovery Adventure Dive does *not* cover professional salvage, and it's important to understand the distinct differences between professional and recreational diver searches and object recovery.

To start, professionals require and complete much more extensive training for their tasks than you will as a recreational diver. This is because professionals often work in very challenging environments – zero visibility, moving water, extreme depth, etc. – and their searches may involve recovering missing persons, weapons or evidence, or large objects (more than approximately 45 kilograms/100 pounds) like automobiles, planes and boats. All of these are outside the scope of recreational search and recovery. (If this type of search interests you, ask your instructor about the PADI Public Safety Diver course.)

Also, professionals engage in underwater search and salvage/recovery for profit and employment. Their work is often subject to work/labor regulations, such as CCOHS in Canada, OSHA in the US, HSE in the UK, Worksafe in New Zealand and workplace regulatory bodies in Australia. Generally, no diving-at-work regulations apply to recreational divers looking for small lost objects.

Objects of Historical Interest

Another consideration that applies to search and recovery is whether you should recover an object at all. This is rarely an issue with something you lost, like your sunglasses, but is a significant issue regarding historical artifacts. These are only removed under specific circumstances, usually under the supervision of an archaeologist with a local government permit. It is often illegal to remove historical artifacts otherwise.

One reason for this is that removing artifacts and disturbing a site (like a shipwreck) destroys historical information archaeologists can gain from where the site is found and its condition, and from scientific recovery and preservation. Even if legal and lacking archaeological significance, removing such objects makes a site less interesting for other divers.

If you find an artifact that may have historical significance on a wreck or other site, the best way to preserve it is to leave it undisturbed, note the location and report it to appropriate local historical authorities for proper documentation and study.

EXERCISE-1

1. Learning search and recovery benefits me as a diver, because (choose all that apply):
   - ☒ a. I can recover small objects I lose.
   - ☒ b. the skills apply beyond looking for lost objects.
   - ☒ c. search and recovery can be a rewarding challenge.
   - ☒ d. it helps me understand more about professional underwater salvage.
2. A crime weapon is thought to have been thrown into a lake in my neighborhood. My buddy and I should see if we can locate it for the local authorities.

   ☐ True ☒ False
3. While searching for a lost wallet, my buddy and I stumble upon a pile of pottery likely made hundreds of years ago. We should recover the pottery and give it to local historical authorities.

   ☐ True ☒ False

How did you do?

1. a, b, c, d. 2. False. Locating weapons and evidence is outside the scope of recreational search and recovery, so leave this search to professionals. 3. False. Document the location and report it to local historical authorities, but leave it undisturbed.

LEARNING OBJECTIVES

By the end of this section, I should be able to answer this question:

1. What are the differences between searching for specific and nonspecific objects?

Searching for nonspecific objects means looking for whatever may turn up, such as trash on a cleanup dive.

Two Types of Search and Recovery

There are actually two types of search: looking for specific objects, and looking for nonspecific objects.

Searching for specific objects means looking for something someone lost or threw in the water. When you do this, you can be generally sure it is in the search area. The dive ends when you find and recover the object, or you reach a dive limit (no stop time, gas supply, cold, etc.). This type of search and recovery requires careful predive planning, and is the focus of the Search and Recovery Adventure Dive, and the PADI Search and Recovery Diver course.

Searching for nonspecific objects (bottom combing) means looking for whatever may turn up. It can be a cleanup dive; you don't have to use search patterns (though doing so can help, because you're more thorough) and finding something doesn't necessarily end the dive.

EXERCISE-2

1. My buddy and I are looking for a fin a friend lost on the previous dive. If we don't hit a dive limit like depth, gas supply or no stop time, normally the dive would end when we find it.

   ☒ True ☐ False

How did you do?

1. True.

LEARNING OBJECTIVES

By the end of this section, I should be able to answer these questions:

1. What's "bottom topography," and how does it affect search and recovery?

2. How does water movement affect search and recovery?

The Search and Recovery Environment

While you can enjoy some specialty activities in only certain dive environments, searching for and recovering lost objects takes place in virtually all of them. Sometimes you dive in a place (such as a pond or harbor) that otherwise wouldn't be attractive for diving due to reduced visibility or little to see other than what you're looking for, and the only reason to make the dive is for the search and recovery of the object.

That said, leave searches in hazardous environments to professionals. An area orientation is always recommended for diving in unfamiliar environments.

Bottom Topography

Bottom topography, which simply means the contours and characteristics you find on the bottom, affects how you search. Flat, open bottoms are easiest to search, but allow water movement to more easily move an object. Irregular bottoms limit your search techniques. Crevices and obstacles may hide objects, but may also prevent water movement from carrying those objects away.

You don't usually get to choose the bottom topography, but you'll learn to choose appropriate search techniques for whatever the topography where you're searching.

Irregular bottom topography limits your search techniques and may have crevices and obstacles that hide objects, but it may also prevent water movement from carrying those objects away.

Water movement tends to bury lost objects over time, but changes in speed and direction can uncover them, too.

Water Movement

Water movement that affects a search includes currents, tide and surge, which may sweep an object away from where it enters the water. This is particularly true in rivers, but applies anywhere the water's flowing.

Water movement tends to bury lost objects over time, but changes in speed and direction can uncover them, too. These are primarily issues for small objects in high water flow, or moderate-sized objects that have been underwater for an extended period.

Surge tends to carry objects toward deeper water.

Water movement can make it hard to control your position during a search, calling for special techniques (discussed later and in detail in the PADI Search and Recovery Diver course). However, current can aid a search by carrying away accidentally kicked-up silt, or silt intentionally fanned off the bottom when looking for something small that may be buried.

EXERCISE-3

1. My buddy and I are searching for a lost snorkel that was dropped onto flat, open bottom. Compared to irregular bottom, with obstructions and all else being the same, which of the following are likely true? (Choose all that apply.)
   - ☐ a. Water motion is less likely to have moved the snorkel.
   - ☒ b. The search will be easier.
   - ☒ c. We have more choice of search techniques.
2. I've been asked to look for a large coin that fell into a large stream with a moderate flow and a sandy bottom. Which are likely considerations in my search? (Choose all that apply.)
   - ☒ a. The coin will likely be downstream from where it went in.
   - ☒ b. Sand may have covered the coin.
   - ☒ c. It may be hard to hold position during the search.
   - ☒ d. The flow can help by carrying away silt when fanning for the coin.

How did you do?

1. b, c. 2. a, b, c, d.

LEARNING OBJECTIVES

By the end of this section, I should be able to answer this question:

1. What are six potential hazards of search and recovery diving?

Unless prohibited in the local area, wear protective gloves, especially if you're feeling your way on the bottom in low visibility.

Potential Search and Recovery Hazards

Searching for lost objects has some potential hazards to avoid. These concerns exist in most forms of diving, but the nature of searching and/or recovering something can make it important to be extra mindful of them.

1. **Sharp objects and debris.** You tend to have more bottom contact during a search, so be more cautious regarding broken glass, wire, rusted metal and anything else than can cut or puncture. Be aware that mud and silt may conceal such objects.

   Be careful when close to the bottom. Unless prohibited in the local area, wear protective gloves, especially if you're feeling your way on the bottom in low visibility.

2. **Entanglement.** This risk is a little higher than with many other specialty activities, because some search techniques use line/rope. Also, some common search environments have fishing line and netting – be especially careful of transparent, monofilament fishing line.

   Move slowly and carefully over the bottom and around objects likely to have line or netting including piers, piles, wrecks, docks, etc. Carry at least one sharp knife/cutting tool; many divers carry two as an extra precaution. When using a line for the search, always use a reel or line caddy to control the line.

3. **Low visibility.** You may be searching in low-visibility water, or you may cause low visibility by kicking up silt while searching. (Try to do this as little as possible, but in some situations it is almost unavoidable.)

   Low visibility increases the risk of buddy separation or disorientation. You should have enough visibility to check your instruments and communicate with your buddy. If the visibility is too poor for this, leave searching to the professionals.

4. **Current.** Currents exist to some extent in every large body of water, as well as in rivers, streams and spring-fed environments. Even relatively small lakes can have currents. As you know from the PADI Open Water Diver course, current can carry you away from a dive boat, search area or your planned exit.

   When diving and searching in currents, be familiar with local conditions and current diving procedures. If you have an unexpected, strong current during a dive, you may decide to limit the search or cancel the dive. Pay attention to tidal currents (search at slack tide if possible) as well a current's direction.

   Try to avoid searching against anything but a very mild current. Begin up-current; use a search pattern that lets

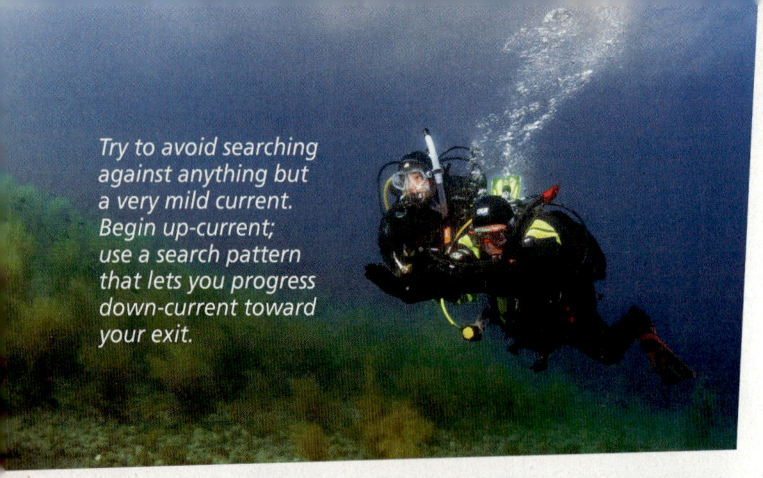

Try to avoid searching against anything but a very mild current. Begin up-current; use a search pattern that lets you progress down-current toward your exit.

you progress down-current toward your exit. (More about search patterns shortly.)

Very strong currents – rivers at flood stage, tidal currents through restricted areas, etc. – are beyond the range of recreational diving.

5. **Falling objects.** This is primarily a potential issue during object recovery. As you'll learn, there's some risk that an object recovered with a lift bag can fall back to the bottom if the bag spills or the rigging fails. But, you greatly reduce this risk simply by staying out from under an object that's being raised.

6. **Boat traffic.** People often lose things where they're boating, so a search may be in an area with boat traffic.

   Clearly mark your search area and location, and use a locally recognized dive flag. If possible, have people at the surface to help direct boats around the search area, and don't assume that boaters see or recognize your dive flag. If a boat sounds close, stay down and deep enough to be safe from its propellers. When you come up, look up and around, and surface cautiously.

Clearly mark your search area and location, and use a locally recognized dive flag. If possible, have people at the surface to help direct boats around the search area, and don't assume that boaters see or recognize your dive flag.

EXERCISE-4

1. My buddy and I are conducting a search that uses a line. We should
   - ☐ a. carry the line in a loose coil.
   - ☑ b. use a reel or line caddy for the line.
2. While conducting a search for a lost fishing rod, my buddy and I hear a boat that sounds like it's coming very close to us. Generally, the best action would be
   - ☑ a. stay deep enough to be safe from its propellers.
   - ☐ b. surface and deploy our surface signaling devices.
   - ☐ c. pull repeatedly on our dive float line.

How did you do?

1. b. 2. a.

You greatly reduce the risk of falling objects simply by staying out from under an object that's being raised.

Planning Search and Recovery Dives

Planning is an important part of all dives, but there are two main reasons for specifically planning the search and recovery portions of a dive, in addition to your general dive plan. Avoid making a search and recovery dive without planning the search/salvage portion adequately.

The first reason is *success*. Successful searches almost always follow thorough, planned search strategies – the best pattern to use (discussed in the next section), where to start, making sure you have the equipment you need and so on. Simply getting in the water and swimming haphazardly to find something tends to have a low success rate. When it works, it's usually more a matter of luck than searching.

LEARNING OBJECTIVES

By the end of this section, I should be able to answer these questions:

1. What are two reasons for planning search and recovery dives?

2. What are the five general steps in planning a search and recovery dive?

The second reason is *safety*. This is part of every dive plan, but as mentioned in the previous section, you want to prepare for and avoid hazards that may be present in the search area. This may be as simple as being sure everyone has gloves, or more complex like having several small boats with dive flags to courteously steer boat traffic away.

Beyond the normal elements of diving, a search and recovery dive has five general steps.

Step One: Define the search objective. Identify the dive purpose, whether it is to search an area, part of a larger search area or raise something that's already located, etc. Be realistic within the limits of ability, equipment, time, etc. You may need to plan more than one dive to find and recover something.

Step Two: Collect and analyze all available information. Try to narrow down the search by learning as much as you can. The more you know about the site, the object and where it was lost, the more efficient the dive and the better prepared you are for potential hazards. Besides what you want for general planning, useful information includes:

In addition to your general dive plan, there are two main reasons for specifically planning the search and recovery portions of a dive: success and safety.

- Expected location, as close as possible where the object was lost
- Size, shape, material and weight of the object
- Any special equipment needed (more about this later)
- Where to attach a lift bag (if needed)
- Bottom topography, visibility, composition, temperature
- Surface conditions
- Possible hazards

Step Three: Diving or snorkeling? Although you usually search and raise something using scuba, sometimes snorkeling is a better choice, such as when looking for a large object in clear, shallow water. Or, you may snorkel for the search and use scuba for the recovery.

Step Four: Dive team. Ideally, you want individuals with search and recovery experience, and who work well together as a team.

Step Five: Briefing. Especially if more than two teams will search and/or recover the object, the briefing is important so everyone understands specific assigned tasks. It usually works best to have an assigned leader who briefs everyone and controls the search to avoid gaps.

The more you know about the site, the object and where it was lost, the more efficient the dive and the better prepared you are for potential hazards.

EXERCISE-5

1. My buddy and I want to specifically plan the search and recovery portion of our dive to increase our chance of success, and to prepare for and avoid hazards that may be present in the search area.
   ☐ True ☐ False
2. My neighbor wants my help finding some expensive golf clubs that "got lost" in a lake after something called a "three putt on a par three." After getting permission to make the dive from the course owners, based on the general steps of planning a search and recovery dive, which of the following would I do first?
   ☐ a. Brief the team on what we'll each do in searching for the clubs.
   ☐ b. Find out how many clubs were lost, what the lake is like and how big the search area is.
   ☐ c. Decide whether we should use scuba or snorkel.
   ☐ d. Find one or more buddies with search and recovery experience who want to team with me.
   ☐ e. Determine the lake's bottom topography, visibility, composition and temperature.

How did you do?

1. True. 2. b.

Underwater Searches

Establishing the Search Area

Before beginning a search, you need to establish the search area, which is part of step two in planning the search. You want to define an area you can be *sure* the object is within, but no larger than necessary. For your starting point, use the most precise estimate available of where the object was lost.

When possible, use natural boundaries to establish the search area (shorelines, edge of a reef, etc.). This makes it easier to stay within your defined area while conducting the search. Defining a square/rectangle shape, which fits many search patterns, also helps.

Measuring the area boundaries can help you choose a search pattern and estimate how many dives (or teams) you need to cover the whole area. There are many types of searches, each with different advantages and disadvantages depending upon what you're looking for, the size of the search area and the conditions. You will learn some of the most popular ones here, practice a small and a large area search pattern on the Search and Recovery Adventure Dive, and learn additional search techniques in the PADI Search and Recovery Diver course. Let's look at some of the patterns that you may practice.

LEARNING

OBJECTIVES

By the end of this section, I should be able to answer these questions:

1. How do I establish a search area?
2. When do I use a *U search* and an *expanding square* compass search pattern, and how do I execute them?
3. When do I use and execute a *circular* search pattern?

When possible, use natural boundaries to establish the search area. Defining a square/rectangle shape, which fits many search patterns, also helps.

The U search is particularly effective for searching a larger area. It works well when searching for small to large objects over flat bottom, though with care, it can also be effective over uneven bottom or in current.

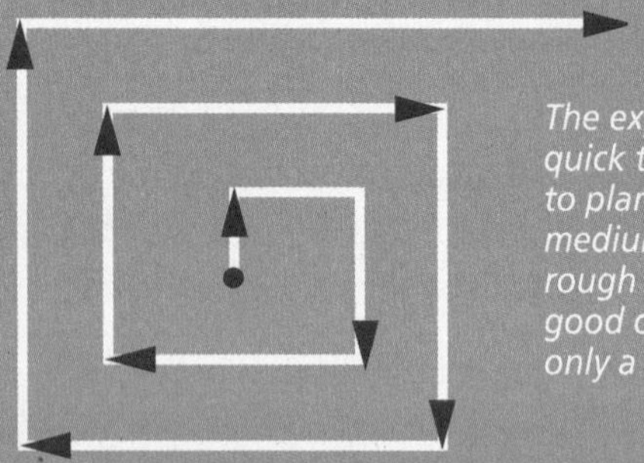

The expanding square is quick to set up and easy to plan. It is well suited for medium-sized objects in rough topography, and is a good choice when there is only a single buddy team.

Compass Search Patterns

Compass search patterns have the advantage of requiring only a compass for navigation and being easy and quick to set up. Two common ones are the *U search* and the *expanding square.*

U Search

The U search is particularly effective for searching a larger area. It works well when searching for small to large objects over flat bottom, though with care, it can also be effective over uneven bottom or in current.

To complete the U pattern, search teams swim along the bottom in a straight line, turn 90 degrees for a short length, and then 90 degrees for a long length. At the end of the long length, they make a right turn, swim a short length, then make another right turn and repeat a long length. This pattern continues, alternating two left turns and two right turns, resulting in a series of U shapes (hence the name) with close overlap.

You adjust the short length that spaces the long search lengths based on the visibility, search area size and object size, but the area searched with each long length should overlap the previous to avoid gaps.

Depending upon the situation, you can measure the legs of the pattern with kick cycles, or even arm spans when looking for something small, in a small area. If there is a current, try to orient the pattern so you swim directly across it, or directly into and with it when swimming the long lengths, and you'll need to account for how it affects your navigation and distance estimation.

If you don't find the object, return to the start point and begin a new pattern in another direction or parallel to the first, until you cover the entire area, find the object, or reach a dive limit.

Expanding Square

The expanding square is quick to set up and easy to plan. It is well suited for medium-sized objects in rough topography, and is a good choice when there is only a single buddy team. It's a popular pattern when you discover you need to look for something while already diving.

Begin the expanding square at the search area center – the best guess where the object is, or was seen last. Swim a short, straight length – for example, three kick cycles. Turn 90 degrees, either right or left, and swim a slightly longer length – for example, six kick cycles. Turn 90 degrees again, always maintaining the same left or right turn as your first, and the next length increased same amount – for our example, nine kick cycles. Continue this process so the pattern forms a straight-lined spiral moving away from the starting point. Overlap the spiral sides slightly to avoid search gaps.

The distance you travel between turns depends on the object size and visibility. The smaller the object and lower the visibility, the shorter the distance you want between turns.

Line-Based Search Patterns

Line-based search patterns take more time and effort to set up, but are less likely to have accidental gaps. Many (but not all) are better choices for obstructed bottoms, and tend to work better in currents, because the line is anchored and helps control navigation more closely. This pattern is usually a good choice when looking for something small in limited visibility.

Circular Search

The circular search is a good choice for finding a small object in a small area. You need a line and reel, because it is nearly impossible to navigate an accurate circle without them. This search works best on a relatively flat bottom free of obstructions.

As with the expanding square, start at the search area center. One buddy anchors the line while the other swims a circle, holding the line taut. After each circle, the team lets out a little more line so that the search continues in widening, overlapping circles. The anchor diver may control the reel, letting out line on each pass, but the search diver may do so to accommodate topography and visibility.

For larger areas, the line may be anchored on a stake or by a second buddy team. This allows the search circles to become large without losing buddy contact. Also, two buddies can swim side by side on the line as they circle, covering a wider area with each pass. The searching team controls the reel.

The circular search is a good choice for finding a small object in a small area. It works best on a relatively flat bottom free of obstructions.

With multiple buddy teams conducting a circular search or other line-based search, rope signals are useful for communicating when out of sight from one another.

Rope Signals

With multiple buddy teams conducting a circular search (one anchoring, the other searching) or other line-based search, rope signals are useful for communicating when out of sight of one another. Here are common rope pull signals:

One pull = *Attention or Stop*; when starting a search, Begin pattern

Two pulls = *Okay?* or *Okay*

Three pulls = *I've finished the leg* (circle or length of pattern)

Four pulls = *Come toward me* or *Let's unite*

Continuous pulls = *Emergency – come to me immediately*

In the PADI Search and Recovery Diver course, you will learn additional search patterns with lines.

EXERCISE-6

1. While gearing up on a dive boat, I accidentally dropped my favorite mask overboard, but fortunately I have a spare. The wind is making the boat swing, so to establish our search area when my buddy and I look for it, we should use ______________ as our starting point.
   - ☐ a. the mooring
   - ☐ b. directly under the boat center
   - ☐ c. the trail line buoy
   - ☐ d. as best we can estimate, where I dropped it

2. My buddy and I need to search for a lost deck chair in a 60-metre by 30-metre/200-foot by 100-foot search area. Of those listed, probably the best choice would be the __________ pattern.
   - ☐ a. circular search
   - ☐ b. expanding square
   - ☐ c. U search

3. Although it's best to use a line and reel for the circular search pattern, with practice I can navigate an accurate circle using my compass.
   - ☐ True ☐ False

How did you do?

1. d. 2. c. 3. False. It is nearly impossible to navigate an accurate circle without a line and reel.

LEARNING OBJECTIVES

By the end of this section, I should be able to answer these questions:

1. Based on the weight of an object, when should I use a lift bag for recovery?
2. What is wrong with using my BCD as a lifting device to recover an object?
3. What three advantages does using a commercially made lift bag to recover an object have over using a homemade lift bag?
4. How do I tie a bowline, sheet bend and two half-hitches, and under what conditions should I be able to tie them?
5. What is the procedure for lifting an object to the surface with a lift bag?
6. Why do I choose a lift bag based on the weight of the object being lifted?
7. Where should I position myself when a lift bag is ascending?
8. Which air source should I use to fill a lift bag?

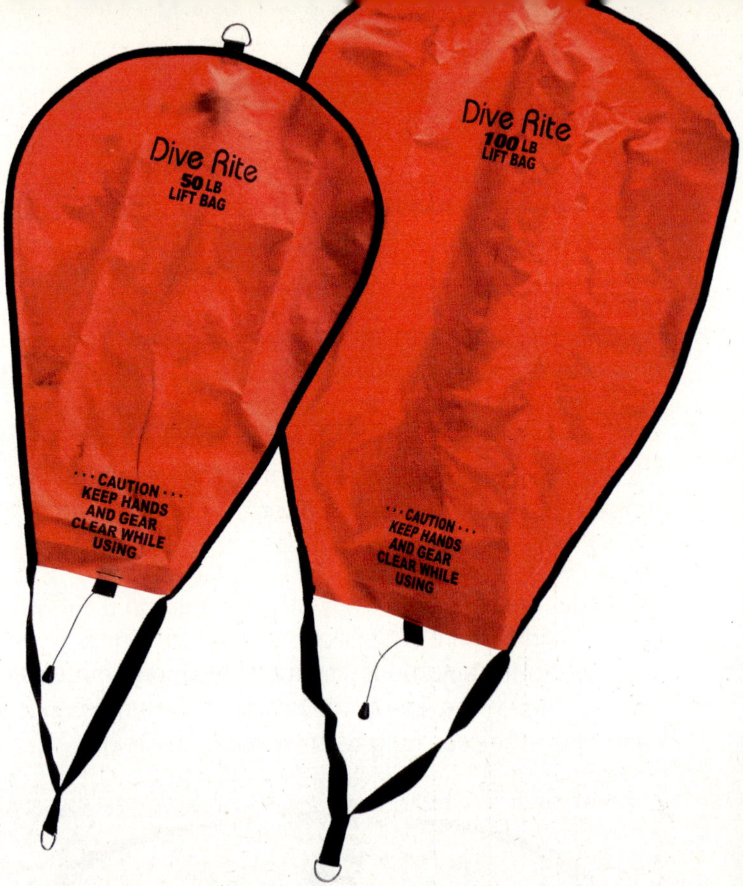

Although lift bags can be improvised, it is better to use a commercially made bag because it's designed for the job. Your PADI Instructor and/or PADI Dive Center or Resort can help you choose an appropriate lift bag.

Recovery Procedures

Lift Bags

Once you find what you're looking for, you want to bring it up. This isn't an issue with small objects (e.g. glasses, wallets, fishing rods, etc.) because you carry them up in your hand or in a mesh bag; this is suitable for objects that weigh no more than 4-7 kilograms/10-15 pounds.

Do *not* use your BCD to lift more weight than you can comfortably swim to the surface. This is important, because doing so risks a rapid, uncontrolled ascent if you were to accidentally lose hold of the recovered object. This creates an unacceptable DCI risk. For recreational recoveries of objects weighing more than this to no more than 45 kilograms/100 pounds, you need to use a *lift bag* – a specially made bag to which you add gas to provide buoyancy to the object you're lifting to the surface.

Although lift bags can be improvised, it is better to use a commercially made bag because it's designed for the job, giving at least three advantages. First, they have built-in dump valve systems so you can release expanding air and control the ascent. Homemade devices generally don't, which can create some hazards. Second, they have rigging to which you attach the object, made to withstand the stress of lifting. This can be a problem with homemade devices. Third, they're made of rugged materials designed for the job to withstand the diving environment. Depending upon what's used, improvised lift devices can fail before or during a lift because the material can't withstand the stresses.

Your PADI Instructor and PADI Dive Center or Resort can help you choose an appropriate lift bag. And, some DSMBs (Delayed Surface Marker Buoys) are large enough to double as small lift bags.

It is possible to improvise a lift bag that works adequately in a pinch. You can learn more about this in the PADI Search and Recovery Diver course.

Preparing for the Lift

The first step after locating an object is to mark it with a buoy and line, which stays attached until the object is safely out of the water. This allows you or another dive team to return to it with a lifting device if you don't have it during the search, and so you don't have to search again if it comes loose and sinks again during the lift.

The first step after locating an object is to mark it with a buoy and line, which stays attached until the object is safely out of the water.

Next, attach the lift bag securely to the object. How you do this depends upon the bag and the object, but most frequently involves clipping the bag to the object, tying it, or a combination of these. If you'll be tying the object to the bag, use nylon line if possible because knots hold well in it. Polypropylene tends to untie more easily, though will work if necessary.

There are literally hundreds of knots you can use, but practically speaking, there are three that will cover more than 90 percent of what you need for recovering an object. You want to be able to tie all three underwater in low visibility by feel while wearing gloves, which takes some practice.

How you attach your lift bag depends upon the bag and the object, but most frequently involves clipping the bag to the object, tying it, or a combination of these.

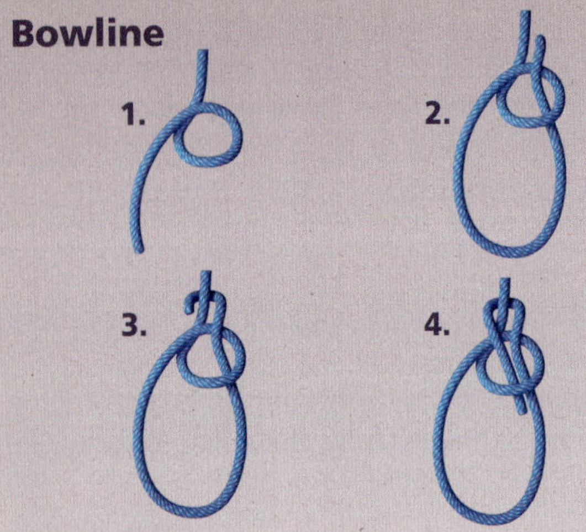

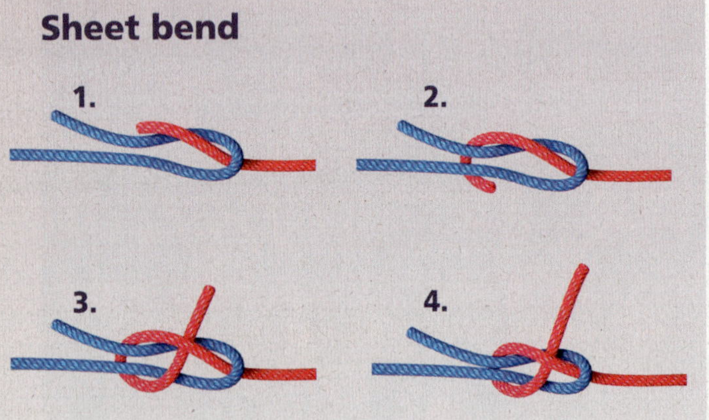

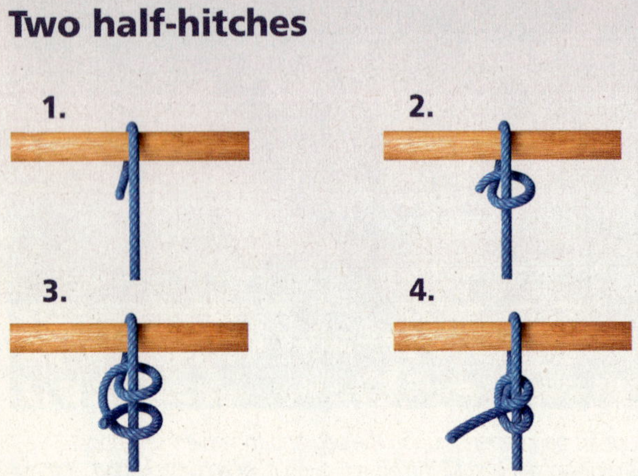

Bowline. This forms a loop with a very secure, but easily untied knot. You usually use it to attach line to an object.

1. Make an overhand loop in the line the size of "eye" desired.
2. Pass the bitter (free) end up through the overhand loop.
3. Bring the bitter end around the standing part (main line) and back down through the overhand loop.
4. Pull the knot tight by holding the bitter end and the loop with one hand, and pulling the standing part with the other.

Sheet bend. You use this knot to attach two lines together; it works well with two different diameters.

1. Form a bight (open end bend) in the thicker of the two lines. Pass the bitter end of the second line up through the bight formed by the first line.
2. Wrap the end of line around the bight.
3. Pass the end over the bight, putting it under its own standing part.
4. Pull taut on both standing parts to set the knot.

Two half-hitches. This is another knot used to attach line to an object.

1. Take a turn around the object. This knot may be combined with a round turn, which is simply passing the rope all the way around the object twice before tying the knot.
2. Bring the bitter end under and over the standing part and back under itself.
3. Continue by passing the bitter end under and over the standing part, then back under itself.
4. Draw tight.

The PADI App shows you how to tie these and other useful knots.

Lifting with the Lift Bag

In planning the recovery, ideally try to choose a lift bag with just enough lift to offset the object's negative buoyancy. As you'll see, this makes lifting easier, because it will be approximately neutral when you inflate the bag to nearly full. This way, expanding

After securing the bag to the object, use your alternate air source or an accessory inflator to put a small puff into the bag. Add gas in small amounts until it is approximately neutral or slightly negative.

As you ascend, expanding gas in the lift bag will increase its buoyancy. Neither you nor your buddy should be under the object. If you cannot control its buoyancy, let it go and swim away in case it sinks. Do not risk making an uncontrolled ascent.

gas escapes from it during ascent, which makes it easier to control the ascent. If this isn't possible, you'll need to vent expanding gas to control the object's ascent.

After securing the bag to the object, use your alternate air source or an accessory inflator, not the second stage from your mouth, to put a small puff into the bag. (In cold water, use an accessory inflator to reduce freezing/freeflow risk.) Pull up on the rigging to be sure it is secure. Then, add gas in small amounts, pulling up periodically to check the buoyancy. If bottom suction (e.g. from a mud bottom) holds the object down, break the suction by pulling up on the object, rather than relying on the lift bag to do so.

Continue filling the bag and checking until everything is approximately neutral or slightly negative, so you can hold it over the bottom. This will help you start and control the ascent. You can also swim the object horizontally to bring it up closer to your exit, near a boat, etc.

When ready, start upward, pulling up on the bag and object. Expanding gas in the bag will increase its buoyancy. **Neither you nor your buddy should be under the object.** If the bag is close to full as you start your ascent, expanding gas will bubble out of the bag's bottom and/or exhaust valve. If not, you will need to vent expanding gas as you ascend to control its buoyancy. You may accompany the bag alongside if you can control the ascent. If you cannot, let it go and swim away in case it sinks.

Do not risk making an uncontrolled ascent.

At the surface, you may add air to the bag to give it ample buoyancy, or attach a second bag. You may also want to secure it to a boat or float while you exit the water.

At the surface, you may add air to the bag to give it ample buoyancy, or attach a second bag.

SEARCH AND RECOVERY DIVER SPECIALTY

At your instructor's discretion, the Search and Recovery Adventure Dive credits toward the PADI Search and Recovery Diver Specialty course. The course gives you more opportunities to develop and practice search and recovery, including:

- Relocating an object from the surface
- Using more search patterns
- Improvising lift devices when necessary
- Practice in small and large search areas

Remember to log your training dives with the PADI Mobile App or at padi.com.

EXERCISE-7

1. My buddy and I plan to raise an object that weighs 10 kilograms/22 pounds. My buddy doesn't think we need a lift bag, but based on accepted recommendations, I do. Who is right?
   - ☒ a. I am.
   - ☐ b. My buddy is.
2. The most serious problem with using my BCD to lift more weight than I can comfortably swim with is that I could drop the object I'm lifting and have a rapid, uncontrollable ascent.
   ☒ True ☐ False
3. My buddy and I are raising a small outboard motor using a commercially made lift bag. The advantages of using this instead of a homemade one include that commercially made ones (choose all that apply):
   - ☒ a. usually have exhaust valves.
   - ☐ b. automatically inflate.
   - ☒ c. have rigging suited to lifting an object.
   - ☒ d. are made of rugged material.
4. Ideally, I should be able to tie a bowline, sheet bend and two half-hitches in low visibility by feel while wearing gloves.
   ☒ True ☐ False
5. Ideally, I should use a lift bag with significantly more lift than the weight of the object I'm bringing up.
   ☐ True ☒ False
6. To inflate a lift bag, I should use
   - ☐ a. my primary second stage from my mouth.
   - ☒ b. my alternate air source or an accessory inflator.
   - ☐ c. my buddy's alternate air source.
7. I'm inflating a lift bag to raise a bicycle to the surface. I should add air until the bag and bicycle
   - ☐ a. ascend rapidly to the surface.
   - ☒ b. are neutral or just slightly negatively buoyant.
   - ☐ c. are about 7 kilograms/15 pounds negatively buoyant.
8. While raising a small outboard motor with a lift bag, my buddy and I should be____________ the motor and bag as we ascend with it.
   - ☒ a. alongside
   - ☐ b. beneath

How did you do?

1. a. 2. True. 3. a, c, d. 4. True. 5. False. Use a lift bag with as close to the same lift as the weight of the object as possible. 6. b. 7. b. 8. a.

seaQuest
AKONA

Knowledge Review – Search and Recovery

Answer the following questions by selecting the best choice (or choices) from those provided. Be prepared to discuss the material at your next training session.

1. A friend tells me that he lost his 48-kilogram/105-pound anchor near the harbor entrance in 35-45 metres/115-150 feet of water. He's looking for divers to recover his anchor. Is this a task for a recreational search and recovery diver?
   - ☐ Yes
   - ☒ No
2. Which of the following are potential hazards for search and recovery diving? (Choose all that apply.)
   - ☒ Sharp objects and debris
   - ☒ Entanglement
   - ☒ Loss of buddy contact
   - ☒ Boat traffic
3. The first step in planning a search and recovery dive is generally to
   - ☐ choose an appropriate site.
   - ☐ select a buddy team.
   - ☐ define the objective.
   - ☒ collect and analyze information.
4. My buddy and I plan to search for a lost mask at a local dive site that has excellent visibility (18 metres/60 feet). I talk to the diver who lost the mask and determine that much of the search area is no deeper than 10 metres/30 feet over sand bottom. Would it be appropriate to search from the surface snorkeling?
   - ☒ Yes
   - ☐ No
5. A diver drops a weight belt off the end of a long pier. My buddy and I know the bottom off the pier is about 12 metres/40 feet deep and is covered with large, irregular protruding rocks. I decide to use a/an __________ search pattern.
   - ☒ expanding square
   - ☐ circular
   - ☐ U pattern
6. On shore after a dive, I realize that my fish identification slates are missing. I last saw them when I surfaced by our float before swimming to shore on the surface. The float is still deployed about 20 metres/yards offshore in 9 metres/30 feet of water on a gently sloping sandy bottom. My buddy and I decide to look for the slates on the next dive and choose to use a/an __________ search pattern.
   - ☐ expanding square
   - ☐ circular
   - ☒ U pattern
7. If I have a line available and am looking for a small object in a relatively small area, over a flat bottom, a circular search pattern may be a good choice.
   - ☒ True
   - ☐ False
8. My buddy and I come across two BCD weight pouches on the bottom. After trying to pick them up, we realize they are heavy and probably weigh more than 8 kilograms/20 pounds each. My buddy signals for me to take one pouch and he'll carry the other to the surface. What should I do?
   - ☐ Agree and inflate my BCD to offset the extra weight so I can ascend.
   - ☒ Disagree, mark the location and leave the weights until we can return with a lift bag.
9. What features of a commercially made lift bag make it desirable for recovering underwater objects? (Choose all that apply.)
   - ☐ Comes with a low-pressure inflator and deflator
   - ☒ Is constructed from heavy-duty materials
   - ☒ Has exhaust valves to vent air on ascent
   - ☒ Has loops or slings for easy rigging

10. Of the knots listed, I will normally use a __________ to form a loop to tie a line to something, and a __________ to tie two lines together.

- ☐ sheet bend; bowline
- ☐ sheet bend; two half-hitches
- ☐ two half-hitches; bowline
- ☐ two half-hitches; sheet bend
- ☐ bowline; two half-hitches
- ☒ bowline; sheet bend

11. I should use my primary second stage to inflate a lift bag, and position myself below the bag and object as I control it on the way to the surface.

- ☐ True
- ☒ False

Student Statement

I completed this Knowledge Review to the best of my ability. For any questions I answered incorrectly or incompletely, I reviewed the explanation provided and now understand the material. In the case of anything about which I still have questions, I will review the material again and, if necessary, discuss it with my instructor at our next session.

☒ I agree ☐ I disagree

Student signature ____________________

Date 10/22/18

scenario

"Yumiko and Lyn were swimming along a shallow reef, when a triggerfish suddenly swam directly at them. The fish turned abruptly, swam back to a smaller patch of reef, then swam toward them again.

Lyn gently tugged Yumiko to the side, indicating they should swim around the patch reef instead of directly over it. A few minutes later, they saw another triggerfish. This time, they swam well around where the fish was swimming, and it didn't behave like the first one.

"What was up with that first triggerfish?" Yumiko asked after the dive. "I've never had one attack me like that before."

"The triggerfish was just protecting its young," said Lyn. "After that first one, I realized the triggerfish in this area may be spawning, so I knew we could avoid making them defensive by staying out of their territories."

- *Would you expect that aquatic marine animals "attack" divers without cause?*
- *How did Lyn turn the inadvertent active encounter with the first triggerfish into a passive encounter with subsequent triggerfish?*

UNDERWATER
NATURALIST
13

UNDERWATER **NATURALIST**

LEARNING OBJECTIVES

By the end of this section, I should be able to answer these questions:

1. How do I define "ecology" and "ecosystem"?

2. What are at least three physical/structural differences between the land environment and the underwater environment?

Ecology is the study of living things. An ecosystem is a natural system functioning together, including all inanimate and animate components.

Introduction to Underwater Naturalist

Coming to know the underwater world means learning about ecology and ecosystems.

Ecology is the study of living things and their interrelationships with each other and their environments. An environment consists of inanimate components such as chemicals and physical factors – for aquatic environments this includes sunlight, minerals dissolved in water, current and waves, etc. The environment also consists of animate (living) components – for aquatic environments this includes coral reefs, organisms that others can feed on, etc.

An ecosystem is a natural system functioning together, including all inanimate and animate components. Each ecosystem has its own climate and life adapted to it. Ecosystems can be broad or specific depending upon what you study. Broad ecosystems have smaller ecosystems within them. Earth is an ecosystem. Each ocean and sea is an ecosystem within planet earth, and a coral reef is an ecosystem within those.

Differences in Terrestrial and Aquatic Ecosystems

The physical differences between the terrestrial and underwater worlds make the aquatic realm quite different, in several ways.

Density is one of the principle differences between terrestrial and aquatic ecosystems. Water is about

800 times denser than air, so it takes more energy to move through water. Only the fastest terrestrial animals must be streamlined; all but the slowest aquatic animals are streamlined. Nonetheless, the fastest animals are terrestrial; the sailfish can swim 110 kph/68 mph, but even that is a bit slower than the cheetah, and considerably slower than the peregrine falcon, which can exceed 320 kph/200 mph in a dive.

Another difference deals with fluid motion. Relatively few terrestrial animals use air-born reproductive strategies, like plants use pollen – but, this is the most common strategy among animals as well as plants in aquatic ecosystems. Almost no terrestrial animals rely entirely on air movement to bring food or to carry them to food, but many aquatic animals rely on water movement to get nourishment.

One difference scuba divers understand intimately is light. Most terrestrial ecosystems have adequate light to support plant life. Only relatively shallow aquatic ecosystems have plant (or algae) life. Air doesn't significantly affect light properties, other than absorbing ultraviolet light. Water absorbs and scatters light over short distances, so that light is not a significant energy source even at depths that still have visible light.

All terrestrial organisms deal with *gravity*. Because of this, terrestrial organisms have rigid support structures (fiber, wood, bone, cartilage, etc.). The larger the organism, the more support it needs; gravity limits the size of terrestrial organisms. Buoyancy in water offsets gravity, so it affects aquatic organisms less, or almost not at all. In fact, many aquatic organisms have no rigid support structures. The largest organisms live in the oceans. Entire ecosystems (e.g., plankton) live suspended in water. Practically speaking, there is no comparable terrestrial ecosystem.

Oxygen is evenly distributed in the atmosphere (about 20.9 percent). Adaptations to low oxygen are primarily to accommodate altitude in terrestrial organisms. Water has less oxygen and it is unevenly distributed; shallow-water environments may have more oxygen than deeper water. Many aquatic organisms have gills, which are significantly more efficient than lungs at gathering oxygen.

The physical differences explain the resulting structural differences between the terrestrial and the aquatic environments. For example, plants tend to dominate terrestrial ecosystems, thanks to rigid structures that combat gravity. They are often massive and difficult to move, making plant eco-

systems stable and long-lived compared to aquatic plant ecosystems. Long-lived plant communities control short-lived animal communities. We tend to describe terrestrial ecosystems in plant terms and geological terms: tropical rain forest, grassland, snow forest, tundra, desert, etc.

On the flip side, animals tend to dominate aquatic ecosystems. Most plants – including algae, which are not technically plants – tend to be small and primarily microscopic. Small aquatic animals consume small aquatic plants, bringing plant energy into the ecosystem. Large, rigid organism structures are bottom-dwelling collections of animals (coral reefs). More than terrestrial ecosystems, aquatic ecosystems are often described in animal terms: coral reef, oyster beds, clam beds, etc. (There are exceptions, such as kelp forests.)

Terrestrial ecosystems tend to have shorter food chains, because they include large animals that eat stable plant food sources directly. Aquatic ecosystems tend to have longer food chains, because more often small animals eat small aquatic plants; and increasingly larger animals consume smaller ones, passing energy up the food chain.

Obviously, there are many more differences between the physical characteristics and structure of terrestrial and aquatic ecosystems, but these are some of the most readily observable ones. Learn more about the differences of the systems in the PADI Underwater Naturalist specialty course at padi.com. You can also learn more by reading oceanography references, such as *Life on an Ocean Planet®*, published by PADI corporate affiliate Current Publishing (currentpublishingcorp.com).

In terrestrial ecosystems (top photos), long-lived plant communities tend to control short-lived animal communities. In aquatic ecosystems (bottom photos), animals tend to dominate. There are exceptions to both, however.

EXERCISE-1

1. An ecosystem is the animate components of a natural system functioning together.

   ☐ True ☐ False

2. The physical and structural differences between terrestrial and aquatic ecosystems include (choose all that apply):

   ☐ a. density.
   ☐ b. oxygen.
   ☐ c. fluid motion.
   ☐ d. organism intelligence.
   ☐ e. gravity.
   ☐ f. light.

How did you do?

1. False. An ecosystem includes both the inanimate and animate components. 2. a, b, c, e, f.

LEARNING

OBJECTIVES

By the end of this section, I should be able to answer these questions:

1.What does the label "hazardous" mean when applied to an organism?

2. What is the most common cause of aquatic animal "attacks"?

3. How do offensive and defensive behaviors in aquatic animals differ?

4. What is an accurate view of "dangerous" aquatic animals?

5. What are four misperceptions people may have about aquatic organisms?

Human Perceptions of Aquatic Life

Hazardous Marine Life

It's important to have and to share accurate perceptions of aquatic life. This is more than an academic exercise, because perceptions shape values. In turn, values shape actions and interactions. People with inaccurate perceptions of aquatic life may therefore act in ways that differ from how they would act with accurate information.

For example, many people think mangrove swamps are muddy wastelands full of pests. Informed that mangroves trap sediment and protect fragile corals, and act as essential nurseries for fish (including important food fish), many of these people would actively oppose mangrove destruction.

Another example is the common perception that sharks are "bad" because they "attack" people. This belief may lead some to think that killing sharks isn't an issue, or worse, that it's beneficial. The opposite is actually true. Most people, when informed that sharks seldom endanger humans and, that attacks are rare

Perceptions are important. Informed that mangroves trap sediment and protect fragile corals, and act as essential nurseries for fish, many people would actively oppose mangrove destruction.

Hazardous simply means that an organism can cause injury to a human.

(even by potentially hazardous species), and that sharks play integral parts in ecosystem balance, will have at least a more balanced view of sharks and their value.

One of the most problematic perceptions is that certain aquatic organisms are hazardous. *Hazardous* simply means that an organism can cause injury to a human. The problem is that this can be used to form a value judgment. An organism's characteristics are adaptations to its environment; these are neither "good" nor "bad." Potentially hazardous organisms, terrestrial or aquatic, behave according to instinct. There is no malice (ill will) when an animal defends its territory or young, or takes prey.

Animal Behaviors

The most common cause of "attacks" is when an animal exhibits defensive behavior. The organism perceives a need to defend itself, its territory, its mate or its young.

Attacks by aquatic animals can be offensive or defensive in nature. *Defensive* actions, as just described, result when a diver appears to be a threat to the organism. The diver initiates the interaction, usually unintentionally. *Offensive* actions are those initiated by the organism. These are much less common, and most frequently result when the animal mistakes a human for prey (excepting crocodilians, humans are not natural prey for any aquatic animals). For example, it's largely thought that surfers have been attacked by great white sharks because, from below, they look much like sea lions – the great white's natural prey.

Many sedentary organisms, like fire coral, use stinging to both protect and feed themselves. Other non-sedentary organisms, like jellyfish, also sting for the same reasons. These are not attacks. The accurate view of "dangerous" aquatic animals is that these organisms are potentially hazardous if humans trigger defensive responses, or inadvertently appear to be food.

You can reduce the risk of aquatic organism injuries by taking these steps:

- **Get local knowledge.** It's your responsibility to know which local creatures may be hazardous.
- **Understand the nature and severity of potential hazards.** For example, failing to protect yourself from sea

The most common cause of "attacks" is when an animal exhibits defensive behavior. The organism perceives a need to defend itself, its territory, its mate or its young.

urchins may result in a painful injury, but it wouldn't typically be life-threatening. Failing to be appropriately cautious of sea snakes, on the other hand, could be life-threatening.

- **Be cautious.** Behave in ways that reduce and avoid risks of triggering defensive or feeding behaviors of higher animals. For example, to avoid moray eel bites, don't reach into holes where they may live.
- **Protect yourself.** Reduce the risk of injury from stinging organisms by wearing exposure protection, by watching where you dive, by avoiding contact with the environment, and by checking anything you may touch with your hands, feet, knees, etc. when contact is unavoidable.

Common Misperceptions

There are four myths and misperceptions that people commonly have about aquatic organisms. As stated earlier, each of these can affect how people value and interact with animals, commonly in negative ways.

People misperceive aquatic *animals as dangerous and harmful* (as just discussed). Animals are *also misperceived as harmless and friendly*, as is the case with domestic pets or other animals. The other extreme is an unrealistic perception of animals being without risk entirely. This is particularly true of animals with two eyes and complex behaviors like dolphins, fish, crabs, etc.

Media and entertainment can create much of this misinformation and misconceptions. For example, you shouldn't try to pet a sea lion (you may get severely bitten) just because you see trainers touch sea lions at the zoo. Similarly, television and movies sometimes portray dolphins as benevolent and concerned with humans. Though there are occasional interactions that have been initiated by dolphins, this impression generally isn't accurate. It is a normal mental mechanism to relate something unfamiliar with something familiar in an attempt to understand it. Regarding aquatic life, this isn't always a good strategy; the better approach is to learn about aquatic life through education and observation.

The third common misperception is that humans sometimes see *animals as nonliving, inanimate objects.* Animals that don't have eyes and don't move (or move very slowly) may seem inanimate or less important than higher-order animals. These include coral, sea urchins, sea fans, sea stars, etc. Due to ignorance, people may treat them as inanimate – such as breaking or standing on living coral. Emotional detachment can cause people to treat even higher-order animals as inanimate, such as playing with an inflated pufferfish as though it were a balloon.

You reduce the risk of aquatic organism injuries by knowing what local organisms may be hazardous, being cautious to avoid triggering defensive or feeding behaviors, by wearing exposure protection and avoiding contact with the environment.

A misperception is seeing animals as nonliving, inanimate objects. This is more common with animals that don't have eyes and don't move quickly.

The fourth common misperception is that humans sometimes see *animals as having human characteristics*. Especially with higher-order animals, some perceptions arise from attributing human characteristics to animals. As with perceptions of being harmless and friendly, television, cinema and other entertainment can create these perceptions. Having animals wear human clothes or nod "yes" to a trainer's questions is one example of this; others are fictional portrayals in which animals recognize when humans are in trouble and come to their aid. Extreme portrayals cause fewer misperceptions; no one thinks a dog can talk just because sometimes they do in the movies.

Ostensibly, it comes down to this: Misperceiving animals' true nature impedes recognizing them for what they really are, and what their importance in the ecosystem is.

Misperceiving animals' true nature impedes recognizing them for what they really are, and what their importance in the ecosystem is.

EXERCISE-2

1. A "hazardous" marine organism is one that
   - ☐ a. intends to cause harm to a human.
   - ☐ b. can cause injury/harm to a human.
   - ☐ c. is naturally bad.
2. Most aquatic animal "attacks" result from the animal
   - ☐ a. mistaking a diver for prey.
   - ☐ b. seeking revenge for something a diver does.
   - ☐ c. feeling the need to defend itself, territory, mate or young.
3. A/an __________ action is initiated by the organism, and is often the result of feeding behavior.
   - ☐ a. defensive
   - ☐ b. offensive
   - ☐ c. mating
   - ☐ d. territorial
4. An accurate view of "dangerous" aquatic animals is that they are potentially hazardous because humans cannot predict their behavior.
   ☐ True ☐ False
5. The common myths that exist about aquatic organisms include that (choose all that apply):
   - ☐ a. they are harmless and friendly, like a domestic pet.
   - ☐ b. they are dangerous and harmful.
   - ☐ c. they have human characteristics.
   - ☐ d. they all see humans as a potential food source.
   - ☐ e. they are nonliving, inanimate objects.

How did you do?

1. b. 2. c. 3. b. 4. False. An accurate view of "dangerous" aquatic animals is that these organisms are potentially hazardous if humans trigger defensive responses, or inadvertently appear to be food. 5. a, b, c, e.

LEARNING

OBJECTIVES

By the end of this section, I should be able to answer these questions:

1. How do I passively interact with aquatic organisms?
2. Can I responsibly touch or handle aquatic life?
3. Why should divers avoid riding aquatic animals?
4. Why should I avoid feeding fish and other aquatic animals?
5. Which diving techniques should I use to preserve bottom-dwelling organisms, and to reduce the effects of disturbing all aquatic life?

Passive interactions are those that have almost no effect, and are interactions in which you don't directly touch, move, disturb or otherwise directly act in a way that affects an organism's normal behaviors and functions.

Responsible Interactions with Aquatic Life

Passive Interactions

Generally speaking, whenever you enter a natural body of water, you will have interactions with aquatic life, intended or not. Some interactions, such as sightseeing, have little effect on aquatic organisms; some interactions, like hunting, may have a tremendous negative effect.

Interactions with aquatic life may be *passive* or *active*. Passive interactions are those that have almost no effect, and are interactions in which you don't directly touch, move, disturb or otherwise directly act in a way that affects an organism's normal behaviors and functions. Active interactions are those with greater effect, because you touch, move, disturb or affect organisms in some way.

Some interactions are clearly passive (e.g., sedately watching the activities at a cleaner station) or clearly active (e.g., picking up a sea star to look at its underside). Some interactions may be passive, active or in between depending on how you carry them out. For example, you can watch fish without disturbing them, you can watch fish by chasing them, or you can watch fish and take an occasional flash photo that disturbs them only momentarily.

Whether an interaction is passive or active may depend on the organism. For example, swimming close to a fish that prepares to flee, hide or defend, etc., is probably an active interaction. Swimming close to a fish that does not alter its normal behavior significantly probably isn't an active interaction.

The best way to passively interact is to primarily observe natural behaviors in a normal environment. You may observe individual animals, as well as interactions between and within species. It's also worth observing interactions between divers and aquatic life (often unintended by the diver). Aquatic life may exhibit curiosity or to the contrary, flee, make territorial displays or assume defensive postures in response to a diver getting too close.

Some interactions may be passive, active or in between depending on how you carry them out.

Touching, Handling

Touching and handling aquatic life are considered active interactions, though they can be done responsibly. To be done responsibly, touching or handling an organism should:

- be done only by people with the education/experience necessary to do so safely for both divers and the organism;
- not cause a significant disruption to the organism's normal behavior;
- only be done if it provides a meaningful learning experience about the organism without compromising its wellbeing.

Obviously, you can't touch or handle all animals and meet these criteria. Some organisms are too fragile (e.g., coral), and others will almost certainly harm you. Some organisms, while not otherwise harmed, will have a significant behavior disruption.

Riding and Feeding

At one time, it was common to see pictures of divers riding animals (turtles in particular). Fortunately, today more people know they shouldn't do this – at the very least, riding an animal frightens it. Air-breathing aquatic animals can also be drowned by riding them for too long, preventing them from surfacing for air. Also, some seemingly harmless and otherwise gentle animals – manta rays and dugongs, for example – may react defensively

Good diving techniques help you preserve bottom-dwelling organisms and reduce disturbing aquatic life. Secure your kit and dive properly weighted, staying neutral and in good trim.

if ridden, raising the risk of injury to the diver. Today, responsible divers don't attempt to ride aquatic creatures.

Feeding aquatic animals is an active interaction that appears positive, but is generally detrimental. It's prohibited in many areas for several reasons.

Feeding wild animals on a frequent basis may disrupt their normal feeding behaviors and patterns, and, it is debated, may also cause animals to associate humans with food. If so, this could present a hazard. It can also be a hazard for animals that lose their normal fear of humans.

The wrong foods can make animals sick, and accidentally ingesting plastic containers used to carry it in can kill them. While feeding predators like sharks and rays does provide opportunities to see creatures you'd normally not see otherwise, this should be done only be trained professionals who understand the complexities of the local ecosystem and proper feeding techniques.

All in all, the best approach for recreational divers is to simply refrain from feeding marine life.

Dive Techniques

Good diving techniques help you preserve bottom-dwelling organisms and reduce disturbing aquatic life. You've heard most of these techniques before:

- Secure your kit so nothing dangles, especially your SPG/console and alternate second stage.
- Maintain neutral buoyancy and good trim. Stay well off the bottom, horizontal, with your legs parallel to the bottom.
- Don't dive over-weighted. As you've learned, diving over-weighted lowers your feet.
- Descend so that you don't reach the bottom with your feet directly below you. Transition to a horizontal swimming position well above the bottom.
- Swim without kicking up sand or silt. This preserves the visibility. Also, sand/silt settling on coral and other organisms can injure them.
- Be cautious about what you touch – stay far enough above the bottom that you don't kick things. If you must touch the bottom, choose an insensitive area like sand, but even then use care because many organisms live in these areas, too.
- Swim slowly and calmly, as if you're part of the environment. This reduces how much you disrupt behaviors.

EXERCISE-3

1. My buddy and I are diving at 15 metres/50 feet and see a shark at the edge of the reef. Chasing the shark so that we can identify it may be an example of an active interaction.
   ☐ True ☐ False
2. My buddy pulls a lobster from its hole to show me its claws. This is acceptable, because we will put it back after I take an close-up photo of it.
   ☐ True ☐ False
3. I should never ride an aquatic animal, because (choose all that apply):
   ☐ a. I may harm it.
   ☐ b. I could inadvertently drown it.
   ☐ c. it might swim too fast.
   ☐ d. it may react defensively and hurt me.
4. Feeding wild aquatic animals (choose all that apply):
   ☐ a. is encouraged in many areas.
   ☐ b. may disrupt normal feeding patterns and behavior.
   ☐ c. may cause the animals to associate humans with food.
   ☐ d. could make the animals sick.
   ☐ e. should only be done by a trained professional.
5. Good diving techniques that help me reduce disturbing aquatic marine life include (choose all that apply):
   ☐ a. maintaining neutral buoyancy throughout the dive.
   ☐ b. securing my gear so nothing dangles.
   ☐ c. being cautious about what I touch.
   ☐ d. swimming quickly so that I can avoid sensitive areas.

How did you do?

1. True 2. False. Touching or handling an organism should only be done by people with the education/experience to do so safely, and in such a way that will not significantly disrupt the organism's normal behavior or its wellbeing. 3. a, b, d. 4. b, c, d, e. 5. a, b, c.

LEARNING OBJECTIVES

By the end of this section, I should be able to answer the following questions:

1. Why are divers "natural" ambassadors for the aquatic environment?
2. As a PADI Diver, what steps can I take to protect the aquatic world?
3. What is Project AWARE?

Aquatic Conservation

Ambassador for Our Environment

Divers like you notice changes to the underwater world. This makes you a natural ambassador for the aquatic environment – a witness to what's happening and with a passion for sharing and doing something about it.

Divers are some of the strongest supporters of aquatic environmental programs and initiatives through:

- volunteer monitoring efforts;
- underwater and beach cleanups;
- supporting marine parks and protected areas;
- supporting legislative actions for sustainable fisheries and protecting endangered habitats and species.

Environmental Responsibility

As a PADI Diver, you join millions of other divers who, together, form a growing force to preserve the underwater world. The worldwide PADI family is committed to preserving underwater environments because a healthy ocean planet is essential for survival.

Divers are some of the strongest supporters of aquatic environmental programs and initiatives, including monitoring efforts, cleanups, supporting protected areas and parks, and supporting legislative actions to protect and preserve aquatic species and habitats.

Photo courtesy of William Goix

Project AWARE® is a nonprofit organization with a defined environmental mission and purpose to create and maintain a clean, healthy and abundant ocean planet. Divers like you support and assist Project AWARE on an international scale.

Project AWARE's 10 Tips for Divers to Protect the Ocean Planet

1. Be a Buoyancy Expert

Underwater plants and animals are more fragile than they appear. The swipe of a fin, bump of your camera or even a touch can destroy decades of coral growth, damage a plant or harm an animal. Streamline your scuba and photo gear, keep your dive skills sharp, perfect your underwater photo techniques and continue your dive training to fine-tune your skills. Always be aware of your body, dive gear and photo equipment to avoid contact with the natural environment.

2. Be a Role Model

New scuba divers are being trained and certified every day. Regardless of your experience level, be sure to set a good example for others when interacting with the environment – while underwater and on land.

3. Take Only Photos – Leave Only Bubbles

Nearly everything natural found underwater is alive or will be used by a living creature. If you take a coral, shell or animal, you can disturb the delicate balance and make the site less worthwhile for divers who come after you.

4. Protect Underwater Life

Choose not to touch, feed, handle, chase or ride anything underwater. Your actions may stress the animal, interrupt feeding and mating behavior or provoke aggressive behavior. Understand and respect underwater life and follow all local laws and regulations.

5. Become a Debris Activist

An astonishing amount of waste makes its way underwater, reaching even the most remote ocean areas. Once there, it kills wildlife, destroys habitats and threatens our health and economy. Don't let your dives go to waste. Remove and report what doesn't belong underwater every time you dive. Make a conscious effort to buy green, buy local and, when possible, buy less.

6. Make Responsible Seafood Choices

Overfishing leads to species declines while harmful fishing practices damage and pollute underwater ecosystems. You play a critical role as a consumer. If seafood is part of your meal selection, ensure you're choosing sustainably sourced species and encourage others, including restaurants and shop owners, to do the same.

7. Take Action

Scuba divers are some of the strongest ocean advocates on the planet. Now more than ever, divers like you are taking a stand. Speak out for conservation, share your underwater images, and report environmental damage to authorities and campaign for change.

8. Be an Eco-tourist

Make informed decisions when choosing and visiting a destination. Choose facilities dedicated to responsible social and environmental business practices that include water conservation, energy reduction, proper waste disposal, use of mooring buoys and respect for local cultures, laws and regulations.

9. Shrink Your Carbon Footprint

Global warming and ocean acidification are putting your favorite animals and the whole ocean planet at risk. Do your part by understanding and reducing your carbon footprint and look for ways to offset what you can't reduce.

10. Give Back

Ocean protection depends on all of our actions, large and small. Investing in the ocean protects our planet and lets the dive adventure live on. Donate or fundraise for ocean protection to fuel the grassroots action and policy change necessary to ensure a clean, healthy ocean planet.

In 1989, PADI introduced Project AWARE as a 10-year project and environmental ethic campaign to harness each diver's potential to advocate for and protect underwater environments. In 1992, Project AWARE Foundation became a registered nonprofit organization with a defined environmental mission and purpose. The organization's longstanding achievements in underwater protection make Project AWARE PADI's preferred nonprofit partner. PADI provides in-kind support to the foundation and encourages divers to join the Project AWARE movement.

Project AWARE's dive volunteers and supporters around the globe work toward a clean, healthy and abundant ocean planet. Whether you choose the Project AWARE version of your PADI certification card, make your voice heard for conservation or take direct action for ocean protection in your community, every action counts. Get involved through your PADI Dive Center or Resort, and visit projectaware.org. Follow Project AWARE's 10 Tips for Divers to Protect the Ocean Planet.

EXERCISE-4

1. As a PADI Diver, I can support aquatic programs and initiatives by (choose all that apply):
   - ☐ a. participating in underwater and beach cleanups.
   - ☐ b. volunteering for monitoring efforts.
   - ☐ c. supporting legislative actions for sustainable fisheries.
   - ☐ d. supporting marine parks and protective areas.
2. Project AWARE's mission is to certify as many divers as possible, because divers will naturally want to protect the aquatic environment.
   - ☐ True ☐ False
3. Project AWARE's 10 Tips for Divers to Protect the Ocean Planet include (choose all that apply):
   - ☐ a. becoming a buoyancy expert.
   - ☐ b. taking only photos, leaving only bubbles.
   - ☐ c. removing debris when I dive.
   - ☐ d. making responsible seafood choices when I eat.

How did you do?

1. a, b, c, d. 2. False. Project AWARE's mission is to protect the oceans with diver support. 3. a, b, c, d.

PADI UNDERWATER NATURALIST SPECIALTY

At your instructor's discretion, the Underwater Naturalist Adventure Dive credits toward the PADI Underwater Naturalist Specialty course. The course gives you additional information and opportunities to apply and practice your underwater naturalist skills and knowledge, including:

- How to interact responsibly with aquatic life
- Understanding aquatic life behavior
- The role of aquatic plants, food chains and predator/prey relationships

Remember to log your training dives with the PADI Mobile App or at padi.com.

Knowledge Review – Underwater Naturalist

Answer the following questions by selecting the best choice (or choices) from those provided. Be prepared to discuss the material at your next training session.

1. The definition of ecology is the study of the interrelationship of living things and their environment.

   ☐ True ☐ False

2. A(n) _________ is defined as a complex of living things and their environment functioning as a unit.

   ☐ ecosystem
   ☐ ecology
   ☐ symbiosis
   ☐ parasite

3. Light penetration, oxygen distribution and air versus water density are three physical characteristics that differ significantly between land ecosystems and aquatic ecosystems.

   ☐ True ☐ False

4. My buddy and I swim along the edge of a coral reef. A damselfish darts out and tries to bite my buddy's arm. Surprised, we quickly swim away from the little fish. After the dive, my buddy says that the fish "did not like me," which is why it tried to bite. Is this a correct perception?

   ☐ Yes – aquatic creatures can attack out of malice, anger and revenge.
   ☐ No – the fish was probably defending its territory.

5. People often inaccurately perceive aquatic life as (choose all that apply):

   ☐ dangerous and harmful.
   ☐ harmless – much like domestic animals.
   ☐ nonliving, inanimate objects.
   ☐ having human characteristics.

6. To interact passively with aquatic organisms, I should avoid (choose all that apply):

   ☐ touching and handling creatures.
   ☐ gathering aquatic life.
   ☐ chasing aquatic animals.
   ☐ underwater photography.

7. There are no circumstances when I should ride an aquatic animal in the wild.

   ☐ True ☐ False

8. As soon as the dive boat moors at a popular dive site, I notice that many reef fish come up to the back of the boat. The divemaster explains that this is not natural behavior and is caused by people feeding the fish. What are other possible consequences of fish feeding? (Choose all that apply.)

   ☐ Divers will see a wider variety of fish.
   ☐ Fish may stop their normal feeding behaviors.
   ☐ Fed species may lose their natural fear of humans.
   ☐ Eating unnatural foods may cause illness.

9. How can I avoid damaging the aquatic environment while diving? (Choose all that apply.)

   ☐ Maintain neutral buoyancy and stay well off the bottom.
   ☐ Swim horizontally and be aware of my fin movement.
   ☐ Streamline my equipment so that hoses and gauges don't dangle.
   ☐ Avoid touching or accidently bumping delicate aquatic creatures.

Student Statement

I completed this Knowledge Review to the best of my ability. For any questions I answered incorrectly or incompletely, I reviewed the explanation provided and now understand the material. In the case of anything about which I still have questions, I will review the material again and, if necessary, discuss it with my instructor at our next session.

☐ I agree ☐ I disagree

Student signature ______________________________

Date ______________________________

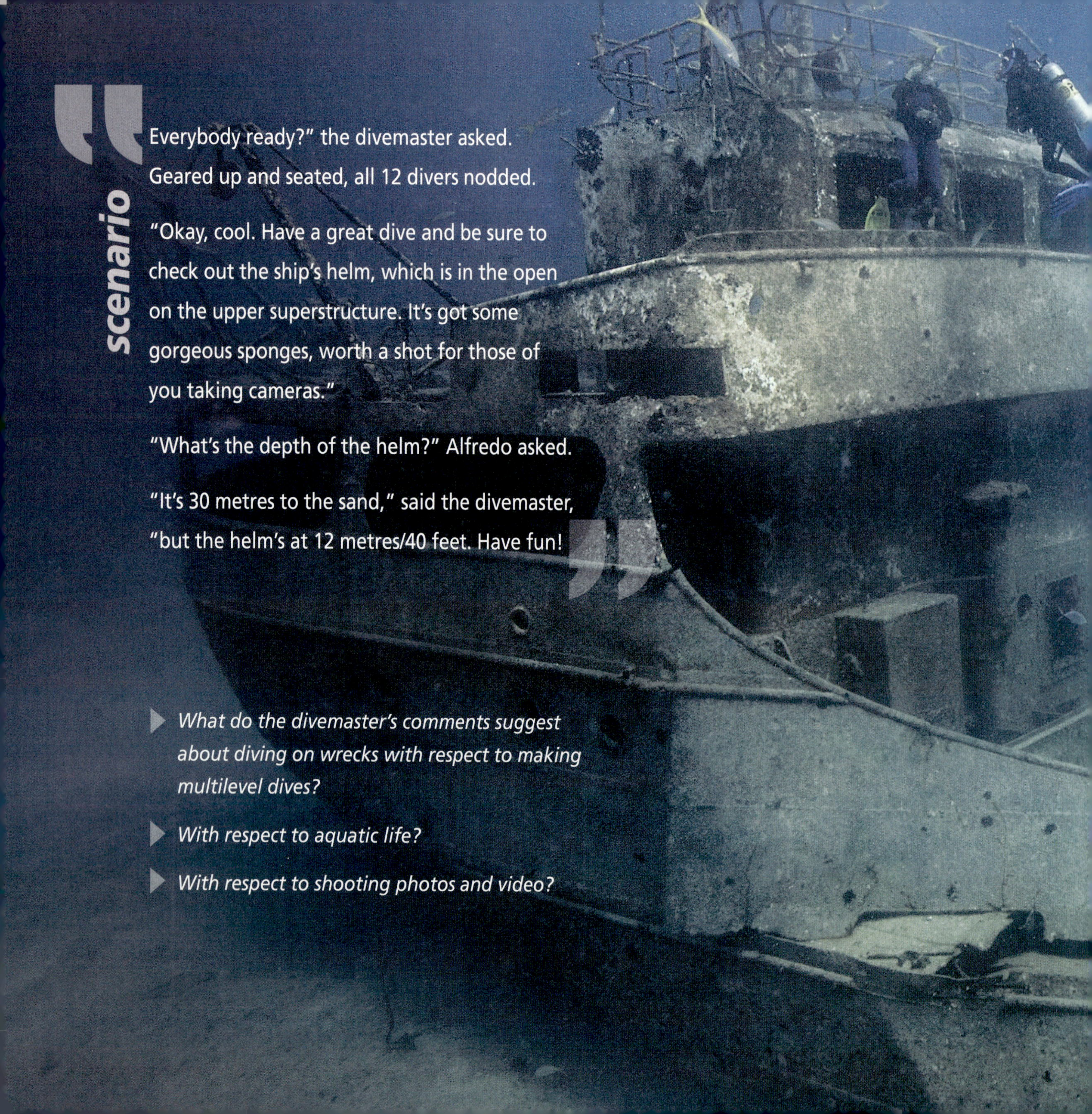

scenario

"Everybody ready?" the divemaster asked. Geared up and seated, all 12 divers nodded.

"Okay, cool. Have a great dive and be sure to check out the ship's helm, which is in the open on the upper superstructure. It's got some gorgeous sponges, worth a shot for those of you taking cameras."

"What's the depth of the helm?" Alfredo asked.

"It's 30 metres to the sand," said the divemaster, "but the helm's at 12 metres/40 feet. Have fun!"

- *What do the divemaster's comments suggest about diving on wrecks with respect to making multilevel dives?*
- *With respect to aquatic life?*
- *With respect to shooting photos and video?*

WRECK DIVING 14

Introduction

The Appeal of Wrecks

No matter where you're diving – salt or fresh water, temperate or tropical, inland or offshore – there's something about diving wrecks that gets most divers excited. Whether a near-intact large ship or the beat-up remnants of a ski boat, wrecks attract divers. You'll probably hear as many reasons as there are divers, but there are four common reasons divers love wreck diving. Even if some of these don't appeal to you, there's a good chance you'll dive with someone who's motivated by them.

1. **Curiosity.** There's something fascinating about wrecks. You start asking yourself about their stories. What caused this wreck to sink? What will we find?

2. **History.** Going a step beyond simple curiosity, some divers like to research wrecks in great detail, especially if little is known. In some cases, wreck diving affords you opportunities to work with archaeologists and historians, and many wrecks are historical resources. This motivates many divers to visit them. The historical nature of many wrecks is also important because some wrecks are fragile; divers play a role in helping to preserve and protect them.

3. **Aquatic life.** Wrecks become artificial reefs that attract aquatic life. In some areas, you only find concentrations of aquatic life on and around wrecks, and some divers are most interested in what lives on wrecks. Be aware that on a wreck you need to take the same precautions regarding aquatic life – avoid harming it and avoid potentially hazardous organisms – as you would on a natural reef.

4. **Imaging.** Wrecks make dramatic backgrounds for video and still imagery of divers and wildlife. Many wrecks are photogenic themselves, making them popular subjects for scenic shots, or locations for diver photos and video. Ask your instructor about the PADI Digital Underwater Photographer course to learn more about underwater imaging.

LEARNING OBJECTIVES

By the end of this section, I should be able to answer these questions:

1. What are four common reasons people wreck dive?

2. What are three reasons artifact recovery is discouraged and not covered in this section, the Wreck Adventure Dive or the PADI Wreck Diver course?

Respecting Wrecks

Every wreck is a unique dive site, so the Wreck Adventure Dive and the PADI Wreck Diver course do not include recovering objects (artifacts) from wrecks. Removing and recovering wreck artifacts is generally discouraged for several reasons.

The first reason is that disturbing a wreck or removing something may be *illegal* (more about this shortly). A second reason is that archaeologists/historians learn from wrecks by studying how objects lie in relation to each other. Simply moving something, much less taking it away, can destroy information. A third reason is that even if it is legal to recover artifacts on wrecks without historical significance, removing them makes the wreck less interesting. Leaving wrecks as you find them is being considerate of the divers who come after you.

EXERCISE-1

1. There are many reasons that wrecks appeal to divers, including (choose all that apply):
   - ☐ a. curiosity.
   - ☐ b. history.
   - ☐ c. aquatic life.
   - ☐ d. for photos and video.

2. My buddy and I are visiting a wreck and find the ship's bell in place below one of the masts. Although we have the means to remove and take it, we leave it because removing it (choose all that apply):
   - ☐ a. may be illegal.
   - ☐ b. destroys information for archaeologists/historians.
   - ☐ c. is inconsiderate of other divers.
   - ☐ d. has a high injury risk.

How did you do?

1. a, b, c, d. 2. a, b, c.

LEARNING OBJECTIVES

By the end of this section, I should be able to answer these questions:

1. Why are there laws about diving on wrecks?

2. What is my responsibility with regard to laws that apply to the wrecks on which I dive?

Even after decades underwater, a wreck's owner or an insurance company usually still claims title to it.

Wreck Diving and the Law

In most areas, diving on wrecks has some legal considerations. Most shipwreck laws originate primarily from either of two concerns: salvage rights and antiquity protection.

The oldest laws concern salvage rights, which determine who owns something lost in the sea, and apply to almost anything, not just shipwrecks. Different areas have different laws, and while many countries allow the finder to keep abandoned property, few wrecks are considered abandoned. Even after decades underwater, the owner or an insurance company usually still claims title.

Antiquity protection laws arose primarily after diving became popular in the 1950s and '60s, because divers ignorantly or uncaringly damaged wreck sites before archaeologists could study them. It was also recognized that in some areas, wrecks are war graves for service people who died in conflict, and should therefore not be disturbed.

Today, most countries have laws that prevent divers from removing anything from or otherwise disturbing historical wrecks. However, what is "historical" varies regionally, and even from wreck to wreck. In some places you need a permit or must dive with a special guide to visit local wrecks or certain wrecks.

Your instructor will explain any laws and regulations that apply to wrecks in your local area. Regardless of where you dive, it's your responsibility to know and follow any local regulations or laws. You can often find these online, but usually the simplest way is to contact a PADI Dive Center or Resort in the area.

EXERCISE-2

1. Most laws involving shipwrecks originate with the hazardous conditions found on local wrecks.
   ☐ True ☐ False

2. I'm planning to wreck dive in a country I've never visited before. It's my responsibility to find out if any laws apply, and to follow those laws.
   ☐ True ☐ False

How did you do?

1. False. Most laws involving shipwrecks originate with salvage rights and antiquity protection. 2. True

LEARNING OBJECTIVES

By the end of this section, I should be able to answer these questions:

1. What are five potential hazards common to wrecks, and how do I avoid them?
2. What five dive planning and equipment considerations should I make for wreck dives deeper than 18 metres/60 feet?
3. What are two reasons why I should obtain a local orientation for an unfamiliar wreck?
4. What are five hazards of entering (penetrating) a wreck, and what causes these hazards?

Respect Our Wrecks

Divers are privileged to have access to underwater sites that are part of our cultural heritage or maritime history. To preserve these sites for future generations, it's important to be informed, dive responsibly and treat shipwrecks with honor and respect. Divers must be responsible when exploring these submerged sites, looking after themselves, the environment and the cultural heritage.

Most countries have laws that prevent divers from removing anything from or otherwise disturbing historical wrecks. In some places you need a permit or must dive with a special guide to visit local wrecks or certain wrecks.

Wreck Diving Hazards and Considerations

Wreck Hazards

Like any dive environment, wrecks have potential hazards. A wreck's hazards, however, may be either unique and/or more present than those found on natural reefs in the same area. They are not difficult to avoid or manage if you're aware of them and prepared. There are five hazards common to wrecks to watch for and avoid.

Sharp objects. Rusted metal, jagged plates, splintered wood, broken glass, etc., are all potential injury sources. Wear an exposure suit and protective gloves (unless prohibited in the local area). Maintain good buoyancy control to reduce contact with the wreck. It's wise to keep immunizations, such as tetanus, current in case you do get cut.

Entanglement. Wrecks may have netting, fishing line or other old line on them. Avoid wrecks that are known to have hazardous amounts of line or netting. On other wrecks, watching where you swim and keeping your gear streamlined helps avoid them. Avoid swimming through or under nets, fishing line or other line, but have a cutting tool with both smooth and serrated edges to handle accidental entanglement too difficult to untangle. Many avid wreck divers have two or more cutting devices.

Aquatic life. Be cautious of the same organisms you would avoid on a natural reef in the same area. Avoid contact by controlling your buoyancy, streamlining your gear and, of course, avoid damaging any sensitive organisms.

Unstable structure. Many wrecks have unstable frames, ceilings, hatches, etc. Avoid diving near such structures, and stay away from those that move easily with current or touch, or that look fragile or not secure. Be aware that war wrecks may have munitions that are still live and dangerous. Do not disturb munitions in any way.

Surge pockets and suction. Water movement through a wreck can cause periodic suction at restricted openings – hatches, holes, etc. – which can be extremely hazardous to divers. Watch for this if surge is present, or reschedule the dive for better conditions.

Deeper Wrecks

Large ships sink in deeper water, so many popular wrecks take you below 18 metres/60 feet. When visiting these wrecks there are five recommendations.

First, it's recommended that you're trained as a PADI Deep Diver. The PADI Deep Diver course gives you experience with the techniques and gear used in deeper diving.

Large ships sink in deeper water, so many popular wrecks take you below 18 metres/60 feet. When visiting these wrecks, it's recommended you have an extra gas supply, account for gas narcosis and plan for reduced dive time at depth. Training as a PADI Deep Diver and a PADI Enriched Air Diver is also recommended.

Common wreck hazards to watch for and avoid include sharp objects, entanglement and any hazardous aquatic life you would find on a local natural reef. Unstable structure, surge pockets and suction are also possible hazards on some wrecks.

Second, it's a good idea to have an extra gas supply. Options for this include using a high-capacity cylinder, wearing a pony bottle or, where appropriate, leaving an extra cylinder and regulator at 5 metres/15 feet to ensure you can make a safety stop or emergency decompression stop. (You learn about these options in the Deep Adventure Dive.)

Third, account for gas narcosis. Keep your objectives simple and avoid task loading. Give yourself ample time.

Fourth, plan for reduced dive time due to faster gas use and/or shorter no stop times. Some wrecks, especially large, relatively intact ones, may allow more dive time with a multilevel profile as you ascend along their structure. The potential for this depends upon the wreck, but on some wrecks you can start your exploration as deep as 30 metres/100 feet and continue shallower all the way to safety-stop depth.

Fifth, it's also useful to be a PADI Enriched Air Diver so you can have longer no stop times, especially on wrecks that don't offer a multilevel profile. Ask your instructor about the PADI Enriched Air Diver course.

An orientation to an unfamiliar wreck can acquaint you with local techniques for diving it, as well as unique points of interest and potential hazards you can find there.

Local Orientation

Whenever possible, it's recommended that you get a local orientation any time you dive somewhere new, and this applies to wrecks as well. There are at least two reasons why you want an orientation to an unfamiliar wreck.

The first reason is that the best techniques for diving a wreck may differ from ones you've used before. A local orientation will usually acquaint you with the preferred local methods.

The second reason is that all wrecks have their own unique points of interest and potential hazards. Different areas have different regulations and community practices regarding wreck diving. A local orientation will help you with these.

Entering a Wreck

Note that the Wreck Adventure Dive does not include or cover entering (penetrating) a wreck. Wreck penetration has distinct hazards that require special training and equipment to manage.

⚠ **Entering a wreck without the special training and equipment required can be extremely hazardous.**

1. **Loss of direction.** You can get disoriented simply by entering some wrecks. Even a wreck that seems easy to find your way through becomes confusing as stirred-up silt destroys the visibility. If the wreck lies at an angle, has collapsed passages and blocking debris, it becomes more confusing. It is very easy to lose your direction inside a wreck.
2. **No direct surface access.** You can't start directly for the surface if you have sudden gas loss or another problem; you have to exit first. Emergency swimming ascents or a buoyant emergency ascent are not options, at least not until you get out into open water.
3. **Restricted passages.** Movement can be limited in small areas within a wreck, making turning difficult or impossible. You're more likely to contact something sharp or abrasive; even recreational divers with special training in penetration (more about this shortly) avoid such areas.
4. **Falling objects.** Your movement can knock objects loose that can fall on you, in your way, or behind you, impeding your exit.
5. **Silt.** Most wrecks have silt or particulate matter spread throughout; it's easy to disturb this silt, reducing the visibility to nearly zero. Even exercising great care, your bubbles can cause silt to dislodge from walls and ceilings, restricting your ability to see.

If you get lost or otherwise trapped inside a wreck, you have only the time until you deplete your gas to find your way out. The deeper you are, the less time you have, so this is a very serious risk.

This doesn't mean you can never enter a wreck, but that to do so you need proper training and equipment, and to follow specific procedures and limits. The PADI Wreck Diver course covers these as appropriate for recreational divers; ask your PADI Instructor for more information if this interests you.

EXERCISE-3

1. My buddy and I are diving on a wreck. The common wreck hazards for us to watch for and avoid include (choose all that apply):
   - ☐ a. sharp objects.
   - ☐ b. entanglement.
   - ☐ c. aquatic life.
   - ☐ d. unstable structure.
   - ☐ e. surge pockets and suction.
2. Two buddies and I are planning to dive on a wreck at 24 metres/80 feet. It would be a good idea to hang an extra cylinder and regulator at 5 metres/15 feet to be sure we have adequate gas for a safety stop or emergency decompression.
   - ☐ True ☐ False
3. I'm diving on an unfamiliar wreck, so I'm getting a local orientation. This benefits me because I can learn (choose all that apply):
   - ☐ a. which artifacts I can remove.
   - ☐ b. points of interest and potential hazards.
   - ☐ c. local methods for diving it.
4. I'm diving on an intact wreck with passages that my buddy and I could enter. We don't enter, however, because we don't have the training and equipment required to avoid hazards that include (choose all that apply):
   - ☐ a. losing our direction inside.
   - ☐ b. no direct access to the surface.
   - ☐ c. restricted passages.
   - ☐ d. falling objects.
   - ☐ e. silt.

How did you do?

1. a, b, c, d, e. 2. True. 3. b, c. 4. a, b, c, d, e.

Wreck penetration has distinct hazards that require special training and equipment to manage. Entering a wreck without the special training and equipment required can be extremely hazardous.

LEARNING OBJECTIVES

By the end of this section, I should be able to answer these questions:

1. What do I evaluate on a wreck when diving on it?
2. What are three ways to navigate on a wreck?
3. Why may my compass be inaccurate on many wrecks?

You'll want to get to know a wreck and how it changes over time. Each time you dive it, generally evaluate it for potential hazards, points of interest and general condition.

Assessing and Navigating a Wreck

When you dive a wreck, you want to get to know it. It also changes over time, so think in terms of evaluating these aspects each time you dive on it.

- **Possible hazards.** Look for the previously discussed hazards, as well as any unusual ones unique to the wreck.
- **Points of interest.** Know where to find the ship's wheel, telegraph, anchor, bell, etc., that give a wreck its personality and tell you something about it. What you may find interesting changes as the wreck ages and as you make new discoveries.
- **General condition.** This affects how you explore a wreck, what areas you want to avoid, etc. Note what's intact and strong versus what appears weak and fragile. Pay attention to this – you'll see it change over time.

Navigating Wrecks

Generally speaking, the more intact a wreck is, the easier it is to navigate on. There are three navigation techniques specific to wreck diving, which you may combine on the same wreck as appropriate to the conditions you find in different areas.

The first technique is to *follow the wreck's layout.* With a largely intact wreck in relatively clear water, you can follow the hull, a rail, etc., using the natural navigation techniques you learn in the Underwater Navigation Adventure Dive.

With a largely intact wreck in relatively clear water, you can navigate by following the wreck's layout, such as the hull, a rail, etc., using natural navigation techniques.

The second technique is *feature reference,* which works well on a wreck that is relatively broken up, or in low visibility on an intact wreck. You note unique features and their relative positions, moving from one to the next and return along the same path, much as you might on a natural reef. It helps to note these features on a slate or in a wet book if necessary.

The third technique is to use a *base line.* This is most useful on a broken up, scattered wreck that lacks distinct features you can use for reference. A base line is simply a straight line through a wreck that you navigate along, exploring to either side to check out what's interesting. In clear, calm water, this may be a general direction. In less ideal conditions, you may opt to use a compass heading – an out-and-back line (reciprocal course). And, in low visibility or in current, you may use a line and reel to create a physical base line.

Compass Accuracy

When using your compass on a wreck, keep in mind that it may be inaccurate at times or, in the extreme, all the time. This is because steel and iron can attract the magnetic compass needle,

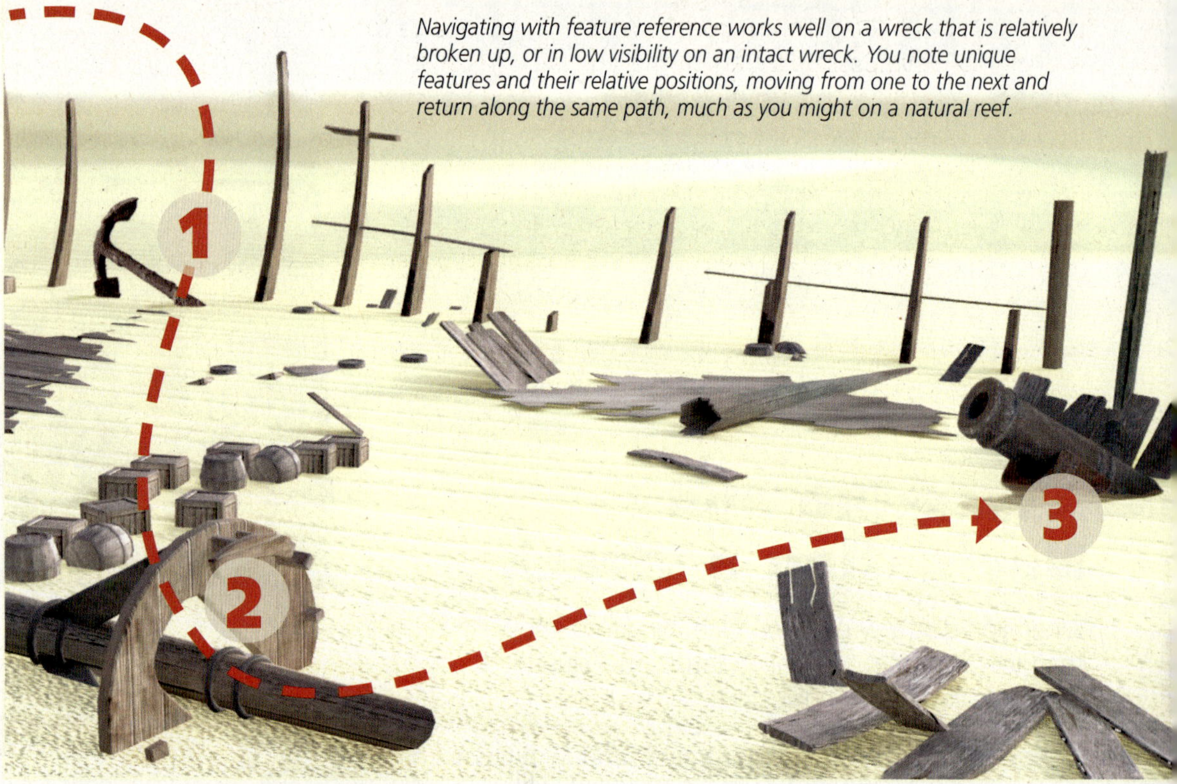

Navigating with feature reference works well on a wreck that is relatively broken up, or in low visibility on an intact wreck. You note unique features and their relative positions, moving from one to the next and return along the same path, much as you might on a natural reef.

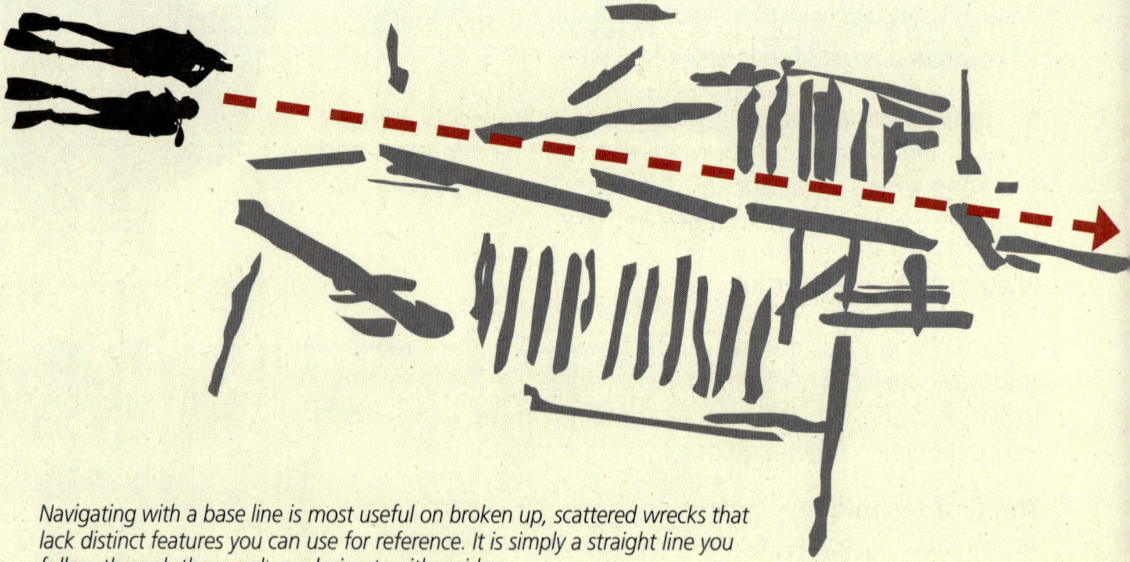

Navigating with a base line is most useful on broken up, scattered wrecks that lack distinct features you can use for reference. It is simply a straight line you follow through the wreck, exploring to either side.

making it swing away from magnetic north. This is as true for an electronic compass as for an analog compass, because its "needle" is a magnetic sensor.

Fortunately, you usually only need to be a bit more than one metre/three feet from steel or iron for your compass to be tolerably accurate and useable for navigation. But, it may still be affected, especially on a wreck that is almost entirely steel or iron.

Be cautious and avoid having your compass too close to metal when using it. It helps to use natural navigation techniques to augment your compass in maintaining your orientation and direction reference.

WRECK DIVER SPECIALTY

At your instructor's discretion, the Wreck Adventure Dive credits toward the PADI Wreck Diver Specialty course. The course gives you more opportunities to develop and practice wreck diving skills, including:

- Researching wreck history
- Mapping wrecks and mapping tools
- General techniques for wreck diving in a current
- Navigating on a wreck
- Practice in small and large search areas
- Recreational wreck penetration equipment and techniques

Remember to log your training dives with the PADI Mobile App or at padi.com.

EXERCISE-4

1. My buddy and I are diving on a wreck. It's my fourth dive on it over five years. Generally, as we explore the wreck we want to evaluate (choose all that apply):
   - ☐ a. possible hazards.
   - ☐ b. points of interest.
   - ☐ c. general condition.
2. Two friends and I plan to dive on a recent, intact wreck in clear, calm water. Our primary navigation method would probably be to (choose all that apply):
   - ☐ a. use dead reckoning.
   - ☐ b. follow the wreck's layout.
   - ☐ c. use feature references.
   - ☐ d. use a base line.
3. I'm diving on an intact 19th-century wood schooner in a cool freshwater lake. I don't need to worry about the hull itself, but should be cautious using my compass near metal fittings and nails that may be made from steel or iron.
   - ☐ True ☐ False

How did you do?

1. a, b, c. 2. b. 3. True

When using your compass on a wreck, keep in mind that it may be inaccurate at times or, in the extreme, all the time. Fortunately, most wrecks allow you to navigate by following their structures as well as by using your compass. A distance of about one metre/three feet or more from steel or iron lets most compasses be tolerably accurate.

Knowledge Review – Wreck Diving

Answer the following questions by selecting the best choice (or choices) from those provided. Be prepared to discuss the material at your next training session.

1. Removing artifacts from wrecks is _______________, because doing so makes wrecks _______________.
   - ☐ a. encouraged/safer
   - ☐ b. discouraged/hazardous
   - ☐ c. encouraged/more interesting
   - ☐ d. discouraged/less interesting
2. In many areas and on many wrecks it is illegal to remove artifacts without a permit.
   - ☐ True
   - ☐ False
3. In some areas you need a permit to dive on wrecks.
   - ☐ True
   - ☐ False
4. You and your buddy are planning a dive on a wreck. To avoid and manage the risks of sharp objects on the wreck, and entanglement, you (choose all that apply):
   - ☐ wear exposure protection.
   - ☐ maintain good buoyancy control.
   - ☐ avoid swimming through/under net, fishing line or other rope/line.
   - ☐ carry a knife or other cutting tool.
5. You're planning a dive to a wreck at 27 metres/90 feet. Which planning/equipment considerations may apply? (Choose all that apply.)
   - ☐ PADI Deep Diver training
   - ☐ Extra gas supply
   - ☐ Narcosis
   - ☐ Short time limits
   - ☐ PADI Enriched Air Diver training
6. Dive techniques, hazards and points of interest may vary from wreck to wreck, so when diving on one that's unfamiliar to you, it's a good idea to get
   - ☐ an extra cutting tool.
   - ☐ a local orientation.
   - ☐ a still or video camera.
   - ☐ its sonar topography.
7. It is extremely hazardous to penetrate a wreck without the special equipment and training required.
   - ☐ True
   - ☐ False
8. When diving a wreck, evaluate (choose all that apply):
   - ☐ possible hazards.
   - ☐ points of interest.
   - ☐ cause of sinking.
   - ☐ general condition.
9. You and your buddy are navigating on a wreck that's broken apart. You can't really determine its structure, nor are there many obviously different features. The navigation method you'd use is probably
   - ☐ following the wreck's layout.
   - ☐ feature reference.
   - ☐ using a base line.

Student Statement

I completed this Knowledge Review to the best of my ability. For any questions I answered incorrectly or incompletely, I reviewed the explanation provided and now understand the material. In the case of anything about which I still have questions, I will review the material again and, if necessary, discuss it with my instructor at our next session.

☐ I agree ☐ I disagree

Student signature ______________________________

Date ______________________________